ENVIRONMENTAL LAW

THIRD EDITION

Other books in the *Essentials of Canadian Law Series*

E S S E N T I A L S   O F
C A N A D I A N   L A W

ENVIRONMENTAL LAW

THIRD EDITION

JAMIE BENIDICKSON
Faculty of Law
University of Ottawa

Environmental Law, third edition
© Irwin Law Inc., 2009

Published in 2009 by

Irwin Law Inc.
14 Duncan Street
Suite 206
Toronto, ON
M5H 3G8

www.irwinlaw.com

ISBN: 978-1-55221-131-1

Library and Archives Canada Cataloguing in Publication

Benidickson, Jamie
    Environmental law / Jamie Benidickson. — 3rd ed.

(Essentials of Canadian law)
Includes bibliographical references and index.
ISBN 978-1-55221-131-1

1. Environmental law — Canada. I. Title. II. Series.

KE3619.B46 2008   344.7104'6   C2008-906353-8
KF3775.ZA2B46 2008

The publisher acknowledges the financial support of the Government of Canada through the Book Publishing Industry Development Program (BPIDP) for its publishing activities.

We acknowledge the assistance of the OMDC Book Fund, an initiative of Ontario Media Development Corporation.

Printed and bound in Canada.

4 5   13 12

SUMMARY
TABLE OF CONTENTS

DETAILED
TABLE OF CONTENTS

FOREWORD

TO THE FIRST EDITION

When I graduated from law school in 1972, nowhere in the curriculum could one find a course called Environmental Law. To the extent that that subject-matter was considered at all, it was through, at most, passing reference in courses such as Municipal Law, Torts, or International Law.

Twenty-five years later, the scene is remarkably changed. All Canadian law schools offer at least one such course. Many offer more. There are specialized law reports and journals, loose-leaf services, newsletters, casebooks, and national and provincial organizations devoted to research, education, and law reform. This flurry of activity reflects society's recognition of the importance of the environment. It also reflects the fact that law is one of the tools essential to environmental protection. Every day, courts and other tribunals in our country are called on to resolve disputes among parties such as governments, agencies, business, and private citizens, each of whom has a role to play in ensuring that our children will have a clean, healthy, and esthetically acceptable planet on which to reside.

As a judge, I appreciate the immense contribution made by my former academic colleagues to the clarification and explanation of law and legal systems. Academics are able to specialize in a way that most judges cannot. Judges must resolve specific cases; academics can take the long, wide view. I often turn to books and articles written by academic commentators to help me understand both the narrow and the broad aspects of a case that I have to decide.

That Professor Benidickson's book will play an integral role in informing readers like me is beyond doubt. It reflects the reality that legal problems about the environment arise in a myriad of settings from the common law to the *Charter*, from international law to statutory interpretation, from criminal liability to contractual arrangements—all these and many other legal areas provide the backdrop for environmental disputes. There are few other problems that require a decision maker to draw upon principles from such a vast array of legal doctrine. Equally important, environmental conflicts are rooted in a social, scientific, and economic context. This book will assist enormously in exposing that context, to, among others, law students, lawyers, regulators, scientists, business people, and judges.

The topics included in this book are broad and rich. Its explanations are clear, not only to those schooled in the law but to other affected professionals. It will help us understand the past. It will help point the way to the future. It will be an invaluable reference for legal professionals and the many others who are engaged in environmental protection endeavours.

Madam Justice Constance Hunt
Alberta Court of Appeal

ACKNOWLEDGMENTS

I would like to thank Elaine Borg, Barry Ditto, Suzanne Shreik, and Gil Yaron for research assistance on the first edition, and Maria Kotsoplous for her work in connection with the second. Carolyn Elliot Magwood, Sean Bawden, Anna Poliszot, and Michelle Jones made substantial contributions to the current revision.

INTRODUCTION

A. LAW AND THE ENVIRONMENT

Environmental protection is always a subject of serious and persistent concern to Canadians, and often ranks ahead of other social and economic issues on the priority list. Evidence of environmental deterioration in the forms of harmful pollution, resource depletion, and the decline or even extinction of species is readily apparent at the national and international levels, despite sometimes significant attempts to address these challenges. Explanations for these disturbing developments vary, with some pointing to the incessant pressure of technology or to the uncontrolled expansion of human population as culprits; others blame deeply entrenched attitudes to nature and long-established patterns of human relationships with the environment and resources.

The suggested responses are equally diverse and occasionally controversial. Means to promote environmental protection include public education, greater spending and investment to safeguard environmental functions, financial incentives and property rights to stimulate individual action, continued technological innovation, and a legal regime designed to prohibit environmentally detrimental activity and to encourage beneficial initiatives. Environmental law is thus a subject of profound importance to a remarkable number of people whether they are concerned individuals, members of environmental public-interest groups, civil servants, corporate officials, technical and scientific ex-

1

perts, or part of the wide range of legal professionals whose practice is affected by environmental considerations.

Each of these constituencies envisages the environmental legal regime from a somewhat different perspective. Not surprisingly, this results in considerable diversity of opinion whenever one contemplates the appropriateness, effectiveness, or utility of law as an instrument of environmental protection. Here it is sufficient to remark that, alongside essentially environmental concerns, general legal values have also influenced the evolution and operation of environmental law in Canada. By way of example, when environmental advocates urge resort to criminal law with the thought that the severity of possible penalties, even including imprisonment, may improve environmental protection, they simultaneously engage the attention of legal professionals with a deeply rooted appreciation of the procedural safeguards embedded in the overall relationship between the state's power as prosecutor and the accused's interest in liberty. Together with concerns about the direct and indirect costs of alternative approaches to environmental protection, tensions such as these constantly reappear in environmental law. They are resolved on an ongoing basis through decision making at the legislative, administrative, judicial, and personal levels.

B. POLICY OBJECTIVES AND LEGAL TECHNIQUES FOR ENVIRONMENTAL PROTECTION

Environmental law, though continuing to evolve rapidly, is not new. However, its focus has clearly shifted over the past century or more from anti-pollution measures associated primarily with local public health and resource conservation. Ecosystem maintenance, biodiversity, and sustainability, concepts that are more thoroughly discussed in chapter 1, now appear more prominently on the list of environmental goals. The shift of attention towards these fundamental ideas reflects advances in scientific understanding of human impacts on the environment and the far greater scope of those impacts: where Ottawa Valley lumbermen were once concerned with the availablity of pine timber in the context of their commercial activity, Canadians are now apprehensive about the maintenance of the boreal forest across the country in light of its role in the economy, its functions in relation to habitat and watersheds, and its contribution to planetary climatic conditions. Similarly, if local fisheries were once threatened by local sources of pollution, we are now aware, following the collapse of the Atlantic cod industry, of the regional devastation that can result from over-harvesting and consumption.

The official objectives of environmental law are often embodied in legislation such as the *Canadian Environmental Protection Act, 1999 (CEPA, 1999)*,[1] which declares that "the protection of the environment is essential to the well-being of Canada." The purposes of the *Canadian Environmental Assessment Act (CEAA)*,[2] which established environmental assessment on a legislated basis at the federal level, are also clearly set out. The *CEAA* is intended "to ensure that the environmental effects of projects receive careful consideration before responsible authorities take actions in connection with them" and "to encourage responsible authorities to take actions that promote sustainable development and thereby achieve or maintain a healthy . . . economy." In addition, the statute seeks to "ensure that projects that are to be carried out in Canada or on federal lands do not cause significant adverse environmental effects outside the jurisdictions in which the projects are carried out." Opportunities for public participation in the environmental assessment process are to be encouraged.

Earlier federal legislation, the *Arctic Waters Pollution Prevention Act*,[3] contains an elaborate discussion of the various competing concerns underlying the scheme. On the one hand, the legislation "recognizes that recent developments in relation to the exploitation of the natural resources of arctic areas, including the natural resources of the Canadian arctic, and the transportation of those resources to the markets of the world are of potentially great significance to international trade and commerce and to the economy of Canada in particular." However, Parliament also expressed the determination "to fulfil its obligation to see that the natural resources of the Canadian arctic are developed and exploited and the arctic waters adjacent to the mainland and islands of the Canadian arctic are navigated only in a manner that takes cognizance of Canada's responsibility for the welfare of the Inuit and other inhabitants of the Canadian arctic." The legislation specifically insisted upon the importance of "the preservation of the peculiar ecological balance that now exists in the water, ice and land areas" of the Arctic

---

1   S.C. 1999, c. 33 [*CEPA, 1999*]. *CEPA, 1999* deals with the regulation of toxic substances, nutrients, ocean dumping, international air and water pollution, waste management, biotechnology, and the environmental management of federal government activity.

2   S.C. 1992, c. 37 [*CEAA*]. Amendments to the legislation, now S.C. 2003, c. 9 are discussed in chapter 12.

3   R.S.C. 1985, c. A-12.

region. This legislative objective, we are now undeniably aware, is being undermined on a daily basis by the impact of climate change on the region.

In the provincial realm, Ontario's *Environmental Protection Act*[4] is intended "to provide for the protection and conservation of the natural environment," while the same province's *Environmental Assessment Act* was enacted to promote "the betterment of the people of the whole or any part of Ontario by providing for the protection, conservation and wise management in Ontario of the environment."[5] Alberta's *Environmental Protection and Enhancement Act* of 1992[6] set out an elaborate statement of purpose. The *AEPEA* is intended "to support and promote the protection, enhancement and wise use of the environment" in the context of a series of associated principles and subobjectives:

- maintaining the integrity of ecosystems and human health and the well-being of society;
- promoting economic growth and prosperity in an environmentally responsible manner and integrating environmental protection and economic decisions in the earliest stages of planning;
- achieving sustainable development;
- preventing and mitigating the environmental impact of development and of government policies, programs, and decisions;
- ensuring opportunities for citizens to provide advice on decisions affecting the environment; and
- encouraging polluters to pay for the costs of their actions.

Manitoba's *Environment Act (MEA)* might be noted as well for expressly incorporating economic goals alongside environmental objectives. Specifically, the *MEA* seeks to "develop and maintain an environmental management system in Manitoba which will ensure that the environment is maintained in such a manner as to sustain a high quality of life, including social and economic development, recreation and leisure for this and future generations."[7] The Yukon *Environment Act* goes so far as to assert the principle that "economic development and the health of the natural environment are inter-dependent."[8] In other cases, limitations that acknowledge that environmental protection measures must accommodate constraints faced by businesses are embodied in regu-

---

4   R.S.O. 1990, c. E.19, s. 3.
5   R.S.O. 1990, c. E.18, s. 2.
6   S.A. 1992, c. E-13.3 [*AEPEA*].
7   *Environment Act*, C.C.S.M. c. E125.
8   The Yukon *Environment Act*, S.Y. 1991, c. 5, s. 5(2)(a) [*YEA*].

lations such as those requiring the use of "practicable means" or the "best available technology economically achievable."

Such statutory formulations of the purposes of environmental law demonstrate that environmental protection regimes are not free-standing or autonomous. Rather, they have evolved in the context of other economic, social, and legal considerations. As will be seen, various factors such as procedural fairness and considerations of proportionality, equitability, and efficiency, influence the design, implementation, and operation of environmental law regimes. Financial responsibility for the cleanup of contaminated lands is one area where these considerations have been subject to intense debate.[9]

Through law, a number of techniques may be employed to achieve the goals of environmental policy. Specified forms of conduct may be subject to clear prohibition, while other activities are permitted or regulated, often in connection with licensing controls. The law may also be used to create economic incentives, or as a means of more directly imposing advance planning and prevention programs to reduce the likelihood of environmental degradation. When damage occurs, however, legal principles and mechanisms regulate the distribution of costs and losses among those responsible, victims, and the general public. There are situations, in fact, where the legal regime may require some form of environmental restoration.

Jurisdictions differ with respect to the general style or orientation of their environmental regimes, with some favouring detailed legislative schemes and others preferring general statements of principle for administrative agencies or the courts to elaborate and refine. Similarly, some jurisdictions favour broad grants of discretionary authority to public officials, while others insist on close scrutiny of agencies to ensure conformity with overall policy.

It is noteworthy that Canadian environmental legislation has to a significant degree been enabling in nature rather than mandatory. That is, statutory powers authorizing designated officials to develop regulations for the protection of the environment are not generally construed as imposing upon those officials an obligation to so act. This principle governed an attempt by a public interest litigant to obtain a declaratory order compelling the lieutenant governor in council to enact regulations dealing with non-returnable beverage containers under legislation providing that such regulations "may" be made and stating that the regulations "shall" be filed by a specified date. In the opinion of the court, the authorization to make regulations was discretionary, and the

---

9   See chapter 11.

obligation to file them was subject to the implied phrase "if enacted."[10] On the other hand when B.C. introduced a tire-recycling scheme on the basis of policy rather than by means of an existing regulation intended for this purpose, the validity of the scheme was undermined.[11]

C. THE SCOPE OF ENVIRONMENTAL LAW

It is not a simple matter to determine the exact composition of a country's environmental regime. Some legal measures affecting the environment will be readily recognizable and agreed on, in that they were designed with environmental goals in mind and essentially operate for this purpose. Statute-based or regulatory standards governing allowable emissions or requiring environmental assessments might be examples of environmental law, narrowly defined. But it is misleading to presume that an inventory of "environmental standards" and "environmental enforcement practices" will identify the full range of issues falling within the ambit of environmental law. Traditional private law doctrines from fields such as tort and contract law also have important environmental implications. Doctrines relating to the rights of riparian owners, nuisance, negligence, and strict liability are prominent examples. Through these long-standing common law claims, water-quality standards may be defended and various forms of pollution that threaten damage to individuals or property may be challenged in court, and so, in some sense, regulated.[12] Moreover, corporate law principles are also extremely relevant to the environmental regime. The same is true for the rules governing taxation, particularly in relation to the deductibility of expenses associated with environmental protection. Today, innovations such as carbon taxes and tradeable emission credits represent additional areas of intersection between taxation, finance and securities law and environmental protection. Planning law and legislation affecting resource use and allocation in the agricultural, fisheries, forest and mining sectors have important environmental implications, although none of these fields is extensively covered here.

Not all measures influencing the operation of an environmental regime take the form of substantive law. Some involve processes for

---

10   *Pim v. Ontario (Minister of Environment)* (1978), 23 O.R. (2d) 45.

11   *Valley Rubber Resources Inc. v. British Columbia (Minister of Environment, Lands and Parks)*, [2001] B.C.J. No. 629 (S.C.).

12   Although the foregoing examples draw upon general principles from the common law, in Quebec, provisions of the *Civil Code (C.C.Q.)* often have similar implications.

environmental decision making. Application procedures relating to environmental licences and approvals for discharges, emissions, and waste management are typical illustrations. Even where such procedures do not actually prevent any particular activity, they are of vital interest in relation to timing, costs, appeals, and the right of other interested persons to participate or intervene in the application process. General statutory principles concerning the filing and disclosure of information also affect the operation of environmental measures.

While some specific legal rules apply exclusively to environmental actions — the level of fines set for violating discharge standards, for example — other rules of significance to environmental protection may apply to several fields of law. Examples of the latter include rules for assessing damages in the context of personal injury that might equally arise in the context of medical malpractice claims or automobile accidents.[13] The rules of civil procedure in each jurisdiction and those governing standing to seek judicial review are of general application, but they are also of direct relevance to the conduct of environmental litigation. Specific standards and approaches to the proof of scientific causation might be applicable to environmental cases,[14] but general developments in the proof of causation may be equally significant. The availability of contingency fees and class-action proceedings are further examples of legal rules that will clearly influence the frequency and character of environmental litigation. But these rules will rarely, if ever, have been adopted or designed with environmental actions specifically in mind.

D. THE INSTITUTIONAL FRAMEWORK FOR ENVIRONMENTAL RESPONSIBILITY

Approximately forty years ago, governments in Canada began to establish departments formally charged with responsibility for environmental protection. Their functions, though prominent, tended to be

---

13   See generally S.M. Waddams, *The Law of Damages* (Toronto: Canada Law Book, 1997).

14   S.E. Gaines, "International Principles for Transnational Environmental Liability: Can Developments in Municipal Law Help Break the Impasse" (1989) 30 Harv. Int'l L.J. 311 at 336–37; L.A. Reynolds, "The Era of Juriscience: Investigating the Relationship between Science, Law and the Environment" (1995) 9 Can. J. Admin. L. & Prac. 61; J. Swaigen & A.D. Levy, "The Expert's Duty to the Tribunal: A Tool for Reducing Contradictions between Scientific Process and Legal Process" (1997–8) 11 Can. J. Admin. L. & Prac. 277.

carried out in a manner that was separate from, and generally subsequent to, the established processes of decision making. Since that time considerable debate has taken place about the appropriate design of institutions to promote timely and integrated attention to the environmental dimensions of projects, programs, and even policies in fields such as transportation, energy, housing, and so on. It was strongly argued by the World Commission on Environment and Development (WCED), for example, that environmental and economic considerations should be integrated in decision making,[15] and as a consequence environmental units or branches often appeared within other governmental agencies. Departments of environment or equivalent exist today at the federal level and in all provinces, however, and remain the central source of policy making in the environmental field, a field that continues to evolve at a sometimes surprising pace.

At the federal level, the *Government Organization Act, 1970* and the *Department of the Environment Act* set out the authority and responsibility of the DOE and departmental officials, including the minister (see figure 1). The scope of departmental responsibility includes matters affecting the preservation and enhancement of the natural environment and resource conservation falling within Parliament's constitutional jurisdiction. Yet interdepartmental coordination and cooperation remain essential because of the wide-ranging nature of environmental issues. Thus, Health Canada and Transport Canada have important responsibilities in connection with some environmental matters, and, by way of an administrative agreement embodied in a memorandum of understanding (MoU), DOE assumed responsibilities for pollution-prevention aspects of the *Fisheries Act*, a statute otherwise under the authority of the Department of Fisheries and Oceans. In the context of prosecution, final authority to proceed with charges often rests with officials of the Department of Justice representing the attorney general of Canada. Natural Resources is another federal department with extensive authority relating to federal environmental responsibilities.

Important contributions have been made to the development of the federal environmental framework by the House Standing Committee on Environment and Sustainable Development through a series of reports on legislative and policy initiatives, including recent studies of Blue-Green Algae, the role of the Commissioner for Environment and Sustainable Development and a five-year review of *CEPA, 1999*.[16]

---

15 World Commission on Environment and Development, *Our Common Future* (Oxford: Oxford University Press, 1987).

16 *A Global Partnership: Canada and the Conventions of the United Nations Conference on Environment and Development* (1993); *It's About Our Health: Towards*

Figure 1 Organization of the Federal Department of the Environment

Source: OECD, *Environmental Performance Reviews: Canada* (OECD, 1995). At the time of publication, departmental reorganization was continuing. New branches will include Environmental Stewardship, Strategic Policy, International Affairs, and Enforcement.

Pollution Prevention (1995); *Harmonization of Environmental Protection: An Analysis of the Harmonization Initiative of the Canadian Council of Ministers of the Environment* (1997); *Enforcing Canada's Pollution Laws: The Public Interest Must Come First* (1998); *Pesticides: Making the Right Choice for the Protection of Health and the Environment* (2000); *The Canadian Environmental Protection Act, 1999: Five-Year Review: Closing the Gaps* (2007); *Strengthening the Role of the Commissioner of the Environment and Sustainable Development* (2007); *Blue-Green Algae (Cyanobacteria) and their Toxins* (2008).

Provincial departments exercise corresponding responsibilities within the scope of their own constitutional powers. British Columbia's *Environmental Management Act*[17] provides an inventory of duties, powers, and functions of the provincial minister in relation to the management, protection, and enhancement of the environment:

- planning, research, and investigation with respect to the environment;
- development of policies for the management, protection, and use of the environment;
- planning, design, construction, operation, and maintenance of works and undertakings for the management, protection, or enhancement of the environment;
- providing information to the public about the quality and use of the environment;
- preparing and publishing policies, strategies, objectives, guidelines and standards for the protection and management of the environment; and
- preparing and publishing environmental management plans for specific areas of British Columbia which may include, but need not be limited to, measures with respect to the following: flood control; drainage; soil conservation; water-resource management; fisheries and aquatic-life management; wildlife management; waste management; and air management.

In other provinces, corresponding functions are performed by the relevant ministry or ministries in conjunction with specialized agencies. An appendix to this volume lists website information for provincial environment ministries.

In addition to federal and provincial departments, the Canadian institutional framework for environmental matters includes several intergovernmental and international bodies such as the Canadian Council of Ministers of the Environment, the International Joint Commission, and the North American Commission on Environmental Co-operation.

E. OVERVIEW OF THE BOOK

This book begins with an examination of basic concepts in environmental law (chapter 1) and a survey of constitutional (including the *Charter of Rights and Freedoms*) considerations (chapters 2 and 3). The international legal context, including the growing significance of trade

---

17   S.B.C. 2003, c. 53, s. 5.

regulation, comes next (chapter 4) and is followed by a review of the common law (chapter 5) as it affects the environment and of the basic regulatory regime (chapters 6 to 9). The volume then addresses a number of specific topics including financial compensation for spills and the restoration of contaminated lands (chapters 10 and 11), environmental assessment (chapter 12), toxic substances (chapter 13), and protected spaces and species (chapter 14). Afterwards, the text turns to more recent innovations including emphasis on individual responsibility and consumer behaviour (chapter 15), alternative dispute resolution (chapter 16), and economic instruments (chapter 17). Following a chapter on sources of environmental information (chapter 18), is a specific discussion of climate change initiatives at the federal, provincial and municipal levels (chapter 19).

The approach throughout emphasizes a description of representative examples from the range of Canadian jurisdictions rather than a comprehensive and detailed examination of any one province or the federal environmental regime. After an issue has been discussed in relation to selected jurisdictions, references for further reading are provided to assist readers to begin to identify some of the relevant provisions in the environmental legislation of other parts of Canada.

BASIC CONCEPTS IN ENVIRONMENTAL LAW

A. ENVIRONMENT

"People," argued the authors of an early report titled *The State of Canada's Environment* "have traditionally tended to view air, water, land, other organisms, and themselves as separate components that could each be understood in isolation from the whole."[1] This limiting assumption, although of steadily diminishing influence, asserts a residual effect in a variety of contexts, including the legal sphere where sectoral legislation governing forests, land-use, and agriculture, for example, coexists alongside new frameworks oriented around environmental protection or ecosystem management.

The way the term *environment* is interpreted or understood in legal settings is directly linked to the scope of environmental protection: environmental protection legislation safeguards environment as defined in that legislation and as interpreted by the courts in the light of legal principles drawn from many different spheres. Thus interpreted, environment may, but frequently does not, correspond with professional, scientific, or popular understandings of the term. By way of example, those prosecuting the hypothetical offence of doing damage to the environment must establish that the damage was inflicted on environment as that term applies in the specific context of the offence. If the

---

1 Environment Canada, *The State of Canada's Environment* (Ottawa: Supply & Services, 1991) at 1–1.

damage was done to some man-made structure, and such structures are excluded from the courts' understanding of environment, then no offence has been committed under the act.[2] Or, if environment is defined as "natural environment," excluding the indoors, them some other legal regime will be required to safeguard the indoor environment.

Courts have also considered the problem of contaminants moving through the natural environment and perhaps affecting private property in the process. One example concerned land situated between a farm and a lake:

> If the farmer uses excessive fertilizer, it could become a contaminant that seeps though the farm soil or runs into the abutting land or seeps into the soil of the abutting land, and through it into the lake. The intervening property owner would have no knowledge either of the contaminant or its location. The contaminant entered the natural environment on the farm and the owner of the in-between lands could not be said to be the owner of the source of contaminant. It would be an undue and improper strain upon the interpretation of the definition of a natural environment in s. 1(1)(k) to read it as being disjunctive and to cover natural movements of contaminant from one part of the natural environment to another.[3]

Also, where one jurisdiction legislates on the grounds that activity within its boundaries might harm the environment of another jurisdiction, courts may be reluctant to enforce the extraterritorial reach of the statute. However, environmental impacts crossing jurisdictional boundaries or extending well beyond national territories are now more widely acknowledged. We know, for example, that agricultural and forest management practices as well as domestic energy and transportation systems profoundly affect global atmospheric conditions and ultimately climate systems.

Each environmental statute must nevertheless be carefully scrutinized to assess its operational scope. This need not alter anyone's personal inclination as to what environmental law should encompass, but it will serve to identify some of the practical legal limits of statutory initiatives presently in place.

---

2   R. v. *Enso Forest Products* (1992), 8 C.E.L.R. (N.S.) 253 (B.C.S.C.), aff'd (1993), 12 C.E.L.R. (N.S.) 221 (B.C.C.A.). See also *British Columbia (Minister of Environment Lands and Parks) v. Alpha Manufacturing* (1996), 132 D.L.R. (4th) 688 (B.C.S.C.), aff'd (1997), 150 D.L.R. (4th) 193 (B.C.C.A.).

3   *Canadian National Railway v. Ontario (Director appointed under the Environmental Protection Act)*, (sub nom. *Re Canadian National Railway*) (1991), 3 O.R. (3d) 609 at 620 (Div. Ct.).

The approach Alberta takes in section 1 of its *Environmental Protection and Enhancement Act* is typical of more recent drafting. There, environment "means the components of the earth and includes (i) air, land, and water, (ii) all layers of the atmosphere, (iii) all organic and inorganic matter and living organisms, and (iv) the interacting natural systems that include components referred to in subclauses (i) to (iii)." The Northwest Territories, in keeping with its own regional priorities, adds snow and ice after air, land, and water. Saskatchewan, on the basis of 2002 amendments to its basic environmental legislation, elaborates the definition of environment to include "interacting natural systems and ecological and climatic interrelationships" among the range of components.[4]

For purposes of environmental assessment, Ontario lists plant and animal life, "including humans" and "the social, economic and cultural conditions that influence the life of humans or a community" as well as "any building, structure, machine or other device or thing made by humans," as components of the environment.[5] This definition, in the opinion of the Divisional Court, is very broad.[6] In its basic environmental protection statute, however, the same province defines natural environment as "the air, land and water, or any combination or part thereof, of the Province of Ontario."[7] In considering this definition and the purpose of the *Ontario Environmental Protection Act*, Gonthier J. acknowledged that "the social importance of environmental protection is obvious, yet the nature of the environment does not lend itself to precise codification."[8]

Another judicial observer remarked: "To variably interpret the 'natural environment' according to the character of surrounding neighbourhoods would . . . create a multitude of natural environments. . . . This . . . appears contrary to . . . the Act, which refers to only one natural environment."[9] This observation was addressed, at least in part, to the risk that a polluter might avoid liability for causing adverse effects by adding contaminants to an already polluted environment. It is not unknown, however, for a single statute to embody more than one def-

---

4   Saskatchewan, *Environmental Management and Protection Act, 2002*, S.S. 2002, c. E-10.21, s. 2 (i).

5   Ontario, *Environmental Assessment Act*, R.S.O. 1990, c. E.18, s. 1.

6   *Municipal Electric Assn. v. Ontario (Environmental Assessment Board)* (1992), 8 C.E.L.R. (N.S.) 147 at 151 (Div. Ct.).

7   Ontario, *Environmental Protection Act*, R.S.O. 1990, c. E.19, s. 1 [*OEPA*].

8   *R. v. Canadian Pacific Ltd.*, [1995] 2 S.C.R. 1028 at 1072.

9   *R. v. Commander Business Furniture Inc.* (1992), 9 C.E.L.R. (N.S.) 185 at 197–98 (Ont. Prov. Div.), Hackett Prov. J.

inition of environment, each applicable for particular purposes under the act.[10]

Also noteworthy in connection with judicial understanding of environment are indications that the courts are sensitive to a range of objectives underlying environmental protection. In weighing the benefits of a municipal noise bylaw against the restrictive effects of the legislation on freedom of expression which is safeguarded in the *Canadian Charter of Rights and Freedoms*, the Supreme Court of Canada endorsed the following observation from the Quebec Court of Appeal: ". . . the citizens of a city, even a city the size of Montreal, are entitled to a healthy environment. Noise control is unquestionably part of what must be done to improve the quality of this environment."[11] Even beyond this clear understanding of environment as a direct contributor to the well-being of the human population, are acknowledgements of the essential well-being of the environment independent of direct human interests. With reference to the toxic substance provisions of the *Canadian Environmental Protection Act*, Justices Lamer and Iacobucci remarked:

> Their scope extends well beyond matters relating to human health into the realm of general ecological protection. Parliament's clear intention was to allow for federal intervention where the environment itself was at risk, whether or not the substances concerned posed a threat to human health and whether or not the aspect of the environment affected was one on which human life depended.[12]

B. POLLUTION

Anti-pollution measures are central features of environmental law, but their application has always been complicated by controversy about the nature of the conduct in question. What is meant by pollution, and particularly what constitutes prohibited levels of pollution, has varied depending on local conditions, scientific or professional analyses, and the judgments of observers, some of whom will be more tolerant than others of "acceptable" levels. Indeed, the argument has occasionally been made that pollution is a socially defined phenomenon, or even something constructed by enforcement officials: "[P]ollution, in other words, is an administrative creation. The broad legal mandate of the

---

10 *Clean Environment Act*, R.S.N.B. 1973, c. C-6.

11 Chamberland J.A. quoted in translation in *Montreal (City) v. 2952-1366 Quebec Inc.*, 2005 SCC 62 at para 99.

12 *R. v. Hydro Quebec*, [1997] 3 S.C.R. 213 at para. 42.

agencies about water pollution control is transformed into policy by senior officials and given practical expression in the setting of pollution standards. ... In this sense, the water authorities create pollution . . . by making the rules whose infraction constitutes pollution."[13] An apparent illustration of such an approach is found in Quebec's *Environment Quality Act* where a pollutant is defined as "a contaminant or a mixture of several contaminants present in the environment in a concentration or quantity greater than the permissible level determined by regulation of the government."[14] Other statutory approaches to defining pollution include that of a British Columbia statute on waste management in which pollution is described as "the presence in the environment of substances or contaminants that substantially alter or impair the usefulness of the environment."[15]

A Saskatchewan statute set forth a more extended explanation in its definition of pollution as alteration of the physical, chemical, biological, or aesthetic properties of the environment, including the addition or removal of any substance that (i) will render the environment harmful to the public health; (ii) is unsafe or harmful for domestic, municipal, industrial, agricultural, recreational, or other lawful uses of the environment; or (iii) is harmful to wild animals, birds or aquatic life.[16] The explicit reference to aesthetic harm, something by no means found throughout environmental laws, is indicative of the potential for different conceptions of pollution in the minds of scientific experts and officials in the legal system.

Other jurisdictions, sometimes without reference to pollution as such, have employed the concepts of contaminant and adverse environmental effects to delineate the harms that anti-pollution legislation is intended to control. In Ontario's *Environmental Protection Act*, adverse effect is defined as one or more of: impairment of the quality of the natural environment for any use that can be made of it; injury or damage to property or to plant or animal life; harm or material discomfort to any person; an adverse effect on the health of any person; impairment of the safety of any person; rendering any property or plant or animal life unfit for human use; loss of enjoyment of normal use of property; and interference with the normal conduct of business.[17] Federal fish-

---

13   K. Hawkins, *Environment and Enforcement: Regulation and the Social Definition of Pollution* (Oxford: Clarendon Press, 1984) at 23.

14   R.S.Q. c. Q-2.

15   *Environmental Management Act*, S.B.C. 2003, c. 53, s. 1(1).

16   *Environmental Management and Protection Act*, S.S. 1983–84, c. E-10.2, s. 2. Now see the *Environmental Management and Protection Act, 2002*, above note 4.

17   OEPA, above note 7, s. 1(1).

eries legislation addresses related dimensions of environmental quality by means of a prohibtion against the deposit of any "deleterious substance" in Canadian fisheries waters, with deleterious substance defined as: "any substance that, if added to any water, would degrade or alter or form part of a process of degradation or alteration of the quality of that water so that it is rendered or is likely to be rendered deleterious to fish or fish habitat or the use by man of fish that frequent that water."[18]

Although the legal concepts of pollution, adverse effects from contaminants, deleterious substances and so on may not appear to embody scientific precision, they should not be seen as arbitrary and subjective: they are utilized and applied in the context of relevant professional knowledge that is subject to ongoing evaluation and reassessment and are continually reviewable through formal judicial procedures. It should also be noted, however, that for these and other reasons, there are important interrelationships between legal responses to pollution and the concept of risk.

There are risks associated with our understanding of the nature or effects of polluting substances: perhaps they are more harmful than assumed. There are risks associated with the presence of such substances in the environment: perhaps they persist longer or travel more broadly than we assume. There are risks associated with environmental exposure to pollutants: perhaps more people will be exposed to a contaminant than we assume, or perhaps those people, children for example, are more susceptible to adverse effects than we assume. Managing risk has thus become an important element of the law's response to pollution.[19]

Pollution is not the only form of damage which an environmental protection regime seeks to address.

C. CONSERVATION

For earlier generations, the term *conservation* was used to describe an important social objective associated with maintaining resource stocks

---

18   *Fisheries Act*, R.S.C. 1985, c. F-14, s. 34.

19   Elizabeth Fisher observes that "it is now common for environmental problems to be characterized in terms of risk and the bulk of environmental regulatory law to be thought of as 'risk regulation'." "Risk and Environmental Law: A Beginner's Guide" in Benjamin J. Richardson & Stepan Wood, *Environmental Law for Sustainability* (Portland, OR: Hart Publishing, 2006) 97. See also, Jeremy D. Fraiberg & Michael J. Trebilcock, "Risk Regulation: Technocratic and Democratic Tools for Regulatory Reform" (1998) 43 McGill L.J. 835.

and capacity. The harm to be avoided in the minds of such conservationists might be described as resource depletion, for they certainly anticipated that resources would be fully utilized on an ongoing basis.[20]

Conservation remains an important element of environmental protection programs and can certainly be found as an objective in environmental and resource legislation. The federal *Fisheries Act*, for example, contains provisions associated with the objective of conservation; proposed revisions, which were never enacted, would have made it explicit that "the conservation of Canada's fisheries and their management on a sustainable basis are central to the economic viability of persons engaged in fishing and fish processors and the well-being of communities that are dependent on fisheries resources."[21] Conservation does, however, figure prominently in the *Oceans Act*.[22] Other legislation envisages conservation in terms of avoiding degradation of essential physical, chemical, and biological characteristics of the environment.[23]

Without defining conservation, the Canadian Council of Ministers of the Environment (CCME) explained conservation strategy as "a guide for the sustainable use of our resources and the environment,"[24] thereby signalling a transition from the historic conception of resource conservation to the current concern with sustainability, be it termed environmental sustainability or sustainable development. It is perhaps in this sense that a number of provinces continue to employ the term in relation to habitat restoration and wildlife protection measures. B.C., for example, has established a Habitat Conservation Trust Fund with responsibility for acquiring and maintaining parts of the province that contribute to wildlife preservation and for supporting community stewardship organizations and research initiatives oriented towards similar ends.[25] Another indication that the concept of conservation may now be interpreted broadly to correspond with the growing comprehensiveness of the contemporary environmental agenda is found in commen-

---

20   As used in the General Regulation under Ontario's *Environmental Assessment Act*, O. Reg. 334, s. 8, to refer to the creation of shelter belts, erosion control, and soil and water conservation, the phrase "conservation services" is in this tradition. For historical background, see S.P. Hays, *Conservation and the Gospel of Efficiency: The Progressive Conservation Movement, 1890–1920* (Cambridge, MA: Harvard University Press, 1968).

21   Bill C-115, *An Act Respecting Fisheries*, 1st Sess., 35th Parl., 1995.

22   S.C. 1996, c. 31

23   *Environmental Protection and Enhancement Act*, S.A. 1992, c. E-133, s. 1.

24   Canadian Council of Ministers of the Environment, *Conservation Strategies: A Compendium of Canadian Experiences* (September 1989) at 7.

25   Online: www2.news.gov.bc.ca/nrm_news_releases/2005WLAP0015-000226. htm.

tary from the Supreme Court of Canada. In *R. v. Sundown*, the Court referred to the Crown's view that conservation extended no further than the scope of protective measures for fish, fur-bearing animals and big game as possibly amounting to "an unnecessarily restrictive definition of conservation."[26] The judgement continued:

> . . . a requirement that cabins be built at least 150 feet away from the shore may be concerned with possible pollution of the lake, the erosion of the shoreline and the effects of that erosion on water quality. It may well be that . . . conservation laws . . . should be construed generously to refer not only to the conservation of game and fish but also to the environment they inhabit. Legislation aimed at preserving habitat and biodiversity, the water quality of ground water and lakes, rivers and streams, topsoil conservancy and the prevention of erosion may be laws in relation to conservation.[27]

Evidence from the international context also suggests that the historic concept of conservation remains sufficiently flexible to encompass emerging environmental challenges. In this vein, Achim Steiner, Director General of the International Union for Conservation of Nature and Natural Resources (IUCN), observed that "Conservation in the 21st Century will need to come to terms with a world that will increasingly struggle with the scale and complexity of our collective impact on the Earth's natural resources." He added in explanation that:

> While species and ecosystems were once our departure points for protecting and restoring nature, we are today forced to recognize that we must redefine our work in terms of systems (e.g. economic, social, and political) and cycles (e.g. hydrological, climate, nutrient). Our ability to influence them will determine whether we can cope with the forces of global change unfolding before our very eyes.[28]

D. SUSTAINABLE DEVELOPMENT

Popularized internationally through the report of the World Commission on Environment and Development (WCED) entitled *Our Common Future*, sustainable development has been widely endorsed within domestic environmental regimes. In Canada this process was initially en-

---

26   *R. v. Sundown*, [1999] 1 S.C.R. 393 at para. 45.
27   *Ibid.*
28   Achim Steiner, Director General, World Conservation Union (IUCN), 22 December 2005.

couraged by the deliberations of a National Task Force on Environment and Economy, which preceded incorporation of sustainable develoment in several federal statutes.[29] Sustainability is now widely regarded as a criterion or performance standard against which various development- al initiatives should be assessed. Indeed, the promotion of sustainable development is among the stated objectives of the North American Free Trade Agreement (*NAFTA*) and its environmental side agreement (see chapter 4). Sustainable development has also been acknowledged in international law as the "need to reconcile economic development with protection of the environment."[30]

The WCED's formulation of sustainable development as develop- ment that "meets the needs of the present without compromising the ability of future generations to meet their own needs" is not without controversy and has been subject to fairly open-ended interpretation. In the words of the National Task Force on Environment and Economy, "environmental and economic planning cannot proceed in separate spheres. Long-term economic growth depends on a healthy environ- ment. It also affects the environment in many ways. Ensuring en- vironmentally sound and sustainable economic development requires the technology and wealth that is generated by continued economic growth."[31] Such an approach suggests the importance of integrating economic and environmental decision making, although the manner in which this is to be accomplished remains to be determined.

In the words of one experienced observer of the policy process from both the domestic and international perspectives:

> Sustainable development is an approach to decision making that takes a long-term focus, incorporates social, economic and environmental factors, and recognizes the interdependence of domestic and global activities. It is an ethical principle that incorporates a commitment to equity between the current generation and those that will follow; and between the poor and the more affluent. It means working to ensure a fair distribution of the costs and benefits of development between the nations of the developed and developing worlds. Sustainable de- velopment is also about ensuring that choices we make as citizens,

---

29 See, for example, the *Canadian Environmental Assessment Act*, S.C. 1992, c. 37 and the *Department of Forestry Act*, S.C. 1989, c. 27.

30 *Case Concerning the Gabčíkovo-Nagymaros Project* (Hungary/Slovakia), [1997] I.C.J. Rep. 3.

31 National Task Force on Environment and Economy, *Report of the National Task Force on Environment and Economy: submitted to the Canadian Council of Re- source and Environmental Ministers, September 24, 1987* by Gerard Lecuyer, Chair (Downsview, ON: National Task Force on Environment and Economy, 1987) at 2.

consumers, producers, and investors are compatible with an excellent quality of life for all Canadians and the global community, now and in the future. However, sustainability is not a fixed endpoint that can be defined.[32]

Legislative elaboration of sustainability incorporates increasing detail without often appearing to specify legally enforceable standards. As discussed in the federal *Auditor General Act*, for example, sustainable development is "a continually evolving concept based on the integration of social, economic and environmental concerns." It may be achieved, according to the statute, in various ways. These include:

a)   the integration of the environment and the economy;
b)   protecting the health of Canadians;
c)   protecting ecosystems;
d)   meeting international obligations;
e)   promoting equity;
f)   an integrated approach to planning and making decisions that takes into account the environmental and natural resource costs of different economic options and the economic costs of different environmental and natural resource options;
g)   preventing pollution; and
h)   respect for nature and the needs of future generations.[33]

For purposes of forest management, British Columbia set out to codify sustainable use as:

a)   managing forests to meet present needs without compromising the needs of future generations;
b)   providing stewardship of forests based on an ethic of respect for the land;
c)   balancing productive, spiritual, ecological, and recreational values of forests to meet the economic and cultural needs of peoples and communities, including First Nations;
d)   conserving biological diversity, soil, water, fish, wild life, scenic diversity, and other forest resources; and

---

32   Richard Ballhorn, "The Role of Government and Policy in Sustainable Development" (2005) 1 Journal of Sustainable Development Law and Policy 19.

33   *Auditor General Act*, R.S.C. 1985, c. A-17, s. 21.1. *Canadian Environmental Protection Act, 1999*, S.C. 1999, c. 33 [*CEPA, 1999*], s. 54 requires the federal minister of the environment to issue objectives, guidelines, and codes of practice adressing sustainable development among other factors. See also the *Environmental Trust Fund Act*, S.N.B. 1990, c. E-9.3, s.3; the *Environment Act*, R.S.N.S. 1994–95, c. 1, s. 2.

e)   restoring damaged ecologies.[34]

Similarly, in Ontario, forest management legislation calls for the use of enforceable indicators of sustainability to replace a prior regime oriented around guidelines and policy statements.[35] Manitoba has also taken steps to recognize the importance of sustainability in provincial decision making. Legislation in that province set out principles and guidelines for sustainable development in the province and called for the development of sustainability indicators.[36]

E. BIODIVERSITY AND ECOLOGICAL INTEGRITY

The international *Convention on Biological Diversity* defined an ecosystem as "a dynamic complex of plant, animal and micro-organism communities and their non-living environment interacting as a functional unit."[37] Thus, reference to ecosystems acknowledges the interconnectedness of biological communities and the surrounding environmental complex of which they are a part. The contrast between an ecosystem approach and a purely sectoral or media-based approach emphasizing air, land, and water in isolation is seen in *CEPA, 1999*'s definition of environment as the components of the Earth including air, land, and water, together with all layers of the atmosphere, all organic and inorganic matter and living organisms, as well as the interacting natural systems that comprise any of these components.[38] As explained by the House of Commons Standing Committee on Environment and Sustainable Development, "the key insight of the ecosystem approach is that it is the integration and interaction among the living and non-living elements of an ecosystem that enable it to function as a unit. If one part is harmed, the entire ecosystem itself may be affected. Sustained life is a property of ecosystem integrity. Individual species cannot exist

---

34   *Forest Practices Code of British Columbia Act*, R.S.B.C. 1996, c. 59. The *Code* was subsequently replaced by the *Forest and Range Practices Act*, S.B.C. 2002, c. 69.

35   *Crown Forest Sustainability Act*, S.O. 1994, c. 25. *Algonquin Wildlands League v. Ontario (Minister of Natural Resources)* (1998), 26 C.E.L.R. (N.S.) 163 (Ont. Div. Ct.), additional reasons at (1998), 27 C.E.L.R. (N.S.) 218 (Ont. Div Ct.), aff'd in relation to sustainability indicators (1998), 29 C.E.L.R. (N.S.) 31 (Ont. C.A.), additional reasons at (2000), 32 C.E.L.R. (N.S.) 233 (Ont. C.A.).

36   *Sustainable Development and Consequential Amendments Act*, S.M. 1997, c. 61. See also *Waste Reduction and Prevention Act*, C.C.S.M. c. W40.

37   *Convention on Biological Diversity*, 5 June 1992, 31 I.L.M. 818, art. 2.

38   Above note 33.

on their own."[39] Arguably then, adoption of the ecosystem focus represents a broadening of the objectives of environmental protection regimes.[40]

The concept of *biological diversity* gives prominence to the importance of variety in terms of life on Earth, with variety including ecological diversity, species diversity, and genetic diversity. "Genetic diversity comprehends variability within a species, measured by variation in genes within a particular variety, subspecies, or breed; species diversity relates to the range of terrestrial living organisms; ecological diversity concerns the variety of habitats, biotic communities, and ecological processes found in the biosphere and the great variety within ecosystems in terms of difference in habitat and ecological processes."[41] As an objective for environmental legislation, biodiversity is increasingly common in Canadian statutes. Thus, for example, the Northwest Territories' *Environmental Rights Act* is intended to further the "integrity, biological diversity and productivity of the ecosystems."[42]

Following consideration by an expert panel, the concept of *ecological integrity* was introduced to national parks legislation in 2000. For purposes of the *Canada National Parks Act*, ecological integrity means "a condition that is determined to be characteristic of its natural region and likely to persist, including abiotic components and the composition and abundance of native species and biological communities, rates of change and supporting processes."[43]

F. THE POLLUTER-PAYS PRINCIPLE

The *polluter-pays* principle emphasizes the responsibility of those who engage in environmentally harmful conduct (either as producers or

---

39 *Report of the House of Commons Standing Committee on Environment and Sustainable Development: It's About Our Health! Towards Pollution Prevention* (Ottawa: Canadian Communication Group, 1995) at 50.

40 For a recent judicial statement endorsing the validity of an ecosystem focus in environmental legislation, see *R. v. Inco Ltd.* (2001), 54 O.R. (3d) 495 (C.A.).

41 P.W. Birnie & A.E. Boyle, *International Law and the Environment* (Oxford: Clarendon Press, 1992) at 483.

42 R.S.N.W.T. 1988 (Supp.), c. 83. For implementation of biodiversity goals in the N.W.T., see Northwest Territories Biodiversity Action Plan: Major Initiatives on Biodiversity (2004), online: www.nwtwildlife.rwed.gov.nt.ca/biodiversity/biodiversity_action_plan.htm. See also *Environmental Bill of Rights, 1993*, S.O. 1993, c. 28, s. 2(2)2; *Environment Act*, S.Y. 1991, c. 5, s. 5.5(1)(a); *Environment Act*, S.N.S. 1994–95, c. 1, s. 2 [*NSEA*]; *CEPA, 1999*, above note 33, s. 3.

43 *Canada National Parks Act*, S.C. 2000, c. 32, s. 2.

consumers) for the costs associated with their activity. They should not be subsidized financially by direct public expenditures for environmental harm, nor should they enjoy indirect advantages from damaging the environment in ways that are not attributed back to them but are instead borne by others. This concept enjoys constitutional status within the European Union[44] and has begun to influence penalty regimes, the design of economic instruments and incentives, and the nature of environmental restoration programs in Canada.

Recognition of the polluter-pays principle is one of the goals of Nova Scotia's *Environment Act* where this concept is explained as "confirming the responsibility of anyone who creates an adverse effect on the environment to take remedial action and pay for the costs of that action."[45] As explained by the Supreme Court of Canada:

> To encourage sustainable development, that principle assigns polluters the responsibility for remedying contamination for which they are responsible and imposes on them the direct and immediate costs of pollution. At the same time, polluters are asked to pay more attention to the need to protect ecosystems in the course of their economic activities.[46]

The extent of liability under the polluter-pays principle and how responsibility might be apportioned remain complex and difficult issues in many circumstances. By general implication from the Supreme Court commentary, it would be necessary to distinguish pollution costs of a direct and immediate nature from those that would not be so described. These matters are occasionally addressed in the particularities of statutory regimes.[47]

G. THE PRECAUTIONARY PRINCIPLE AND POLLUTION PREVENTION

From its German origins in relation to good household management, the *precautionary principle* has evolved to encompass a cluster of basic principles with both substantive and procedural implications. It in-

---

44 *Single European Act*, 1986, article 25, 1992 adding article 130R 2.

45 NSEA, above note 42, s. 2(c).

46 *Imperial Oil Ltd. v. Quebec (Minister of the Environment)*, [2003] 2 S.C.R. 624 at para. 24.

47 For an inventory of federal and provincial legislation where the principle of polluter pays is incorporated either explicitly or by implication, see *Imperial Oil Ltd. v. Quebec (Minister of the Environment)*, ibid. at para. 23.

cludes, for example, the proposition that early preventive action is appropriate even in the absence of scientifically documented need when delay would impose increased costs and greater risks of environmental harm. Precaution also entails recognition of the importance of leaving wide margins of tolerance or room for manoeuvre to permit natural adaptation to human interference. In addition, the precautionary principle implies a shift in the onus of proof to those who propose initiatives, innovations, and activities whose environmental impact is not fully understood.[48] The precautionary principle accordingly offers guidance on managing the relationships between scientific uncertainty, the potential for adverse effects, and the legal or administrative decision-making process. Scientific uncertainty as it affects decision making about adverse environmental impacts may take several forms. These include conceptual uncertainty or shortcomings in our understanding of causation, as well as limitations in our ability to sample and take measurements, or deficiencies in modelling procedures.[49]

The principle of precaution has been formulated in a number of ways and enjoys varying degrees of acceptance. In international law, the *Rio Declaration on Environment and Development* clearly raised the visibility of precautionary claims in stating that "[w]here there are threats of serious or irreversible damage, lack of full scientific certainty shall not be used as a reason for postponing cost-effective measures to prevent environmental degradation."[50]

There are growing indications of formal recognition of the precautionary idea in Canada, in *CEPA, 1999*, for example. The use of the precautionary principle in decision making is also a goal associated with sustainable development in Nova Scotia's environmental legislation so that "where there are threats of serious or irreversible damage, the lack of full scientific certainty shall not be used as a reason for postponing measures to prevent environmental degradation."[51] In confirming the authority of a Quebec town to regulate pesticide use within its municipal boundaries, a majority of the Supreme Court of Canada

---

48   T. O'Riordan & J. Cameron, *Interpreting the Precautionary Principle* (London: Earthscan Publications, 1994) at 16–18. For a recent illustration of the precautionary approach in Canada, see *Dillon v. Ontario (Director, Ministry of the Environment)* (2001), 36 C.E.L.R. (N.S.) 141 (O.E.A.B.).

49   Vern R. Walker, "The Siren Song of Science: Toward a Taxonomy of Scientific Uncertainty for Decisionmakers" (1991) 23 Conn. L. Rev. 567.

50   *Rio Declaration of the United Nations Conference on Environment and Development*, 14 June 1992, 31 I.L.M. 874, Principle 15.

51   *NSEA*, above note 42, s. 2(b)(ii). See also *Endangered Species Act*, S.N.S. 1998, c. 11, ss. 2(1)(h) and 11(1).

suggested that the legitimacy of the bylaw was enhanced insofar as the bylaw's preventive approach respected the precautionary principle in international law.[52]

In consideration of the challenges of implementing precautionary decision making in a consistent manner across the wide range circumstances for which it is responsible, the government of Canada formulated a set of guiding principles.[53] As summarized below, these suggest some of the factors relevant to putting precaution into operation:

1. The precautionary approach is a legitimate and distinctive decision-making tool within risk management.
2. It is legitimate for decisions to be guided by society's chosen level of protection against risk.
3. Sound scientific information and its evaluation must be the basis for applying the precautionary approach, particularly with regard to (i) the decision to act or not to act (i.e., to implement precautionary measures or not), and (ii) the measures taken once a decision is made.
4. The scientific evidence required should be established relative to the chosen level of protection. Further, the responsibility for producing the information base (burden of proof) may be assigned. It is recognized that the scientific information base and responsibility for producing it may shift as the knowledge evolves.
5. Mechanisms should exist for re-evaluating the basis for the decisions and for providing a transparent process for further consultation.
6. A greater degree of transparency, clearer accountability and increased public involvement are appropriate.
7. Precautionary measures should be subject to reconsideration, on the basis of the evolution of science, technology and society's chosen level of protection.
8. Precautionary measures should be proportional to the potential severity of the risk being addressed and to society's chosen level of protection.
9. Precautionary measures should be non-discriminatory and consistent with measures taken in similar circumstances.
10. Precautionary measures should be cost-effective, with the goal of generating (i) an overall net benefit for society at least cost, and (ii) efficiency in the choice of measures.

---

52 *114957 Canada Ltée (Spraytech, Société d'arrosage) v. Hudson (Town)*, 2001 SCC 40 at paras. 31–32.

53 Government of Canada, *A Canadian Perspective on the Precautionary Approach* (Discussion Document, September 2001).

11. Where more than one option reasonably meets the above characteristics, then the least trade-restrictive measure should be applied.

There has also been extensive discussion of *pollution prevention*, often known simply as "P2."[54] Pollution prevention is envisaged as a reorientation of environmental protection efforts so as to reduce or avoid the creation of environmental contaminants in the first instance rather than trying to control and contain their impact later. The federal government's working definition of pollution prevention is "the use of processes, practices, materials, products, substances or energy that avoid or minimize the creation of pollutants and waste, and reduce the overall risk to the environment or human health."[55] (See Figure 1.1.)

Figure 1.1 The Environmental Protection Hierarchy

Source: Environment Canada, *Pollution Prevention: A Federal Strategy for Action* (Minister of Supply and Services Canada, 1995) at 3. Also available at www. ec.gc.ca/pollution/strategy/en/p3.cfm

Nova Scotia is among those jurisdictions that have explicitly embraced the principle of pollution prevention, describing it, along with waste reduction, as "the foundation for long-term environmental protection." Specifically, the Nova Scotia statute provides that pollution prevention includes: "the conservation and efficient use of resources . . . the promotion of the development and use of sustainable, scientific and technological innovations and management systems, and . . . the importance of reducing, reusing, recycling and recovering the products of our society."[56]

---

54 Canadian Council of Ministers of the Environment, *National Commitment to Pollution Prevention* (Canadian Council of Ministers of the Environment, 1993).

55 *CEPA, 1999*, above note 33, s. 3(1).

56 *NSEA*, above note 42, s. 2(b)(iii).

Individual decisions within the overall realm of environmental law are generally influenced—whether explicitly or implicitly—by underlying concepts and principles such as those introduced here. The list might certainly be extended to include, for example, intergenerational equity or adaptive management,[57] but the concepts reviewed above are certainly the most prominent. Their dynamic character or recent vintage have significantly contributed to the pace of change in the environmental law field.

Insofar as the concepts introduced here constitute norms, they may be considered to be objectives or standards against which the performance of an environmental protection regime may be assessed. Indeed, there are indications that biodiversity and sustainability have begun to assume such a status in the minds of many observers.[58] It should be noted, however, that there is considerable room for debate about whether such goals are being effectively pursued. Some of the other concepts, such as the polluter-pays principle or that of precaution, are more likely to perform instrumental functions; that is, rather than being ends in themselves, they may be useful in reaching other objectives.

FURTHER READINGS

ATTRIDGE, I., ed., *Biodiversity Law and Policy in Canada: Review and Recommendations* (Toronto: Canadian Institute for Environmental Law and Policy, 1996)

BALLHORN, RICHARD, "The Role of Government and Policy in Sustainable Development" (2005) 1 Journal of Sustainable Development Law and Policy 19

CORDONIER SEGGER, MARIE-CLAIRE, ed., *Sustainable Justice: Reconciling Economic, Social and Environmental Law* (Boston: Martinus Nijhoff, 2005)

ELDER, P.S., "Biological Diversity and Alberta Law" (1996) 34 Alta. L. Rev. 293

---

57   C. Walters, *Adaptive Management of Renewable Resources* (New York: McMillan, 1986); Bradley C. Karkkainen, "Adaptive Ecosystem Management and Regulatory Penalty Defaults: Toward a Bounded Pragmatism" (2003) 87 Minn. L. Rev. 943.

58   Robert B. Keiter, "Conservation Biology and the Law: Assessing the Challenges Ahead" (1994) 69 Chicago-Kent L. Rev. 911; Richardson & Wood, *Environmental Law for Sustainability*, above note 19.

ELDER, P.S., & W.A. ROSS, "How to Ensure That Developments Are Environmentally Sustainable" in J.O. Saunders, ed., *The Legal Challenge of Sustainable Development* (Calgary: Canadian Institute of Resources Law, 1990) 124–140

FISHER, ELIZABETH, "Shifting Environmental Law: A Beginner's Guide" in Benjamin J. Richardson and Stepan Wood, eds., *Environmental Law for Sustainability* (Portland: Hart Publishing, 2006) 97

JARDINE, CINDY G., "Risk and Risk Management Frameworks for Human Health and Environmental Risks" (2003) 6 Journal of Toxicology and Environmental Health 569

LEVY, A.D., & J. SWAIGEN, "The Expert's Duty to the Tribunal: A Tool for Reducing Contradictions between Scientific Process and Legal Process" (1998) 11 C.J.A.L.P. 277

O'RIORDAN, T., & J. CAMERON, eds., *Interpreting the Precautionary Principle* (London: Earthscan Publications, 1994)

Report of the House of Commons Standing Committee on Environment and Sustainable Development: It's About Our Health! Towards Pollution Prevention (Ottawa: Canadian Communication Group, 1995)

REYNOLDS, L.A., "The Era of Juriscience: Investigating the Relationship Between Science, Law and the Environment" (1995) 9 Canadian Journal of Administrative Law and Practice 61

SCOTT, DAYNA NADINE, "The Burden of Proof: The Precautionary Principle and Its Potential for the 'Democratization of Risk'" in Law Commission of Canada, *Law and Risk* (Vancouver: UBC Press, 2005) 50

TRUDEAU, HELENE, "Du droit international au droit interne: l'emergence du principe de precaution en droit de l'environnement" (2003) 28 Queen's Law Journal 455

VANDER ZWAAG, D., "The Precautionary Principle in Environmental Law and Policy" (1999) 8 J. Envtl. L. & Prac. 355

THE CONSTITUTIONAL ALLOCATION OF ENVIRONMENTAL RESPONSIBILITIES AND INTERJURISDICTIONAL COORDINATION

A. INTRODUCTION

Although pollution of Canada's lakes and rivers was certainly under discussion in the Confederation era, environment is not specifically mentioned in the documentation that formally established the constitutional framework. There was therefore no assignment of responsibility for the environment as such to either the provinces or the federal government. Accordingly, constitutional authority over the environment is divided on the basis of a number of heads of power, essentially as formulated at the time of Confederation in what is now known as the *Constitution Act, 1867.* In *Friends of the Oldman River Society v. Canada (Minister of Transport)*[1] Justice La Forest of the Supreme Court of Canada discussed the difficulty these arrangements present for those who seek to identify and allocate responsibility for environmental matters in the Canadian process of constitutional adjudication:

> The environment, as understood in its generic sense, encompasses the physical, economic and social environment touching several of the heads of power assigned to the respective levels of government. . . .

---

1   [1992] 1 S.C.R. 3.

It must be recognized that the environment is not an independent matter of legislation under the *Constitution Act, 1867* and that it is a constitutionally abstruse matter which does not comfortably fit within the existing division of powers without considerable overlap and uncertainty.[2]

La Forest J. then emphasized the necessity of linking environmental initiatives at either the federal or the provincial level to an existing head of power, under the *Constitution Act*, further noting that "the extent to which environmental concerns may be taken into account in the exercise of a power may vary from one power to another." As an example he indicated that the federal government's environmental authority in relation to the management of fisheries, a resource, will not necessarily correspond with the environmental role permitted in association with federal constitutional power over such activities as navigation or railways.

The foregoing confirms that responsibility for important environmental questions has not been allocated with the level of constitutional certainty often thought to be desirable from the perspective of legislators, policy makers, and anyone seeking to ensure governmental accountability in this field. This is partly a consequence of the original omission dating from 1867, but it is also a result of the processes of constitutional interpretation and of the changing perceptions of the nature of environmental problems and appropriate policy responses. Al Lucas writes, for example, that it is "constitutionally meaningless" to attempt to determine conclusively whether the federal or the provincial government has jurisdiction over air pollution. An answer to the question would, he explains, "depend not only on factual matters such as the source, nature and consequences of particular air pollution, but also on the precise form and scope of any law aimed at it."[3]

This is a useful reminder that constitutional analysis in Canada requires one to determine or specify the subject of the allocation or the specific matter one wishes a particular level of government to regulate.[4] One might be concerned with the availability of a particular instrument or technique of environmental control such as criminal law, general

---

2   *Ibid.*, at para 86.

3   A.R. Lucas, "Harmonization of Federal and Provincial Environmental Policies: The Changing Legal and Policy Framework" in J.O. Saunders, ed., *Managing Natural Resources in a Federal State: Essays from the Second Banff Conference on Natural Resources Law* (Toronto: Carswell, 1986) 33 at 34.

4   D. Gibson, "Environmental Protection and Enhancement under a New Constitution" in S.M. Beck & I. Bernier, eds., *Canada and the New Constitution: The Unfinished Agenda*, vol. 2 (Montreal: Institute for Research on Public Policy, 1983) 113 at 117–23.

regulatory schemes, or licensing controls such as quotas and emission standards. Alternative instruments might include zoning and land-use restrictions, positive programs with respect to wilderness protection, or cleanup initiatives directed towards the rehabilitation of contaminated sites. The potential utility of each of these forms of legal intervention often induces people to focus on the availability of such powers as justification for environmental protection measures by the level of government entitled to use them. But most of these general techniques are applicable in relation to subjects other than the environment.

The risk in focusing on legal instruments can be that the government with the interest in safeguarding the environment may not be the government with the most effective tools. This difficulty partly explains the persistence of analysis centred on a preoccupation with so-called environmental media or sectors: air, land, water. Yet this sectoral approach is also problematic because administrative measures frequently involve interrelationships outside the subject being regulated. A third model sometimes put forward associates constitutional authority with the territory to be affected. Thus, national parks, Indian reserves, coastal waters, or federal lands are sometimes identified as zones within which environmental responsibility might be neatly allocated.[5] However, the interrelationship between activity within and without any areas of this type demonstrates the limitations of geographic demarcation schemes as a basis for assigning legislative responsibilities.

Given the overlapping nature of spheres of constitutional responsibility affecting the environment and the further difficulties presented by environmental externalities or spillovers, clear and definitive answers as to which government has power to deal with the environmental dimensions of different fields of activity or even classes of physical things have been slow to emerge. Nonetheless, before describing some non-constitutional mechanisms of intergovernmental coordination, we will consider the bases on which claims about the allocation of constitutional authority are typically formulated.

B. SOURCES OF FEDERAL ENVIRONMENTAL AUTHORITY

Certain specific heads of constitutional power provide the federal government with legislative authority encompassing associated environmental

---

5   *Canadian Environmental Protection Act, 1999*, S.C. 1999, c. 33 [*CEPA, 1999*]. Part 9 addresses environmental issues on "federal lands."

measures. Powers concerning the regulation of trade and commerce (section 91[2]), navigation and shipping (section 91[10]), seacoast and inland fisheries (section 91[12]), federal works and undertakings (section 91[29] and section 92[10]), and Indians and lands reserved for the Indians (section 91[24]) are notable examples. However, the scope of environmental measures linked to the exercise of such powers is not unlimited. The courts remain sensitive to the existence of provincial powers and have formulated procedures for resolving conflicts.

In *R. v. Northwest Falling Contractors Ltd.*[6] the Supreme Court of Canada upheld a federal *Fisheries Act* provision prohibiting the deposit of deleterious substances into water frequented by fish, despite arguments that this measure invaded the realm of provincial responsibility for property and civil rights under section 92(13) of the *Constitution Act*. The validity of the federal measure rested on the close linkage between the prohibition and the potential for harm to fish, a connection based on the definition of *deleterious substance* as one posing the prospect of harm to fish or their habitat. The fate of another, more broadly worded *Fisheries Act* provision illustrated, however, that the scope of the fisheries' power to support federal environmental initiatives is subject to constraints. When the federal government declared that "[n]o person engaging in logging, lumbering, land clearing or other operations, shall put or knowingly permit to be put, any slash, stumps or other debris into any water frequented by fish or that flows into such water, or on the ice over either such water, or at a place from which it is likely to be carried into either such water," the legislation was struck down for its failure to link the prohibited conduct to actual or potential harm to the fishery.[7] The existence or threat of such harm was thus determined to be an essential precondition of federal jurisdiction in this area.

Federal authority in connection with trade and commerce, and in connection with international agreements, has also failed to provide broad support for federal initiatives in the environmental area. The courts have historically interpreted the trade and commerce power in a restrictive manner, so that it permits federal regulation of international and interprovincial but not intraprovincial trade.[8] And it has long been established that the federal government cannot, simply by entering into international agreements, extend the scope of its domestic jurisdiction over a matter that would otherwise fall within provincial jurisdiction.[9] In situations where pollution originating in one province will have an

---

6   [1980] 2 S.C.R. 292.
7   *R. v. Fowler*, [1980] 2 S.C.R. 213.
8   *Labatt Breweries v. Canada (A.G.)*, [1980] 1 S.C.R. 914.
9   *Canada (A.G.) v. Ontario (A.G.)*, [1937] A.C. 326 (P.C.).

external impact on neighbouring provinces or internationally, however, the federal government can assert jurisdiction resulting from the lack of extraterritorial competence on the part of the provinces.[10]

Potentially more expansive sources of federal authority in relation to environmental matters include the general or residual power for the peace, order, and good government of Canada (POGG) and the criminal law power (section 91[27]). The POGG power, and in particular its "national concern" branch, has been considered for some time as a promising foundation for extensive federal jurisdiction in the environmental field. In *R. v. Crown Zellerbach Canada Ltd.*, the constitutionality of federal provisions dealing with dumping in coastal waters was challenged by a company charged for activity in a British Columbia bay.[11] After determining that provisions of the federal *Ocean Dumping Control Act*[12] could not be upheld constitutionally under any of the specific powers listed in section 91, Justice Le Dain assessed the statutory scheme against the "national concern" doctrine relating to the federal POGG power. To satisfy the "national concern" test, the subject matter of the statute must have "a singleness, distinctiveness, and indivisibility that clearly distinguishes it from matters of provincial concern and a scale of impact on provincial jurisdiction that is reconcilable with the fundamental distribution of legislative power under the Constitution."[13] Taking account of a series of considerations, including the implications of provincial inaction or inability to address the problems of ocean dumping, the extent to which the federal measures affected provincial jurisdiction, and the nature of marine pollution itself, Justice Le Dain concluded that such pollution, given its "predominantly extra-provincial as well as international character and implications" qualified as a matter of national concern.

But there was apprehension that the breadth of the authority potentially available under the "national concern" test might threaten the essential and underlying balance of the federation. The tension was in fact apparent in the dissenting judgment of Justice La Forest in *Crown Zellerbach*:

> All physical activities have some environmental impact. Possible legislative responses to such activities cover a large number of the

---

10   *Interprovincial Co-operative v. R.*, [1976] 1 S.C.R. 477; P.W. Hogg, *Constitutional Law of Canada*, 2d ed. (Toronto: Carswell, 1985) at 598.

11   [1988] 1 S.C.R. 401.

12   Provisions originally found within ocean dumping legislation are now found in *CEPA, 1999*, above note 5, Part 7.

13   *Crown Zellerbach*, above note 11 at 432.

enumerated legislative powers, federal and provincial. To allocate the broad subject-matter of environmental control to the federal government under its general power would effectively gut provincial legislative jurisdiction. [14]

The challenge for the courts, he concluded, "will be to allow the federal Parliament sufficient scope to acquit itself of its duties to deal with national and international problems while respecting the scheme of federalism provided by the Constitution."

Commentators had speculated, however, that in addition to securing the foundations of the ocean-dumping provisions of CEPA, the "national concern" test as applied in Crown Zellerbach might offer constitutional support for other matters addressed in the federal legislation, including toxic substances.[15] When, in fact, the constitutionality of CEPA's toxic substance provisions was judicially examined, the national concern branch of the POGG power was not the basis on which the legislation was upheld.

In Canada (A.G.) v. Hydro-Québec, the Quebec Court of Appeal ruled that environmental protection, as a subject which is itself an aggregate of other matters falling within both federal and provincial competence, lacks the "singleness, distinctiveness and indivisibility" necessary to satisfy the national concern as formulated in Crown Zellerbach.[16] A majority of the Supreme Court subsequently upheld the toxic substance provisions of CEPA on the basis of the federal criminal power.[17]

In attempting to prevent the conception of the criminal law power from becoming too all-encompassing, the courts have generally looked for the characteristic of blameworthiness in the relevant conduct and a formal prohibition against it. The consequence has been that federal legislation of a regulatory nature not amounting to actual prohibition of blameworthy conduct has not found constitutional shelter under the criminal law power. "Criminal sanctions designed to prohibit certain wrongful conduct are constitutional," explained Paul Emond, "whereas sanctions used to regulate conduct are not."[18] Recent jurisprudence—even before the Supreme Court's Hydro-Québec deci-

---

14   Ibid. at 455.
15   Lucas, above note 3 at 366.
16   Canada (A.G.) v. Hydro-Québec (1995), 17 C.E.L.R. (N.S.) 34 at 52–53 (Que. C.A.).
17   Canada (A.G.) v. Hydro-Québec, [1997] 3 S.C.R. 213.
18   P. Emond, "The Case for a Greater Federal Role in the Environmental Protection Field: An Examination of the Pollution Problem and the Constitution" (1972) 10 Osgoode Hall L.J. 647 at 664.

sion—suggested some softening in the rigidity of such traditional constraints on the criminal power.[19]

When Hydro-Quebec was charged in 1990 with dumping PCBs (polychlorinated biphenyls) contrary to interim regulations made pursuant to sections 34 and 35 of *CEPA*'s toxic substance provisions, the utility defended on the grounds that neither the statutory provisions nor the regulations were within the constitutional scope of federal law-making authority. Briefly stated, section 34 provided for the regulation of toxic substances as determined under *CEPA*. Toxic substances were those that had been shown to have potential for harmful effects on the environment or constituted a danger to the environment on which human life depends or represented a danger in Canada to human life or health. As itemized in section 34, the list of considerations specifically subject to the regulation of toxic substances ran from (a) to (x) where (x) authorized "any other matter necessary to carry out the purposes of this Part" of *CEPA*. Section 35 allowed temporary orders equivalent to regulations under section 34 to be made when the ministers of health and environment believed immediate action was required. The *Chlorobiphenyls Interim Order* was one of these.

In the deliberations of the Supreme Court, the legitimacy of the various impugned provisions under the criminal law power became central. In the forcefully expressed view of four dissenting judges: "While the protection of the environment is a legitimate public purpose which could support the enactment of criminal legislation, we believe the impugned provisions of the Act are more an attempt to regulate environmental pollution than to prohibit or proscribe it. As such, they extend beyond the purview of criminal law and cannot be justified under s. 91(27)."[20]

The majority opinion, written by La Forest J., took a more generous approach to the criminal law power as "plenary in nature." With respect to the validity of the underlying objective, La Forest identified environmental protection as "a public purpose of superordinate importance."[21] In considering the scheme of *CEPA*'s toxic substance provisions, he was satisfied that they were consistent with established judicial understanding of criminal law: "These listed substances, toxic in the ordinary sense, are those whose use in a manner contrary to the regulations the Act ultimately prohibits. This is a limited prohibition applicable to a limited number of substances. The prohibition is

---

19   *RJR-MacDonald Inc. v. Canada (A.G.)*, [1995] 3 S.C.R. 199.
20   *Canada (A.G.) v. Hydro-Québec*, above note 17 at 246.
21   *Ibid.* at 266.

enforced by a penal sanction and is undergirded by a valid criminal objective, and so is valid criminal legislation."[22]

In addition to the grounds available to the federal government, provincial governments also possess legitimate bases for environmental regulation under the enumerated heads of power in section 92.

C. SOURCES OF PROVINCIAL ENVIRONMENTAL JURISDICTION

Provincial authority to enact environmental protection measures derives principally from power in relation to "Property and Civil Rights in the Province" (92[13]) and "Generally all Matters of a merely local or private Nature in the Province" (92[16]). Further potentially relevant sources of provincial constitutional authority include: the management and sale of public lands and timber (92[5]); municipal institutions (92[8]); licensing for local, municipal, and provincial revenue (92[9]); local works and undertakings [92(10)]; and the enforcement powers enumerated in section 92(15). In addition, section 92a of the *Constitution Act, 1982*, known as the natural resources amendment, is relevant to environmental law-making insofar as it confers on each provincial legislature exclusive authority to make laws in relation to the

> development, conservation and management of non-renewable natural resources and forestry resources in the province, including laws in relation to the rate of primary production therefrom; and . . . development, conservation and management of sites and facilities in the province for the generation and production of electrical energy.

Apart from these enumerated powers, the courts have recognized provincial legislative authority deriving from rights of ownership or proprietary rights over natural resources.[23]Collectively, these sources of legislative power provide the provinces with a strong constitutional basis for the extensive range of regulatory initiatives each has taken in relation to environmental protection. Yet certain constraints must be acknowledged, beginning with the geographic restriction of provincial authority within provincial boundaries. In *Interprovincial Cooperative*, an attempt by Manitoba to create a statutory right of action against pollution that originated upstream in the neighbouring provinces of Saskatchewan and Ontario was found unconstitutional by the Supreme

---

22   *Ibid.* at 308.
23   *Constitution Act, 1867* (U.K.), 30 & 31 Vict., c. 3, s. 109.

Court.[24] In a complex decision, a plurality of the judges determined that the extraterritorial origin of the pollution removed it from the legislative reach of Manitoba, despite the acknowledged fact of injury to that province's fishery. The delimitation of provincial boundaries is therefore of considerable importance to the applicability of environmental regulatory regimes,[25] although there are recent indications that provinces are anxious to extend the protective reach of their environmental laws.

From the perspective of those industries that face actual compliance obligations, shared or overlapping environmental jurisdiction may entail inconvenience, uncertainty, additional expense, or still more serious consequences, including prosecution. Some of those facing prosecution, especially in such federally regulated industries as interprovincial transportation, have argued that on this basis they are not subject to provincial environmental requirements and that, somewhat like the federal Crown and its agents, they enjoy a form of interjurisdictional immunity.

It has been confirmed that federally regulated industries enjoy no such immunity.[26] In *R. v. Canadian Pacific Ltd.*, the company was charged under the Ontario *EPA* in connection with the adverse environmental effects of smoke, a contaminant, which resulted from a controlled burn of weeds along the railway right of way. The railway's claim that the *EPA* unconstitutionally interfered with the management of a federally regulated undertaking was rejected. The statute was one of general application in the province, not directed at the management of the railway; and, though it affected the railway's clearing operations, it did not have an impermissible impact on CP's essential functions. Similarly, it was determined that an interprovincial trucking company was subject to provincial PCB transport regulation. As Mackinnon A.C.J.O. explained:

> In the same way that the province can regulate speed limits and the mechanical conditions of vehicles on the roads of the province for the protection and safety of other highway users, it can set conditions for the carriage of particular toxic substances within the province, provided that the conditions do not interfere in any substantial way with

---

24 *Interprovincial Co-operative*, above note 10. See also *Mathias Colomb Band of Indians v. Saskatchewan Power Corp.* (1994), 13 C.E.L.R. (N.S.) 245 (Man. C.A.).

25 *Reference Re Offshore Mineral Rights (British Columbia)*, [1967] S.C.R. 792; *Canada (A.G.) v. British Columbia (A.G.)*, [1984] 1 S.C.R. 388; *Reference Re Seabed & Subsoil of Continental Shelf Offshore Newfoundland*, [1984] 1 S.C.R. 86.

26 *R. v. Canadian Pacific Ltd.*, [1995] 2 S.C.R. 1028.

the carrier's general or particular carriage of goods, and are not in conflict either directly or indirectly with federal legislation in the field.[27]

D. MUNICIPAL GOVERNMENT AND THE ENVIRONMENT

As "creatures of the provinces" for constitutional purposes, municipal and local governments lack constitutional autonomy. Their executive and legislative powers are exercised on the basis of delegation, primarily by means of provincial legislation. But once conferred, such powers include the capacity to enact fully enforceable bylaws reflecting the decisions of municipal or local officials. As subordinate instruments, such bylaws cannot exceed the scope or contradict the intent of corresponding provincial legislation. Thus, in *Superior Propane Inc. v. York (City)*, a municipal bylaw designed to regulate propane storage and distribution in the interests of public safety was struck down. The Ontario Court of Appeal concluded that the municipal initiative was in conflict with a comprehensive scheme of regulations under the provincial *Energy Act* and, accordingly, the bylaw was *ultra vires*.[28]

It is evident nevertheless that municipal authority in the environmental context is both vital and extensive. Local authority to regulate and manage the environment has been classified in relation to six sets of powers: environment powers; public health powers; planning and zoning powers; business licensing and regulation powers; dangerous substances powers; and plenary powers.[29] This range of responsibility requires some further consideration, even if the limited scope of this text precludes detailed discussion of local environmental protection regimes.[30]

---

27 *R. v. TNT Canada Inc.* (1986), 37 D.L.R. (4th) 297. In *Canadian Western Bank v. Alberta*, 2007 SCC 22 at para. 77, the Supreme Court emphasizes that interjurisdictional immunity is of limited application.

28 (1995), 23 O.R. (3d) 161 (C.A.), leave to appeal to S.C.C. refused (1996), 19 C.E.L.R. (N.S.) 270 (S.C.C.). For a more recent example of conflict between a municipal bylaw and provincial regulation, see *Peacock v. Norfolk (County)* (2006), 81 O.R. (3d) 530 (C.A.).

29 L.A. Reynolds, "Environmental Regulation and Management by Local Public Authorities in Canada" (1993) 3 J. Envtl. L. & Prac. 41.

30 For a comprehensive review of municipal law in Canada see I.M. Rogers, *The Law of Canadian Municipal Corporations*, 2d ed. (Toronto: Carswell, 1971). See also Y. Duplessis & J. Hetu, *Les pouvoirs des municipalités en matière de protection de l'environnement*, 2d ed. (Cowansville, QC: Editions Y. Blais, 1994).

Judicial consideration of municipal decision making in the environmental area suggests a willingness to acknowledge the importance of action at the local government level. This is true both in relation to the treatment of the scope of municipal authority and in relation to judicial review of the exercise of that authority when it has been established on the basis of statutory interpretation.

When the town of Hudson, Quebec, enacted a pesticide bylaw without specific legislative authority to do so, it became necessary to ascertain whether such authority could be found within a general provision of the province's *Cities and Towns Act*.[31] This provision, similar to that found in other jurisdictions, stated simply: "The Council may make bylaws to secure peace, order, good government, health and general welfare in the territory of the municipality, provided such bylaws are not contrary to the laws of Canada, or of Quebec, nor inconsistent with any special provision of this act or of the *Charter*."

The court's finding that the bylaw in question was within the scope of this general authority is widely regarded as enhancing the role of municipalities in relation to environmental, health, and other matters.

In an earlier decision, *Rascal Trucking*,[32] after the court had concluded that a specific municipal act provision dealing with nuisance applied to a municipal resolution that had been challenged, Justice Major endorsed the following observation:

> Courts must respect the responsibility of elected municipal bodies to serve the people who elected them and exercise caution to avoid substituting their views of what is best for the citizens for those of municipal councils. Barring clear demonstration that a municipal decision was beyond its powers, courts should not so hold.

Thus, the court concluded as a matter of administrative law that judicial review of municipal decisions should be conducted according to the deferential standard of patent unreasonableness and not on the basis of the more intrusive standard of correctness.

In relation to judicial respect for the environmental responsibilities of municipal government and, of course, for the significance of environmental considerations themselves, it is equally noteworthy that

---

31 *114957 Canada Ltée (Spraytech, Société d'arrosage) v. Hudson (Town)*, 2001 SCC 40.

32 *Nanaimo (City) v. Rascal Trucking Ltd.*, 2000 SCC 13. Subsequent developments have once again altered the Supreme Court of Canada's approach to the standard of review of administrative decisions. See *Dunsmuir v. New Brunswick*, 2008 SCC 9.

a Montreal bylaw regulating noise survived a challenge grounded on the constitutional right to freedom of expression.[33]

Municipal environmental efforts require supporting resources that are not always available. Even major cities and large metropolitan areas have lamented financial limitations that have restricted their capacity to pursue desirable initiatives. Some level of assistance, at least in terms of research, information, and policy guidance is available through the Federation of Canadian Municipalities, which has taken some steps to encourage local government action in relation to waste management, water quality, air pollution, climate change, toxics, and other issues.[34]

E. ABORIGINAL RIGHTS, RESOURCES, AND THE ENVIRONMENT

The constitutional framework governing environmental and resource issues extends beyond the allocation of powers between the federal and provincial governments to encompass the relationship between those governments and the aboriginal peoples of Canada, including the Indian, Inuit and Metis communities. This observation is grounded in section 35(1) of the *Constitution Act, 1982* which asserts that "[t]he existing aboriginal and treaty rights of the aboriginal peoples of Canada are hereby recognized and affirmed."

The importance of section 35 for resource management and the environment was demonstrated in the *Sparrow* decision, where the Supreme Court of Canada established a strict test for the extinguishment of aboriginal rights, that is, inherent rights associated with aboriginal occupancy preceding European settlement.[35] "The test of extinguishment to be adopted, in our opinion, is that the Sovereign's intention must be clear and plain if it is to extinguish an aboriginal right."[36] Legislation or regulation affecting aboriginal rights is not precluded, for "[r]ights that are recognized and affirmed are not absolute," but regulation must be enacted "according to a valid objective" such as "conservation and resource management." In other words, legislative authority

---

33   *Montreal (City)* v. *2952-1366 Quebec Inc.*, 2005 SCC 62.

34   For an illustration of significant municipal actions, see the pesticides discussion in chapter 13. See also the City of Toronto sewer bylaw No. 457-2000 introducing pollution prevention requirements and Edmonton's "Toward a Cleaner River" initiative.

35   *R. v. Sparrow*, [1990] 1 S.C.R. 1075.

36   *Ibid.* at para 37.

in areas associated with aboriginal rights is subject to close judicial scrutiny under section 35: moreover, courts have repeatedly underlined the significance of the Crown's honour and fiduciary duties in relation to aboriginal peoples.

In *Sparrow*, a Musqueam Indian was charged for fishing salmon illegally with a net whose dimensions exceeded those established in the Musqueam Band Indian Food Fishing Licence, which had been issued in accordance with regulations under the federal *Fisheries Act*. The defence put forward by the accused was that he enjoyed an aboriginal right to fish that overrode the licence restrictions. As explained by the court, the initial step in cases of this kind is for the party asserting an aboriginal right to demonstrate its existence and to show that its exercise has been interfered with by the regulation being challenged.[37] It then falls to the Crown to justify the interference. This exercise will require the Crown to show a valid legislative objective, pursued through means that are consistent with or respectful of the existence of the aboriginal right and that interfere as little as possible with that right.[38]

In subsequent decisions, the S.C.C. has returned to the question of limitations on section 35 rights concerning resource use and conservation. In *Nikal*, the relationship between aboriginal fishing rights and resource conservation programs was explicitly addressed:

> The aboriginal right to fish must be balanced against the need to conserve the fishery stock. This right cannot automatically deny the ability of the government to set up a licensing scheme or program as part of a conservation program since the right's exercise depends on the continued existence of the resource.[39]

In *Gladstone*,[40] in the context of charges of selling herring spawn on kelp without a licence against Heiltsuk Indians who asserted an aboriginal right to fish commercially, the S.C.C. observed:

> Where the aboriginal right is one that has no internal limitation [so that it is clear when that right has been satisfied and other users can be allowed to participate in the fishery] . . . the doctrine of priority requires that the government demonstrate that, in allocating the resource, it has taken account of the existence of aboriginal rights and al-

---

37   As discussed below, certain protections now extend to aboriginal rights that are claimed or asserted rather than established.

38   *Sparrow*, above note 35.

39   *R. v. Nikal*, [1996] 1 S.C.R. 1013 at para. 94.

40   *R. v. Gladstone*, [1996] 2 S.C.R. 723.

located the resource in a manner respectful of the fact that those rights have priority over the exploitation of the fishery by other users.[41]

In connection with the distribution of the fisheries resource after conservation goals and aboriginal uses have been satisfied, the Court identified several relevant criteria or appropriate objectives including "the pursuit of economic and regional fairness, and the recognition of the historical reliance upon, and participation in, the fishery by non-aboriginal groups."[42]

In a subsequent decision, the S.C.C. again elaborated on the range of legislative objectives that might justify infringement of aboriginal rights. Protection of the environment or endangered species was specifically listed among such objectives, along with resource development, the building of infrastructure, and settlement.[43]

The existence of constitutionally required safeguards is no longer confined to aboriginal rights whose existence has been established. Thus, in two cases from British Columbia where extensive land claims remain unresolved, the S.C.C., with reference to section 35, insisted upon a duty of consultation (and of appropriate accommodation).[44] It is also noteworthy that Metis aboriginal rights in relation to hunting have been recognized.[45]

Although the scope of aboriginal rights remains to be determined in many parts of the country, especially in relation to self-government, acknowledged and asserted aboriginal interests in land and resources will have an important influence on the design and operation of resource management and environmental protection regimes in various parts of Canada.[46]

Treaty rights and land-claim agreements, that is, governing documents derived from negotiation and mutual consent, also affect the nature and extent of aboriginal participation in resource and environ-

---

41   *Ibid.* at para 62.
42   *Ibid.* at 187.
43   *Delgamuukw v. British Columbia*, [1997] 3 S.C.R. 1011 at 1111.
44   *Haida Nation v. British Columbia (Minister of Forests)*, [2004] 3 S.C.R. 511; *Taku River Tlingit First Nation v. British Columbia (Project Assessment Director)*, [2004] 3 S.C.R. 550. For a recent illustration of the possible scope of the duty to consult, see *Hiawatha First Nation v Ontario (Minister of Environment)*, [2007] O.J. No. 506 (Div. Ct.).
45   *R. v. Powley* (2001), 53 O.R. (3d) 35 (C.A.); appeal and cross-appeal dismissed, 2003 SCC 43.
46   *Canada (A.G.) v. Inuvialiut Regional Corp.* (1994), 119 D.L.R. (4th) 373 (F.C.A.); *Quebec (A.G.) v. Canada (National Energy Board)*, [1994] 1 S.C.R. 159.

mental management.[47] Modern treaties typically address, sometimes in great detail, issues associated with decision making over land use, environmental assessment and approvals, and the relationship of these processes to traditional aboriginal interests. Historic treaties, even when largely silent on such matters, may also be of significance as the first *Marshall* decisions demonstrate.[48]

In a situation not unlike that in *Sparrow*, in *Marshall,* a Mi'kmaq Indian was charged with catching eels by means of a prohibited net during the close season and then selling these without holding a commercial licence to do so. The accused's defence rested on an interpretation of treaties dating from the mid-eighteenth century, and specifically a *Treaty of Peace and Friendship (1860)* in which a Mi'kmaq chief agreed "not to traffick, barter or exchange any commodities in any manner but with such persons or the managers of such truck houses as shall be appointed or established by His Majesty's governor." A majority of the S.C.C. concluded that the treaty preserved "a treaty right to continue to obtain necessaries through hunting and fishing by trading the products of those traditional activities subject to restrictions,"[49] stating further that "necessaries" was equivalent to "a moderate livelihood."[50] Marshall, not being subject to the close season rule or the licence requirement, was acquitted. The court subsequently clarified its initial *Marshall* judgment by emphasizing that, like aboriginal rights, the treaty right that had been recognized could be subject to both regulation and licensing where such measures are justified. Justification requires a valid legislative objective, appropriate consultation, minimal infringement of the right affected, and consideration of the special trust relationship of the government toward aboriginal peoples.[51]

F. INTERGOVERNMENTAL COORDINATION AND ENVIRONMENTAL PROTECTION

Suggestions to change the manner in which responsibilities for environmental protection have been allocated among governments in Canada are not uncommon. On the one hand, promoters of greater centraliza-

---

47   *Cree Regional Authority v. Canada (Federal Administrator)*, [1992] 1 F.C. 440 (T.D.); *Eastmain Band v. Canada (Federal Administrator)*, [1993] 1 F.C. 501 (T.D.).

48   *R. v. Marshall* (1999), 138 C.C.C. (3d) 97 (S.C.C.).

49   *Ibid.* at 129.

50   *Ibid.* at 107.

51   *R. v. Marshall* (1999), 139 C.C.C. (3d) 391 (S.C.C.).

tion of environmental regulation and control are inclined to cite the benefits of uniformity, consistency, comprehensiveness, and economies of scale as virtues. On the other hand, decentralists or those committed to local and provincial powers claim the virtues of innovation, experimentation, and sensitivity to local conditions as benefits of a multijurisdictional system. They might claim, for example, that it is easier to experiment in smaller jurisdictions and that successful experiments can then be implemented more comprehensively. Or they might argue that diversity of environment requires diversity of responses. But the concern is then expressed that smaller governments are perhaps more vulnerable to being "captured" by polluters and might be induced to compromise; on the other hand, standards set centrally might be subject to the pressures of the lowest common denominator that animates the search for agreement and so environmental protection might be undermined. In some contexts this quest for consistency at a low level of environmental protection is described as the "race for the bottom."

Although a growing number of members of the legal community recognize an "environmental imperative" or "the imperatives of nature itself," the persistence of divided jurisdiction and constitutional constraints on both federal and provincial governments causes most observers to insist upon the importance of intergovernmental mechanisms in getting the job done. They do so in Canada for reasons explained clearly twenty-five years ago: "[E]nvironmental management" does not, under the existing situation, constitute a homogeneous constitutional unit. Instead, it cuts across many different areas of constitutional responsibility, some federal and some provincial."[52]

Overlap and ambiguity in the scope of federal and provincial constitutional authority respecting the environment present challenges of coordination in the interests of reducing costly duplication, avoiding gaps, and generally promoting consistency. In the face of increasingly urgent and wide-ranging environmental challenges such as those presented by climate change and biodiversity loss, the costs of dysfunctional constitutional arrangements are incalculable. To minimize the impact of this ambiguity and dysfunction, numerous mechanisms—both informal and statutorily prescribed—have been employed to enhance intergovernmental coordination. These include simple information exchange and ongoing consultations, negotiation of formal agreements—on a bilateral or multilateral basis—concerning environmental responsibilities, the delegation of authority from one government to another, and the de-

---

52 D. Gibson, "Constitutional Jurisdiction over Environmental Management in Canada" (1973) 23 U.T.L.J. 54 at 85.

velopment of joint-decision-making bodies and procedures whereby one government can adopt the outcome of another's processes.

1) Intergovernmental Consultation

In addition to ongoing communication between environmental officials in one jurisdiction and their counterparts elsewhere, several institutions facilitate coordination of policy and decision making. In the 1980s a national task force consisting of government, industry, and representatives of environmental groups contributed to the formation of multistakeholder "round tables" in many jurisdictions.[53] One of these, the National Round Table on the Environment and the Economy (NRTEE), includes participants from the federal and a number of provincial governments. While not a decision-making body as such, the NRTEE continues to make significant contributions to a variety of environmental issues through research and consultation exercises.

Certain pieces of federal legislation also provide for mechanisms to encourage coordination by means of consultation. Section 6 of the *CEPA, 1999*, for example, calls for the creation of a National Advisory Committee (formerly the Federal-Provincial Advisory Committee) "[f]or the purpose of enabling national action to be carried out and taking co-operative action in matters affecting the environment and for the purpose of avoiding duplication in regulatory activity among governments." Consisting of representatives from the federal departments of environment and health, from each of the provincial governments, and from aboriginal government representatives, the National Advisory Committee provides a forum for discussion of a range of issues.

The most important institution today in terms of intergovernmental consultation on environmental matters is the Canadian Council of Ministers of the Environment (CCME). The CCME is an offshoot of the Canadian Council of Resource and Environment Ministers (1971), which itself was a reconfiguration of the Canadian Council of Resource Ministers (1964). To address the problem of regulatory costs on Canadian business in the environmental field, the CCME has undertaken several examinations of regulatory arrangements with a view to promoting increased harmonization. In 1993, the CCME's *Statement of Interjurisdictional Cooperation on Environmental Matters* argued that "[t]he increased complexity of environmental issues, particularly their interjurisdictional impacts, requires coordinated responses from both

---

53   *Report of the National Task Force on Environment and Economy* (Downsview: Canadian Council of Resource and Environment Ministers, 1987).

orders of government; and . . . [e]ffective interjurisdictional cooperation leads to certainty and predictability of environmental regulation, and promotes public confidence and sound economic planning."[54] This statement was one of the antecedents of the harmonization accord discussed later in this chapter.

2) Intergovernmental Bilateral Agreements

The federal government has occasionally negotiated bilateral agreements with specific provinces concerning the administration of particular features of the environmental law regime. Over thirty years ago, all provinces but Newfoundland, Quebec, and British Columbia signed federal-provincial "Accords" for the protection and enhancement of environmental quality. Renewals updated and extended the life of some of these agreements, and arrangements have been negotiated in relation to other matters.

In 1991 Alberta and the federal government signed an accord on environmental quality that addressed, among other issues, enforcement arrangements:

13. Canada and the Province agree to appoint officers designated by either government to facilitate inspection for compliance with national effluent and emission standards and guidelines. Appropriate arrangements for inspection of facilities would be determined by specific agreements.

14. (1) Canada agrees to take enforcement action pursuant to this Accord:
(a) at federal facilities unless otherwise agreed to under Clause 13, above;
(b) at the request of the Province; or
(c) where the Province cannot, or for some reason fails to fulfil its obligations pursuant to the Accord, with respect to matters of federal jurisdiction administered by the Province.

(2) In instances where Canada for some reason fails to take enforcement action under subsection 1, paragraph (a) or (b) with respect to federal requirements, Canada and Alberta may agree that Alberta take action as required on behalf of Canada.[55]

---

54 Canadian Council of Ministers of the Environment, *Statement of Interjurisdictional Cooperation on Environmental Matters* (1993).

55 *Canada-Alberta Accord for the Protection and Enhancement of Environmental Quality*, 8 October 1991, quoted in D. Tingley, "Conflict and Cooperation on

Agreements in relation to the *Fisheries Act* include the *Canada-Alberta Administrative Agreement for the Control of Deposits of Deleterious Substances under the Fisheries Act* (June 1994) and the *Canada-Saskatchewan Administrative Agreement for the Control of Deposits of Deleterious Substances under the Fisheries Act* (September 1994).

CEPA, 1999 section 9 authorizes federal-provincial agreements concerning the administration of the Act. Administrative agreements are described as "working arrangements" between governments to streamline the administration of regulations. The *Canada-Saskatchewan Administrative Agreement* (15 September 1994) addresses the administration of seven federal regulations within the province.[56] The *Canada-Quebec Pulp and Paper Administrative Agreement* (2000-2005) established a joint committee and provided for reporting procedures and information exchange in relation to federal regulation of the pulp and paper sector under *CEPA, 1999* and the *Fisheries Act.*

Pursuant to *CEPA, 1999* section 10, when the federal Minister of the Environment and a provincial government agree that provincial law is equivalent to *CEPA, 1999* regulations on toxic substances and that citizens' rights to require investigation of an alleged offence are similar to those established under *CEPA, 1999*, the federal government may declare that the federal regulations do not apply in that province other than to federal works, undertakings, and lands. In 1994 the first federal-provincial equivalency agreement dealing with four federal regulations was concluded with Alberta.[57]

3) The Harmonization Accord and the Agreement on Internal Trade

In January 1998, following half a decade of discussion under the general auspices of the CCME, the federal, provincial, and territorial governments (excluding Quebec) signed a Canada-wide Accord on

---

the Environment" in D.M. Brown, ed., *Canada: The State of the Federation 1991* (Kingston: Queen's University Institute of Intergovernmental Relations, 1991) 131 at 135–36.

56   Online: www.mb.ec.gc.ca/pollution/e00s63.en.html.

57   *Agreement on the Equivalency of Federal and Alberta Regulations for the Control of Toxic Substances in Alberta* (June 1994), available as *Alberta Equivalency Order*, S.O.R./94-752, C. Gaz. 1994. II. 4056. For discussion of this and other federal-provincial agreements, see Canada, House of Commons, Standing Committee on Environment and Sustainable Development, "Enforcing Canada's Pollution Laws: The Public Interest Must Come First" at c. 3 (1998) and Commissioner of the Environment and Sustainable Development, *Annual Report 1999* at c. 5, "Streamlining Environmental Protection Through Federal-Provincial Agreements."

Environmental Harmonization.[58] The stated objectives of the harmonization initiative are to enhance environmental protection, to promote sustainable development, and to improve environmental management from the perspective of effectiveness, efficiency, accountability, predictability, and clarity. These goals are to be accomplished by means of cooperation and the delineation of governmental roles and responsibilities. Overlapping environmental management of activities is to be prevented; gaps and weaknesses are to be filled. Thirteen principles, set out as follows, were incorporated within the accord:

1. those who generate pollution and waste should bear the cost of prevention, containment, cleanup, or abatement (polluter-pays principle);
2. where there are threats of serious or irreversible environmental damage, lack of full scientific certainty shall not be used as a reason for postponing cost-effective measures to prevent environmental degradation (precautionary principle);
3. pollution prevention is the preferred approach to environmental protection;
4. environmental measures should be performance-based, results-oriented, and science-based;
5. openness, transparency, accountability, and the effective participation of stakeholders and the public in environmental decision making is necessary for an effective environmental management regime;
6. working cooperatively with Aboriginal people and their structures of governance is necessary for an effective environmental management regime;
7. Canada-wide approaches on how to meet the objectives of this accord will allow for flexible implementation required to reflect variations in ecosystems and local, regional, provincial, and territorial conditions;
8. decisions pursuant to the accord will be consensus-based and driven by the commitment to achieve the highest level of environmental quality within the context of sustainable development;
9. nothing in this accord alters the legislative or other authority of the governments or the rights of any of them with respect to the exercise of their legislative or other authorities under the Constitution of Canada;
10. legislation, regulations, policies, and existing agreements should accommodate the implementation of this accord;

---

58 Online: www.ccme.ca.

11. the environmental measures established and implemented in accordance with this Accord will not prevent a government from introducing more stringent environmental measures to reflect specific circumstances or to protect environments or environmental values located within its jurisdiction;

12. this Accord and sub-agreements do not affect aboriginal or treaty rights;

13. all Canadians should be confident that their environment is respected by neighbouring Canadian jurisdictions.

A number of sub-agreements have been formulated to implement the principles of the Accord in a series of designated subject areas. To date, sub-agreements have been developed with respect to environmental standards, environmental inspections and enforcement, and environmental assessment. A statement of guiding principles has been drafted to address issues involved in monitoring and reporting. Task groups continue to examine other matters.

The Canadian Environmental Law Association (CELA) unsuccessfully sought judicial review of the decision of the federal minister of environment to sign the Accord and accompanying sub-agreements.[59] CELA had argued that any proposed realignment of federal and provincial roles and responsibilities for environmental management pursuant to the Accord was beyond the authority of the minister under existing federal legislation. Alternatively, CELA had argued that insofar as the agreements constituted an undertaking to not act in certain circumstances, the minister's authority was unlawfully fettered.

In the context of interprovincial trade, other efforts have been made to address the problems of inconsistent and conflicting environmental standards within Canada's comparatively small domestic market. Thus, the *Agreement on Internal Trade* (AIT) addresses environmental protection and extends general rules of entry, non-discrimination, transparency, and so on to this area while simultaneously calling on all parties to maintain high standards.[60] Although the thrust of the AIT is directed at economic competitiveness, the institutions and processes associated with the agreement offer an additional forum for encouraging the coordination of environmental protection initiatives.

---

59 *Canadian Environmental Law Assn. v. Canada (Minister of the Environment)* (1999), 34 C.E.L.R. 159.

60 B. Schwartz, "Assessing the Agreement on Internal Trade: The Case for a 'More Perfect Union'" in D.M. Brown & J.W. Rose, eds., *Canada: The State of the Federation 1995* (Kingston: Queen's University Institute of Intergovernmental Relations, 1995) 189.

FURTHER READINGS

BANKES, N., "*Delgamuukw*, Division of Powers and Provincial Land and Resource Laws: Some Implications for Provincial Resource Rights" (1998) 32 U.B.C. L. Rev. 317

CASTRILLI, J., "*R. v. Hydro Québec*: The Criminal Law Power May Hinder the Future of Federal Protection of the Environment" (1997) 9 C.R. (5th) 312

CURRAN, D., & M.M'GONIGLE, "Aboriginal Forestry: Community Management as Opportunity and Imperative" (1999) 37 Osgoode Hall L.J. 711

DONIHEE, JOHN, & Priscilla Kennedy, *Wildlife and the Canadian Constitution*: Wildlife Paper #4 (Calgary: Canadian Institute of Resources Law, 2006)

HARRISON, K., *Passing the Buck: Federalism and Canadian Environmental Policy* (Vancouver: University of British Columbia Press, 1996)

HOEHN, F., *Municipalities and Canadian Law: Defining the Authority of Local Governments* (Saskatoon: Purich Publishing, 1996)

LECLAIR, J., "Aperçu de virtualités de la compétence fédérale en droit criminel dans le contexte de la protection de l'environnement" (1996) 27 R.G.D. 137

MAINVILLE, ROBERT, BRIAN A. CRANE, & MARTIN W. MASON, *First Nations Governance Law* (Markham, ON: LexisNexis Canada, 2006)

RANKIN, M., "Environmental Regulation and the Changing Canadian Constitutional Landscape" in G. Thompson, M.L. McConnell, & L.B. Huestis, eds., *Environmental Law and Business in Canada* (Aurora, ON: Canada Law Book, 1993) 31–51

CHAPTER 3

ENVIRONMENTAL RIGHTS

A. HUMAN AND CONSTITUTIONAL RIGHTS TO ENVIRONMENTAL QUALITY

Debate over a human right to environmental quality, or about whether constitutional protection of environmental rights (or for some level of environmental quality for human or possibly even non-human populations) does or can exist raises legal analysis to a high plane of abstraction. The attraction of rights or constitutional safeguards for environmental interests lies in the improved position of environment in the legal hierarchy in both practical and symbolic ways. Proponents envisage environmental rights as a philosophical and practical advance that would not only acknowledge the fundamental importance of environmental preservation as a public value, but also facilitate enforceability by helping to overcome existing obstacles to environmental protection. These obstacles include constraints on opportunities for participation in judicial and administrative decision making, broad delegations of discretion conferred upon government officials, and the significant weight or priority accorded to property interests in cases of conflict with other values of the community.

While discussion of environmental rights has not been prominent in Canada, the subject has certainly not been ignored. In the words of the Law Reform Commission of Canada, for example, "a fundamental and widely shared value is indeed seriously contravened by some environmental pollution, a value which we will refer to as the *right to a safe environment.*"[1] Recently, in discussing a provision of Quebec's *Environmental Quality Act* dealing with a statutory entitlement to a healthy environment and to which we will shortly refer, the Supreme Court of Canada stated:

> To ensure that this right may be effectively exercised, and that the duties created to give effect to it are executed, the Act provides for a variety of mechanisms for taking action. Various schemes are established for authorizing and monitoring activities that could threaten the environment. Others prohibit or restrict the emission of contaminants and impose obligations to decontaminate.[2]

Environmental rights are sometimes further classified on the basis of a distinction between procedural and substantive rights, with the former being confined to safeguards for the participation of environmental advocates and the latter implying some actual change in priorities and therefore in the expected outcome of environmentally significant decisions. The distinction is aptly summarized in an early Canadian commentary on environmental rights:

> Those who search for a right to environmental quality hope it will confer more than a right to participate or some requirement of due process or natural justice before environmentally harmful decisions are taken. They want a right which will dictate a decision in favour of environmental protection in difficult cases. They hope this right will be equivalent to a civil liberty, on the one hand, constraining government actions harmful to the environment, and, on the other, equivalent to a property right, restraining the use of private property in ways that are incompatible with sound ecological management.[3]

A more recent synthesis of the continuing debate pulls together some of the uncertain ingredients of environmental rights while it also identifies direct linkages between environmental rights and the essentials of ecological management. With regard to matters of scope and design associated with environmental rights, questions along these lines arise:

> Is such a right individual or collective? Is it a positive or a negative right? Can we conceptualize such rights as anthropocentric (i.e., hu-

---

1   Law Reform Commission of Canada, *Crimes Against the Environment* (Ottawa: The Commission, 1985) at 8.

2   *Imperial Oil Ltd. v. Quebec (Minister of the Environment)*, [2003] 2. S.C.R. 624 at 640.

3   J. Swaigen & R.E. Woods, "A Substantive Right to Environmental Quality" in J. Swaigen, ed., *Environmental Rights in Canada* (Toronto: Butterworths, 1981) 195 at 200.

man rights to environmental quality) or ecocentric (animal rights, species' rights or rights for nature)? Do these rights extend to future generations? Are there duties that accompany the rights . . . ?[4]

The extent to which positive measures must be contemplated to ensure simple survival is set out in relation to essential ecological functions:

> to supply the essentials of life, it is necessary to maintain essential biological processes. Thus, for example, humans need to have photosynthesis continue to supply atmospheric oxygen, and to maintain hydrological cycles to supply fresh water. Second, the only known way to maintain essential biological processes is to maintain functioning ecosystems . . . . To maintain functioning ecosystems (i.e., natural processes) scientific consensus tells us to do things such as: preserve biological diversity; maintain soil fertility and the productive capacity of the land; protect the oceans; receive sunlight only at wavelengths to which the planet's biology is accustomed; maintain climatic stability; and protect ourselves and our environment from toxic contamination.[5]

Before examining Canadian developments in the law in this area, it is worthwhile to note related initiatives in other jurisdictions and to touch on international considerations.

Attempts have been made in a number of jurisdictions around the world to confer constitutional status on environmental interests or to establish environmental rights on a legislative basis. One survey suggests that over fifty countries have included some form of environmental right in a *Bill of Rights* or equivalent proclamation. By way of example, the South African *Bill of Rights* states that:

> Everyone has the right . . . to an environment that is not harmful to their health or well-being; and to have the environment protected for the benefit of present and future generations, through reasonable legislative and other measures that prevent pollution and ecological degradation, promote conservation, and secure ecologically sustainable development and use of natural resources while promoting justifiable economic and social development.[6]

---

4   E. Hughes & D. Iyalomhe, "Substantive Environmental Rights in Canada" (1998–1999) 30 Ottawa L. Rev. 229 at 232. For an exploration of tentative answers to some of these questions, see Erin Eacott, "A Clean and Healthy Environment: The Barriers and Limitations of this Emerging Right" (2001) 10 Dal. J.Leg. Stud. 74 at 89–94.
5   Hughes & Iyalomhe, *ibid.* at 236.
6   *Constitution of the Republic of South Africa 1996*, ch. 2, s. 24.

Provisions of the treaty arrangements under which the European Union is constituted establish that European community policy on the environment will contribute to pursuit of the following objectives:

- preserving, protecting, and improving the quality of the environment;
- protecting human health;
- utilizing natural resources prudently and rationally; and
- promoting measures at the international level to deal with regional or worldwide environmental problems.[7]

Moreover, the treaty requires that "Community policy on the environment shall aim at a high level of protection taking into account the diversity of situations in the various regions of the Community."[8] In fact, Europe's constitutional framework incorporates several fundamental principles of environmental law by requiring that policy:

> shall be based on the precautionary principle and on the principles that preventive action should be taken, that environmental damage should as a priority be rectified at source and that the polluter should pay. Environmental protection requirements must be integrated into the definition and implementation of other Community policies.[9]

Several U.S. state constitutions also incorporate environmental rights. Under Pennsylvania's constitution, for example, "[t]he people have a right to clean air, pure water, and to the preservation of the natural, scenic, historic, and esthetic values of the environment." Public natural resources in the state are "the common property of all the people, including generations yet to come." Moreover, the state is expected to conserve and maintain these resources for the benefit of all the people in its capacity as trustee.[10]

Statements supporting the principle of a human right to environmental quality may also be found in the international context. In the words of the *Stockholm Declaration, 1972*, "[m]an has the fundamental right to freedom, equality and adequate conditions of life, in an environment of a quality that permits a life of dignity and well-being, and he bears a solemn responsibility to protect and improve the environ-

---

7 *Treaty Establishing the European Community*, art. 174, [2002] O.J. C 325/33. The treaty is now known as the *Treaty on the Functioning of the European Union*.

8 *Ibid.*

9 *Treaty on European Union*, 7 February 1992, 31 I.L.M. 247, art. 130 R.

10 Pa. Const. art. I, 27, cl. 1, quoted in E. Brandl & H. Bungert, "Constitutional Entrenchment of Environmental Protection: A Comparative Analysis of Experiences Abroad" (1992) 16 Harv. Envtl. L. Rev. 1 at 15–16.

ment for present and future generations."[11] Legal principles for environmental protection proposed in conjunction with the work of the WCED articulate as a fundamental human right that "[a]ll human beings have the fundamental right to an environment adequate for their health and well-being."[12]

It has been generally understood, however, that although environmental rights may be derived from existing treaty rights such as the right to life, health, and property, international law has not incorporated an independent right to environmental quality.[13] Ongoing developments, including some at the regional level, nevertheless suggest directions for further discussion and elaboration. In 1994, a Special Rapporteur operating under the auspices of the United Nations Sub-Commission on Prevention of Discrimination and Protection of Minorities, presented a *Draft Declaration of Principles on Human Rights and the Environment* as an appendix to her report.[14] In 1998, the *Aarhus Convention* on access to information and public participation, in particular, referred in the statement of its objective to "the right of every person of present and future generations to live in an environment adequate to his or her health and well-being."[15] In the following year, the *Protocol of San Salvador* to a human rights convention previously developed by the Organization of American States entered into force. It declared that "[e]veryone shall have the right to live in a healthy environment" and called upon State Parties to "promote the protection, preservation and improvement of the environment."[16] Despite such developments, the rights-based approach to environmental protection has advanced only modestly and remains subject to persistent criticisms and reservations.[17]

---

11   *Declaration of the United Nations Conference on the Human Environment*, 16 June 1972, 11 I.L.M. 1416, principle 1.
12   Quoted in World Commission on Environment and Development, *Our Common Future* (Oxford: Oxford University Press, 1987) at 348.
13   P.W. Birnie & A.E. Boyle, *International Law and the Environment* (Oxford: Clarendon Press, 1992) at 192.
14   Karrie A. Wolfe, "Greening the International Human Rights Sphere? An Examination of Environmental Rights and the Draft Declaration of Principles on Human Rights and the Environment" (2003) 13 J. Envtl. L. & Prac. 109.
15   Convention on Access to Information, Public Participation in Decision-Making and Access to Justice in Environmental Matters, Aarhus, Denmark, 25 June 1998.
16   *Additional Protocol to the American Convention on Human Rights in the Area of Economic, Social, and Cultural Rights "Protocol of San Salvador,"* 14 November 1988, San Salvador, (1989) 28 I.L.M. 156, Article 11.
17   Wolfe, above note 14.

B. THE *CHARTER* AND ENVIRONMENTAL LAW

No express recognition of a right to environmental quality or protection exists in Canadian constitutional instruments. Yet the absence of an explicit reference to the environment has not precluded argument that environmental rights exist implicitly within other constitutional provisions.

Since the time of its enactment as Part 1 of the *Constitution Act, 1982*, the *Canadian Charter of Rights and Freedoms* has profoundly influenced judicial decision making and legislative development in many fields. This is so because the rights and freedoms articulated in the *Charter* are applicable to the Parliament of Canada, the provincial legislatures, and the federal and provincial governments in relation to all matters within the constitutional authority of each and are enforceable through judicial proceedings.[18] Not surprisingly, the implications of *Charter* jurisprudence for environmental matters have attracted considerable attention.

Sections 7 and 15 initially appeared most promising to those seeking to ground substantive environmental rights within the *Charter*. The former confirms that "[e]veryone has the right to life, liberty and security of the person and the right not to be deprived thereof except in accordance with the principles of fundamental justice," while the latter provides that "[e]very individual is equal before and under the law and has the right to the equal protection and equal benefit of the law without discrimination" on the basis of a non-comprehensive listing of prohibited grounds.

The scope of interests protected under the phrase "life, liberty and security of the person" is still under consideration. It encompasses freedom from threats to one's physical integrity, including risks to health,[19] but excludes property and economic interests.[20] Accordingly, people whose property or perhaps livelihoods suffer because of environmental contamination or degradation resulting from the decisions of an institution subject to the *Charter*'s application will have limited recourse under the *Charter*, whereas those exposed to health risks in the same circumstances might envisage a *Charter* claim. The prospects of success in each case are dependent on satisfactory proof of a causal connection between the injury alleged and the impugned decision or official action.

---

18 *Canadian Charter of Rights and Freedoms*, Part 1 of the *Constitution Act, 1982*, being Schedule B to the *Canada Act 1982* (U.K.), 1982, c. 11, s. 32 [*Charter*].
19 *R. v. Morgentaler*, [1988] 1 S.C.R. 30.
20 *Reference Re Criminal Code ss. 193 & 195.1(1)(c)*, [1990] 1 S.C.R. 1123.

In *Operation Dismantle*, where a public interest group challenged a decision of cabinet to allow cruise missile tests in northern Canada on the grounds that this increased the risk of nuclear war, the S.C.C. found that there was an insufficient link between the decision to permit the testing and the alleged harm.[21] The court acknowledged, however, that in appropriate circumstances the analysis of a possible right's violation could proceed.

In *Manicom v. Oxford*[22] resident landowners in the vicinity of a site that had been approved by the Ontario Cabinet for waste disposal challenged the decision on several grounds, including the assertion that the approval violated their interest in life, liberty, and security of the person and was not made in accordance with the "principles of fundamental justice" as required by section 7. The Divisional Court rejected the plaintiffs' claim on the grounds that property interests were not protected under section 7 of the *Charter*. In a dissenting opinion, one member of the court concluded that the matter should have been left to the trial judge to determine whether the allegations made, including allegations of adverse health effects, could be substantiated:

> The landowners' claim that the provincial Cabinet decision to permit the construction of the waste disposal site poses a direct threat to them, a specific segment of the population . . . . Moreover, the landowners do not claim only that their right to life, liberty and security will be violated by the Cabinet decision; they also claim that the decision to violate these rights was not made in accordance with the principles of fundamental justice.[23]

Two subsequent cases concerning alleged health risks related to municipal water treatment also suggest that a genuine health hazard resulting from a decision of government could constitute a violation of constitutionally protected interests within the scope of section 7.[24]

It must be borne in mind that the concept of fundamental justice is central to proceedings under section 7. As underlined most recently by the Supreme Court of Canada: "Claimants whose life, liberty or security of the person is put at risk are entitled to relief only to the extent that their complaint arises from a breach of an identifiable principle of fundamental justice."[25] A section 7 claim asserted by residents of a First

---

21   *Operation Dismantle Inc. v. R.*, [1985] 1 S.C.R. 441.
22   (1985), 52 O.R. (2d) 137 (Div. Ct.).
23   *Ibid.* at 155–56.
24   *Locke v. Calgary (City)* (1993), 15 Alta. L.R. (3d) 70 (Q.B.); *Millership v. Kamloops (City)*, 2003 BCSC 82.
25   *Chaoulli v. Quebec (A.G.)* (2005), 254 D.L.R. (4th) 577 at para. 199 (S.C.C.).

Nation Reserve seeking redress for the effects of toxic mould in reserve housing which had been located, designed and constructed under the supervision of the Crown foundered on precisely this ground.[26]

Moreover, even where infringement of section 7 interests can be shown to have taken place in a manner contrary to "principles of fundamental justice," the government will have the opportunity to justify that infringement under section 1 of the *Charter* as being a "reasonable limit prescribed by law as can be demonstrably justified in a free and democratic society." In *Reference Re S. 94(2) of the Motor Vehicle Act (British Columbia)*, Lamer J. concluded that an offence imposing absolute liability on the accused will violate section 7 if and to the extent that it has the potential for depriving life, liberty, or security of the person.[27] In response to some observations by the British Columbia Court of Appeal about the importance of environmental legislation, he remarked that the public interest might be a justification under section 1 for absolute liability offences, depending on the specific circumstances:

> I think the balancing under section 1 of the public interest against the financial interests of a corporation [charged with an absolute liability offence, and if entitled to claim section 7 protection] would give very different results from that of balancing public interest and the liberty and security of the person of a human being.
>
> Indeed, the public interest as regards "air and water pollution offences" requires that the guilty be dealt with firmly, but the seriousness of the offence does not in my respectful view support the proposition that the innocent *human* person be open to conviction, quite the contrary.[28]

The equality rights provisions in section 15 of the Charter have also proven difficult to apply in relation to environmental matters. For example, the applicability of section 15 to environmental claims was once considered to involve claims of discrimination based on differential treatment according to jurisdiction, geography, economic activity, and so on. In *Aluminum Co. of Canada Ltd. v. Ontario (Minister of the Environment)*, a case arising in connection with refillable container regulations, the aluminum can manufacturer contended that the regulations discriminated to the economic advantage of steel manufacturers and imposed economic detriment on the aluminum industry. After concluding that the protection afforded by the *Charter's* equality provisions was not available to corporations, the court further observed that

---

26   *Grant v. Canada (A.G.)* (2005), 77 O.R. (3d) 481 (S.C.J.).

27   [1985] 2 S.C.R. 486.

28   *Ibid.* at 518.

economic discrimination was not a prohibited form of discrimination.[29] Subsequent judicial interpretation restricted the scope of section 15 by insisting upon reference to the enumerated or analogous grounds, not including territory:

> A complainant under section 15(1) must establish that he or she is a member of a discrete and insular minority group, that the group is defined by characteristics analogous to the enumerated grounds of discrimination set out in section 15(1), and that the law has a negative impact. In determining whether a group is analogous to those that are enumerated within section 15(1), of the *Charter*, . . . [a court must focus] on the larger context by searching for indicia of discrimination such as "stereotyping, historical disadvantage or vulnerability to political and social prejudice."[30]

Section 7 and section 15 claims were combined prominently in litigation over the constitutionality of certain provisions of the federal *Nuclear Liability Act*, which established a compensation scheme for victims of nuclear accidents while limiting the liability of a nuclear plant operator to $75 million for any particular incident. Plaintiffs in the case[31] argued that the effect of limited liability was to increase the exposure of the public to risk of nuclear accident by encouraging the proliferation of nuclear reactors and by reducing the operator's incentive to take appropriate care and safety measures. This, it was alleged, infringes the public's constitutionally protected interest in security of the person under section 7. With regard to section 15, plaintiffs argued that those in closest proximity to nuclear reactors were most exposed to physical risk and thereby suffered discrimination, and that all victims of a nuclear incident—being limited in their total damage claims—suffered discrimination in comparison with victims of other accidents who are not similarly limited in their ability to seek financial compensation.

At trial, Wright J. of the Ontario Court of Justice (General Division) rejected both lines of analysis. Citing regulatory controls on the nuclear industry, he concluded that the required link between the *Nuclear Liability Act* and reduced levels of safety that would increase the likelihood of a nuclear incident had not been established. In relation to section 15, Wright J. observed that the *Nuclear Liability Act* does not discriminate as that concept is understood within the meaning of the section.

---

29 *Aluminum Co. of Canada v. Ontario (Minister of the Environment)* (1986), 55 O.R. (2d) 522 (Div. Ct.).

30 *Haig v. Canada (Chief Electoral Officer)*, [1993] 2 S.C.R. 995 at 1043–44, L'Heureux-Dubé J.

31 *Energy Probe v. Canada (A.G.)* (1994), 17 O.R. (3d) 717 (Gen. Div.).

Although the jurisprudence will continue to evolve in this area, one experienced environmental lawyer provided a frank summary of the limitations presented by or the obstacles facing the rights paradigm in the context of environmental protection. First, insofar as human rights are generally perceived to involve safeguards from state interference (so-called negative rights), it is not clear how this applies to environmental protection, which will rarely take the form of a contest between government and the individual. State action appears to be an essential component of environmental protection, for the right to a healthy environment is a classic illustration of a right that must be enjoyed collectively or not at all. Moreover, human rights safeguards have generally operated in the context of relatively immediate and relatively severe threats to the individual, while the adverse effects of environmental degradation are frequently gradual, cumulative, and often difficult to link causally to individual victims, sometimes including members of future generations. There are additional limitations in the sense that the appropriate scope of environmental rights remains unresolved. Fundamentally, however, "the mere assertion of a right fails to give sufficient guidance in making the hard choices of pollution control."[32]

Hard choices will also arise in relation to the allocation of limited environmental resources rather than their direct degradation. Such a situation arose in R. v. Kapp where commercial fishermen — mainly non-aboriginal — in British Columbia challenged communal fishing licenses issued to aboriginal bands to allow them exclusive, short-term access to salmon in the mouth of the Fraser River. An equality rights challenge to those licenses under section 15 (1) failed. In the view of the Supreme Court of Canada, the communal fishing licenses constituted a "law, program, or activity" within the meaning of section 15(2) which "has as its object the amelioration of conditions of disadvantaged individuals or groups." A distinction between groups such as the preference embodied in the communal fishing licenses will not constitute unlawful discrimination where it serves an ameliorative or remedial purpose in favour of a disadvantaged group.[33]

Somewhat ironically perhaps, constitutional safeguards also serve to constrain the ability of government to intrude into private decision making or to coerce and punish individuals accused of wrongdoing, including environmentally harmful conduct. Thus, in the environmental context, claims about Charter rights are used simultaneously to pro-

32   D. Saxe, Environmental Offences: Corporate Responsibility and Executive Liability (Aurora, ON: Canada Law Book, 1990) at 18–20.
33   R. v. Kapp, 2008 SCC 41.

mote and to check environmental protection measures. One common form of attack by defendants has been to suggest that, where individual liberty is in question as a consequence of the prospect of imprisonment for conviction, the entitlement to "fundamental justice" includes prohibition against vague or uncertain offence provisions. The test for assessing vagueness claims under section 7 is that "a law will be found unconstitutionally vague if it so lacks in precision as not to give sufficient guidance for legal debate."[34]

In *R. v. Canadian Pacific Ltd.*, the railway was charged with a violation of section 13 of Ontario's *Environmental Protection Act* which states:

> Notwithstanding any other provision of this Act or the regulations, no person shall deposit, add, emit or discharge a contaminant or cause or permit the deposit, addition, emission or discharge of a contaminant into the natural environment that, (*a*) causes or is likely to cause impairment of the quality of the natural environment for any use that can be made of it.[35]

The railway alleged that aspects of the section were so vague and broad that they failed to establish a standard of sufficient intelligibility to allow citizens to regulate their conduct. CP challenged the provision in its entirety and specifically criticized the concepts of contaminant, impairment, natural environment, and the expression "for any use that can be made of it."

Writing for six members of the Supreme Court of Canada, Gonthier J. was fully satisfied that the legislative language under attack survived the vagueness challenge. General observations accompanying the decision are equally, if not more, significant. Gonthier J. remarked that, in the environmental protection context, "a strict requirement of drafting precision might well undermine the ability of the legislature to provide for a comprehensive and flexible regime."[36] Precise legislative codification of environmental hazards, he added, might even impede rather than promote understanding of the prohibited conduct. Having examined environmental legislation from several provinces, and after noting that virtually all of the regimes in place might have been vulnerable to challenge if the grounds on which the Ontario provision was criticized for vagueness were valid, Gonthier J. explained his view of the legislative options and their significance:

34   *R. v. Nova Scotia Pharmaceutical Society*, [1992] 2 S.C.R. 606.
35   *Environmental Protection Act*, R.S.O. 1980, c. 141, s. 13 (1)(a). Now see R.S.O. 1990, c. E-19, s. 14.
36   *R. v. Canadian Pacific Ltd.*, [1995] 2 S.C.R. 1028 at 1073.

In the area of environmental protection, legislators have two choices. They may enact detailed provisions which prohibit the release of particular quantities of enumerated substances into the natural environment. Alternatively, they may choose a more general prohibition of "pollution" and rely on the courts to determine whether, in a particular case, the release of a substance into the natural environment is of sufficient magnitude to attract legislative sanction. The latter option is, of course, more flexible and better able to accommodate developments in our knowledge about environmental protection. However, a general enactment may be challenged . . . for failing to provide adequate notice to citizens of prohibited conduct.[37]

This does not necessarily mean that detailed technical provisions are therefore the best means of alerting citizens about prohibited conduct. "If a citizen requires a chemistry degree to figure out whether an activity releases a particular contaminant in sufficient quantities to trigger a statutory prohibition," Gonthier J. continued, "then that prohibition provides no better fair notice than a more general enactment." The court concluded that an objective approach is applicable to the notice aspect of the vagueness analysis. "[W]ould the average citizen, with an average understanding of the subject matter of the prohibition, receive adequate notice of prohibited conduct?"[38]

C. THE LEGISLATIVE BASIS OF ENVIRONMENTAL RIGHTS

Several provinces and territories have established environmental rights through legislation. Though lacking the authority of constitutional entrenchment, such measures embody a number of crucial principles, including, on occasion, formal recognition of human entitlements to environmental security or a healthy environment.

Quebec's *Environmental Quality Act (EQA)*, as previously noted, affirms that "[e]very person has a right to a healthy environment and to its protection, and to the protection of the living species inhabiting it, to the extent provided for by this act and the regulations, orders, approvals, and authorizations issued under any section of this act."[39] In *Calvé v. Gestion Serge Lafrenière inc.* riparian owners secured an inter-

---

37 *Ibid.* at 1073–74.
38 *Ibid.* at 1074.
39 *Environmental Quality Act*, R.S.Q. 1977, c. Q-2, s. 19, as am. by S.Q. 1978, c. 64, s. 4.

locutory injunction limiting fish production and the phosphorous discharge level of an aquaculture plant that had been operating pursuant to provincial approvals. Plaintiffs, also invoking protections embodied in the *Civil Code of Quebec*, had argued that the approvals were unreasonable in the circumstances of a lake already known to be experiencing eutrophication and were contrary to the letter and spirit of the *EQA*. A unanimous Court of Appeal, in upholding (with modifications) the interlocutory injunction issued at the trial level, remarked that in order for the statutory right to environmental quality to be respected, some judicial remedy was required.[40]

Quebec, more recently, has further enhanced environmental rights at the provincial level by means of amendments to the Quebec *Charter of human rights and freedoms*. This "quasi-constitutional" instrument now provides that "[e]very person has a right to live in a healthful environment in which biodiversity is preserved, to the extent and according to the standards provided by law."[41] While the contents of the new right are circumscribed by the state of the law, this right offers reinforcement to the existing legal framework by providing potentially forceful remedies to those whose right has been violated.

Pursuant to the *Environmental Rights Act* of 1990, "the people of the Northwest Territories have the right to a healthy environment and a right to protect the integrity, biological diversity and productivity of the ecosystems in the Northwest Territories."[42] The legislation more specifically confirms the right of any person resident in the territories "to protect the environment and the public trust from the release of contaminants" thus granting standing to private individuals to seek injunctive relief, a remedial order, or compensation for breaches of the law. The statute also ensures that such a plaintiff be provided with relevant information. With reference to the public trust as embodied in the *Environmental Rights Act*, territorial courts have observed that:

> Wildlife management, indeed environmental policy in general takes on a special significance in the Northwest Territories. The legislature has deemed the collective interest of the people of the Territories in the quality of the environment and the protection of the environment for future generations to be a "public trust."[43]

---

40   [1999] J.Q. no. 1334.

41   R.S.Q. c. C-12, s. 46.1.

42   *Environmental Rights Act*, R.S.N.W.T. 1988 (Supp.), c. 83, as amended by S.N.W.T. 1999 c. 21. Provision is made in the *Nunavut Act* for the applicability of legislation from the former jurisdiction.

43   *R. v. Ram Head Outfitters*, [1995] N.W.T.J. No. 29 (Terr. Ct.).

The Yukon *Environment Act* asserts the right of the people of the Yukon to "a healthful natural environment" and that it is "in the public interest to provide every resident in the Yukon with a remedy adequate to protect the natural environment."[44] Saskatchewan had also initiated discussion on legislation concerning a *Charter of Environmental Rights and Responsibilities*, which in its initial form was less explicit on the issue of rights. The draft legislation simply affirmed that "the health and integrity of the environment is of paramount concern to Saskatchewan residents" and that "the health and integrity of the environment must be sustained for the benefit of present and future generations of Saskatchewan citizens."[45]

A somewhat different approach was later taken in Ontario where the *Environmental Bill of Rights, 1993 (OEBR)* noted "the inherent value of the natural environment" and the people's "right to a healthful environment." In the protection, conservation, and restoration of the environment, the *OEBR* distinguished between government and individual roles; the former was acknowledged to have primary responsibility, but the people should have means to ensure that these goals are realized in "an effective, timely, open and fair manner."[46] Yet, because these assertions are made in the preamble to the *OEBR* rather than in the substantive provisions of the legislation itself, they lack the full authority of actual legislative provisions.

However, the *OEBR*'s purposes as enunciated in section 2 do encompass environmental protection, conservation, and "where reasonable," restoration as well as sustainability and protection for "the right to a healthful environment," all to be accomplished "by the means provided in this Act."[47] Those means include a requirement for designated Ontario ministries to prepare a statement of environmental values (SEV) explaining how the *OEBR*'s purposes will be applied when the ministry makes decisions that might significantly affect the environment. Designated ministries must also explain how they propose to integrate objectives of the *OEBR* with "other considerations, including social, economic and scientific considerations, that are relevant to their decision making."[48] Other provisions confirm or establish a variety of public rights to participate in environmental decision making in Ontario:

---

44 S.Y. 1991, c. 5, ss. 6 & 7.
45 Bill 48, *An Act to Provide a Charter of Environmental Rights and Responsibilities*, 2d Sess, 22d Leg., Saskatchewan, 1992.
46 *Environmental Bill of Rights, 1993*, S.O. 1993, c. 28.
47 *Ibid.*, s. 2.
48 *Ibid.*, s. 7. The Statement of Environmental Values may be found online: www.ene.gov.on.ca/envision/ebr.

- the right to get notice of, and to comment on, proposed policies, Acts, regulations, and instruments that may affect the environment;
- the right to seek leave to appeal certain ministry decisions;
- the right to ask a minister to change or eliminate existing environmental policies, Acts, regulations, and instruments;
- the right to ask a ministry to consider the need for new policies, Acts, and regulations;
- the right to ask a ministry to investigate contraventions of environmental Acts, regulations, and instruments;
- the right to sue those responsible for harming a public resource; and
- the right to sue for damages in the case of direct economic or personal loss resulting from an environmentally harmful public nuisance.

In addition, the *OEBR* facilitates access to information and public accountability through the creation of an environmental registry[49] and the appointment of an environmental commissioner for the province as an officer of the Legislative Assembly.[50] The commissioner's operations encompass responsibilities for:

- reviewing implementation of the *OEBR*;
- reviewing ministerial compliance with the *OEBR*;
- providing guidance on request to ministries concerning compliance with the *OEBR*;
- providing assistance on request concerning public educational programs regarding the *OEBR*;
- providing advice and assistance to the public concerning opportunities for participating in decision making as provided for in the *OEBR*;
- reviewing the use of the environmental registry;
- reviewing the exercise of ministerial discretion under the *OEBR*; and
- reviewing the public's use of rights of participation provided under the *OEBR*.

The environmental commissioner enjoys extensive powers of inquiry in connection with the performance of these responsibilities[51] and reports annually to the speaker of the legislature.[52]

---

49   *Ibid.*, s. 5. See online: www.ene.gov.on.ca/envision/ebr.
50   *Ibid.*, Part III.
51   *Ibid.*, s. 60.
52   *Ibid.* s. 58; The Environmental Commissioner of Ontario's annual reports may be found at www.eco.on.ca/english.ar.

In conjunction with a 10-Year Review of the *OEBR*, the commissioner, in 2003–2004, formulated a series of recommendations intended to update and strengthen environmental rights in Ontario.[53] These call for explicit recognition of emerging environmental principles such as polluter pay, more regular revision and stricter adherence to Ministry Statements of Environmental Values, and greater accountability for decisions to exempt decisions from disclosure on the EBR Registry. Modifications were also proposed that would facilitate use of current procedures that permit applications to be made for review of existing instruments, for investigations of alleged contraventions, and for leave to appeal certain environmental decisions.

At the federal level, *CEPA, 1999* also addressed a number of issues relating to public participation and provided for an environmental registry relating to matters under the Act.[54] In addition, pursuant to earlier federal legislation, designated federal departments are required to prepare sustainable development strategies for presentation to the House of Commons. To monitor and report on departmental progress towards sustainable development, the office of federal commissioner of the environment and sustainable development (CESD) was created to work with the auditor general of Canada, whose responsibilities include bringing to the attention of the House of Commons any cases where "money has been expended without due regard to the environmental effects of those expenditures in the context of sustainable development."[55] A resident of Canada may petition the auditor general about an environmental matter associated with the sustainable development responsibilities of designated departments. Within fifteen days such inquiries are to be forwarded to the appropriate minister who must acknowledge the petition and then prepare a reply, generally within 120 days of receiving the petition from the auditor general.[56]

The CESD reports annually on the use that is being made of the federal environmental petition process and conducts audits on selected responses. For the reporting period 1 July 2004 through to 30 June 2005, thirty-seven environmental petitions were directed to thirty-one federal departments or agencies.

---

53 Environmental Commissioner of Ontario, *Looking Forward: The Environmental Bill of Rights* (Toronto: Environmental Commissioner of Ontario, 2004).

54 *CEPA, 1999*, Part 2. A number of these public participation provisions are noted and discussed elsewhere in this volume.

55 *Auditor General Act*, R.S.C. 1985, c. A-17, s. 7(1)(f).

56 *Ibid.*, s. 22.

FURTHER READINGS

ANDREWS, W., "The Environment and the Canadian Charter of Rights and Freedoms" in N. Duplé, ed., *Le droit à la qualité de l'Environnement: un droit en devenir, un droit à définir* (Montreal, Québec/ Amérique, 1988)

BIRNIE, P.W., & A.E. BOYLE, *International Law and the Environment*, 2d ed. (Oxford: Oxford University Press, 2002)

BOYLE, A.E., & M.R. ANDERSON, eds., *Human Rights Approaches to Environmental Protection* (New York: Clarendon Press, 1996)

GAGE, ANDREW, "Public Health Hazards and Section 7 of the *Charter*," (2003) 13 J. Envtl. . L. & Prac. 1

GIBSON, N., "The Right to a Clean Environment" (1990) Sask. L. Rev. 54

HUGHES, E., & IYALOMHE, D., "Substantive Environmental Rights in Canada" (1998–1999) 30 Ottawa L. Rev. 229

LINDGREN, R., & P. MULDOON, *The Environmental Bill of Rights: A Practical Guide* (Toronto: Emond Montgomery, 1995)

STEVENSON, C.P., "A New Perspective on Environmental Rights after the *Charter*" (1983) 21 Osgoode Hall L.J. 390

SWAIGEN, J., & R.E. WOODS, "A Substantive Right to Environmental Quality" in J. Swaigen, ed., *Environmental Rights in Canada* (Toronto: Butterworths, 1981) 195

WINFIELD, M.S., "A Political and Legal Analysis of Ontario's Environmental Bill of Rights" (1998) 47 U.N.B.L.J. 325

THE INTERNATIONAL CONTEXT OF CANADIAN ENVIRONMENTAL LAW

A. INTERNATIONAL ENVIRONMENTAL LAW AND ORGANIZATIONS

Nations around the world have had long-standing concerns about the impact on their domestic environments of transboundary air and water pollution, as well as about offshore tanker spills inflicting economic and ecological damage on their coastal regions and resources. In addition, indications of environmental deterioration in areas of common interest outside national boundaries such as the oceans, the Antarctic, and the atmosphere sheltering the planet have encouraged efforts to identify effective international responses, including legal measures. To some degree, pressure in this direction is even increased by the thought that environmental deterioration constitutes a threat to both peace and security.[1]

The United Nations Conference on the Human Environment (Stockholm, 1972), the report of the World Commission on Environment and Development, *Our Common Future* (1987), the UN Conference on Environment and Development in Rio de Janeiro (1992) and the *Johannesburg Declaration* following the World Summit on Sustain-

---

1   A. Daniel, "Environmental Threats to International Peace and Security: Combatting Common Security Threats Through Promotion of Compliance with International Environmental Agreements" (1994) Canadian Council for International Law 134–46.

able Development (2002) have been landmarks in the development of principles of international environmental law.[2] Principle 21 from the Stockholm Convention is a particularly prominent example of attempts to formulate environmental norms:

> States have, in accordance with the Charter of the United Nations and the principles of international law, the sovereign right to exploit their own resources pursuant to their own environmental policies, and the responsibility to ensure that the activities within their jurisdiction or control do not cause damage to the environment of other states or of areas beyond the limits of national jurisdiction.

The evolution of international law affecting the environment is ongoing (see table 4.1). As explained by the international legal scholar Alexandre Kiss, evolution of "environmental governance" involves the interrelated emergence of legal norms and management institutions:

> The international legal ordering of environmental protection includes the two components: on the one hand, legal norms intended to govern the behaviour of states and other actors of international law and on the other hand international regulation creating international bodies and determining their functions. The two sides of governance interact: different forms of international co-operation, conferences or permanent institutions create international legal norms the implementation of which needs new forms of international organisms. The co-operation is to be undertaken at a world-wide level as well as in regional frameworks. Such forms can be considered as the world Constitution governing environmental matters.[3]

Public international law, the principles governing relations between and among nations, derives from several sources—agreement, customary international law, and general principles of law. All are independent sources of international obligations. For example, over sixty years ago, in connection with an arbitration between Canada and the United States concerning liability for damage from air pollution from smelting facilities in Trail, British Columbia, an international tribunal stated that "no State has the right to use or permit the use of its territory in such a manner as to cause injury by fumes in or to the territory of another or the persons or property therein, when the case is of

---

2   *Johannesburg Declaration on Sustainable Development*, online: www.un.org/esa/sustdev/documents/Johannesburg%20Declaration.doc.

3   Alexandre Kiss, "The Legal Ordering of Environmental Protection" in Ronald MacDonald & Douglas Johnston, eds., *Towards World Constitutionalism: Issues in the Legal Ordering of the World Community* (Boston: Martinus Nijhoff, 2005) 567.

Table 4.1:   International Environmental Treaties

1971	*Convention on Wetlands of International Importance*, 30 January–3 February 1971, 11 I.L.M. 963
1972	*Declaration of the United Nations Conference on the Human Environment*, 16 June 1972, 11 I.L.M. 1419 *Convention on the Prevention of Marine Pollution by Dumping of Wastes and Other Matter*, 13 November 1972, 11 I.L.M. 1294
1973	*Convention on International Trade in Endangered Species of Wild Fauna and Flora*, 3 March 1973, 12 I.L.M. 1085 *International Convention for the Prevention of Pollution from Ships*, 2 November 1973, 12 I.L.M. 1319
1976	*Convention on Civil Liability for Oil Pollution Damage Resulting from Exploration for and Exploitation of Seabed Mineral Resources*, 17 December 1976, 16 I.L.M. 1450
1978	Protocol *of 1978 Relating to the International Convention for the Prevention of Pollution from Ships, 1973*, 16 February 1978, 17 I.L.M. 576 *Great Lakes Water Quality Agreement of 1978*, 22 November, 1978, Can. T.S. 1978 No. 20
1979	*Convention on Long-Range Transboundary Air Pollution*, 13 November 1979, 18 I.L.M. 1442
1982	*World Charter for Nature*, UNGA Res. 37/7 *Convention on the Law of the Sea*, 10 December 1982, 21 I.L.M. 1261
1985	*Vienna Convention for the Protection of the Ozone Layer*, 22 March 1985, 26 I.L.M. 1529
1986	*Agreement between Canada and the United States on Transboundary Movement of Hazardous Waste*, 28 October 1986, T.I.A.S. 11099
1987	Protocol *on Substances that Deplete the Ozone Layer*, 16 September 1987, 26 I.L.M. 1550 Protocol *to the 1979 Convention on Long-Range Transboundary Air Pollution Concerning the Control of Nitrogen Oxides or their Transboundary Fluxes*, 31 October 1988, K.A.V. 2371
1989	*Basel Convention on the Control of Transboundary Movements of Hazardous Wastes and their Disposal*, 22 March 1989, 29 I.L.M. 657
1991	*Convention on Environmental Impact Assessment in a Transboundary Context*, 25 February 1991, 30 I.L.M. 802 *Agreement between the Government of the United States of America and the Government of Canada on Air Quality*, 13 March 1991, 30 I.L.M. 678
1992	*Framework Convention on Climate Change*, 9 May 1992, 31 I.L.M. 849 *Convention on Biodiversity*, 5 June 1992, 31 I.L.M. 818
1997	*Conference of the Parties to the F.C.C.C.: Kyoto Protocol*, 10 December 1997, 37 I.L.M. 22
2000	*Stockholm Convention on Persistent Organic Pollutants*, 9 March 2001, 40 I.L.M. 531

serious consequence and the injury is established by clear and convincing evidence."[4] Here one can discern some indication of the origins of Stockholm Principle 21 quoted above.[5]

Today, however, treaties or conventions as they are also known are increasingly used to embody the text of environmental agreements between states. Such agreements may be reached on a bilateral basis—between neighbouring countries, for example—or they may involve many signatories. Formal agreements of this nature dealing with such subjects as the law of the sea, the protection of endangered species, transboundary movement of hazardous wastes, prevention of pollution from ships, and so on are the primary forms of international environmental law. These agreements will often directly influence the shape of domestic environmental regimes. Indeed, some commentators have speculated about a process of "internationalization" of environmental regulation.[6] This is in part a consequence of various forms of recognition in the international context of a range of fundamental environmental principles: intergenerational equity, common heritage of humankind, prevention, precaution, polluter pays, common but differentiated responsibilities, and prior notification, among others.[7]

The process for incorporating international law into Canada's domestic legal regime varies as between customary and treaty law; the former is presumed to apply automatically in the absence of conflict with statute or judicial precedent, while treaty obligations are implemented only by means of legislative enactment.[8] Consistent with the division of powers under the *Constitution Act, 1867*, domestic Canadian responsibility for treaty implementation is divided between the federal government and the provinces depending on the subject matter in question.[9]

---

4   *Trail Smelter Arbitration* (1941), 3 U.N. Rep. Int. Arb. Awards 1908 at 1965.

5   See Rebecca M. Bratspies & Russell A. Miller, *Transboundary Harm in International Law: Lessons from the Trail Smelter Arbitration* (New York: Cambridge University Press, 2006).

6   R.W. Hahn & K.R. Richards, "The Internationalization of Environmental Regulation" (1989) 30 Harv. Int'l L.J. 421.

7   David Hunter, James Salzman, & Durwood Zaelke, *International Environmental Law and Policy* (New York: Foundation Press, 1998) c. 8.

8   For judicial suggestion of the possible relevance of international environmental law developments to the legal powers of Canadian municipalities, see *114957 Canada Ltée (Spraytech) v. Hudson (Town)*, 2001 SCC 40 at paras. 31–32. See also Jerry V. DeMarco & Michelle L. Campbell, "The Supreme Court of Canada's Progressive Use of International Environmental Law and Policy in Interpreting Domestic Legislation" (2004) 13 R.E.C.I.E.L.320.

9   *Canada (A.G.) v. Ontario (A.G.)*, [1937] A.C. 326 (P.C.). For information on Canadian participation in international environmental agreements, see online: www.ec.gc.ca/international/multilat/compendium_e.htm.

Although nation states remain the principal players in international environmental matters, intergovernmental and non-governmental organizations have a significant and influential role in fostering cooperation between states in relation to discussion and research on environmental issues. Some of these bodies, such as the International Maritime Organization and the World Meteorological Organization, are associated with the United Nations. These and other institutional mechanisms provide research, technical support, and monitoring, or facilitate dispute resolution and enforcement, or contribute to continuing refinement of the legal regime itself.

The United Nations Environment Program (UNEP), whose secretariat is located in Nairobi, Kenya, was created following the 1972 Stockholm Conference. According to the resolution of the United Nations General Assembly bringing it into existence, UNEP was intended to serve as "a focal point for environmental action" by offering coordination, advice, and policy guidance within the UN system of agencies and institutions and by promoting international environmental cooperation.[10] As organizer of a three-year program of negotiations, UNEP facilitated agreement on an international convention to eliminate or restrict production of certain pesticides and industrial chemicals that are not only highly toxic but stable and persistent in the environment. The pollutants initially targeted as Persistent Organic Pollutants (POPs) are aldrin, chlordane, DDT, dieldrin, endrin, heptachlor, mirex, toxaphene, PCBs, hexachlorobenzene, dioxins, and furans.[11]

Outside the United Nations framework, various international bodies with regional focus or otherwise concerned with the common interests of their members have incorporated environmental considerations within their mandates. In the case of the Organisation for Economic Co-operation and Development (OECD), in which Canada participates along with some two dozen other industrialized nations, environmental matters are addressed under the auspices of an environment committee. A certain amount of policy advice is provided alongside research initiatives and valuable detailed analyses of environmental conditions in the member states.[12]

The involvement of environmental non-governmental organizations (ENGOs) in international environmental law and policy should also be noted. Organizations such as Greenpeace International, Friends

---

10   P.W. Birnie & A.E. Boyle, *International Law and the Environment* (Oxford: Clarendon Press, 1992) at 42.

11   See online: http://irptc.unep.ch/pops.

12   Birnie & Boyle, above note 10 at 71; see OECD, *Environmental Performance Reviews: Canada* (Paris: OECD, 2004).

of the Earth, and the World Wildlife Fund have participated actively in research, public information, and awareness campaigns to promote both domestic and international responses to environmental issues such as species protection and resource conservation. ENGO representatives quite frequently have observer status or some other formal affiliation with intergovernmental organizations. The long-established International Union for Conservation of Nature and Natural Resources (IUCN), has been particularly important for its ongoing contributions to international law-making. Some other ENGOs have been more oriented towards litigation.

B. INTERNATIONAL INSTITUTIONS AND ENVIRONMENTAL PROTECTION IN CANADA

Many examples of the influence of international considerations on Canadian environmental law and policy could be identified.[13] The following are important illustrations.

1) Great Lakes Water Quality, Diversion and Exports

For the roughly fifty million North Americans living on either side of the Great Lakes, the condition of the region is a paradigm test of the effectiveness of contemporary responses to environmental protection. The experience of the Great Lakes region contributed significantly to North American understanding of the complexity of environmental challenges. Thus, cross-media effects (those that transfer from one media — air, land, or water — to another), the role of non-point (generalized) sources of pollution such as pesticide use in forest management and agriculture, acid rain, and long-range transport of airborne pollutants, persistent toxicity, invasive species and sustainability are on the broader agenda to some degree because they were encountered in the Great Lakes Region and in part were brought to public attention through work associated with the International Joint Commission (IJC).

The IJC is the creation of Article VII of the *Treaty Between the United States and Great Britain Relating to Boundary Waters, and Questions Arising Between the United States and Canada* [*Boundary Waters Treaty*] of 1909, an agreement reached in response to significant Canada–U.S. border irritants, including proposals by civic officials from Chicago to

---

13   See discussion below of *CITES*, transboundary waste, etc.

divert water south from the Great Lakes for sewage disposal[14] and disputed access to the hydroelectric power potential at Niagara Falls. It operates as a binational panel or administrative agency consisting of three commissioners from Canada and three from the United States whose responsibilities centre on water-related conflicts between the two North American countries that—one way or another—share some three hundred rivers.

The IJC's functions have been classified as quasi-judicial, investigative, and arbitral. In relation to the assessment and approval of works that might affect the natural level and flow of boundary waters, the commission exercises quasi-judicial authority. Decisions are to reflect a commitment to the "equal and similar rights" of the parties and an established hierarchy of uses. The IJC was also authorized to undertake investigative work on the basis of a reference from the parties and to make recommendations to the two national governments. In addition, and subject to the advice and consent of the U.S. Senate, which has never been given, the IJC has an arbitration function for the resolution of disputes connected with its jurisdiction.

Until comparatively recently, the IJC's work emphasized flooding and diversions. Concerns about water quality tended to be of secondary importance through to the 1960s even though the *Boundary Waters Treaty* of 1909 explicitly addressed pollution and some important pioneering work on water quality was actually undertaken. Article IV embodies the agreement of the parties "that . . . waters . . . defined as boundary waters and waters flowing across the boundary shall not be polluted on either side to the injury of health or property on the other."

Since 1964, when the Canadian and U.S. governments referred issues of pollution of Lake Erie, Lake Ontario, and the international section of the St. Lawrence River to the IJC for investigation, the commission has become increasingly active in relation to the Great Lakes environment. The study's finding that "grave deterioration of water quality on each side of the boundary" was "causing injury to health and property on the other side"[15] led to the *Great Lakes Water Quality Agreement (GLWQA)* of 1972.

In outline, this original agreement enumerated both general and specific water-quality objectives, identified a series of programs to be undertaken for preventive and remedial purposes, authorized the parties to proceed with implementation according to their own legislative

---

14 Jamie Benidickson, *The Culture of Flushing: A Social and Legal History of Sewage* (Vancouver: UBC Press, 2007) c. 8.

15 *Great Lakes Water Quality Agreement*, 15 April 1972, T.I.A.S. No. 7312.

regimes, and accorded to the IJC certain functions relating to information gathering and exchange, coordination, monitoring of progress, and making recommendations.

According to the general water-quality objectives, the waters were to be made:

a) free from substances that enter the waters as a result of human activity and that will settle to form putrescent or otherwise objectionable sludge deposits, or that will adversely affect aquatic life or waterfowl;
b) free from floating debris, oil, scum, and other floating materials entering the waters as a result of human activity in amounts sufficient to be unsightly or deleterious;
c) free from materials entering the waters as a result of human activity producing colour, odour, or other conditions in such a degree as to create a nuisance;
d) free from substances entering the waters as a result of human activity in concentrations that are toxic or harmful to human, animal, or aquatic life;
e) free from nutrients entering the waters as a result of human activity in concentrations that create nuisance growths of aquatic weeds and algae.[16]

In 1978 a revised agreement reaffirmed the basic objectives but added several extremely important elements to the definition of the task ahead. First, although the 1972 agreement had broadened the scope of operation beyond the narrowly defined 1909 definition of boundary waters to encompass tributary waters of the Great Lakes system, the 1978 agreement further extended the challenge to what was known as the "Great Lakes Basin Ecosystem," defined as "the interacting components of air, land, water and living organisms, including man, within the drainage basin of the St. Lawrence River."[17] Second, by 1978, with measures taking hold to deal with phosphates and municipal sewage, the parties singled out toxics for more elaborate attention.[18] The 1978 agreement recognized a toxic substance as "a substance which can cause death, disease, behavioural abnormalities, cancer, genetic mutations, physiological or reproductive malfunctions or physical deformities in any organism or its offspring, or which can become poisonous after concentration in the food chain or in combination with other

16 *Ibid.*, art. II.
17 *Great Lakes Water Quality Agreement of 1978*, 22 Nov. 1978, Can. T.S. 1978 No. 20, art. I(g).
18 *Ibid.*

substances."[19] Early candidates included mercury, DDT, mirex, PCBs, and dioxin.[20]

Moreover, by 1978, the parties had adopted an overall statement of purpose: "to restore and maintain the chemical, physical, and biological integrity of the waters of the Great Lakes Basin Ecosystem." To that end they adopted as a policy the principle that "[t]he discharge of toxic substances in toxic amounts be prohibited and the discharge of any or all persistent toxic substances be virtually eliminated."[21]

In 1987 the *GLWQA* was amended by a protocol setting out a process for rehabilitating the overall ecosystem by means of more localized remediation mechanisms.[22] Following a comprehensive process of review and assessment, the Commission advanced recommendations in 2006 for further institutional changes in Great Lakes water quality management and called for a Binational Action Plan which would:

> Make provision for clear and achievable goals, accountability, binational coordination, program integration, adaptive management, data management, substantive reporting, research, monitoring and surveillance.
>
> Include activities to manage excess nutrients; address existing and emerging chemicals of concern; improve spills prevention and response; control and prevent invasive species; restore and preserve hydrological processes; understand and prevent impacts from groundwater pollution; protect, create and restore habitat; adapt to climate change; monitor atmospheric sources of pollution; reduce the impact of shoreline development and urban sprawl; and improve the condition of nearshore waters.[23]

Concern about water quantity issues has also arisen in connection with a series of export and diversion proposals.[24] In its February 2000 report, *Protection of the Waters of the Great Lakes*,[25] the IJC responded to a reference from the governments of Canada and the United States requesting an examination of the way in which the levels and flows of

---

19   *Ibid.*, art. I(v).

20   *Ibid.*

21   *Ibid.*, art. II.

22   For further discussion, see chapter 11.

23   International Joint Commission, *Advice to Governments on Their Review of the Great Lakes Water Quality Agreement: A Special Report to the Governments of Canada and the United States* (Ottawa: International Joint Commission, 2006).

24   Peter Annin, *The Great Lakes Water Wars* (Washington, DC: Island Press, 2006).

25   International Joint Commission, *Protection of the Waters of the Great Lakes: Final Report to the Governments of Canada and the United States* (Ottawa: International Joint Commission, 2000).

waters within the boundary and transboundary basins and in relation to shared aquifers might be affected by:

- existing and potential consumptive uses of water;
- existing and potential diversions of water in and out of the transboundary basins, including withdrawals of water for export;
- the cumulative effects of existing and potential diversions, and removals of water, including removals in bulk for export;
- the current laws and policies as may affect the sustainability of the water resources in boundary and transboundary basins.

Following investigation by binational interdisciplinary study teams and an extensive program of public consultation, the IJC published findings and recommendations. With regard to water removals, the commission recommended that the governments of the U.S. states bordering the Great Lakes and the Canadian provinces of Ontario and Quebec should not permit a proposed water removal from the Great Lakes to proceed unless the project proponent is able to demonstrate that the integrity of the Great Lakes ecosystem would not be endangered by the removal and that

- there are no practical alternatives for obtaining the water;
- full consideration has been given to the potential cumulative impacts of the proposed removal, taking into account the possibility of similar proposals in the foreseeable future;
- effective conservation practices will be implemented in the place to which the water would be sent;
- sound planning practices will be applied with respect to the proposed removal;
- there is no net loss to the area from which the water is taken and, in any event, there is no greater than a 5 percent loss; and
- the water is returned in a condition that, using the best available technology, protects the quality of and prevents the introduction of alien invasive species into the waters of the Great Lakes.

On the basis of extensive discussion involving the Great Lakes states and provinces, an agreement has been concluded for the purpose of implementing a decision-making process that would apply principles along these lines with respect to water-taking and diversion proposals in the basin.[26]

---

26 *Great Lakes-St. Lawrence River Basin Sustainable Water Resources Agreement* (13 December 2005).

2) The Arctic Circumpolar Environment

The Arctic and its inhabitants are particularly vulnerable or susceptible to certain forms of environmental damage and contamination. As was explained by the House of Commons Standing Committee on Environment and Sustainable Development over a decade ago:

> One reason for this vulnerability is that contaminants persist longer in the Arctic because cold temperatures, persistent ice cover and low levels of solar radiation retard natural degradation processes. Another reason is that organisms at the top of the food chain tend to have long lifespans and, as a result, more time to accumulate contaminants they ingest in their tissues. These characteristics place northerners, who eat the food they hunt or fish, especially at risk by exposing them to potentially high levels of contamination.[27]

In addition, the location of the Arctic region exposes it to particularly disruptive impact:

> Not only does being downwind and downstream from major industrial centres expose the North to surprisingly high levels of pollution, but climate models also imply that the effects of global warming will be most pronounced at higher latitudes. Furthermore, because polar regions receive more ultraviolet radiation due to a naturally thin ozone layer, emission of chlorofluorocarbons (CFCs) have always had the greatest effect in these areas.[28]

Concern about the impact of climate change in the Arctic has continued to intensify on the basis of actual northern experience and scientific study.[29] To address some issues associated with environmental contamination, the *Arctic Waters Pollution Prevention Act (AWPPA)* was specifically enacted with a view to "the preservation of the peculiar ecological balance that now exists in the water, ice and land areas of the Canadian arctic."[30] Through regulations on the construction and operation of ships and on their cargo, as well as by means of controls on deposits of waste in the Arctic, the *AWPPA* establishes a framework safeguarding the fragile environment of Canada's northern waters. Can-

---

27 *Report of the House of Commons Standing Committee on Environment and Sustainable Development: It's About Our Health! Towards Pollution Prevention* (Ottawa: Canada Communication Group, 1995) at 191–92. See also A. Saunders, *For Generations to Come: Contaminants, the Environment and Human Health in the Arctic* (Conference Report) (Ottawa: Canadian Polar Commission, 1997).

28 *Ibid.*

29 *Arctic Climate Impact Assessment*, online: www.acia.uaf.edu.

30 R.S.C. 1985, c. A-12.

ada has also pursued a program on northern contaminants and other measures associated with wildlife protection and habitat preservation which derive, at least in part, from international undertakings.[31]

Canada has also collaborated with other northern countries in signing the *Arctic Environmental Protection Strategy*.[32] In connection with this initiative, Canada, the Russian Federation, the United States, Denmark, Sweden, Finland, Iceland, and Norway agreed in 1996 to form an Arctic Council.[33] The Council's objectives include coordination of northern environmental monitoring, wildlife preservation and management, and emergency response programs. Specific programs or initiatives, sometimes circumpolar in extent and sometimes focused on particular northern regions such as that of the Russian Federation have targetted PCB wastes, offshore oil and gas operations, atmospheric mercury releases, and biodiversity monitoring.

The Arctic Council has now joined the chorus of voices calling attention to climate change. At its 2004 meeting in Iceland, the organization adopted the *Reykjavik Declaration* in which it encouraged its member states "to take effective measures to adapt and manage the environmental, economic and social impact of climate change and ultraviolet radiation, *inter alia* through enhancing the access of Arctic residents to information, decision makers and institutional capacity-building."[34] In light of the Arctic's distinctive regional features, including the extensive presence of indigenous populations, some legal researchers have begun to directly address the possibility that—in a manner roughly analogous to previous developments in the antarctic—a dedicated international Arctic environmental treaty might be desirable.[35]

---

31 For a detailed review of implementation measures, see Commissioner of the Environment and Sustainable Development, *2004 October Report*, c. 1, online: www.oag-bvg.gc.ca/internet/English/aud_parl_cesd_2004_e_1125.html. On the vulnerability of the Arctic to chemical contaminants, see Leonard Downey & Terry Fenge, eds., *Northern Lights Against POPs: Combatting Toxic Threats in the Arctic* (Montreal: McGill-Queen's University Press, 2003).

32 14 June 1991, 30 I.L.M. 1624.

33 *Declaration on the Establishment of the Arctic Council*, 19 September 1996, 35 I.L.M. 1382. See Timo Koivurova & David VanderZwaag, "The Arctic Council at 10 Years: Retrospect and Prospects" (2007) 40 U.B.C. L. Rev. 121.

34 The Reykjavik Declaration on the occasion of the Fourth Ministerial Meeting of the Arctic Council (24 November 2004), online: http://arctic-council.org/filearchive/Reykjavik_Declaration.pdf [Reykjavik Declaration].

35 Linda Nowlan, *Arctic Legal Regime for Environmental Protection*, IUCN Environmental Law and Policy Papers No. 44 (Bonn: IUCN, 2001).

3) Controlling Acid Rain

Acid rain, more formally known as acid deposition, which derives from the reaction of sulphur dioxide and nitrogen oxides with atmospheric water vapour, has been acknowledged as an environmental concern for a long time. Nevertheless, the nature and extent of its environmental and human health effects have been the subject of controversy and debate. Legal responses to the problem have also been greatly complicated by the interjurisdictional diffusion of responsibility and by diplomatic considerations.

European scientific initiatives demonstrated long ago that the transmission of air pollutants associated with acid rain occurs over great distances. This understanding helped to lay the foundations for a 1979 *Convention on Long Range Transboundary Air Pollution* (LRTAP) to which Canada and the United States were signatories along with some thirty European nations. On the basis of this framework agreement to reduce air pollution in general, several more detailed protocols were negotiated in relation to specific substances: sulphur (Helsinki Protocol, 1985, and Oslo Protocol, 1994); nitrogen oxides (Sophia Protocol, 1988); and volatile organic compounds (Geneva Protocol, 1991); further sulphur reductions (Oslo Protocol, 1994); heavy metals (Aarhus Protocol, 1998); more rigorous sulphur, NOx, VOCs, and ammonia controls (Gothenburg Protocol, 1999).

When bilateral discussions between Canada and the United States produced only limited substantive progress, the government of Canada and the seven provincial governments eastward from and including Manitoba reached agreement in 1985 on a schedule to reduce SO_2 emissions to half of their 1980 levels by 1994. The initiative involved significant public spending to support modernization of smelters and power production facilities that were the principal source of emissions.[36] Inco, Falconbridge, Algoma Steel, and Ontario Hydro accounted for over 70 percent of Ontario's total emissions in 1983, and these operations became the subject of specific regulatory emission limits under Ontario's Countdown Acid Rain Program.[37]

The success of the Ontario program by no means marked the end of major efforts directed towards the problem of acid rain. In October 1998, energy and environment ministers from the federal, provincial, and territorial governments signed the *Canada-Wide Acid Rain Strat-*

---

36 G.B. Doern & T. Conway, *The Greening of Canada: Federal Institutions and Decisions* (Toronto: University of Toronto Press, 1994) at 158–63.

37 *Inco Regulation*, O. Reg. 660/85; *Algoma Regulation*, O. Reg. 663/85; *Ontario Hydro Regulation*, R.R.O. 1990, Reg. 355; *Falconbridge Regulation*, O. Reg. 661/85.

egy for Post-2000 with a view to "meet the environmental threshold of critical loads for acid deposition across Canada." As outlined in table 4.2, Ontario, Quebec, New Brunswick, and Nova Scotia have adopted new reduction targets.

Table 4.2:   SO$_2$ reduction targets for Ontario, Quebec, New Brunswick, and Nova Scotia

	Eastern Canada Acid Rain Program Cap	New Target under *The Canada-Wide Acid Rain Strategy*	Timeline for New Target
Ontario	885 kt	442.5 kt (50% reduction) announced January 2000	2015*
Quebec	500 kt	300 kt (40% reduction) announced November 1997	2002
		250 kt (50% reduction) announced April 2001	2010
New Brunswick	175 kt	122.5 kt (30% reduction)	2005
		85 kt (50% reduction) announced March 2001	2010
Nova Scotia	189 kt	142 kt (25% reduction)	2005
		94.5 kt (50% cumulative reduction total)	2010

* Ontario has proposed and is consulting on the proposal to advance this timeline to 2010

Source: Canadian Council of Ministers of the Environment, "Five Year Review of the Canada-Wide Acid Rain Strategy for Post-2000" (January 2006), online: www.ccme.ca/assets/pdf/5_year_review_acid_rain_strategy_e1.0_web.pdf

In view of the important transboundary dimensions of the acid rain problem, Canada and the United States concluded a bilateral *Air Quality Agreement* in 1991.[38] This agreement required Canada and the United States to set objectives and to pursue the implementation of air pollution reduction measures, including measures directed towards sulphur dioxide and nitrogen oxides. Domestic activities are now to be assessed from the perspective of potential transboundary air pollution, and—alongside notification and consultation requirements—mitigative measures are required. The agreement established an air quality committee and designated the International Joint Commission as the body responsible for making progress reports available for public com-

---

38   *Agreement Between the Government of the United States of America and the Government of Canada on Air Quality*, 13 March 1991, 30 I.L.M. 678. See Environment Canada, *2004 Progress Report: U.S.–Canada Air Quality Agreement*, online: www.ec.gc.ca/pdb/can_us/2004CanUs/pdf/AirQualityeng.pdf.

ment. Disputes not resolved through negotiations may be referred to the IJC.[39]

Pursuant to the *Canadian Environmental Protection Act*, the federal government consulted with the provinces to reach a series of federal—provincial agreements on sulphur dioxide and nitrogen oxides reductions, and the provinces affected, for their part, took steps to fulfil their obligations. SO_2 emissions have fallen dramatically, and thus acid rain may be regarded as an example of a comprehensive regulatory response to a serious cause of environmental deterioration. However, on the basis of scientific research, it is far less clear that recovery is proceeding at satisfactory rates. Indeed, water, soil, and forest damage from acid rain now appears to be far more persistent than earlier, more optimistic predictions had anticipated.[40]

CEPA part V provided a mechanism for the federal government to regulate (in relation to Canadian sources of international air pollution, or anticipated violations of international agreements to control or abate pollution) in cases where attempts to have the situation addressed by provincial action have been unsuccessful.[41] *CEPA, 1999* preserves such authority.[42] There are a number of international air agreements that might lead to the power being used: the *Canada–US Air Quality Agreement*, 1991; the *Climate Change Convention*, 1992; the Montreal Protocol, 1987, and the *Geneva Convention on Long-Range Transboundary Air Pollution*, 1979.

4) Protecting the Ozone Layer

The ozone layer, an atmospheric band some nine to fifty kilometres above the Earth's surface, provides a protective filter against harmful ultraviolet radiation. This layer is vulnerable to deterioration brought about by the decomposition at high altitudes of certain substances, notably chlorofluorocarbons and halons. Through further chemical interaction, these substances deplete the protective ozone shield.[43]

Ozone depleting substances (ODSs) were widely used in a variety of important economic applications such as refrigeration and fire suppression, especially within industrialized economies. The detrimental impact of ozone depletion on human health and the environment is

---

39   *Ibid.*
40   For descriptive information, see online: www.ec.gc.ca/acidrain/index.
41   *Canadian Environmental Protection Act*, R.S.C. 1985 (4th Supp.), c. 16 [*CEPA*].
42   *Ibid.*, part 7, division 6.
43   For descriptive information on the stratospheric ozone situation, see online: www.ec.gc.ca/ozone/EN/index.cfm?intCat=158.

global in nature, a situation that highlights the importance of a comprehensive international response.

The environmental regime to protect the ozone layer derives from the 1985 *Vienna Convention for the Protection of the Ozone Layer*. Although essentially a framework agreement creating no concrete remedial agenda, the convention stimulated ongoing research and established a conference of the parties and a secretariat for the purpose of gathering and disseminating research and with responsibility for refining the convention through protocols, annexes, and amendments. Given the limitations of scientific knowledge at the time, the convention heralded the precautionary era at the international level. As well, with its formulation of adverse effects as "changes in the physical environment or biota, including changes in climate, which have significant deleterious effects on human health or on the composition, resilience and productivity of natural and managed ecosystems, or on materials useful to mankind," the convention's commitment to a broadly conceived ecosystem approach is notable.[44]

The *Montreal Protocol on Substances that Deplete the Ozone Layer* was signed in 1987 and entered into force on 1 January 1989.[45] It established targets for reducing the production and consumption of specified groups of ODSs and subjected these substances to a control regime accompanied by reporting obligations, a commitment to research on ODS containment techniques, and alternatives to controlled substances. In addition, the Montreal Protocol addressed the risk that non-parties posed to the integrity and effectiveness of the arrangements by banning trade between parties and non-parties in relation to controlled substances shipped in bulk and products containing controlled substances, as well as to goods produced with controlled substances. To encourage the participation of developing nations, many of whom wished to increase rather than lower levels of ODS use and production, the Montreal Protocol offered delayed compliance along with financial and technical incentives to facilitate implementation.

Amendments to the protocol at London in 1990 and again at Copenhagen in 1992 accelerated (subject to an exception for "essential uses") the phasing-out of substances on the original ODS list and extended coverage to new substances on the basis of evolving scientific understanding about the rate of ozone depletion.[46] The protocol has been

---

44   *Vienna Convention for the Protection of the Ozone Layer*, 22 March 1985, 26 I.L.M. 1529, art. 1(2).
45   16 September 1987, 26 I.L.M. 1550 [Montreal Protocol].
46   29 June 1990, 30 I.L.M. 541; 23–25 November 1992, 32 I.L.M. 874.

either ratified or approved by 189 parties.[47] UNEP, while acknowledging continuing challenges, reports significant improvements attributable to the agreement:

> Without the Protocol, by the year 2050 ozone depletion would have risen to at least 50% in the northern hemisphere's mid latitudes and 70% in the southern mid latitudes, about 10 times worse than current levels. The result would have been a doubling of UV-B radiation reaching the earth in the northern mid latitudes and a quadrupling in the south. The amount of ozone-depleting chemicals in the atmosphere would have been five times greater. The implications of this would have been horrendous: 19 million more cases of non-melanoma cancer, 1.5 million cases of melanoma cancer, and 130 million more cases of eye cataracts.[48]

Within Canada, initiatives pursuant to the Montreal Protocol have included both federal and provincial legislation and regulations intended to eliminate certain uses of ODSs, to control imports and exports, and to govern the handling and maintenance of various forms of equipment where ODSs have historically been used.[49]

5) Climate Change, Global Warming, and the Kyoto Protocol

As atmospheric concentrations of greenhouse gases (GHG) (including carbon dioxide (CO_2), methane (CH_4), and nitrous oxide (N_2O)) have

---

47 A progress report on the protocol may be found online: www.globalcentres.org/cgcp/english/html_documents/ads/coll-e.htm.

48 UNEP, Ozone Secretariat, "Basic Facts and Data on the Science and Politics of Ozone Protection" (Backgrounder) (November 2005) online: www.unep.org/ozone/pdf/Press-Backgrounder.pdf . See also Donald Kaniaru, ed., *The Montreal Protocol: Celebrating 20 Years of Environmental Progress* (London: Cameron May, 2007).

49 *CEPA Regulations*: S.O.R./89-351; S.O.R./90-127; S.O.R./90-583; S.O.R./90-584; S.O.R./93-214; consolidated and revised in 1998 *Ozone-Depleting Substances Regulations*, Alta. Reg. 125/93; *Ozone-Depleting Substances Regulations*, B.C. Reg. 53/93; *Ozone-Depleting Substances Control Act, 1993*, S.S. 1993, c. O-8.1; *Ozone-Depleting Substances Control Regulations*, R.R.S. c. O-8.1, Reg.1; *Ozone-Depleting Substances Act*, S.M. 1989–90, c. 38; *Ozone-Depleting Substances Regulations*, Man. Reg. 103/94; *Ozone-Depleting Substances Regulations*, R.R.O. 1990, Reg. 356; *Ozone Layer Protection Regulations*, N.S. Reg. 54/95; *Ozone-Depletion Substances Regulations*, N.B. Reg. 92-119; N.B. Reg. 93-202; N.B. Reg. 95-170; *Ozone-Depleting Substances and Replacement Regulations*, E.C. 619-94; and *Environment Act*, S.Y. 1991, c. 5, s. 145. For an unsuccessful prosecution of a CFC importer, see *R. v. Haas* (1993), 139 A.R. 180 (Prov. Ct.). More recently a number of convictions have been secured.

increased since the pre-industrial era, climate change has been observed. Prominent initial indications included global warming or a general rise in average temperatures around the planet. Other indications of climate change include the increasing frequency of extreme weather occurrences, floods and droughts, alpine and polar melting and shifts in ocean currents. Despite some uncertainty about the pace and nature of future developments, particularly at the regional level, global climate change is expected to continue as a consequence of discernable human influence. As expressed in the Fourth Assessment Report of the Intergovernmental Panel on Climate Change, "(c)ontinued greenhouse gas emissions at or above current rates would cause further warming and induce many changes in the global climate system during the 21st century that would *very likely* be larger than those observed during the 20th century."[50] The social, economic, and ecological impact of global warming and climate change is not precisely understood, but the immensity of the risk and challenge is such that international attempts to promote legal, institutional, and behavioural responses are intense.

In 1988 the United Nations General Assembly identified climate change as a "common concern of mankind,"[51] and in the same year the World Meteorological Society and UNEP established an intergovernmental panel on climate change (IPCC) to undertake an assessment of available evidence. In the 1992 meetings of the UN Conference on Environment and Development at Rio de Janeiro, a *Framework Convention on Climate Change* was opened for signature. The *FCCC*, which entered into force in 1994, articulated as an international objective the "stabilization of greenhouse gas concentrations in the atmosphere at a level that would prevent dangerous anthropogenic interference with the climate system." The desired level is to be achieved in a timeframe "sufficient to allow ecosystems to adapt naturally to climate change, to ensure that food production is not threatened and to enable economic development to proceed in a sustainable manner."[52]

The *FCCC* set out a series of commitments on information exchange, technical and scientific cooperation, and education and training applicable to all parties, and specified additional undertakings for developed and developing country parties. Developed country parties, including Canada, are specifically committed to "adopt national policies and take corresponding measures on the mitigation of climate change, by limit-

---

50   Intergovernmental Panel on Climate Change, *Climate Change 2007: The Physical Science Basis-Summary for Policymakers* (Geneva: Intergovernmental Panel on Climate Change Secretariat, 2007) at 13.

51   UNGA 43/53.

52   *Framework Convention on Climate Change*, 9 May 1992, 31 I.L.M. 849, art. 2.

ing . . . anthropogenic emissions of greenhouse gases and protecting and enhancing . . . greenhouse gas sinks and reservoirs."[53]

Within the context of the *FCCC*, further negotiations were pursued through the mechansim of Conference of the Parties (COP).[54] On 11 December 1997, the Kyoto Protocol was agreed to at COP-3. The most prominent innovation of the Kyoto Protocol was the adoption of quantitative objectives for greenhouse gas (GHG) reductions by developed nations. Specifically, on the basis of varying individual commitments, those countries undertook to reduce their overall GHG emissions by 5.2 percent below 1990 levels in the period 2008 to 2112. For its part, Canada commited to a 6 percent reduction from the 1990 baseline, and ratified the Protocol in 2002.

The Protocol does not require the adoption of any particular policy in connection with the emissions reduction goal, although all efforts to implement commitments should be designed to minimize adverse social, environmental, and economic impacts on developing nations. The Kyoto agreement, however, did provide for several flexible mechanisms including an emissions trading system and cooperative arrangements involving developed nations (joint implementation) or involving developed and developing nations (clean development mechanism).

The formula for entry into force of the Kyoto Protocol required ratification by fifty-five parties so long as the developed countries that have ratified account for at least 55 percent of 1990 emissions by developed countries. These requirements were met on 16 February 2005.[55] International negotiations concerning future commitments to GHG emissions reductions are ongoing.[56]

Canada's response to climate change is more fully discussed in Chapter 19.

C. INTERNATIONAL TRADE AND THE ENVIRONMENT

The promotion of international trade raises a difficult set of issues for the design and operation of domestic environmental protection regimes.

---

53   *Ibid.*, art. 4(2)(a).
54   For ongoing coverage of the negotiations process, see the Earth Negotiations Bulletin, online:www.iisd.ca/enbvol/enb-background.htm.
55   Meinhard Doelle, "The Cat Came Back, or the Nine Lives of the Kyoto Protocol" (2006) 16 J. Envtl. L. & Pol'y 261.
56   Steven Bernstein *et al.*, eds., *A Globally Integrated Climate Policy for Canada* (Toronto: University of Toronto Press, 2008).

Strong divergences of opinion have separated certain advocates of environmental protection from others committed to trade liberalization, with adherents to each perspective frequently assuming that the two interests are antithetical and that in the case of conflict their own preferred objective should prevail. Others argue that the free trade and environmentalist communities share the common objective of minimizing waste and maximizing the efficient use of resources. "The trade approach," it is sometimes argued, "seeks to do so through control of the end product and its consumption—that is, the 'finished' end of the production cycle—while the more apparently environmental perspective focuses on the conservation of the 'raw' end of the production cycle."[57]

With general acceptance of the legitimacy of environmental imperatives and trade policy goals, especially in relation to development, attention has been more positively directed towards reconciliation of environmental and trade promotion regimes and on mechanisms to ensure the benefits of each.[58] Environmentalists, for example, often see important advantages in being able to utilize powerful trade sanctions to enforce environmental standards, while those committed to trade liberalization industriously pursue their efforts to ensure that environmental protection measures do not interfere unduly with international trade. The underlying challenge then becomes the need for institutions and processes to resolve conflicts when they arise.

1) The *General Agreement on Tariffs and Trade* (GATT) and the World Trade Organization (WTO)

The sophistication of decision-making and dispute-resolution institutions in international trade law, in comparison with more recently developed international efforts to address environmental concerns, resulted in a situation in which trade-environment reconciliation was often attempted in the context of trade regimes. Of the latter, the most

---

57   M.L. McConnell, "International Trade and Environmental Law" in G. Thompson, M.L. McConnell, & L.B. Huestis, eds., *Environmental Law and Business in Canada* (Aurora, ON: Canada Law Book, 1993) 343 at 345. See also Canada, Department of Foreign Affairs and International Trade, *Framework for Conducting Environmental Assessments of Trade Agreements* (Ottawa: Department of Foreign Affairs and International Trade, 2001); Donald McRae, "Trade and the Environment: Competition, Cooperation or Confusion?" (2003) 41 Alta. L. Rev. 745.

58   Canada is among the group of nations that endeavours systematically to evaluate trade agreements from an environmental perspective. See Canada, Department of Foreign Affairs and International Trade, *Handbook for Conducting Environmental Assessments of Trade Negotiations* (Ottawa: Foreign Affairs Canada, 2004).

notable was the 1947 *General Agreement on Tariffs and Trade (GATT)*, encompassed as of January 1995 within the framework of the World Trade Organization (WTO). Other agreements have been reached within the WTO framework, and multilateral negotiations continue.

GATT and several subsequent rounds of multilateral negotiations elaborated a set of rules to regulate tariff and non-tariff barriers to trade among contracting parties. Subject to specified exceptions, a *most-favoured nation* rule was implemented, meaning that trade restrictions had to operate on a *non-discriminatory* basis as between one *GATT* member and another.[59] Products imported by a *GATT* contracting party were to be accorded *national treatment*; that is, imports could be treated no less favourably in relation to taxes and regulations than goods produced domestically by the importing nation.[60] In addition, Article XI provided that "[n]o prohibitions or restrictions other than duties, taxes or other charges, whether made effective through quotas, import or export licences or other measures, shall be instituted or maintained by any contracting party on the importation of any product of the territory of any other contracting party or on the exportation or sale for export of any product destined for the territory of any other contracting party." However, *GATT* itself provided certain exceptions which came to be regarded as providing some scope for environmental measures within the overall framework. In particular, in Article XX, *GATT* itself identified exceptions in the case of measures "necessary to protect human, animal or plant life or health"; and measures "relating to the conservation of exhaustible natural resources if such measures are made effective in conjunction with restrictions on domestic production or consumption," so long as the measures did not in the words of Article XX's "chapeau" constitute a "disguised restriction on international trade" or an "arbitrary or unjustifiable discrimination between countries where the same conditions prevail."

Interpretation of Article XX eventually suggested comparatively limited scope for these provisions as mechanisms with which to defend environmental measures. Interpretation of "necessary," for example, directed decision making towards the least trade restrictive alternative. That is, given two or more equally effective mechanisms for protecting human life or health, only the approach involving the least restrictions on trade will be considered necessary in the context of the *GATT* exceptions.[61]

---

59   *General Agreement on Tariffs and Trade*, 30 October 1947, Can. T.S. 1947 No. 27, art. I.

60   *Ibid.*, art. III.

61   *Thailand: Restrictions on Importation of and Internal Taxes on Cigarettes*, B.I.S.D. (1990) 37th Supp. 200.

It was also understood that measures defended on the grounds that they "relate to" conservation must meet the test of being "primarily aimed at" conservation.[62] Commentators have observed that the determination to restrict exemptions to measures that are least restrictive of international trade has produced "a very rigorous kind of test that may result in measures taken for genuinely environmental purposes being nevertheless found to violate the *GATT* . . . . The strong implication is that avoidance of trade-restricting impacts must be a paramount consideration in domestic choices between alternative instruments of environmental protection."[63]

The possibility that interpretation of the Article XX exemptions might tilt overwhelmingly towards trade objectives was confirmed in 1998. In a decision concerning a challenge to U.S. legislation seeking to protect endangered species of sea turtles from dangerous shrimp harvesting practices, the *Shrimp-Turtle* panel reported that:

> If an interpretation of the chapeau of Article XX were to be followed which would allow a member to adopt measures conditioning access to its market for a given product upon the adoption by the exporting members of certain policies, including conservation policies, *GATT* 1994 and the WTO Agreement could no longer serve as a multilateral framework for trade among members as security and predictability of trade relations under these agreements would be threatened.[64]

In addition, proceedings under *GATT* established the scope of measures "necessary to protect human, animal or plant life or health" as confined to measures intended to safeguard these interests within the jurisdiction of the importing state. Thus, measures intended to safeguard species outside the enacting jurisdiction — on the high seas, for example — could not be saved by the Article XX(b) exemption. This was the decision reached in the controversial *Tuna-Dolphin* decision when a *GATT* panel concluded that U.S. legislation could not be saved by the exemption. The United States had introduced an embargo against tuna from Mexico on the grounds that that country's fishing practices led to the killing of excessive numbers of dolphins contrary to the U.S.

---

62 *In the Matter of Canada's Landing Requirement for Pacific Coast Salmon and Herring*, 16 October 1989, 2 T.C.T. 7163.

63 M.J. Trebilcock & R. Howse, *The Regulation of International Trade* (London: Routledge, 1995) at 338.

64 *United States – Import Prohibition of Certain Shrimp and Shrimp Products* WT/DS58/R, 15 May 1998 (Panel Report) at para. 7.45. This decision is often referred to as *Shrimp-Turtle*.

Marine Mammal Protection Act.[65] A subsequent *GATT* panel decision arising from European concerns about other provisions in the same U.S. legislation suggested a greater degree of tolerance for extraterritorial environmental protection.[66] It did so on the basis that there were no prohibitions in "general international law" against measures relating to matters located outside a country's own territory, and because there were no indications in the *GATT*'s background documentation to suggest the framers had intended to exclude extraterritorial environmental initiatives from the scope of Article XX.

More recent indications suggest that application of Article XX principles in the WTO context will ease or eliminate certain highly restrictive interpretations and thus permit greater scope for the justification of environmental and conservation measures. This increased flexibility results from procedural changes and the evolution of the jurisprudence effected by the WTO Appellate Body (WTOAB). Procedurally, the WTOAB has indicated a willingness in appropriate circumstances to receive *amicus curiae* briefs from environmental NGOs. This may permit panel access to a wider range of relevant perspectives on trade and environmental relationships than disputing parties are able to provide.

In a report that severely criticized the panel in *Shrimp-Turtle* quoted above, the WTOAB emphasized the legitimate nature of the policies and interests embodied in Article XX.[67] Accordingly, "the right to invoke one of those exceptions is not to be rendered illusory." The goal of interpretation would be to strike a balance between "the right of a member to invoke an exception under Article XX and the duty of that same member to respect the treaty rights of the other members."[68]

The appropriate approach to the Article XX exceptions, reflecting "the fundamental structure and logic" of the Article is now said to be two-tiered. First, provisional justification by reason of characterization of the measure under Article XX (g) is called for. Second, further appraisal of the same measure will be undertaken with reference to the introductory clauses of Article XX.[69]

With respect to Article XX (g) in *Shrimp-Turtle* itself, the WTOAB provided several indications that the tests for provisional justification would be more accommodating to environmental considerations than

65 *United States – Restrictions on Imports of Tuna*, 16 August 1991, 30 I.L.M 1594.

66 *Dispute Settlement Panel Report on United States Restrictions on Imports of Tuna* (July 1994), 33 I.L.M. 839.

67 *United States – Import Prohibition of Certain Shrimp and Shrimp Products* WT/DS58/AB/R, 12 October 1998 (Appellate Body).

68 *Ibid.* at para. 156.

69 *Ibid.* at paras. 118–19.

the preceding *GATT* approach. In connection with "exhaustible natural resources" these may be either living or non-living and with respect to the former, it is enough that migratory species migrate or pass through the waters of a state for there to be a "sufficient nexus" to support protective measures. Insofar as those measures must "relate to" conservation, "a close and genuine relationship of ends and means" replaces the more restricted "primarily aimed at" requirement.[70]

Article XX (b) — "necessary to protect human, animal or plant life or health" — may also be more liberally viewed in light of the WTOAB's discussion of "necessary" in the *Asbestos* report of 12 March 2001. When Canada argued against a French decree banning asbestos on the ground, amongst others, that controlled use was a "reasonably available" alternative to the prohibition, the WTOAB noted the undisputed right of members of the WTO to determine the level of health protection they consider appropriate. France, having chosen to halt the spread of asbestos-related health risks, "could not reasonably be expected to employ any alternative measure if that measure would involve a continuation of the very risk that the Decree seeks to halt."[71]

Where a measure otherwise inconsistent with *GATT* principles is provisionally justified under either Article XX (b) or (g) exemptions, a second tier analysis must still be conducted under the "chapeau." In this regard, the three factors to be addressed are: (a) the existence of discrimination; (b) the arbitrary or unjustifiable character of such discrimination; and (c) whether the discrimination occurs between countries where the same conditions prevail.[72]

In addition to disputes that might arise between parties to the WTO framework on the basis of the domestic environmental measures of one that might be challenged as trade-restricting by another, there may be situations in which conflicts arise between the terms of multilateral environmental agreements such as the Montreal Protocol and obligations associated with the WTO regime. General rules of international law, notably in relation to treaty interpretation, would be brought to bear in such circumstances. A training manual prepared by UNEP outlines some possible outcomes:

> Applying these rules, it would follow that the trade restrictions established under post-1994 agreements, such as the 2000 Biosafety Protocol and the 2001 POPs Convention, would prevail over incon-

---

70   *Ibid.* at para. 136.
71   *European Communities – Measures Affecting Asbestos and Asbestos-Containing Products* WT/DS135/AB/R, 12 March 2001 at paras. 168 and 174.
72   *Shrimp-Turtle*, (Appellate Body) above note 68 at para. 150.

sistent obligations established under the 1994 GATT (to the extent that they are inconsistent) when the states involved are parties to both the MEA as well as the GATT. In the case when a state is not a party to the relevant MEA, the obligations of the GATT might prevail, to the extent that the GATT obligations are inconsistent. The situation is slightly more complex in the case of pre-1994 MEAs, such as the Montreal Protocol. . . . With the GATT 1947 being re-adopted as the GATT 1994 at the Uruguay Round of trade negotiations, the trade agreement is at least technically, the *lex posterior.* However, the ruling of the WTO Appellate Body in the Shrimp/Turtle dispute suggests that trade restrictions in most MEAs, like the 1987 Montreal Protocol . . . are unlikely to fall afoul of the GATT 1994 requirements. Moreover, some MEAs may also be seen as *lex specialis* rules (i.e., more specific rules) than those embodied in the GATT.[73]

2) The Canada–United States and North American Free Trade Agreements

The *Canada–United States Free Trade Agreement*, covering bilateral trade in goods and services, came into force in January 1989. It incorporated *GATT* principles, including Article XX, but otherwise provided little explicit direction concerning environmental protection measures.[74] However, when Canada, the United States, and Mexico embarked on negotiations for a North American free trade pact in 1991, environmental considerations figured prominently. This high level of interest and attention may be explained by a combination of factors. For their part, environmentalists were anxious to try to avoid some of the limitations that had emerged under the *GATT* regime and were concerned that existing environmental safeguards might be undermined if trade provisions and economic integration measures promoted a "race to the bottom." At the same time, free trade advocates were apprehensive that, by manipulating environmental standards or enforcement practices, a party to *NAFTA* might gain an advantage over other trading partners that could lower export prices unfairly or induce investors to migrate to a perceived "pollution haven" in order to avoid the costs of environmental protection. Their interest in environmental measures was thus

---

73 Lal Kurukulasuriya & Nicholas A. Robinson, eds., *Training Manual on International Environmental Law* (Nairobi: Division of Policy Development and Law, UNEP, 2006) at 334–35.

74 Arguably, article 904 of the *Canada–United States Free Trade Agreement*, 22 December 1987, 27 I.L.M. 281, dealing with energy goods, could be construed as environmental in nature.

part of a wider preoccupation with maintaining a "level playing field" in relation to trade matters and investment decisions.

NAFTA[75] addresses these fears in several provisions, including the preamble where the parties express their commitment to pursuing the commercial and economic objectives of the agreement in a manner that is consistent with environmental protection and conservation, sustainable development, and a strengthened development and enforcement of environmental law and regulations. Detailed provisions deal with other aspects of the relationship between environmental measures and trade and investment.

NAFTA establishes that, to the extent that inconsistency exists between the specific trade obligations set out in a number of specified international environmental agreements and NAFTA, the terms of the environmental agreements shall take precedence.[76] Where such agreements allow a choice among equally effective and reasonably available options, however, a party intending to rely on this provision must select the alternative that involves the least level of inconsistency with NAFTA.[77] NAFTA also acknowledges the possibility that a party to the agreement might wish to adopt sanitary or phytosanitary measures that are more stringent than established international standards, guidelines, or recommendations in order to protect human, animal, or plant life or health in its territory. Circumstances in which such action would be permissible under NAFTA are set out.[78]

Environmental considerations are also discussed in relation to investment in the agreement, which confirms the understanding of the parties that "it is inappropriate to encourage investment by relaxing domestic health, safety or environmental measures." Thus, in the words of the agreement itself: "[a] Party should not waive or otherwise derogate from, or offer to waive or otherwise derogate from, such measures as an encouragement for the establishment, acquisition, expansion or retention in its territory of an investment of an investor."[79]

Another provision of NAFTA's investment chapter has already raised significant controversy from the perspective of environmental

---

75   *North American Free Trade Agreement*, 8 and 17 December 1992, 32 I.L.M. 605 [*NAFTA*].

76   *Convention on International Trade in Endangered Species of Wild Fauna and Flora*, 3 March 1973, 12 I.L.M. 1085 [*CITES*]; *Basel Convention on the Control of Transboundary Movements of Hazardous Wastes and Their Disposal*, 22 March 1989, 28 I.L.M. 657; Montreal Protocol, above note 45.

77   *NAFTA*, above note 75, art. 104.

78   *Ibid.*, arts. 712 & 713.

79   *Ibid.*, art. 1114.

law and regulation. Except when employed for a public purpose, on a non-discriminatory basis, and in accordance with due process of law, and where compensation is provided, Article 1110 prohibits *NAFTA* parties from taking measures that are "tantamount to expropriation." An investor-state dispute resolution process permits aggrieved companies to sue member states for redress. The particular controversy associated with Article 1110 relates to the uncertain ambit of measures "tantamount to expropriation." Although state confiscation of physical property is readily understood as expropriation, it is less clear within the *NAFTA* context that other forms of government action such as regulation making or contractual behaviour are encompassed. In the U.S., however, a strong tradition of concern for the status of contracts as a form of property and with "regulatory takings" supports the expectation that companies that suffer losses when contracts are interfered with or regulations altered may be entitled to compensation. On the other hand, of course, environmentalist concern has been expressed that a "regulatory chill" may be created by the prospect that any alteration of the regulatory framework could give rise to compensation claims.

Although the expropriation and compensation provisions of the *NAFTA* remain controversial, a number of cases have already arisen. When the Canadian government banned trade in the fuel additive MMT, the exclusive North American producer, Ethyl Corporation of Richmond, Virginia, claimed on behalf of its Canadian subsidiary that its assets had been "indirectly expropriated." In other words, ending the MMT business was equivalent to an expropriation. This dispute was settled on the basis of a $19-million payment for costs and lost profits and repeal of the MMT ban.[80] In another case, S.D. Myers, an Ohio-based company involved in PCB disposal, challenged Canadian regulations prohibiting the transborder shipment of PCB wastes for treatment in the United States.[81] A more recent dispute between an American investor and Mexico, *Metalclad v. United Mexican States*, resulted in the first successful claim against a host jurisdiction under Chapter 11, accompanied by a comparatively broad interpretation of the scope of compensable expropriation.[82]

---

80 J. Soloway, "Environmental Regulation as Expropriation: The Case of NAFTA's Chapter 11" (2000) 33 Can. Bus. L.J. 92 at 114–19.

81 *Ibid.*

82 Award, Case No. ARB (AF)/97/1 (30 August 2000), online: www.naftaclaims. com. The decision was ultimately subject to judicial review in British Columbia, *United Mexican States v. Metalclad Corp.* (2001), 89 B.C.L.R. (3d) 359. See Chris Tollefson, "*Metalclad v. United Mexican States* Revisited: Judicial Oversight

Disputes between *NAFTA* parties, including disagreements about the operation of environmental measures, are to be resolved by a dispute-settlement mechanism established under the agreement. The influence of other jurisprudence relating to trade and environment conflicts—including decisions under *GATT*—will continue to be felt. Nevertheless, *NAFTA*'s assigning of the burden of proof to the challenging party, as well as its allowing of the use of scientific experts on panels,[83] suggests that environmental protection measures could be less vulnerable to trade-based challenges under *NAFTA* than they had been under *GATT*.

In addition to *NAFTA* itself, a side agreement was concluded between Canada, the United States, and Mexico in 1993. The stated objectives of the *North American Agreement on Environmental Cooperation (NAAEC)* are to

a) foster the protection and improvement of the environment in the territories of the Parties for the well-being of present and future generations;

b) promote sustainable development based on cooperation and mutually supportive environmental and economic policies;

c) increase cooperation between the Parties to better conserve, protect, and enhance the environment, including wild flora and fauna;

d) support the environmental goals and objectives of the *NAFTA*;

e) avoid creating trade distortions or new trade barriers;

f) strengthen cooperation on the development and improvement of environmental laws, regulations, procedures, policies, and practices;

g) enhance compliance with, and enforcement of, environmental laws and regulations;

h) promote transparency and public participation in the development of environmental laws, regulations, and policies;

i) promote economically efficient and effective environmental measures; and

j) promote pollution prevention policies and practices.

NAAEC, in addition to establishing the Commission for Environmental Cooperation (located in Montreal), articulates a series of obligations. Of particular interest is Article 3, which recognizes each party's right "to establish its own levels of domestic environmental protection and en-

---

of NAFTA's Chapter Eleven Investor-State Claim Process" (2002) 11 Minn. J. Global Trade 183.

83   *NAFTA*, above note 75, arts. 2014 & 2015.

vironmental development policies and priorities" while indicating that each "shall ensure that its laws and regulations provide for high levels of environmental protection and shall strive to continue to improve those laws and regulations." The parties have also agreed to environmental research, reporting, and educational initiatives, to appropriate environmental impact assessment, and to promotion of economic instruments for achieving environmental goals efficiently.[84]

Enforcement obligations also figure prominently in the side agreement. Thus, each party is to ensure "appropriate access" to "fair, open and equitable" administrative, quasi-judicial, or judicial proceedings where those with recognized legal interests can pursue their claims.[85] Moreover, in pursuit of effective environmental enforcement and compliance, the parties are committed to appropriate governmental action[86] although nothing in the agreement authorizes a party to undertake environmental law enforcement activities in another's territory.[87] The *NAFTA* environmental side agreement now makes a party's "persistent pattern of failure . . . to effectively enforce its environmental law" the basis for invoking a dispute-settlement mechanism leading potentially to significant sanctions. However, critics of environmental enforcement practices will be discouraged from advancing their complaints by broadly crafted exceptions to the notion of failing to enforce effectively. Specifically, a party will not fail the standard where the conduct of officials in a particular case "reflects a reasonable exercise of their discretion in respect of investigatory, prosecutorial, regulatory or compliance matters" or where action or inaction "results from *bona fide* decisions to allocate resources to enforcement in respect of other environmental matters determined to have higher priorities."[88] In addition, a complaints process allows individuals and non-governmental organizations to make submissions to the secretariat concerning the alleged failure of a party to enforce its environmental law effectively.[89]

---

84 *North American Agreement on Environmental Cooperation*, 12 and 14 September 1993, 32 I.L.M. 1480, art. 2. Now see *Ten Years of North American Environmental Cooperation: Report of the Ten-year Review and Assessment Committee to the Council of the Commission for Environmental Cooperation* (15 June 2004)

85 *Ibid.*, arts. 6 & 7.

86 *Ibid.*, art. 5.

87 *Ibid.*, art. 37.

88 *Ibid.*, art. 45.

89 *Ibid.* For further discussion of the complaints process, see *Bringing the Facts to Light: A Guide to Articles 14 and 15 of the North American Agreement on Environmental Cooperation* (CEC, 2000). For an example of a "factual record" relating to Canada, see *BC Hydro Final Factual Record* (CEC, 2000). These and other materials are available online: www.cec.org.

In order to facilitate the application of *NAAEC* in Canada, the federal government entered into negotiations with the provinces for an intergovernmental agreement on *NAAEC*. The first such agreement was concluded with Alberta on 15 August 1995, thereby providing for that province's involvement in implementing and further elaborating *NAAEC*. Quebec and Manitoba subsequently signed the *Canadian Intergovernmental Agreement*.

D. CONCLUSION

Canada's domestic environmental record is now under scrutiny from external observers who have not always been favourably impressed. Canadian wilderness rivers such as the Great Whale and Tatshenshini that have been threatened by development, timber-cutting practices in the domestic forest industry, and depletion of fish and wildlife resources have been subjects of concern for an international audience. Canada's performance in relation to climate change obligations under the Kyoto Protocol is now equally a matter for international attention. This scrutiny, along with more systematic and comparative assessments by agencies such as the OECD, indicate that Canada's domestic environmental protection regime will become a matter of wider interest in the international community. Thus, international pressure and expectations must be added to the list of factors influencing Canadian policy in the environmental arena.

FURTHER READINGS

BERNSTEIN, S., *et al.*, eds., *A Globally Integrated Climate Policy For Canada* (Toronto: University Of Toronto Press, 2008)

BIRNIE, P.W., & A.E. BOYLE, *International Law and the Environment*, 2d ed. (Oxford: Oxford University Press, 2002)

BRUNNÉE, J., *Acid Rain and Ozone Layer Depletion: International Law and Regulation* (Dobbs Ferry, NY: Transnational Publishers, 1988)

BRYCE, J.T., "Controlling the Temperature: An Analysis of the Kyoto Protocol" (1999) 62 Sask. L. Rev. 379

CAMERON, J., "Future Directions in International Environmental Law" (1996) 19 Dal. L.J. 122–38

COOPER, ERNEST W.T., & NATHALIE CHALIFOUR, *CITES, Eh? A Review of Canada's Implementation of CITES under WAPPRIITA* (Toronto: WWF Canada, 2004)

CORDONIER SEGGER, M-C., & C.G. WEERAMANTRY, *Sustainable Justice: Reconciling Economic, Social and Environmental Law* (Boston: Martinus Nijhoff, 2005)

NOWLAN, LINDA, & CHRIS ROLFE, *Kyoto, POPs and Straddling Stocks: Understanding Environmental Treaties* (Vancouver: West Coast Environmental Law, 2003)

PEREZ, OREN, *Ecological Sensitivity and Global Legal Pluralism: Rethinking the Trade and Environment Conflict* (Oxford: Hart Publishing, 2004)

PHARAND, D., "The Case for an Arctic Region Council and a Treaty Proposal" (1992) 23 R.G.D. 164

REIF, L.C., "International Environmental Law" in G. Thompson, M.L. McConnell, & L.B. Huestis, eds., *Environmental Law and Business in Canada* (Aurora, ON: Canada Law Book, 1993) c. 4

SANDS, PHILIPPE, *Principles of International Environmental Law*, 2d ed. (New York: Cambridge University Press, 2003)

SMITH, D.A., "The Implementation of Canadian Policies to Protect the Ozone Layer" in G.B. Doern, ed., *Getting It Green: Case Studies in Canadian Environmental Regulation* (Toronto: C.D. Howe Institute, 1990) 111–28

VOGEL, D., & A.M. RUGMAN, "Environmentally Related Trade Disputes between the United States and Canada" (1997) American Review of Canadian Studies 271

WOLD, CHRIS, *et al.*, *Trade and the Environment: Law and Policy* (Durham, NC: Carolina Academic Press, 2005)

ZAELKE, DURWOOD, DONALD KANIARU, & EVA KRUZIKOVA, *Making Law Work: Environmental Compliance and Sustainable Development* (London: Cameron May, 2005)

CIVIL LIABILITY FOR ENVIRONMENTAL HARM

The civil courts have a long history of dealing with disputes that would readily be acknowledged today as environmental in nature. Nuisance claims, along with negligence, strict liability, trespass, and riparian rights have all been asserted—occasionally in combination—on behalf of those seeking judicial protection from the effects of conduct that has resulted, or that may result in the future, in some form of environmental damage.[1] Intermittently, courts have provided strong encouragement for private claims of this nature. Justice Rinfret remarked, for example, that "[p]ollution is always unlawful and, in itself, constitutes a nuisance."[2] Nevertheless private litigants have faced significant obstacles in pursuing environmental claims. The challenges naturally include specific doctrinal requirements, but encompass as well complex evidentiary burdens, and the costs of litigation, possibly including responsibility for defendants' costs where environmental claims ultimately fail. Some of the constraints—notably in connection with class actions—have recently been addressed through statutory reforms.

---

1   Analogous claims arise under the *Civil Code of Quebec* (C.C.Q.). See, for example, chapter III, section III, Articles 980, 981, & 982 concerning riparian rights and water quality.

2   *Groat v. Edmonton (City)*, [1928] S.C.R. 522 at 532.

A. COMMON LAW CAUSES OF ACTION

1) Nuisance

The common law doctrine of nuisance affords some protection to persons whose use and enjoyment of land is unreasonably interfered with by the actions of another, typically though not exclusively a neighbour. The cause of the plaintiff's complaint might be toxic fumes, chemicals or smoke, unpleasant odours, or excessive light or noise, while the interference experienced might involve actual physical damage to property, personal injury or risk to health and safety, or discomfort or inconvenience.

The courts' central concern in nuisance is to determine whether the activity complained of substantially and unreasonably interferes with the plaintiff's own reasonable use of the land:

> [I]t is the impact of the defendant's activity on the plaintiff's interest which is the focus of attention and not the nature of the defendant's conduct. The interference must be unreasonable in the sense that the plaintiff should not be required to suffer it, not that the defendant failed to take appropriate care. By the same token, if the level of interference is unreasonable, it is irrelevant that the defendant was taking all possible care. Furthermore, it makes no difference that in his mind he was making reasonable use of his land, or that his operation was beneficial to the community. The plaintiff satisfies the substantive requirement of the tort if he can point to tangible damage resulting from the defendant's activity or a significant degree of discomfort or inconvenience.[3]

A judicial formulation of the requirements drawing upon a scholarly synthesis indicates that actionable nuisance

> must be such as to be real interference with the comfort or convenience of living according to the standards of the average man. . . . Moreover, the discomfort must be substantial and not merely with reference to the plaintiff; it must be of such a degree that it would be substantial to any person occupying the plaintiff's premises, irrespective of his position in life, age, or state of health; it must be an "inconvenience materially interfering with the ordinary comfort physically of human existence, not merely according to elegant or

---

3   J.P.S. McLaren, "Annotation" (1976) 1 C.C.L.T. 29 at 300.

dainty modes and habits of living, but according to plain and sober and simple notions among the [Canadian] people."[4]

A few examples will help to illustrate the applicability of the doctrine in an environmental context.

Nuisance doctrine has been successfully invoked against an operation whose fumes and emissions damaged the plaintiff's commercial gardens,[5] and by an orchard owner whose fruit trees experienced damage attributable to the use of salt for de-icing an adjacent highway.[6] Another successful plaintiff was a corporate landlord whose use of his property was materially interfered with and whose ability to earn rents was undermined by excessive noise and vibration following the introduction of new equipment by a long-established manufacturing plant in a mixed residential and industrial neighbourhood.[7] A homeowner in Quebec succeeded under a provision of the province's *Civil Code* roughly comparable to nuisance against the operators of a telecommunications tower that had the effect of attracting birds to the neighbourhood. The combined impact of the noise and the smell of excrement—on and off her property—interfered with the resident's ability to enjoy her yard, thereby lessening the value of her property.[8] Noise, smoke, litter, and offensive odours emanating from a rural landfill operation led to an injunction and a substantial award of damages.[9]

Notwithstanding such successful claims, the courts clearly recognize a number of defences, and plaintiffs in nuisance face a number of other significant obstacles. Defendants may seek to undermine the plaintiff's case with evidence indicating that plaintiffs are abnormally

4   Morden J. in *Walker v. Pioneer Construction Co.* (1975), 8 O.R. (2d) 35 at 48 (H.C.J.), quoting with approval from *Clerk and Lindsell on Torts*, 11th ed. (London: Sweet & Maxwell, 1954) at 564.
5   *Walker v. McKinnon Industries Ltd.*, [1949] O.R. 549 (H.C.J.), var'd [1950] O.W.N. 309 (C.A.).
6   *Schenck v. Ontario* (1981), 34 O.R. (2d) 595 (H.C.J.), aff'd (1984), 49 O.R. (2d) 556 (C.A.), aff'd (*sub nom. Schenck v. Ontario (Minister of Transportation & Communications)*), [1987] 2 S.C.R. 289.
7   *340909 Ontario Ltd. v. Huron Steel Products* (1990), 73 O.R. (2d) 641 (H.C.J.).
8   *Bolduc v. Bell Mobilité Cellulaire* (1994), 17 C.E.L.R. (N.S.) 102 (C.Q.). For a convenient overview of Quebec's environmental law framework, see Lorne Giroux and Paule Halley, "Environmental Law in Quebec" in Elaine Hughes, Alastair R. Lucas, and William A. Tilleman, *Environmental Law and Policy*, 3d ed. (Toronto: Emond Montgomery, 2003) c. 4. Issues around fault and compliance with approvals in the nuisance context arose recently in *Barette c. Ciment St-Laurent*, [2003] J.Q. no 5273 (S.C.).
9   *Nippa v. C.H. Lewis (Lucan) Ltd.* (1991), 7 C.E.L.R. (N.S.) 149 (Ont. Gen. Div.), (1991), 7 C.E.L.R. (N.S.) 163 (C.A.).

sensitive to interference[10] or perhaps that the plaintiff consented in some way to the nuisance.[11] Prescriptive rights may be acquired by defendants who are able to show that the activity complained of and otherwise amounting to a nuisance was carried out continuously for a period of twenty years or more to the knowledge of the plaintiffs or their predecessors who failed to take action against it.[12] Defendants may also seek to immunize their operations against nuisance claims on the grounds that the activity complained of is the inevitable consequence of express statutory authorization and was accordingly given implicit legislative protection.

In *Tock v. St. John's (City) Metropolitan Area Board*,[13] where a blocked sewer operated by the defendant municipality resulted in flood damage to the plaintiff homeowner, the Supreme Court of Canada considered the defence of statutory authority. The Court was divided in its analysis of the appropriate treatment of inevitable consequences, with three members proposing to restrict the defence to damage caused by actions specifically required by legislation. Another member of the Court suggested that the defence would be available if the defendant could establish that no other methods of carrying out the work would have avoided damage. In a third opinion, two justices indicated that consideration of statutory authority should be incorporated in the general calculus of reasonableness in a nuisance analysis. "[G]iven all the circumstances, [is it] reasonable to refuse to compensate the aggrieved party for the damages he has suffered?" In *Tock* the defendant municipality was unable to satisfy the Court's requirements and could not avail itself of the defence in the context of the following statutory provision:

> 154. (1) The council may . . . construct, acquire, establish, own and operate
>
> (a) a public water supply system . . .
>
> (b) a public sewerage system . . . and
>
> (c) a storm drainage system . . .
>
> (2) For the purposes of subsection (1) the council may
>
> (a) acquire any waters required for the purpose of providing a sufficient supply of water for the town, and
>
> (b) acquire by purchase or expropriation any lands adjacent to such waters to prevent pollution of those waters.

---

10 *MacNeill v. Devon Lumber Co.* (1987), 82 N.B.R. (2d) 319 (C.A.).

11 *Pattison v. Prince Edward Region Conservation Authority* (1988), 3 C.E.L.R. (N.S.) 212 (Ont. C.A.).

12 *Russell Transport Ltd. v. Ontario Malleable Iron Co.*, [1952] O.R. 621 (Co. Ct.).

13 [1989] 2 S.C.R. 1181.

> (3) For the purpose of exercising its powers under subsection (1) the council may lay out, excavate, dig, make, build, maintain, repair and improve all such drains, sewers, and water supply pipes as the council deems necessary.[14]

This language was considered by the Court to be permissive and not mandatory.

The Supreme Court subsequently affirmed the traditional view of the defence of statutory authority when it endorsed the following description:

> The defendant must negative that there are alternate methods of carrying out the work. The mere fact that one is considerably less expensive will not avail. If only one method is practically feasible, it must be established that it was practically impossible to avoid the nuisance. It is insufficient for the defendant to negative negligence. The standard is a higher one. While the defence gives rise to some factual difficulties, in view of the allocation of the burden of proof they will be resolved against the defendant.[15]

Defendants may, however, enjoy more explicit immunity from nuisance claims on the basis of express legislative exclusions. These are especially common in relation to agricultural operations. A typical example of such a "right to farm" provision is from Saskatchewan:

> The owner or operator of an agricultural operation is not liable to any person in nuisance with respect to the carrying on of the agricultural operation, and may not be prevented by injunction or other order of any court from carrying on the agricultural operation on the grounds of nuisance where the owner or operator uses normally accepted agricultural practices.[16]

Although "right to farm" legislation does not operate to exempt farm operations from environmental legislation, some provinces have extended agricultural immunity to restrictive local bylaws. Virtually all provinces adopted "right to farm" legislation in some form or other.[17]

---

14   *The Municipalities Act*, S.N. 1979, c. 33, s. 154.

15   *Ryan v. Victoria* [1999] 1 S.C.R. 201 at para. 55, quoting Sopinka J. from *Tock*, above note 13 at 1226.

16   *Agricultural Operations Act*, R.S.S. 1995, c. A-12.1, s. 3(1). For consideration of this issue in Ontario, see *Pyke v. TriGro Enterprises* (2001), 55 O.R. (3d) 257 (C.A.).

17   *Agricultural Operations Practices Act*, S.N.B. 1999, c. A-5.3; *Agricultural Operations Practices Act*, R.S.A. 2000, c. A-7; *Agricultural Operations Protection Act*, R.S.N.S. 1989, c. 2; *Farm Practices Act*, S.N.S. 2000, c. 3; *Farm Practices Protection Act*, C.C.S.M. c. F45; *Act Respecting the Preservation of Agricultural Land and*

Plaintiffs contemplating a claim in nuisance may also have to confront an awkward and uncertain distinction between private and public nuisance, the latter more difficult to pursue though arguably more relevant to environmental protection. Anchored in the proprietary interests of potential plaintiffs, the private nuisance claim as described above offers the prospect of redress against environmental harm almost in direct proportion to the self-interest of the individuals affected. In contrast, public nuisance doctrine provides a basis for legal action against the perceived causes of environmental harm when that harm involves injury to or interference with public rights, a situation in which individual litigants have no automatic entitlement or standing to pursue a claim.

In cases of public nuisance, the attorney general is presumed to be the most suitable party to initiate litigation on behalf of the general interests of the community. Individuals seeking to proceed with public nuisance claims on behalf of the wider community—in effect to represent the public interest for purposes of the litigation—have been required as a condition of standing to obtain the attorney general's permission to proceed or to demonstrate that they have suffered special damages as a result of the defendant's interference with public rights.

The potentially restrictive application of the special damages test is illustrated in *Hickey v. Electric Reduction Co.*,[18] where commercial fishermen in Placentia Bay, Newfoundland, were denied standing to proceed in public nuisance against an industrial polluter on the grounds that despite commercial losses their right to fish in public waters was simply "a right in common with all Her Majesty's subjects."

In a more recent decision, the relationship between public and private nuisance was also considered. In *Sutherland v. Vancouver International Airport Authority*, residents of a Richmond, British Columbia, subdivision launched nuisance proceedings in response to aircraft noise. The noise levels interfered with speech outside the plaintiffs' homes, affecting their use of patios, gardens and other outdoor amenities. The trial judge found that the aircraft noise inside the house "interfered to a degree transcending annoyance." The British Columbia Court of Appeal, while upholding the finding that the noise of the airport constituted nuisance, ultimately accepted the government's argument that the nuisance was statutorily authorized and overturned the ruling. In

---

Agricultural Activities, R.S.Q., c. P-41.1; *Farm Practices Protection (Right to Farm) Act*, R.S.B.C. 1996, c. 131; *Agricultural Operations Act*, S.S. 1995, c. A-12.1; *Farming and Food Production Protection Act, 1998*, S.O. 1998, c. 1; *Farm Practices Act*, R.S.P.E.I. 1988, c. F-4.01.

18   (1971), 2 Nfld. & P.E.I.R. 246 (Nfld. T.D.).

so doing, however, the B.C.C.A. directly addressed the argument that since the conduct to which the residents objected constituted public nuisance it could only be challenged with the consent of the attorney general:

> In my opinion, the plaintiffs succeeded in establishing the elements of private nuisance: unreasonable and substantial interference with the use and enjoyment of their lands. They are not to be denied a remedy because the defendants' conduct in the circumstances also amounts to a public nuisance.[19]

2) Negligence

To succeed in negligence, the plaintiff must establish that the defendant's failure to meet a standard of care to which the plaintiff was entitled has caused damage for which compensation is being sought. In the environmental context, claims of this nature might arise in connection with physical injury or property damage following on the defendant's use or handling of contaminants or other hazardous substances.

A plaintiff advancing a civil claim in negligence must first establish that the defendant owed that party a duty of care. In *Donoghue v. Stevenson*, Lord Atkin explored the "general conception of relations giving rise to a duty of care" and remarked:

> The rule that you are to love your neighbour becomes in law, you must not injure your neighbour; and the lawyer's question, Who is my neighbour? receives a restricted reply. You must take reasonable care to avoid acts or omissions which you can reasonably foresee would be likely to injure your neighbour. Who, then, in law is my neighbour? The answer seems to be — persons who are so closely and directly affected by my act that I ought reasonably to have them in contemplation as being so affected when I am directing my mind to the acts or omissions which are called in question.[20]

It must then be demonstrated that the defendant's conduct fell short of the standard of care reasonably expected in the circumstances. Such standards may be derived by the court from an examination of applicable statutory requirements, on the basis of normal practices, or in light of the conduct that would be expected from a reasonable person. Those holding themselves out as experts or professionals in a particular field

---

19   *Sutherland v. Vancouver International Airport Authority*, 2002 BCCA 416 at para. 34.

20   [1932] A.C. 562 at 580 (H.L.).

will be charged with a higher standard of care, as will anyone undertaking an activity, however desirable, which poses risks to others. Plaintiffs in negligence will face the further requirement of demonstrating that the defendant's breach of a duty or standard of care was the cause of their injury, and that the damage complained of was not so remote as to have been unforeseeable.

In contrast with riparian claims and trespass actions, negligence requires the plaintiff to provide proof of damages. Physical injury and property damage, however difficult they may be to quantify, have long been considered compensable. In the absence of personal injury or property damage, however, purely economic losses have not ordinarily been recoverable.[21] This limitation may now be softened by a Supreme Court of Canada decision holding that expenditures taken to safeguard property interests or to preserve bodily integrity may constitute recoverable economic loss even in the absence of actual physical damage or personal injury.[22]

Negligence principles have figured prominently in another stream of environmental cases where claims are not made directly against those originally responsible for environmental damage but against others whose acts or omissions subsequently exposed the plaintiffs to economic losses. The *Sevidal v. Chopra* litigation arose in connection with the purchase of a residential property that had been contaminated several decades earlier with radioactive soil.[23] At the time of the agreement of purchase and sale, the vendors failed to disclose that radioactive soil dating from experimental research work in the 1940s had been found in the vicinity. Nor did they disclose additional information that came to their attention between the date of the agreement and the date of closing to the effect that the Atomic Energy Control Board had found radioactive contamination on their property. Prior to closing, the purchasers read newspaper reports concerning radioactive soil in the area, but not on the property they intended to buy. However, on the basis of assurances from an official of the AECB, they decided to proceed with the transaction. The AECB was found liable for negligently misrepresenting the condition of the property under the doctrine of *Hedley Byrne & Co. Ltd. v. Heller & Partners Ltd.*[24] Liability of this kind has made governments extremely cautious about certifying the environmental condition of land. For their part, the vendors were

---

21 *Rivtow Marine Ltd. v. Washington Iron Works* (1973), [1974] S.C.R. 1189.
22 *Winnipeg Condominium Corp. No. 36 v. Bird Construction Co.*, [1995] 1 S.C.R. 85.
23 (1987), 64 O.R. (2d) 169 (H.C.J.).
24 (1963), [1964] A.C. 465 (H.L.).

found liable in deceit for failing to disclose a dangerous latent defect in the property.

In *Heighington v. Ontario*, provincial officials were found liable in negligence for failing to remedy radioactive contamination of the soil although the condition of the soil was known to them, and the *Public Health Act* as then in existence imposed a duty on the Department of Health to abate conditions injurious or dangerous to public health. "In all the circumstances," stated the Ontario Court of Appeal, "the provincial officials were negligent in that, in breach of the *Public Health Act*, they failed to take reasonable steps to cause to be removed such radioactive material, including contaminated soil, as might endanger the health of future occupants of the land."[25]

Claims have also been made against legal professionals for failing to detect environmental liabilities in real estate transactions or for failing to protect their clients against such liabilities. In a recent B.C. case, legal advisors to a property development firm were found to have breached the duty of care owed in circumstances where they neither discovered a pollution abatement order relating to the land in question nor insisted on appropriate contractual safeguards in the agreement. As the court determined that these failings were not in fact the cause of the plaintiff's losses, the action was dismissed.[26]

There are also indications of increasing resort to allegations of regulatory negligence against public officials whose conduct or decisions may appear to be causally connected to some form of environmental injury.[27] The general principles applicable to such claims, including an important distinction exempting policy decisions (as distinct from operational responsibilities), from the realm of liablility were discussed in *Just v. British Columbia*:

> As a general rule, the traditional tort law duty of care will apply to a government agency in the same way that it will apply to an individual. In determining whether a duty of care exists, the first question to be resolved is whether the parties are in a relationship of sufficient proximity to warrant the imposition of such a duty. In the case of a government agency, exemptions from this imposition of duty may occur as a result of the nature of the decision made by the government agency. That is, a government agency will be exempt from the

---

25   (1989), 69 O.R. (2d) 484 at 486 (C.A.).

26   *Fraser Park South Estates v. Lang Michener Lawrence and Shaw* (2001), 84 B.C.L.R. (3d) 65 (C.A.).

27   *Tottrup v. Alberta (Minister of Environmental Protection)*, [2000] A.J. No. 435 (C.A.); *Quebec (A.G.) v. Girard*, [2004] J.Q. no 13624 (C.A.).

imposition of a duty of care in situations which arise from purely policy decisions.

In determining what constitutes a policy decision, it should be borne in mind that such decisions are generally made by persons of a high level of authority in the agency, but may also be made by persons of a lower level of authority. The characterization of such a decision rests on the nature of the decision and not on the identity of the actors. As a general rule, decisions concerning budgetary allotments for departments or government agencies will be classified as policy decisions. Further, it must be recalled that a policy decision is open to challenge on the basis that it is not made in the *bona fide* exercise of discretion. If after due consideration it is found that a duty of care is owed by the government agency and no exemption by way of statute or policy decision-making is found to exist, a traditional torts analysis ensues and the issue of standard of care required of the government agency must next be considered.[28]

In the context of claims against government agencies and officials, notice requirements and limitation periods are important considerations.[29]

3) Strict Liability

Originating as an application of nuisance principles in the 1866 decision of Mr. Justice Blackburn in *Rylands v. Fletcher*, the doctrine of strict liability for damages caused when dangerous substances escape from the defendant's lands to injure the lands of another now offers potential relief in circumstances involving environmental harm.[30] Injury to persons or property resulting from the escape of such substances as sewage, industrial chemicals, pesticides, fuels, and gases may be compensable notwithstanding the exercise of reasonable care by the defendant to prevent the escape.

Blackburn J.'s formulation of the principle of liability indicated that "the person who for his own purposes brings on his lands and collects and keeps there anything likely to do mischief if it escapes, must keep it in at his peril." Those failing to contain the cause of such mischief are "*prima facie* answerable for all the damage which is the natural conse-

28 *Just v. British Columbia* (1989), 64 D.L.R. (4th) 689 at 708 (S.C.C.). See also *Cooper v. Hobart*, [2001] 3 S.C.R. 537; *Edwards v. Law Society of Upper Canada*, [2001] 3 S.C.R. 562; *Holland v. Saskatchewan*, 2008 SCC 42.

29 *Public Authorities Protection Act*, R.S.O. 1990, c. P-38; *Proceedings Against the Crown Act*, R.S.O. 1990, c. P-27. *Berendsen v. The Queen*, 2001 SCC 55.

30 (1866), L.R. 1 Ex. 265, confirmed by (1868), L.R. 3 H.L. 330.

quence of its escape." In confirming this interpretation, the House of Lords qualified the application of the rule by confining it to situations involving the "non-natural" use of land. That consideration has been variously approached by succeeding generations of judicial interpreters who have endeavoured to comply with Lord Moulton's observation that "[i]t is not every use to which land is put that brings into play that principle. It must be some special use bringing with it increased danger to others, and must not merely be the ordinary use of the land or such a use as is proper for the general benefit of the community."[31] Thus, even dangerous uses, if common or generally accepted in a particular locale, might not give rise to liability under the doctrine in *Rylands v. Fletcher*, while potentially harmful activities carried on for the general benefit of the community rather than for private advantage or profit might equally fall within the exceptions to the rule.[32]

The doctrine in *Rylands v. Fletcher* was recently reconsidered by the House of Lords in a prominent controversy involving a tannery whose solvent-handling practices eventually resulted in the contamination of an underground aquifer used for municipal supply purposes by the Cambridge Water Company.[33] The House of Lords was emphatic in rejecting a lower court finding to the effect that the use and storage of substantial quantities of industrial chemicals was a natural or ordinary use of land in the context of the industrial community in which the tannery was located. Lord Goff remarked:

> Indeed I feel bound to say that the storage of substantial quantities of chemicals on industrial premises should be regarded as an almost classic case of non-natural use; and I find it very difficult to think that it should be thought objectionable to impose strict liability for damage caused in the event of their escape.[34]

More fundamentally, the House of Lords in *Cambridge Water* considered whether it was necessary for the plaintiff to establish foreseeability of harm of the relevant type in a claim under the *Rylands v. Fletcher* principle and concluded that this was indeed an essential ingredient of the tort. On the basis that the contamination of water supplies resulting from spilled chemicals travelling a significant distance underground was not foreseeable during the period (pre-1976) when the defendants were using the solvents in question, the tannery escaped liability. More sophisticated contemporary knowledge and

---

31 *Rickards v. Lothian*, [1913] A.C. 263 at 280 (P.C.).
32 For example, *Danku v. Fort Frances (Town)* (1976), 14 O.R. (2d) 285 (Dist. Ct.).
33 *Cambridge Water Co. Ltd. v. Eastern Counties Leather Plc.*, [1994] 2 A.C. 264 (H.L.).
34 *Ibid.* at 309.

scientific understanding—resulting in part from extensive research undertaken by water authorities in the investigation of the *Cambridge Water* contamination—will increasingly extend the limits of foreseeable environmental harm, thus broadening the scope of liability.

4) Breach of Statutory Duty

The Supreme Court of Canada in *Canada v. Saskatchewan Wheat Pool* discussed the suggestion that breach of statute would in itself constitute the basis of tortious action for which damages might be recoverable. The decision indicated firmly that breach of statutory duty ought not to be regarded as an independent source of liability. Rather, proof of the breach and resulting damages may be evidence of negligence, with the statutory formulation of the duty serving to indicate "a specific, and useful, standard of reasonable conduct."[35] Consistent with this analysis, in *McGeek Enterprises v. Shell Canada*, an Ontario court found that the defendant's breach of the provincial *Gasoline Handling Act* was insufficient to ground liability in negligence.[36]

5) Trespass

Intentional and direct entry onto another person's land, or placing or allowing some substance or material onto that land, may constitute a trespass in the absence of such lawful justification or excuse as consent or licence, necessity, or statutory authorization. Thus, in *Hole v. Chard Union*,[37] defendants committed a trespass by discharging refuse and sewage into a stream passing directly through the plaintiff's property. The requirement of directness, however, has sometimes precluded trespass claims of an environmental nature when substances—sprayed insecticides, for example—have drifted onto plaintiffs' lands. Trespass, being actionable per se without proof of damage, entitles the plaintiff to recover nominal or general damages for the fact of the interference or to injunctive relief, which may be particularly appropriate in the case of a continuing trespass. Arguments concerning the rejuvenation or extension of this historic cause of action have recently emerged in

---

35   *Canada v. Saskatchewan Wheat Pool*, [1983] 1 S.C.R. 205 at 228. Now see *Ingles v. Tutkaluk Construction Ltd.*, [2000] 1 S.C.R. 298. As recently underlined by the Supreme Court of Canada, "the proper remedy for breach of statutory duty by a public authority, traditionally viewed, is judicial review for invalidity:" *Holland v. Saskatchewan*, above note 28 at para. 9.

36   *McGeek Enterprises v. Shell Canada* (1991), 6 O.R. (3d) 216 (Gen. Div.).

37   [1894] 1 Ch. 293 (C.A.).

connection with the use of genetically modified organisms, especially in western Canada.[38]

6) Riparian Rights

Landowners whose property borders a natural watercourse are entitled under the doctrine of riparian rights to take action to preserve the natural quantity and quality of the adjacent water subject to the reasonable use of other riparians. The principle was articulated in *John Young v. Bankier Distillery Co.*, where Lord MacNaghten explained that a riparian owner is "entitled to the water of his stream, in its natural flow, without sensible diminution or increase and without sensible alteration in its character or quality."[39]

Defendants have sometimes asserted the importance, reasonableness, or utility of the activity which an aggrieved riparian seeks to enjoin. In *McKie v. K.V.P. Co.*, where objection was taken to pollution from a pulp mill, arguments of this kind were advanced and emphatically rejected by the trial judge who awarded damages and an injunction against the defendant company: "Some evidence was given on behalf of the defendant to show the importance of its business in the community, and that it carried it on in a proper manner. Neither of these elements is to be taken into consideration in a case of this character, nor are the economic necessities of the defendant relevant to be considered."[40] In the aftermath of the company's final appeal to the Supreme Court of Canada, however, the Ontario legislature dissolved the injunction, confining the riparian plaintiffs to damages alone.[41]

B. ASSESSING THE COMMON LAW

As forums for dealing with private claims concerning the environment, the courts offer all the attractions regularly associated with formal adversarial procedures. Litigation initiated by aggrieved individuals defending property-based interests has strong advocates.[42] One experienced observer has expressed some of the attractions this way:

---

38   *Monsanto Canada Inc. v. Schmeiser*, [2004] 1 S.C.R. 902; *Hoffman v. Monsanto Canada Inc.*, 2005 SKQB 225, aff'd (2007), 28 C.E.L.R. (3d) 165 (Sask. C.A.).
39   [1893] A.C. 691 at 698 (H.L.).
40   *McKie v. K.V.P. Co.*, [1948] O.R. 398 at 410 (H.C.J.).
41   *The KVP Company Limited Act*, 1950, S.O. 1950, c. 33.
42   E. Brubaker, *Property Rights in the Defence of Nature* (London: Earthscan Publications, 1995).

The injured person can initiate action on his own, without the need to rely on any government agency to protect his interest. He controls the choice of lawyers, medical and other scientific experts to assist him. The parties themselves or their legal advisors maintain control over the timing and choice of strategies through every stage of the negotiations. Except in the case of infants and certain persons deemed by law to be incapable of making informed judgments without assistance, the decision of the plaintiff whether to accept a settlement offer need not be approved by any bureaucracy. Moreover, if the matter goes to trial, it is decided by an independent judiciary designed, at least in theory, to be above political or partisan pressures, and whose decisions are subject to appeal to higher courts.[43]

Yet those who have experienced such litigation, and other commentators, including presiding judges, have identified important limitations in the ability of traditional courts to resolve modern environmental controversies in a fully satisfactory and conclusive manner.

The constraints take several forms. Some are procedural in nature. They concern such questions as who is eligible to proceed with this litigation; or, as it is ordinarily expressed, does the would-be plaintiff have standing? Other obstacles to private litigation include the expense associated with lengthy and often complex proceedings involving expert witnesses and potential liability for legal costs.[44] Certain difficulties also arise in connection with the burden of proof, notably in situations where scientific evidence is inconclusive or where expert opinion is divided. Cases of this kind are further complicated by the long latency periods sometimes required for actual damage to appear from exposure to toxic substances.[45] Additional reservations are expressed on occasion about remedial constraints: damages will often be difficult to calculate and are widely considered an inadequate form of compensation where serious environmental harm has taken place. Moreover, with

---

43 J. Swaigen, "The Role of the Civil Courts in Resolving Risk and Uncertainty in Environmental Law" (1991) 1 J. Envtl. L. & Prac. 199 at 208.

44 *Canadian Environmental Law Assn. v. Canada (Minister of the Environment)* (1999), 34 C.E.L.R. (N.S.) 159 (F.C.A.). See also C. Tollefson, "When the Public Interest Loses: The Liability of Public Interest Litigants for Adverse Costs Awards" (1995) 29 U.B.C. L. Rev. 303; C. McCool, "Costs in Public Interest Litigation: A Comment on Professor Tollefson's Article, 'When the Public Interest Loses'" (1996) 30 U.B.C. L. Rev. 309; C. Tollefson, Darlene Gilliland, & Jerry DeMarco, "Towards a Costs Jurisprudence in Public Interest Litigation" (2004) 83 Can. Bar Rev. 473.

45 To some degree difficulty of this nature may be alleviated by statute. See, for example, *Limitations Act*, S.O. 2002, c. 24, Sched. B, s. 17: "There is no limitation period in respect of an environmental claim that has not been discovered."

the exception of injunctive relief, judicial remedies generally come into play after the damage has occurred, a situation that is immensely frustrating to those who are anxious to emphasize preventive approaches to environmental problems.

As environmental law overall evolves to reflect such emerging principles as sustainability, pollution prevention, polluter pay, and precaution, the common law will come under close scrutiny for its congruence and ability to keep pace. That courts are aware of a series of new challenges on the common law horizon has recently been acknowledged by the Supreme Court of Canada where Binnie J. remarked in *British Columbia v. Canadian Forest Products Ltd.*:

> It seems to me there is no legal barrier to the Crown suing for compensation as well as injunctive relief in a proper case on account of public nuisance, or negligence causing environmental damage to public lands, and perhaps other torts such as trespass, but there are clearly important and novel policy questions raised by such actions. These include the Crown's potential liability for inactivity in the face of threats to the environment, the existence or non-existence of enforceable fiduciary duties owed to the public by the Crown in that regard, the limits to the role and function and remedies available to governments taking action on account of activity harmful to public enjoyment of public resources, and the spectre of imposing on private interests an indeterminate liability for an indeterminate amount of money for ecological or environmental damage.[46]

There have been indications however of some legislative willingness to address some of the uncertainties and limitations of the common law framework in the environmental context.

C. STATUTORY CIVIL LIABILITIES

A number of recent legislative measures have established new statutory civil liabilities for environmental damage. For example, the Alberta *Environmental Protection and Enhancement Act* created a civil cause of action for the benefit of any person who suffered loss or damage as a result of conduct constituting an offence for which the defendant was convicted under the Act.[47] Although the plaintiff is still required to proceed with the action in a court of competent jurisdiction, the ef-

---

46   *British Columbia v. Canadian Forest Products Ltd.*, 2004 SCC 38 at para. 81.
47   R.S.A. 2000, c. E-12, s. 219 [*AEPEA*].

fect of the statute is to relieve plaintiffs of the obligation to show that the defendant owed them a duty of care, or of establishing the relevant standard of care which the defendant failed to meet. In cases of conduct contravening the *AEPEA*, the Act also offers injunctive relief to "[a]ny person who has suffered, is suffering or is about to suffer loss or damage."[48]

In a somewhat similar manner, the Ontario *Environmental Bill of Rights* resolves the standing problem in public nuisance claims:

> No person who has suffered or may suffer a direct economic loss or direct personal injury as a result of a public nuisance that caused harm to the environment shall be barred from bringing an action without the consent of the Attorney General in respect of the loss or injury only because the person has suffered or may suffer direct economic loss or direct personal injury of the same kind or to the same degree as other persons.[49]

Other statutory liabilities for losses and the costs of preventing or cleaning up damage arising in the context of spills are described in chapter 10.

D. CLASS ACTION LEGISLATION

Since environmental damage frequently entails injury to numerous parties or potential plaintiffs, provisions to facilitate proceedings on behalf of multiple victims are of considerable importance. In addition to rules of procedure allowing for "representative" actions and the inherent jurisdiction of the courts relating to their proceedings, considerable attention has been directed to legislation establishing the framework for class actions.[50]

In *Comité d'environnement de la Baie v. Société d'électrolyse et de chimie Alcan*, the Quebec Court of Appeal, with reference to the province's class action legislation, authorized a class action on behalf of 2400 property owners seeking some $20 million compensation for damages attributed to particulate emissions from the defendant's oper-

---

48 *Ibid.*, s. 225. See also *Canadian Environmental Protection Act, 1999*, S.C. 1999, c. 33, ss. 39–41.

49 *Environmental Bill of Rights, 1993*, S.O. 1993, c. 28, s. 103(1).

50 *Class Proceedings Act*, S.O. 1992, c. 6; *Class Proceedings Act*, R.S.B.C. 1996, c. 50; *Class Actions Act*, S.S. 2001, c. C-12.01; *Western Canadian Shopping Centres Inc. v. Dutton*, 2001 SCC 46.

ations.[51] The court recognized the existence of distinctions between various members of the applicant class in relation to exposure and the extent of damages, but it found sufficient common ground in relation to technical evidence and the standard of care to justify permitting an action which, given the comparatively small size of individual losses, would not otherwise have proceeded. As the court expressed its assessment of the relevant considerations:

> The class action recourse seems to me a particularly useful recourse in appropriate cases of environmental damage. Air and water pollution rarely affect just one individual or one piece of property. They often cause harm to many individuals over a large geographic area. The issues involved may be similar in each claim but they may be complex and expensive to litigate, while the amount involved in each case may be relatively modest. The class action, in these cases, seems an obvious means for dealing with claims for compensation for the harm done when compared to numerous individual law suits, each raising the same issues of fact and law.[52]

Despite this sympathetic account of the objectives of environmental class actions, certification has not been readily available in other jurisdictions: applicants for certification under class proceedings legislation must satisfy all necessary preconditions in order to succeed in having the class of litigants recognized.

Section 5 of Ontario's statute of class proceedings indicates that a class action shall be certified where a class proceeding would be the *preferable* means to resolve *common issues* on behalf of an *identifiable class of persons* relating to a cause of action disclosed in the pleadings by a qualified plaintiff or defendant. Those experienced in environmental class action litigation suggest that certification is generally more easily obtained in the context of a discrete environmental incident rather than in relation to ongoing pollution. In *Cotter v. Levy*, although the composition of the class of appropriate plaintiffs was contested, the Plastimet fire in Hamilton was an event well suited to certification.[53] On the other hand, in *Hollick v. Metro Toronto*, the circumstances proved to be more problematic for the would-be plaintiffs. In *Hollick*, the certification application was made on behalf of roughly 30,000 persons who might have been affected over an extended period of years by exposure to noxious fumes and gases associated with the City of Toronto's Keele

---

51   [1990] R.J.Q. 655.
52   *Ibid.* at 660.
53   *Cotter v. Levy*, [2000] O.J. No. 1086 (S.C.J.).

Valley landfill site. After initial success on the certification application, the plaintiffs suffered reversal in the divisional court which held that there was no identifiable class of persons and in the Court of Appeal where a majority of the court found "no common issue to justify the certification of a class action because the individuals' lives have been affected, or not affected, in a different manner and degree." On further appeal, the Supreme Court of Canada was satisfied as to the existence of an identifiable class and as to the existence of common issues. It concluded, however, that a class action was not the *preferable* procedure for the resolution of those issues.

The preferability analysis set out by the court had three aspects relating to the principal advantages of class actions: economical use of judicial resources, improved access to justice, and the potential to encourage modification of the tortfeasor's behaviour. Despite its conclusion that these goals would not be achieved by certification of the *Hollick* class action, the courts emphasized that environmental class actions are not necessarily precluded by the analysis. Each application for certification must be tested on its own facts.[54] Another major application immediately presented an opportunity for such further testing.

In *Pearson v. Inco Ltd.*, claims for physical, emotional, property and business damages were brought against several defendants by a large group of residents of Port Colborne, Ontario where an Inco refinery was alleged to have emitted a range of substances, including nickel oxide, arsenic and lead. In addressing the application for certification of the proceedings as a class action, Justice Nordheimer highlighted the complexities of the case. He anticipated that the matter would:

> inevitably disintegrate into the need for thousands of individual trials with potentially tens, if not hundreds, of thousands of individual issues to be resolved. Consequent on that reality, will be the need for examinations for discovery of each and every one of the 20,000 members of the proposed class. In an action for damages arising from contamination, it is necessary to determine the exposure of each of the claimants to the contaminants. There is also a need to know the individual claimant's health history and their personal habits as they would relate to possible exposure to the contaminants. Further compounding the complexity of such a claim in this case is that there is considerable variation in contaminant levels across the area of concern.

---

54 *Hollick v. Metro Toronto (Municipality)* (1999), 32 C.E.L.R. (N.S.) 1 (Ont. C.A.), aff'd [2001] S.C.J. No. 67.

At the Ontario Court of Appeal, a more limited group of Port Colborne residents succeeded in obtaining certification to pursue the class action in relation to a more narrowly-circumscribed common issue associated with losses to property values.[55]

Initiatives intended to facilitate litigation on behalf of classes or groups of victims of environmental harm continue in provinces with and without class action legislation.[56]

FURTHER READINGS

BRANCH, WARD, *Class Actions in Canada*, looseleaf (Aurora, ON: Canada Law Book, 2005–)

BRUNNÉE, J., "Individual and Group Enforcement of Environmental Law in Québec" (1992) 41 U.N.B.L.J. 109

EMOND, D.P., "Environmental Law and Policy: A Retrospective Examination of the Canadian Experience" in I. Bernier & A. Lajoie, eds., *Consumer Protection, Environmental Law, and Corporate Power* (Toronto: University of Toronto Press, 1985) 89

DEMARCO, J., D.GILLILAND, & CHRIS TOLLEFSON, "Towards a Public Interest Costs Jurisprudence" (2004), 83 Can. Bar Rev. 473

FAIETA, M.D., *et al.*, *Environmental Harm: Civil Actions and Compensation* (Toronto: Butterworths, 1996)

FAIETA, M.D., "Civil Liability for Environmental Torts" (2004) Ann. Rev. Civil Lit. 21-58

KALMAKOFF, J.J., "'The Right to Farm': A Survey of Farm Practices Protection Legislation in Canada" (1999) 62 Sask. L. Rev. 225

---

55   *Pearson v. Inco Ltd.*, [2005] O.J. No. 4918 (C.A.), leave to appeal to S.C.C. refused, [2006] S.C.C.A. No. 1.

56   *Windsor v. Canadian Pacific Railway*, 2006 ABQB 348; *Paron v. Alberta (Environmental Protection)*, 2006 ABQB 375. In Nova Scotia, despite the absence of class action legislation, residents of the Sydney Tar Ponds area sought to pursue a class action on a common law basis. See Wagner & Associates, online: www.wagnerslawfirm.com, and *MacQueen v. Ispat Sidbec Inc.*, 2006 NSSC 208. For a thoughtful discussion of Saskatchewan's new class action legislation, see Martin Olszynski, "*Hoffman v. Monsanto Canada Inc.*: Looking for a Generous Approach to the Elephant in the Garden" (2005) 16 J. Envtl. L. & Prac. 53.

MCLAREN, J.P.S., "The Common Law Nuisance Actions and the Environmental Battle: Well-Tempered Swords or Broken Reeds?" (1972) 10 Osgoode Hall L.J. 513

MCLEOD-KILMURRAY, H., "*Hollick* and Environmental Class Actions: Putting the Substance into Class Action Procedure" (2002–3) 34 Ottawa L.R. 263

NADON, O., "Civil Liability Underlying Environmental Risk-Related Activities in Quebec" (1998) 24 C.E.L.R. (N.S.) 141

ONTARIO, LAW REFORM COMMISSION, *Report on the Law of Standing* (Toronto: Ontario Law Reform Commission, 1989)

TOLLEFSON, CHRIS, "Costs and the Public Interest Litigant: *Okanagan Indian Band* and Beyond" (2006) 19 Can. J. Admin. L. & Prac. 39

WILDSMITH, B.H., "Of Herbicides and Human Kind: Palmer's Common Law Lessons" (1986) 24 Osgoode Hall L.J. 161

CHAPTER 6

ENVIRONMENTAL REGULATIONS AND APPROVALS

The proliferation of environmental regulations is consistent with a general tendency described by Justice Cory, formerly of the Supreme Court of Canada:

> Regulatory measures are the primary mechanisms employed by governments in Canada to implement public policy objectives . . . . It is difficult to think of an aspect of our lives that is not regulated for our benefit and for the protection of society as a whole. From cradle to grave, we are protected by regulations; they apply to the doctors attending our entry into this world and to the morticians present at our departure . . . . The more complex the activity, the greater the need for and the greater our reliance upon regulation and its enforcement.[1]

Although critics might dispute Justice Cory's concluding assertion, an explanation along the lines he sets out might well be offered to account for the extensive body of regulations that has been formulated to protect the environment from various forms of degradation.

The basic purposes of an environmental protection regime are typically embodied in statutory schemes and in statements of official policy. In Canada actual performance requirements are generally established by regulation or administrative guidelines. This chapter addresses some of the issues associated with designing such standards before turning to the relationship between standards and the permits

---

1   R. v. Wholesale Travel Group Inc., [1991] 3 S.C.R. 154 at 220–22.

or approvals usually required by those whose operations entail impacts on or discharges into the natural environment of air, land, and water.

A. STANDARD-SETTING

1) Introduction

Standard-setting in the environmental context has been described as "the process of deciding how much pollution will be allowed to enter the environment each year."[2] Yet it is important to appreciate that pollution standards are established—explicitly or implicitly—in the context of underlying goals relating to environmental quality. Standards are technical instruments intended to promote or maintain certain objectives, whether those objectives are expressed in terms of environmental quality and human health, biological diversity, economic development and resource productivity, sustainability, or something else. Thus, an important relationship exists between environmental principles such as those described in Chapter 1, and legislative and regulatory practice. By way of example, if sustainability is an intended policy outcome, it will be appropriate to incorporate measures for assessing sustainability in regulatory standards; or, in situations involving certain health risks, it may be appropriate to incorporate the precautionary principle into the standard-setting process.

Standards may be formulated in various ways, some directed at allowable emission levels (emission standards), others based on actual measurements of environmental quality in the relevant media, whether air, water, or land (ambient-quality standards), or possibly in terms of operational practices or design and technology requirements (design standards).[3]

Each of these approaches has a contribution to make, although their comparative merits are subject to heated discussion. Advocates of emission standards or limits applicable to particular industrial operations and other dischargers of pollutants point to their obvious administrative and legal convenience. Monitoring is comparatively straightforward and violators are far more readily identifiable than in the case of environmental quality objectives where the relationship be-

---

2   D. Macdonald, *The Politics of Pollution* (Toronto: McClelland & Stewart, 1991) at 159.

3   For a useful overview of approaches to pollution control, see N. Haigh, *EEC Environmental Policy and Britain*, 2d ed. (London: Institute for European Environmental Policy, 1989).

tween observed environmental deterioration and any specific source or sources among hundreds of discharges is rarely so clear. Yet ambient-quality standards have the virtue of maintaining the regulatory focus on overall results whereas emission limits (especially those formulated in terms of effluent concentrations or production ratios) have sometimes failed to address the fundamental issue of levels of overall pollution that are acceptable in light of broader goals such as sustainability or biodiversity.[4] In other words, environmental deterioration may continue to occur even though dischargers are meeting emission standards. Design standards may appear attractive from business and administrative perspectives in that, once the appropriate technology or process has been identified, one can readily determine whether it has been adopted or implemented. Critics of technology standards, however, lament the separation of the manner of environmental protection from results, especially in areas where the environmental risk is severe but technical performance standards are bounded by such concepts as "practicable" or "economically achievable." From the perspective of economic efficiency, other observers regard technology-based standards as excessively costly in comparison with the alternatives that might be developed if industry were given economic incentives to innovate.[5]

The Canadian tendency has been to control pollutant discharges on the basis of emission standards or limits for specified substances. Limits may ultimately be expressed in various ways; they may be stated, for example, in terms of effluent concentrations or in terms of linkages to production levels. Alternatively, absolute discharge levels may be established on daily, seasonal, or annual bases. A zero-discharge standard or even outright bans on the use of particular toxic substances are not unknown, and may become more common as further evidence accumulates to demonstrate that the assumption that pollutants are gradually rendered harmless through diffusion is unreliable. By way of example, an excerpt from federal *Chlor-Alkali Mercury Release Regulations* follows:

> 3. (1) The quantity of mercury that the owner or operator of a plant may release into the ambient air from that plant shall not exceed

---

4   Macdonald, above note 2; S. Boehmer-Christiansen, "Environmental Quality Objectives Versus Uniform Emission Standards" in D. Freestone & T. Ijlstra, eds., *The North Sea: Perspectives on Regional Environmental Co-operation* (London: Graham and Trotman, 1990) c. 12. The differences between ambient quality standards and emission limits, correspond in some respects to the debate between proponents of overall emission reductions and intensity targets in relation to greenhouse gases.

5   See chapter 17.

(a) 5 grams per day per 1000 kilograms of rated capacity, where the source of the mercury is the ventilation gases exhausted from cell rooms;

(b) 0.1 gram per day per 1000 kilograms of rated capacity, where the source of the mercury is the hydrogen gas stream originating from denuders;

(c) 0.1 gram per day per 1000 kilograms of rated capacity, where the source of the mercury is the ventilation gases exhausted from end boxes; and

(d) 0.1 gram per day per 1000 kilograms of rated capacity, where the source of the mercury is the gases exhausted from retorts.

(2) Notwithstanding paragraph (1)(c), no mercury shall be released directly into the ambient air from a tank.

(3) Notwithstanding subsection (1), the total amount of mercury that the owner or operator of a plant may release into the ambient air from the sources specified in subsection (1) shall not exceed 1.68 kilograms per day.

(4) Measurements shall be taken of the amount of mercury released into the ambient air per day from sources specified in subsection (1) by taking the arithmetical average of not less than three measurements conducted for each source in the same day in accordance with the appropriate method, or any other method the results of which can be confined by the appropriate method, described in *Standard Reference Methods for Source Testing: Measurement of Emissions of Mercury from Mercury Cell Chlor-Alkali Plants*, Department of the Environment Report EPS–1–AP–76–1 dated November 1976, as amended from time to time.

(5) Each measurement of mercury released shall be conducted under normal operating conditions and the minimum continuous sampling duration shall be

(a) two hours in respect of cell rooms; and

(b) one hour in respect of all other sources specified in subsection (1).[6]

---

6   *Chlor-Alkali Mercury Release Regulations*, S.O.R. 90/130, as am. by *Canadian Environmental Protection Act Omnibus Amendment Order*, 1993–1, S.O.R. 1 94–364. For a detailed examination of standard-setting procedure in relation to pesticides, see Chapter 3, "The Standard Setting Framework," in Kathleen Cooper *et al.*, *Environmental Standard Setting and Children's Health* (Canadian Environmental Law Association and the Ontario College of Family Physicians, Environmental Health Committee, May 2000), online: www.cela.ca/publications/cardfile.shtml?x=1114 .

Canadian practice has been typical of many jurisdictions in that discharge standards often lack clear and explicit linkages to overall objectives for environmental quality or to the condition of the receiving medium. However, certain quality objectives do exist for air and water. These can serve as benchmarks or background signals for those responsible for the detailed operation of the regulatory and approvals regime, triggering responses or influencing decisions even if they are not directly enforceable.[7]

In the aftermath of the Harmonization Accord and sub-agreements, including a sub-agreement on Canada-wide standards (CWS), discussions have been undertaken with a view to identifying areas in which timely and concerted action is required on a national basis. Smog-related initiatives across the country are in part a result of the signing of the *Canada-wide Standards for Particulate Matter (PM) and Ozone* in June 2000.

As described by the CCME, it is possible for CWSs to include qualitative or quantitative standards, guidelines, objectives, and criteria relating to health and environmental protection. "CWSs will include a numeric limit (for example, ambient discharge, or product standard), a commitment and timetable for attainment, a list of preliminary actions to attain the standard, and a framework for reporting to the public."[8] The standards themselves lack legal force and may be implemented in each jurisdiction according to that jurisdiction's own preferences.

2) Air

In relation to air, the federal government has for some time produced a set of non-binding *Ambient Air Quality Objectives* for several key pollutants, including suspended particulate matter. For each of the designated pollutants, three concentration levels were established on an annual, daily, and hourly basis. The *tolerable* level suggested a threshold at which a response is required in the interests of public health. The *acceptable* level (roughly approximating WHO guidelines) indicated adequate protection against environmental and health effects. The *desirable* level represents a long-term goal for air-quality improvement.[9] As expressed by one group of observers, "a level of pollution may be

---

7   See Canadian Council of Ministers of the Environment, *Comprehensive Air Quality Management Framework for Canada* (November 1993).

8   Canada-wide Standards, CCME, online: www.ccme.ca/ourwork/environment. html?category_id=108.

9   *Ambient Air Quality Objectives*, C. Gaz. 1989, I.3642. *National Ambient Air Objectives for Particulate Matter* (1998). Executive Summary online:www.hc-sc.gc.ca/

considered unacceptable, but still tolerable, or it may be acceptable, but better air quality would be desirable."[10]

In addition to such objectives for ambient air quality at sites throughout Canada, and as discussed in connection with the international context, various targets have been established under international agreements for reductions in total emissions of sulphur, NOx, VOCs, and heavy metals. Increasingly, stringent emission controls are anticipated as part of a long-term federal agenda to promote cleaner vehicles, engines, and fuels.[11]

At the provincial level, regulations or guidelines concerning air quality[12] and regulations covering emissions elaborate the regime in considerable detail.[13]

3) Water

In relation to water quality, objectives have been formulated through planning procedures undertaken by the federal and provincial governments. These are often regional in scope or oriented around a particular drainage area such as the Fraser River or the St. Lawrence.

In 1986 Ontario introduced a Municipal/Industrial Strategy for Abatement (MISA), an initiative that has been described as the "keystone" of that province's attempts to control the discharge of contaminants into surface waters.[14] MISA's ultimate objective is the "virtual

---

ewh-semt/alt_formats/hecs-sesc/pdf/pubs/air/naaqo-onqaa/particulate_mat-
ter_matieres_particulaires/summary-sommaire/98ehd220.pdf.

10 D. Estrin & J. Swaigen, *Environment on Trial*, 3d ed. (Toronto: Emond Montgomery, 1993) at 481.

11 Department of the Environment, "Federal Agenda on Cleaner Vehicles, Engines and Fuels," Canada Gazette Part 1, 17 February 2001, 452; Canada, *The Government of Canada's Interim Plan 2001 on Particulate Matter and Ozone* (April 2001).

12 For a province by province comparison of standards for selected contaminants, see Alberta Environmental Protection, *A Comparison of Alberta's Environmental Standards* (March 1999).

13 Pursuant to recent regulatory amendments, Ontario Regulation 346 has been replaced by O. Reg 419/05 "Air Pollution – Local Air Quality." The new air quality regulation whose sectoral implementation is to be phased in over a fifteen year period brings Ontario practice closer to air quality assessment methodologies developed by the U.S. Environmental Protection Agency. Further changes are intended to increase compatibility between provincial monitoring and reporting requirements under O. Reg. 127/01 and the federal National Pollutant Release Inventory. See chapter 18.

14 Ontario, Ministry of the Environment, *Municipal/Industrial Strategy for Abatement (MISA): A Policy and Program Statement of the Government of Ontario on*

elimination" of persistent toxic contaminants (including toxic metals and toxic organics) from all discharges into Ontario's waterways.

Significantly, MISA approached the problems of analysis and regulation by focusing on municipalities and several industrial sectors: electric power, inorganic chemicals, iron and steel manufacturing, metal casting, mines, petroleum refining, pulp and paper, and organic chemical manufacturing. Industrial operations in each of the designated sectors were first required to monitor their discharges of a specified list of contaminants. Detailed abatement regulations have been based on the monitoring results.[15]

The regulations are established on the basis of the best available technology, and they are subject to revision as new developments occur. The objective of virtual elimination is therefore to be achieved through ongoing evaluation and step-by-step reductions.

Although this text offers no discussion of water allocation issues, it should be noted that issues of water distribution and supply are of growing importance across the country.[16]

4) Drinking Water

Drinking water supplies in Canada are drawn from both surface and groundwater sources, demonstrating vital connections between environmental protection and human health. Recent illnesses and tragic deaths as well as other indications of contamination have resulted in greater public attention to issues surrounding drinking water quality.[17]

Controlling Municipal and Industrial Discharges into Surface Waters (Toronto: Ministry of the Environment, 1986).

15   Petroleum refining: O. Reg. 537/93; pulp and paper: O. Reg. 760/93; industrial minerals: O. Reg. 561/94; metal casting: O. Reg. 562/94; metal mining: O. Reg. 560/94; electric power generation: O. Reg. 215/95; organic chemical manufacturing: O. Reg. 63/95; inorganic chemicals: O. Reg. 64/95; iron and steel manufacturing: O. Reg. 214/95.

16   Marcia Valiante, "The Great Lakes Charter Annex, 2001" (2003) 13 J. Envtl. L. & Prac. 47; Arlene Kwasniak, "Quenching Instream Thirst: A Role for Water Trusts in the Prairie Provinces" (2006) 16 J. Envtl. L. & Prac. 211; Nigel Bankes & Arlene Kwasniak, "The St. Mary's Irrigation District Licence Amendment Decision" (2005) 16 J. Envtl. L. & Prac. 1; D.W. Schindler and W.F. Donahue, "An impending water crisis in Canada's western prairie provinces," www.pnas.org/cgi/doi/10.1073/pnas.0601568103.

17   Background or issue papers prepared for the Walkerton Inquiry provide a comprehensive overview of legal, constitutional, technical, and social aspects of the drinking water supply system, largely with reference to Ontario in a comparative context. See online: www.walkertoninquiry.com/part2info/commissuepapers/-index.html.

Municipal water supply systems, many of which were introduced by private enterprise in the nineteenth century, largely came under public ownership and operation in the twentieth. Municipal waterworks provide local water treatment and distribution services within an overall framework established at the provincial level. In addition to matters relating to the administration and financing of waterworks and other operational considerations including technical and staffing requirements for different types and sizes of facilities, drinking water quality standards may also be prescribed. *Guidelines for Canadian Drinking Water Quality*, formulated and revised through the ongoing deliberations of federal and provincial specialists, set out relevant parameters. Several provinces have incorporated the essence of these guidelines into provincial regulations.[18]

In the aftermath of the Walkerton, Ontario, and North Battleford, Saskatchewan incidents, policy reviews were conducted across the country[19] often leading to legislative or regulatory reforms intended to safeguard sources of drinking water supply.[20]

B. PERMITS, LICENSING, AND APPROVALS

Depending on the nature and scope of a proposed activity, environmental licences, permits, or approvals will be required as a precondition to development or operations. Such authorizations provide relief from the blanket prohibitions against harmful discharges that are fre-

---

18 *Drinking Water Protection Regulation*, B.C. Reg. 200/2003, as amended by B.C. Reg. 300/2004, 352/2005; *Potable Water Regulation*, A. Reg. 277/2003; *Quebec Drinking Water Regulation*, c. Q-2, r. 4.1; *Potable Water Regulation-Clean Water Act*, N.B. Reg., 93-203; *Safe Drinking Water Act, 2002*, S.O. 2002, c. 32 and *Ontario Drinking Water Quality Standards*, O.Reg. 169/03; *Water Regulations, 2002*, R.R.S., c.E-10.21, Reg.1; *Drinking Water Safety Regulation*, Man. Reg. 40/2007; *Water and Wastewater Facilities and Public Drinking Water Supplies Regulations*, N.S. Reg 186/2005.

19 Alberta, *Water for Life: Alberta's Strategy for Sustainability* (Edmonton: Alberta Environment, 2003); British Columbia, *A Water Conservation Strategy for British Columbia* (Victoria: Ministry of the Environment, 1999); Newfoundland and Labrador, *Source to Tap: Water Supplies in Newfoundland and Labrador* (St. John's: Newfoundland & Labrador Department of Environment, 2001); Nova Scotia, *A Drinking Water Strategy for Nova Scotia* (Halifax: Ministry of the Environment & Labour, 2002); Northwest Territories, *Managing Drinking Water Quality in the Northwest Territories* (Yellowknife: Policy, Planning and Evaluation, 2003).

20 *Drinking Water Protection Act*, S.B.C. 2001, c. 9; *Clean Water Act*, S.O. 2006, c. 22; Règlement sur la qualité de l'eau potable, L.R.Q., chap.Q-2, r.18.1.1.

quently found in basic environmental legislation. In actual operational situations the permitting process therefore plays an important role in implementing or elaborating general standards set out in objectives or embodied in regulations.

In Ontario, several environmental statutes deal with permit requirements, but the *Environmental Protection Act* is illustrative:

> No person shall, except under and in accordance with a certificate of approval issued by the Director,
>
> (a) construct, alter, extend or replace any plant, structure, equipment, apparatus, mechanism or thing that may discharge or from which may be discharged a contaminant into any part of the natural environment other than water; or
>
> (b) alter a process or rate of production with the result that a contaminant may be discharged into any part of the natural environment other than water or the rate or manner of discharge of a contaminant into any part of the natural environment other than water may be altered.[21]

Other approvals, licences, or permits under the *OEPA* deal with small-scale sewage systems and waste management while a parallel scheme under the *Ontario Water Resources Act* addresses discharges to water.[22]

Through the approvals process, each of the relevant environmental ministries seeks to ensure compliance with applicable environmental legislation, regulation, policies, and guidelines. "At least in theory," one experienced commentator has explained, "the system is intended to ensure that activities which discharge potential contaminants into the air, water or onto the land, are subject to technical scrutiny to ensure that pollution controls are utilized and contamination of the environment minimized."[23] It must be emphasized, however, that to a considerable degree it is the terms and conditions attached to individual approvals which establish the detailed legal requirements for operations. And it is also noteworthy that environmental regulations are not always uniformly applicable in any given jurisdiction. For example, long-established enterprises continuing historic operations that predate the introduction of regulatory standards and approval requirements may be exempt from the regulatory regime on the basis of acquired rights,

---

21   *Environmental Protection Act*, R.S.O. 1990, c. E.19, s. 9 [*OEPA*].

22   R.S.O. 1990, c. O.40. See *Environmental Quality Act*, R.S.Q. c. Q-2, s. 22 [*EQA*].

23   R.M. Fishlock, "Orders and Approvals of the Ontario Ministry of the Environment" (Paper presented to Canadian Bar Association – Ontario, 1991 Institute of Continuing Legal Education, *Environmental Law: An Environmental Primer*, 19 January 1991).

while new applicants are automatically expected to perform according to higher contemporary standards.[24]

The details of the licensing processes vary depending upon the circumstances. But applications accompanied by supporting documentation will generally proceed through stages of technical review leading to a draft approval or certificate accompanied by a series of conditions. Conditions attached to approvals may deal with various aspects of the applicant's site and operations. Some will address administrative considerations such as entry and inspection, the disclosure of information, reporting, and monitoring. Operating standards detailing authorized emission levels will be set and may be accompanied by a description of actions to be taken in the event that they are exceeded.

The scope of matters to be addressed in conditions accompanying an approval is established initially by legislation or regulation. A permit under British Columbia's *Environmental Management Act* illustrates how the authorization process may be used to impose specific operational requirements on applicants:

> A director may issue a permit authorizing the introduction of waste into the environment subject to requirements for the protection of the environment that the director considers advisable and, without limiting that power, may do one or more of the following in the permit:
>
> (a) require the permittee to repair, alter, remove, improve or add to works or to construct new works and to submit plans and specifications for works specified in the permit;
>
> (b) require the permittee to give security in the amount and form and subject to conditions the director specifies;
>
> (c) require the permittee to monitor, in the manner specified by the director, the waste, the method of handling, treating, transporting, discharging and storing the waste and the places and things that the director considers will be affected by the discharge of the waste or the handling, treatment, transportation or storage of the waste;
>
> (d) require the permittee to conduct studies and to report information specified by the director in the manner specified by the director;
>
> (e) specify procedures for monitoring and analysis, and procedures or requirements respecting the handling, treatment, transportation, discharge or storage of waste that the permittee must fulfill;
>
> (f) require the permittee to recycle certain wastes, and to recover certain reusable resources, including energy potential from wastes.[25]

---

24   *Lafarge Canada v. Quebec (Procureur-général)*, [1994] J.Q. no 591 (C.A.).

25   *Environmental Management Act*, S.B.C. 2003. c. 53, s. 14(1) [BCEMA].

Statutory authority to require financial assurances in connection with approvals is also common.[26] The assurances may take a variety of forms including cash, letters of credit, or an approved bond. They are intended to relate to specified action in connection with works including "measures appropriate to prevent adverse effects upon and following the cessation or closing of the works."[27] Requirements for pollution-liability insurance coverage may sometimes be included,[28] together with other financial terms.[29]

As is commonly the case, Alberta's *EPEA* appears to rely heavily on regulations to establish the range of issues that may be expected in an approval.[30] However, extensive authority is regularly conferred on the senior official responsible for decisions about approvals. Thus, the Alberta legislation, in addition to providing for regulations respecting terms and conditions, indicates that the director "may issue an approval subject to any terms and conditions the director considers appropriate" while explicitly stating that such terms and conditions "may be more stringent, but may not be less stringent, than applicable terms and conditions provided for in the regulations."[31] The director or manager as the case may be clearly enjoys a substantial grant of discretionary power concerning the issuance of certificates of approval and also in regard to the alteration, revocation, or suspension of such certificates.[32]

The existence of discretion in the environmental regulatory-approvals process is sometimes regarded critically. Some commentators have identified the scope of discretion as potentially problematic for companies attempting to negotiate a suitable response where pollution has occurred, while others consider that the absence of legislative precision facilitates corporate evasion of desirable environmental norms.[33]

---

26   *OEPA*, above note 21, Part XII. Details on the administration of the financial assurances provisions may be found in *Guidelines for Financial Assurance: (Part X-A), Ontario Environmental Protection Act* prepared by the Policy and Planning Branch of the Ontario Ministry of the Environment in February 1988 and now revised.

27   *OEPA*, *ibid.*, s. 132(1)(c).

28   Environmental liability coverage has rarely been required by the Ontario's MOE as a condition of an approval. M.D. Faieta, "Liability Insurance for Environmental Contamination in Ontario" (1991) 2 C.I.L.R. 125 at 127.

29   See also *Environmental Protection and Enhancement Act*, R.S.A. 2000, c. E-12 [*AEPEA*].

30   *AEPEA*, *ibid.*, s. 85(1)(a) and 86(1)(a).

31   *Ibid.*, s. 68 (2) & (3).

32   *OEPA*, above note 21, s. 9(4) & (5).

33   H. Poch, *Corporate and Municipal Environmental Law* (Toronto: Carswell, 1989) at 161. The tendency to use individualized negotiations involving a significant measure of official discretion in the approvals process has also been described

Yet there are reasons for maintaining discretion and for the bargaining and negotiation that accompany its exercise. Such reasons derive from the uncertainties that pervade environmental issues:

> [T]he fisheries officials who drafted legislation that prohibited putting slash, stumps or other debris into water frequented by fish knew very well that this prohibition could not be automatically enforced. To do so would be scientifically and technically unreasonable and politically unacceptable. The difficulties are that it is unclear in what circumstances such debris is harmful to fish (though in some cases it is clearly harmful), it is unclear what alternate technologies are available for avoiding the putting of debris in water if logging and land clearing are to be permitted, and it is impossible to determine if the harm to fish will outweigh the social benefits derived from the logging or clearing land.[34]

Situations of this kind require individualized decision making within the overall legal framework.

With regard to certain substances and industrial processes, sufficient information has become available since the foregoing observations were made to move towards more clearly formulated controls, but for vast numbers of substances and industrial uses, the description has continuing validity.

Applicants have often experienced frustrating delays in the approvals process. Some of the delays may be attributed to deficiencies contained in applications and thus might have been avoided by more careful advance preparation on the part of the applicant. However, when a substantial backlog developed in one province, environmental officials acknowledged the existence of inherent delays in the process which have "at times, compromised the competitiveness of businesses."[35] The desire to reduce administrative complexity and delays has prompted recent legislative measures to standardize or eliminate the need for certain forms of approvals. Thus, Ontario took steps to streamline certain approvals and to exempt other activities from ordinary approvals requirements. The activities eligible for one or other of these forms of

---

as one of the major recent trends in Quebec's environmental regime. See L. Giroux, "L'approche legislative: Ses tendances et ses limites selon l'expérience du Québec" (1992) 2 J. Envtl. L. & Prac. 55.

34   A.R. Thompson, *Environmental Regulation in Canada: An Assessment of the Regulatory Process* (Vancouver: Westwater Research Centre, University of British Columbia, 1980) at 35–36.

35   F. Carnerie, *The Approval Process: A Regulatory Regime in Transition* (Toronto: Canadian Institute of Environmental Policy, 1992) at 15.

treatment are activities whose environmental impact is considered to be "predictable and controllable" so long as they are conducted in a manner that is consistent with rules to be set out in regulations (the "permit by rule" model).[36] The attraction of such streamlining where impact is properly classified as "predictable and controllable" or exemptions for activities whose impacts are deemed insignificant should be set against the loss of flexibility in tailoring licence approvals to distinctive local circumstances, and against the risk of cumulative impacts.[37]

C. APPEAL MECHANISMS AND PUBLIC PARTICIPATION

Decisions with respect to approvals and licences may ordinarily be appealed by the applicant to a senior environment official or to an administrative body with authority to review and amend the initial determination. The composition of appeal bodies will be set out in statutory provisions together with a statement of the powers and duties of the appellate institution. Time limits on the filing of appeals, or notices of objection as they are sometimes known, will also be specified in legislation or regulations. Basic procedures and such related matters as costs awards will generally be addressed alongside the fundamental issue of the availability of an administrative appeal.[38] In the Quebec case, for example, an unsuccessful applicant for a certificate of authorization under the *Environment Quality Act*[39] is entitled under section 96 of the *EQA* to a process resembling appeal proceedings before the Territory and Environment Division of the Administrative Tribunal of Quebec.

Opportunities for wider public participation in the development of environmental regulations and in decisions concerning permit and

---

36   *Environmental Approvals Improvement Act*, S.O. 1997, c. 7.
37   David McRobert indicates that to the extent some certificate of approval requirements are replaced by standardized approvals there will also be a reduction in opportunities for public participation pursuant to the Environmental Bill of Rights. D. McRobert, "The Nuts, Bolts and Rest of the Machinery: An Update on Ontario's Environmental Bill of Rights and the Work of the Environmental Commissioner" (*Insight Information*, September 2001) 20–22.
38   *AEPEA*, above note 29, Part 4; Alta. Reg. 114/93; *BCEMA*, above note 25, Part 8; *Environment Act*, S.N.S. 1994–95, c. 1, Part XIV; *Clean Environment Act*, R.S.N.B. 1973, c. C-6, s.14; *OEPA*, above note 21, Part XIII; *Canadian Environmental Protection Act, 1999*, S.C. 1999, c. 33, ss. 243–27 [*CEPA, 1999*]. Not all tribunals are authorized to award costs. See *Ontario (Director, Environmental Protection Act) v. Becker Milk Co.* (2005), 78 O.R. (3d) 556 (S.C.J.).
39   *EQA*, above note 22.

licensing approvals have historically been limited.[40] The former case reflects a long-standing assumption about the nature of the legislative process, while the traditional exclusion of the public from deliberations relating to individual permit or licence applications has been premised on the assumption that members of the public are not ordinarily affected by a matter between the applicant and regulatory officials or that public interests, including environmental interests, are adequately represented by such officials.[41]

Recent developments such as environmental bills of rights and specific statutory requirements for public notice and comment have often, though not universally, increased the scope for public participation in both settings. In Saskatchewan, the *Environmental Management and Protection Act* provides that "[e]xcept in circumstances that are considered by the Lieutenant Governor in Council to be an emergency, the minister shall seek advice and provide a reasonable opportunity for the public to be heard respecting any prescribed regulation or any prescribed amendment to a regulation under this Act."[42]

Alberta's *EPEA* also provides opportunities in specified circumstances for persons other than the holder of an approval to participate in appeal proceedings involving decisions of the director, provided that the person is "directly affected by the Director's decision."[43] In *Kostuch v. Alberta Environmental Appeal Board*, an environmental advocate sought standing before the board in connection with a decision of the director to extend a previously approved date of commencement for construction of a cement plant in the vicinity of an area she used for recreational pursuits.[44] The decision of the EAB to deny standing was upheld by the Alberta Court of Queen's Bench, following the reasoning of the Court of Appeal in relation to similar language in another statute. The Court of Appeal had stated: "When considered in the context of the regulatory scheme, it is apparent that the right of appeal is con-

---

40 For background, see J.F. Castrilli & C.C. Lax, "Environmental Regulation-Making in Canada: Towards a More Open Process" in J. Swaigen, ed., *Environmental Rights in Canada* (Toronto: Butterworths, 1981) 334. *Pim v. Ontario (Minister of the Environment)* (1978), 23 O.R. (2d) 45 (Div. Ct.).

41 *Sierra Club of Western Canada v. British Columbia* (1984), 11 Admin. L.R. 276 (B.C.S.C.); *Sea Shepherd Conservation Society v. British Columbia* (1984), 55 B.C.L.R. 260 (S.C.).

42 *Environmental Management and Protection Act, 2002*, S.S. 2002, c. E-10.21, s. 81(3). A similar provision appears in the *Manitoba Environment Act*, C.C.S.M. c. E125, s. 41(2).

43 *AEPEA*, above note 29, s. 91(1).

44 *Kostuch v. Alberta (Environmental Appeal Board)* (1996), 182 A.R. 384 (Q.B.).

fined to persons having a personal rather than a community interest in the matter."[45]

The Alberta Court of Appeal elaborated its approach to the interpretation of "directly affected" in relation to environmental appeals by public interest representatives:

> The use of the modifier "directly" with the word "affected" indicates an intent on the part of the Legislature to distinguish between persons directly affected and indirectly affected. An interpretation that would include any person who has a genuine interest would render the word "directly" meaningless, thus violating fundamental principles of statutory interpretation.[46]

On an exceptional basis, the Ontario *Environmental Bill of Rights, 1993* (OEBR) provides an opportunity for public involvement in appeal proceedings where these are otherwise available in relation to certain designated instruments, including statutory permits and other authorizations. Any person resident in Ontario with an interest in the decision on such instruments may, on a timely basis, seek leave to appeal from the relevant appellate body. While the interest necessary to support a leave application under the *OEBR* is therefore broader than the "directly affected" test, the granting of leave to appeal is subject to a severe two-part test. Leave to appeal should be granted only where, in light of relevant law and policy, there is good reason to believe that the decision was unreasonable and where it appears that significant environmental harm could result from that decision.[47]

In *Re Residents Against Co. Pollution Inc.*, numerous applications were made under the *OEBR* for leave to appeal air-emissions and sewage-works approvals issued to Petro Canada in connection with the proposed expansion of the company's Mississauga refinery.[48] Applicants argued variously that the director's decision had not been based on a holistic, ecosystem approach; that guidelines respecting the separation of residential and industrial land had not been followed; that source

45   *C.U.P.E. Local 30 v. WMI Waste Management of Canada Inc.* (1996), 34 Admin. L.R. (2d) 172 at 178 (Alta. C.A.).

46   *Friends of the Athabasca Environmental Assn. v. Alberta (Public Health Advisory & Appeal Board)* (1996), 181 A.R. 81 at 84 (C.A.).

47   *Environmental Bill of Rights, 1993*, S.O. 1993, c. 28, ss. 38 and 41.

48   (1996), 20 C.E.L.R. (N.S.) 97 (O.E.A.B.). See also *Federation of Ontario Naturalists v. Ontario (Director, Ministry of the Environment)* (1999), 32 C.E.L.R. (N.S.) 92 (O.E.A.B.); *Friends of the Jock River v Ontario (Director, Ministry of the Environment)* (2002), 44 C.E.L.R. (N.S.) 69 (O.E.R.T.); *Simpson v. Ontario (Director, Ministry of the Environment)* (2005), 18 C.E.L.R. (3d) 123 (O.E.R.T.).

and ambient air-quality testing were ignored in favour of modelling estimates, and so on, all of which factors were presented as evidence of unreasonableness. In the view of the appeal board, these considerations failed to satisfy the first element of the test for granting leave to appeal. However, the board did accept that procedural irregularities, lack of public notice, and a condition of the air approval concerning the retention of records were such that no director, acting reasonably, would have decided as the director did in this case. In turning to the second test of significant harm to the environment, the EAB (now the Environmental Review Tribunal) ruled that the possibility of such harm (in this case associated with SO_2 concentrations in an apartment building) was sufficient. The board accordingly granted leave to appeal in relation to the issues of record retention and the sulphur-dioxide risk.

In *Dawber*, another comparatively rare example of a successful application for leave to appeal under the *OEBR*, the Environment Review Tribunal agreed that principles such as ecosystem protection, precaution and public participation found in the ministry's policy Statement of Environmental Values could be relevant to the determination of unreasonableness even where regulatory standards had been met:

> The Tribunal does not agree that approval of a CofA based upon compliance with numerical standards in regulations is automatically or necessarily a reasonable decision if reliance upon those standards results in a failure to observe provisions in other laws and policies also applicable to the decision.[49]

In reaching this conclusion, the tribunal carefully analysed the scope and limitations of its own authority:

> The . . . laws and policies that apply to the Directors' decisions are not themselves the subject of the test . . . and the Tribunal is not seized with the task of assessing the reasonableness or adequacy of their content, at least not directly. The Tribunal does not have the mandate to require changes to those laws and policies or to impose upon the Directors a duty to achieve a higher standard of environmental protection than those laws and policies require. Instead, the reasonableness of the Directors' decisions must be assessed in the context of the legal regime within which they occur . . . . However, it is appropriate

---

49 *Dawber v. Director (Ministry of the Environment)*, [2007] O.E.R.T.D. No. 25 at para. 31.

to inquire whether and to what extent the Directors' decisions considered, incorporated and reflected relevant law and policies.[50]

Even in the absence of appeal mechanisms, interested individuals and public interest groups may be entitled to seek judicial review of the decision maker's exercise of its statutory powers in relation to licensing approvals and also in connection with administrative orders and environmental assessment. Judicial review proceedings permit courts to enquire into the manner in which administrative decisions have been taken with a view to ensuring that procedural requirements have been fulfilled, that the tribunal's conduct has been free of bias as that concept is understood in administrative law, and that no reviewable errors have been made in relation to questions of jurisdiction, law, fact, and discretion. Distinctive administrative law remedies may be available.[51]

Access to judicial review is dependent on the standing of the applicant, that is, on the recognition of the applicant's eligibility to present its concerns before the court. Liberalized rules of standing that developed initially in relation to constitutional claims and later extended to administrative action in the *Finlay* decision[52] have been influential in establishing the concept of public interest standing and thereby facilitating access to the courts. On a discretionary basis, the courts may grant public interest standing to an applicant who is either directly affected or genuinely interested as a citizen in a serious and justiciable issue that would not otherwise be brought to trial in a reasonable and effective manner.[53] Although the Supreme Court of Canada has confirmed that the principles applicable to public interest standing should be interpreted in a liberal and generous manner, there are clear indications that public interest standing cannot be open-ended.[54]

---

50   *Ibid.* at para. 28. In a judicial review challenge to the decision, the Ontario Divisional Court concluded that the Tribunal's decision to grant leave to appeal where the Statement of Environmental Values had not been applied by the Director was a reasonable one. *Lafarge Canada Inc. v. Ontario (Environmental Review Tribunal),* [2008] O.J. No. 2460.

51   On the availability of the entitlement of third party complainants to interlocutory relief where the validity of an environmental approval was in question, see *Calvé v. Gestion Serge Lafrenière inc.,* [1999] J.Q. no 1334 (C.A.).

52   *Finlay v. Canada (Minister of Finance),* [1986] 2 S.C.R. 607.

53   For the application of this test to grant standing in environmental cases, see *Western Canada Wilderness Committee v. British Columbia (Minister of Environment & Parks)* (1988), 2 C.E.L.R. (N.S.) 245; *Reese v. Alberta (Ministry of Forestry, Lands & Wildlife)* (1992), 123 A.R. 241 (Q.B.); *Friends of the Island Inc. v. Canada (Minister of Public Works),* [1993] 2 F.C. 229 (T.D.).

54   *Canadian Council of Churches v. Canada (Minister of Employment & Immigration),* [1992] 1 S.C.R. 236.

In a number of cases, prospective environmental litigants have failed to obtain public interest standing on the grounds that the issues involved were neither constitutional nor truly administrative,[55] or because the applicant had failed to satisfy the tests of being directly affected by or genuinely interested in the alleged wrong.[56] Public interest standing on the *Finlay* principles has also been restricted formally to government action, with one court observing that "[p]ublic interest standing should not be conferred to enable a party to sue a private individual or corporation."[57]

CEPA, 1999 provides for public participation in connection with a wide range of government decision making, including the development of regulations, and the issuance of approvals and orders under the act. Opportunities to file objections or to request the formation of boards of review are consistent with the statutory duty of the government of Canada to "encourage the participation of the people of Canada in the making of decisions that affect the environment."[58] Participation is facilitated in part by the creation in connection with *CEPA, 1999* of an Environmental Registry.[59] Section 13(1) outlines information to be included:

> The Environmental Registry shall contain notices and other documents published or made publicly available by the Minister, and shall also include, subject to the *Access to Information Act* and the *Privacy Act*,
>
> (a) notices of objection and of any approval granted under the Act;
> (b) a copy of every policy and of every proposed regulation or order made under this Act; and
> (c) copies of documents submitted to a court by the Minister relating to any environmental protection action.

---

55 *Hunter v. Saskatchewan* (1994), 122 Sask. R. 161 (Q.B.).

56 *Shiell v. Atomic Energy Control Board* (1995), 17 C.E.L.R. (N.S.) 286 (Fed.T.D.); *Manitoba Naturalists Society Inc. v. Ducks Unlimited Canada* (1991), 79 Man. R. (2d) 15 (Q.B.).

57 *Shiell v. Amok Ltd.* (1987), 58 Sask. R. 141 (Q.B.).

58 *CEPA, 1999*, above note 38, s. 2(1)(e).

59 *Ibid.*, s. 12; online: www.ec.gc.ca/ceparegistry.

FURTHER READINGS

ELGIE, S.A.G., "Environmental Groups and the Courts: 1970–1992" in G. Thompson, M.L. McConnell, & L.B. Huestis, eds., *Environmental Law and Business in Canada* (Aurora, ON: Canada Law Book, 1993) at 185

FRANSON, M.A.H., R.T. FRANSON, & A.R. LUCAS, *Environmental Standards: A Comparative Study of Canadian Standards, Standard Setting Processes and Enforcement* (Edmonton: Environment Council of Alberta, 1982)

HOEY, K., & A.J. ROMAN, "The Regulatory Framework" in G. Thompson, M.L. McConnell, & L.B. Huestis, eds., *Environmental Law and Business in Canada* (Aurora, ON: Canada Law Book, 1993) at 53

LAPLANTE, B., "Environmental Regulation: Performance and Design Standards" in G.B. Doern, ed., *Getting It Green: Case Studies in Canadian Environmental Regulation* (Toronto: C.D. Howe Institute, 1990) at 59

LEVY, A.D., "The Scope of Liability and Exercise of Discretion in Recent Decisions of the Ontario Environmental Appeal Board" (1996) 6 J. Envtl. L. & Prac. 223

THOMPSON, A.R., *Environmental Regulation in Canada: An Assessment of the Regulatory Process* (Vancouver: Westwater Research Centre, University of British Columbia, 1980)

CHAPTER 7

ADMINISTRATIVE COMPLIANCE MECHANISMS

A. COMPLIANCE AND ADMINISTRATIVE ENFORCEMENT

Beyond the underlying framework of environmental standards that a business in any given industry may be expected to meet after the required approvals and authorizations have been obtained, lie questions relating to compliance and eventually to the implications of non-compliance; that is, what levels of compliance are being achieved and what are the consequences of failing to satisfy (or even disregarding) applicable environmental norms? These considerations arise naturally in the environmental context where observers of the legal regime are anxious to ascertain the relationship between formal statutory requirements and actual behaviour.

Alternative strategies for encouraging environmental performance have been actively debated: some commentators advocate a conciliatory approach, while others have promoted a sanctions-based or penal model of enforcement.[1] The discussion has been influenced not only by evidence of the potential effectiveness of these general alternatives in

---

1 K. Hawkins, *Environment and Enforcement: Regulation and the Social Definition of Pollution* (Oxford: Clarendon Press, 1984) is a classic reference work on the general debate. Canadian developments are surveyed in D. Chappell, *From Sawdust to Toxic Blobs: A Consideration of Sanctioning Strategies to Combat Pollution in Canada* (Ottawa: Supply & Services, 1989).

environmental terms, but also by external developments affecting the context in which enforcement efforts are undertaken. The introduction of the *Charter of Rights and Freedoms* with its continually evolving implications for administrative procedures, prosecutorial practices, and penalty regimes, and an appreciation of administrative enforcement costs in periods of fiscal restraint are notable examples of such influences.[2]

The compliance mechanisms considered in this chapter include a range of measures to monitor environmental performance, to issue warnings and administrative orders, and even to impose penalties through an administrative process. Other approaches to compliance such as the prosecution of offences or the use of voluntary agreements are discussed in chapters 8 and 16 respectively.

B. REPORTING OBLIGATIONS

The terms and conditions applicable to operating licences and permits will frequently impose regular reporting obligations that provide officials with information on an ongoing basis concerning the normal operations of approved sites and facilities. Water treatment facilities will be expected to conduct regular testing and report results. The operators of waste disposal sites may be required to report the nature and volume of materials collected by or delivered to them. In addition, statutory reporting obligations are now common in connection with spills and other irregular discharges of contaminants. The *OEPA* requires every person who discharges or causes or permits the discharge of a contaminant "out of the normal course of events" that causes or is likely to cause an adverse effect to notify the ministry forthwith.[3] Specific notification requirements apply in Ontario when a pollutant is spilled, that is, discharged, into the natural environment from or out of a structure, vehicle, or other container in a manner that is abnormal in quality or quantity in light of all the circumstances of the discharge.[4] Reporting obligations may be found in other provincial legislation, especially relating to gasoline and other fuels, and in such federal statutes as the *Fisheries Act*[5] and *CEPA, 1999*. Under the latter there is a statutory requirement to report imposed on some individuals, while the legisla-

---

2   *Canada (Director of Investigation & Research, Combines Investigation Branch) v. Southam Inc.*, [1984] 2 S.C.R. 145; *R. v. Wholesale Travel Group Inc.*, [1991] 3 S.C.R. 154.

3   *Environmental Protection Act*, R.S.O. 1990, c. E.19, s. 15 [*OEPA*].

4   *Ibid.*, s. 92.

5   R.S.C. 1985, c. F-14, s. 38(4) [*FA*].

tion permits others to report both releases and likely releases of toxic substances.[6]

A legal issue of considerable sensitivity is possible prosecutorial use of information provided by those subject to regulatory reporting requirements on the grounds that it may violate the principle against self-incrimination and therefore be inconsistent with fundamental justice under the *Charter*. As expressed by Chief Justice Lamer: "Any state action that coerces an individual to furnish evidence against him- or herself in a proceeding in which the individual and the state are adversaries violates the principle against self-incrimination. Coercion, it should be noted, means the denial of free and informed consent."[7]

In *R. v. Fitzpatrick*, the Supreme Court of Canada considered the principle in the context of charges of catching and retaining fish in excess of a fixed quota brought against a British Columbia fisherman where the only evidence presented by the prosecution was a "hail report" and a "daily fishing log." The accused had been required by section 61 of the *Fisheries Act* to provide these reports to authorities. Justice La Forest, writing for the Court, concluded that the principle against self-incrimination was not offended by the use of the reports for prosecutorial purposes. In the context of a regulated industry, the fisherman and the state were not in an adversarial relationship, nor were the reports obtained through coercion since the accused, having chosen to participate in a licensed industry, could be presumed to know of and to have accepted the conditions under which the information was made available to fisheries officers.[8]

Further insights into the relationship between the principle against self-incrimination and regulatory reporting requirements emerge from subsequent decisions. As Justice Iacobucci remarked in *White*:[9]

> The residual protections provided by the principle against self-incrimination as contained in s. 7 are specific, and contextually-sensitive . . . . The principle against self-incrimination demands different things at different times, with the task in every case being to determine exactly what the principle demands, if anything, within the particular context at issue.

In *Jarvis*,[10] the Court explained that the context may be determined by the "predominant purpose" of the reporting. In the absence of an "adver-

---

6 *Canadian Environmental Protection Act, 1999*, S.C. 1999, c. 33, ss. 95–96 [*CEPA, 1999*].
7 *R. v. Jones*, [1994] 2 S.C.R. 229 at 249.
8 *R. v. Fitzpatrick* (1996), 18 C.E.L.R. (N.S.) 237 (S.C.C.).
9 *R. v. White*, [1999] 2 S.C.R. 417 at para. 45.
10 *R. v. Jarvis*, [2002] 3 S.C.R. 757.

sarial relationship" in the context of regulatory reporting, no violation of the principle against self-incrimination, and thus of section 7 of the *Charter*, would arise from subsequent prosecutorial use of the information.

C. INSPECTIONS

Inspections are an additional mechanism available to administrative officials seeking information on the compliance status of businesses that are operating within the framework of an environmental permit and regulatory system. The terms and conditions of licences will frequently contain provisions concerning ongoing inspections of operations. However, environmental legislation itself regularly provides for inspections by designated officials who are authorized to "enter and inspect" certain premises in connection with the administration of the environmental regime, or, as it is expressed in *CEPA, 1999*, for the purpose of ensuring compliance with the Act and regulations.[11]

Routine administrative inspections may be conducted for a number of purposes other than investigation of possible statutory violations with a view to prosecution. Inspections may be undertaken

- to locate and identify pollution;
- to confirm compliance with statutes, regulations, certificates of approval, or administrative orders;
- to identify, contain, clean up, and prevent future repetitions of incidents such as emissions or spills;
- to examine opportunities to reduce pollution or for preventive and corrective action;
- to discuss and attempt to resolve neighbourhood complaints about pollution;
- to determine whether proposed construction or alterations should be approved; and
- to ensure that pollution control equipment has been constructed as applied for and approved.[12]

---

11   *CEPA, 1999*, above note 6, s. 218(1). See also *OEPA*, above note 3, s. 165, S.O. 1998, c.35, s. 25; *Ontario Water Resources Act*, R.S.O. 1990, c. O.40, s. 24, S.O. 1998, c. 35, s. 29; *Pesticides Act*, R.S.O. 1990, c. P.11, S.O. 1998, c. 35, s. 26, *Environmental Management Act*, S.B.C. 2003, c. 53; *Environmental Protection and Enhancement Act*, R.S.A. 2000, c. E-12, s. 26; *Environment Act*, S.N.S. 1994–95, c. 1, s. 119(1); *Environment Act*, S.M. 1987–88, c. 26, s. 20; *Saskatchewan Environmental Management and Protection Act, 2002*, S.S. 2002, c. E-10.21, s. 2.3(2) [EMPA].

12   D. Saxe, *Inspections and Searches in the Environmental Context* (Toronto: Environment Ontario, 1987).

Statutory powers of inspection typically authorize inspectors or abatement officials at any reasonable time to enter non-residential premises to determine whether environmental contaminants have caused or threaten to cause adverse effects, or to enter such premises in the reasonable belief that waste will be found there. Premises in or from which the official reasonably believes a contaminant is or may be released into the environment are also subject to inspection, as are places that are or should be subject to an environmental licence, permit, or approval. Other locations which, in the reasonable belief of the inspector, are likely to contain documentation relating to regulated or approved activities may also be entered without warrant pursuant to the inspection power.[13]

Having entered the premises, officials may undertake a range of activities in furtherance of the inspection. Depending on the legislative particulars in each jurisdiction, they may, for example, take photographs or audiovisual recordings, operate equipment or machinery; conduct tests and take samples, or make reasonable oral or written inquiries.[14]

In the context of constitutionally protected interests in privacy, extensive authority of this nature is controversial. It is justified, however, in relation to administrative objectives that can perhaps be achieved only through inspection. As expressed by La Forest J. in *Thomson Newspapers*, the citizen's expectations of privacy vary depending on the activity in which he or she is engaged, and it is generally accepted that regulation serves, at least in part, to maintain compatibility between individual self-interest and the collective goals or aspirations of the community. Inspection provides one mechanism for ensuring that balance:

> In many cases, this regulation must necessarily involve the inspection of private premises or documents by agents of the state. The restaurateur's compliance with public health regulations, the employer's compliance with employment standards and safety legislation, and the developer's or homeowner's compliance with building codes or zoning regulations, can only be tested by inspection, and perhaps

13 *OEPA*, above note 3, s. 156 (1)(d); *Environment Act*, S.N.S. 1994–95, c. 1, ss. 119(1)(a)–(e) [*NSEA*]; *Environmental Protection and Enhancement Act*, R.S.A. 2000, c. E-12 [*AEPEA*]; *EMPA*, above note 11, s. 2.3(2)(c); *CEPA, 1999*, above note 6, s. 218; *FA*, above note 5, ss. 38(3)–(3.5).

14 *OEPA*, *ibid.*, ss. 156(1)(n)–(t); *AEPEA*, *ibid.*, s.188(5). The powers of provincial officers under the *OEPA*, the *Ontario Water Resources Act*, and the *Pesticides Act* were substantially enhanced by the *Environmental Statute Law Amendment Act*, S.O. 1998, c.35; *EMPA*, *ibid.*, s. 2.3(9).

unannounced inspection, of their premises. Similarly, compliance with minimum wage, employment equity and human rights legislation can often only be assessed by inspection of the employer's files and records.[15]

Even if the validity of inspection functions has been acknowledged in this way, the uncertain boundary between inspection for regulatory purposes and investigations associated with the anticipated use of prosecutorial powers remains extremely sensitive.[16]

Noting in a comprehensive introdution to the *CEPA, 1999* that inspections and investigations are clearly distinguished within the legislation, Meinhard Doelle explains the purpose and use of the former:

> Inspections are carried out to verify compliance with the CEPA . . . . Inspections are generally authorized as a condition for permitting the use of a given substance under conditions set out in regulations. Under section 218, inspections may be carried out at any reasonable time as long as the enforcement officer has reasonable ground to believe that the place to be inspected contains a substance to which the CEPA applies. Dwelling places can only be entered with a search warrant or the consent of the occupant. The CEPA provides for search warrants for inspections in cases where access is refused. It is important to note that such refusal may lead to prosecution itself, turning an inspection into an investigation. According to the compliance policy, inspections will be carried out according to a program of inspections complemented by spot checks. In addition to general compliance, inspections may be carried out as follow-up to warnings, directions, Ministerial orders, environmental compliance orders, injunctions, environmental alternative measures, and court orders that require further action by an offender. Decisions about inspections may also be influenced by information provided by members of the public, whistle blowers, and by alterations made at facilities subject to control under the CEPA.[17]

Some jurisdictions have resorted to publicity concerning the compliance status of licensed and approved operations on the assumption that the knowledge of shareholders, consumers, financial associates, or the public generally will spur business officials to remedy deficien-

---

15   *Thomson Newspapers Ltd. v. Canada (Director of Investigation & Research)*, [1990] 1 S.C.R. 425 at 507, La Forest J.

16   *R. v. Inco Ltd.* (2001), 54 O.R. (3d) 495 (C.A.). This case is discussed in chapter 8.

17   Meinhard Doelle, *Canadian Environmental Protection Act & Commentary: 2005/2006* (Markham, ON: LexisNexis Butterworths, 2005) 42–43.

cies. British Columbia's environment department historically released a *Noncompliance Report* which identified those operations found to be out of compliance with waste-management permits and provincial environmental regulations during the relevant period. Indications of repeated non-compliance by permit holders also increase the accountability of public authorities who are more likely to be called on to defend their enforcement record, particularly in periods of financial retrenchment when resources to finance enforcement must be carefully allocated.[18]

D. ADMINISTRATIVE ORDERS

Authority to issue administrative orders promoting compliance with environmental legislation is common across Canada. Such orders may operate to control sources of existing pollution, to terminate specified activities, or to impose preventive or remedial obligations. Administrative compliance powers of this nature are customarily conferred upon senior officials, including the minister of an environment department, to be exercised in statutorily prescribed circumstances. The validity or legality of these instruments thus demands that they be used only in a manner that conforms to their legislative origins. As a matter of practice, apart from emergency situations, administrative orders are generally resorted to after discussion and consultation have failed to resolve an environmental situation.

The Supreme Court of Canada recently considered the use of an administrative order issued against a Quebec company whose property was contaminated.[19] The specific authority under which the order had been issued reads in part:

> Where the Minister believes on reasonable grounds that a contaminant is present in the environment in a greater quantity or concentration than that established by regulation . . . he may order whoever had emitted, deposited, released or discharged . . . all or some of the contaminant to furnish him with an environmental character-

---

18 Following the 2001 B.C. provincial election, the name of the ministry was changed to the Ministry of Water, Land, and Air Protection. Now see online: www.env.gov.bc.ca/main/prgs/compliancereport.html. Compliance reports for Ontario may be found online: www.ene.gov.on.ca/envision/compliance/compliance.htm; for Alberta, online: www3.gov.ab.ca/env/protenf/compliance/reports/index.html; and for Quebec, online: www.mddep.gouv.qc.ca/Infuseur/mois_condamnations.asp.

19 *Imperial Oil v. Quebec*, [2003] 2 S.C.R. 624 [*Imperial Oil*].

ization study, a programme of decontamination or restoration of the environment describing the work proposed for the decontamination or restoration of the environment and a timetable for the execution of the work.[20]

When the company against whom an administrative order had been issued pursuant to this provision challenged it, the court noted frankly: "As discretionary and broad as the power to make orders appears to be, nonetheless important procedural requirements circumscribe it." Following a detailed review of the specific requirements applicable in the circumstances of the case, LeBel J. provided valuable general insights into the nature of administrative authority in the environmental context:

> When the Minister has to make a specific decision concerning someone subject to the law, he must comply with precise procedural obligations .... Generally speaking, those obligations require that he give notice to the person concerned, receive and review the representations and information submitted by that person and give reasons to that person for his decision. The effect of this procedural framework is that the Minister must carefully and attentively examine the observations submitted to him. However, that obligation is not equivalent to the impartiality that is required of a judge or an administrative decision-maker whose primary function is adjudication. In performing his functions, the Minister is involved in the management of an environmental protection system. He must make decisions in a context in which the need for the long-term management of environmental problems plays a prominent role, and in which he must ensure that the fundamental legislative policy on which the interpretation and application of environment quality legislation are based is implemented. The Minister has the responsibility of protecting the public interest in the environment, and must make his decisions in consideration of that interest.[21]

Insofar as failure to comply with administrative orders constitutes an offence, a party wishing to challenge such orders should generally do so directly by means of judicial review as was done in *Imperial Oil*, or on the basis of a statutory right of appeal where available. An alternative way to challenge an administrative order in the context of enforcement proceedings is known as *collateral attack*, but such an approach is contentious and potentially problematic.[22] In *R. v. Consoli-*

---

20   *Environment Quality Act*, R.S.Q. c. Q-2, s. 31.42.

21   *Imperial Oil*, above note 19 at para. 34.

22   *R. v. Consolidated Maybrun Mines Ltd.*, [1998] 1 S.C.R. 706.

dated *Maybrun Mines Ltd.*, the accused ignored an environmental order concerning PCB containment measures at an abandoned mine site until charged with failing to comply. Elements of the defence included an attack on the original justification for the order and on its reasonableness, prompting the court to distinguish between a challenge that the decision maker lacked jurisdiction to make the order from the outset and a challenge to the effect that otherwise lawful jurisdiction had been exercised without reasonable grounds. Only the former challenge could be pursued on the basis of collateral attack. General observations by the S.C.C. emphasize the status of administrative orders in the environmental context in relation to the rights of those to whom such orders are directed:

> It is clear from a review of the Environmental Protection Act that its purpose is not simply to repair damage to the environment resulting from human activity, even if we assume that repairs will always be possible, but primarily to prevent contamination of the province's environment. Such a purpose requires rapid and effective means in order to ensure that any necessary action is taken promptly. This purpose is reflected both in the scope of the powers conferred on the Director and in the establishment of an appeal procedure designed to counterbalance the broad powers conferred on the Director by affording affected individuals an opportunity to present their points of view and assert their rights as quickly as possible.[23]

With reference to several provincial regimes, the following discussion illustrates various circumstances in which administrative orders may be employed.

1) Control Orders

Control orders, as they have generally been known in Ontario, permit statutorily appointed officials to require designated parties to implement measures to control the illegal discharge of a contaminant into the natural environment where that discharge has been established on the basis of a written report. It is a precondition of any control order that a prohibited contaminant has been discharged into the natural environment, or that a discharge contravening section 14 or the regulations is occurring.[24]

---

23   *Ibid.* at para. 59.
24   *OEPA*, above note 3, s. 7. The power was originally conferred on directors, presumptively a small class of senior officials. In practice, the category was extended to facilitate the issuance of orders. The 1998 *Environmental Statute Law*

Monitoring obligations, equipment installation or replacement, and operational procedures are among the types of measures typically included in such orders.[25] Orders of this nature may be directed to the owner or previous owner of the source of the contaminant, to a person who was or is in occupation of the source of contaminant, or to a person who has or had "charge management or control" of the source of contaminant.[26] The designated recipient of a control order is entitled to fifteen days' notice, accompanied by the director's reasons for proposing the order and by the report on which it is based.[27] The person to whom the order is directed may thereupon make submissions to the director or may appeal to Ontario's Environmental Review Tribunal.[28]

The appeal will not automatically trigger a stay of the Ontario order. Instead, the appeal board has discretion on the application of a party to stay the order, but it may not do so in cases where a stay would produce danger to the health or safety of any person, impairment or serious risk of impairment of the quality of the natural environment, or injury or damage or serious risk of injury or damage to any property or to plant or animal life.[29]

In Alberta, comparable authority to issue what is known as an enforcement order is available to the provincial director, based on the director's opinion that a contravention of the *Environmental Protection and Enhancement Act* has occurred.[30]

2) Stop Orders

Although a control order may be used for the purpose of stopping the discharge of a contaminant into the natural environment,[31] an alternative exists in the form of a stop order. Such orders, also written and accompanied by reasons, require immediate compliance on the part of

---

Amendment Act provided some clarification of the statutory basis upon which abatement officers might issue field orders. The anticipated implementation of further amendments suggests restriction of the availability of control orders to situations involving "adverse effects." See S.O. 2005, c. 12, s. 1(4).

25 *OEPA, ibid.,* s. 124.

26 *Ibid.,* s. 7.

27 *Ibid.,* s. 127.

28 *Ibid.,* ss. 127, 140, and 143. In the exercise of this authority, the Environmental Review Tribunal is the successor to the Environmental Appeal Board.

29 *Ibid.,* s. 143.

30 *AEPEA,* above note 13, ss. 200 and 102; see also *NSEA,* above note 13, s. 125; *EMPA,* above note 11, s. 4; *Environment Act,* C.C.S.M. c. E125, s. 24.

31 *OEPA,* above note 3, s. 124 (1)(b); see also *NSEA, ibid.,* s. 126.

the person to whom they are served.[32] Yet the preconditions of a stop order are more restrictive than those of a control order, and for this reason, stop orders have been used comparatively infrequently. Before issuing a stop order the director must—on reasonable and probable grounds—be of the opinion that an existing discharge of contaminant is occurring in such a way that it constitutes an immediate danger to human life, health, or property.[33]

3) Preventive Orders

In the absence of statutory contraventions, but in anticipation of pollution, administrative orders may also be used to prevent or minimize environmental damage.[34] Orders of a preventive nature require reasonable and probable grounds[35] and are typically subject to appeal.[36]

The pollution prevention order under British Columbia's former *Waste Management Act* illustrates this type of environmental protection authority.[37] Where a manager was satisfied on reasonable grounds that the manner in which an activity was carried out was such that the release of a substance would likely cause pollution of the environment, the manager had authority to order any of the following to be done at the expense of the person to whom the order was directed:

a) provide to the manager information the manager requests relating to the activity, operation, or substance;
b) undertake investigations, tests, surveys, or any other action the manager considers necessary to prevent the pollution and to report the results to the manager;
c) acquire, construct, or carry out any works or measures that are reasonably necessary to prevent the pollution;

---

32 *OEPA, ibid.*, ss. 8 and 129.
33 *Canada Metal Co. v. MacFarlane* (1973), 1 O.R. (2d) 577 (H.C.J.). For recent consideration by the Ontario Environmental Review Tribunal of an order in the nature of a stop order, see *Echo Bay Milling Ltd. v. Ontario (Director, Ministry of the Environment)* 2003 CarswellOnt 4335 (E.R.T.).
34 *OEPA*, above note 3, s. 18, as amended by S.O. 2005, c. 12, ss. 1(8) & (9); *AEPEA*, above note 13, ss. 102 & 103.
35 See *R. v. Consolidated Maybrun Mines Ltd.* (1992), 9 C.E.L.R. (N.S.) 34 (Ont. Prov. Div.), rev'd in part (1993), 12 C.E.L.R. (N.S.) 171 (Ont. Gen. Div.) [*Maybrun*].
36 *OEPA*, above note 3, s. 140; *AEPEA*, above note 13, s. 84. Nova Scotia's authority in connection with an emergency situation appears to have comparable applicability: *NSEA*, above note 13, s. 128.
37 *Waste Management Act*, R.S.B.C. 1996, c. 482 repealed by the *Environmental Management Act*, S.B.C. 2003, c. 53, s. 174, effective 8 July 2004.

d) adjust, repair, or alter any works to the extent reasonably necessary to prevent the pollution.

One or more of the following could have been served with an order of this kind, although the manager's powers could not be exercised in relation to any aspect of an activity or operation that was in compliance with existing regulations and approvals:

a) a person who previously had or or had at the time possession, charge, or control of the substance;
b) a person who previously did anything or who was at the time doing anything that could have caused the release of the substance;
c) a person who previously owned or occupied or at the time owned or occupied the land on which the substance was located.

The nature of these orders is such that courts will construe statutory powers to impose preventive measures strictly. As explained in relation to the *OEPA*, "it authorizes state intervention into the activity of a person on his own land before any offence has been committed, and without providing any offsetting protection or benefit by compliance." In other words, the director may "intrude with his own view of risk management while leaving the person with full responsibility for the risk."[38]

4) Remedial Orders

Remedial orders are now also commonly in place to require cleanup and restoration measures.[39] In light of the tendency to associate their use with emergency situations where delay entails the risk of continuing environmental damages, cleanup orders are not always subject to pre-compliance appeal or judicial review.[40] Where water supplies have suffered or are at risk remedial obligations may include the provision of alternative supplies.

5) Environmental Protection Orders under *CEPA, 1999*

At the federal level, *CEPA, 1999* provides for Environmental Protection Compliance Orders (EPCOs) that are roughly equivalent to the types of administrative order available under provincial legislation. These orders

---

38   *Maybrun*, above note 35 at 41 (Ont. Prov. Div.).
39   *AEPEA*, above note 13, s. 102(3)(e); *OEPA*, above note 3, s. 17; *Contaminated Sites Remediation Act*, C.C.S.M. c. C205, s. 17.
40   *OEPA, ibid.*, s. 122.

are confined in their application to circumstances in which enforcement officers reasonably believe that contraventions of the Act have occurred or will occur in relation to a range of designated activities largely related to substances governed by the Act.[41] Orders "reasonable in the circumstances and consistent with the protection of the environment and public safety" may require that measures be taken to:

- refrain from doing anything in contravention of CEPA, 1999 or the regulations, or do anything to comply with the Act or regulations;
- stop or shut down any activity, work, undertaking, or thing for a specified period;
- cease the operation of any activity or any part of a work, undertaking or thing until the enforcement officer is satisfied that the compliance will be achieved.

EPCOs may be directed to any person who causes or contributes to the alleged contravention or who owns or has the charge, management, or control of the substance or any product containing the substance to which the alleged contravention relates or the property on which the substance or product is located.[42]

6) Fairness and the Allocation of Liability for Administrative Orders

Simply by way of introduction to a subject that is more fully discussed in Chapter 11 in connection with contaminated lands, it is useful to note the existence of debate over the allocation of liability for compliance amongst a range of potentially responsible parties. Pursuant to the various statutory schemes, it is possible that directions may be issued to people to remedy pollution that originated prior to the passage of the legislation authorizing the orders or directed at those who were not directly responsible for the environmental damage to which they may be required to respond.[43] Legislation may be used to clarify the manner in which departmental officials should exercise their discretion in addressing orders in these circumstances. Alberta, for example, has enumerated factors that are to be given consideration by the director in deciding to issue an environmental protection order to a person responsible for a contaminated site:

---

41   CEPA, 1999, above note 6, ss. 234–71.
42   Canada v. IPSCO Recycling Inc., [2003] F.C.J. No. 1950 at paras. 84–86 (Fed. Ct.).
43   British Columbia Hydro and Power Authority v. British Columbia (Environmental Appeal Board), [2005] S.C.J. No. 2.

(a) when the substance became present in, on, or under the site;
(b) in the case of an owner or previous owner of the site,
    (i) whether the substance was present in, on, or under the site at the time that person became an owner;
    (ii) whether the person knew or ought reasonably to have known that the substance was present in, on, or under the site at the time that person became an owner;
    (iii) whether the presence of the substance in, on, or under the site ought to have been discovered by the owner had the owner exercised due diligence in ascertaining the presence of the substance before he became an owner, and whether the owner exercised such due diligence;
    (iv) whether the presence of the substance in, on, or under the site was caused solely by the act or omission of an independent third party;
    (v) the price the owner paid for the site and the relationship between that price and the fair market value of the site had the substance not been present in, on, or under it;
(c) in the case of a previous owner, whether that owner disposed of his interest in the site without disclosing the presence of the substance in, on, or under the site to the person who acquired the interest;
(d) whether the person took all reasonable care to prevent the presence of the substance in, on, or under the site;
(e) whether a person dealing with the substance followed accepted industry standards and practice in effect at the time or complied with the requirements of applicable enactments in effect at the time;
(f) whether the person contributed to further accumulation or the continued release of the substance on becoming aware of the presence of the substance in, on, or under the site;
(g) what steps the person took to deal with the site on becoming aware of the presence of the substance in, on, or under the site;
(h) any other criteria the Director considers to be relevant.[44]

A task force report prepared for the Canadian Council of Ministers of the Environment on factors relevant to the allocation of liability for contaminated sites subsequently proposed a very similar series of considerations for adoption in other jurisdictions.[45]

---

44   *AEPEA*, above note 13, s. 114(2).
45   Canadian Council of Ministers of the Environment, Core Group on Contaminated Site Liability, *Contaminated Site Liability Report: Recommended Principles for*

Even in the absence of legislative guidance, decision makers have addressed the problem of apportioning responsibility for environmental costs under administrative regimes. In *Re 724597 Ontario Ltd.*, more familiarly known as *Appletex*, the Ontario Environmental Appeal Board examined the question of allocating cleanup, waste removal, and decommissioning costs under a director's order aimed at the environmental problems associated with an abandoned wool knitting and dyeing mill.[46] The order, issued in 1993, was directed at the company itself, its president, and two investors whose involvement dated from 1989 as part of an initiative to restore the bankrupt operation. Noting the possibility of "a high degree of unpredictability and potential unfairness"[47] in the manner in which director's orders under the *EPA* might be issued, the board sought guidance in the CCME principles. These, it concluded, require decision makers to examine the particular circumstances of each case rather than adopting a "deep pockets" solution. Ultimately, following a review of the application of the CCME principles to the *Appletex* situation, the EAB amended the director's order in relation to several of the parties, largely revoking the liability of one of the individuals.[48]

The introduction of "fairness" and "equity" to decisions on the allocation of liability under administrative orders remains controversial from several perspectives. Observers question, for example, the evidentiary, procedural, and administrative cost implications of a shift towards fault-based determinations. In addition, the long-term effect of the CCME principles on the number of orphaned or abandoned sites and on the quality of cleanup measures appears to be uncertain.[49] Nevertheless, courts have acknowledged that it is legitimate for decision makers to take account of the fairness factors:

> First, the Tribunal determines the issue of jurisdiction, which is whether or not an order can be made against a party. If it determines that it has jurisdiction to make an order, the next stage is to determine whether it should make an order. In exercising its discretion, the Tribunal is entitled to consider issues of fairness.[50]

---

a Consistent Approach across Canada (23 March 1993).

46   *Re 724597 Ontario Ltd.* (1994), 13 C.E.L.R. (N.S.) 257 (O.E.A.B).

47   *Ibid.* at 284.

48   An appeal by the director was dismissed. *Re 724597 Ontario Ltd.* (1995), 18 C.E.L.R. (N.S.) 137 (Ont. Div. Ct.), leave to appeal refused (11 March 1996), (Ont. C.A.) [unreported].

49   J.D. Coop, "Beyond *Appletex*: The Status of 'Fairness' Litigation and the Challenges Posed by the Doctrine of 'Fairness'" (1996) 7 J. Envtl. L. & Prac. 115.

50   *Montague v. Ontario (Ministry of Environment)*, [2005] O.J. No. 868 (Div. Ct.).

E. ADMINISTRATIVE MONETARY PENALTIES

Although breaches of regulatory provisions, including environmental legislation, have traditionally been viewed as matters for prosecutorial action, statutory enactments over roughly the past decade have introduced an alternative process in the form of administrative penalty mechanisms, occasionally described as administrative monetary penalties (AMP). AMP provisions should be distinguished from ticketable offences where the manner of initiating the proceedings is modified but the matter remains within the jurisdiction of the courts.[51]

Sanctions resulting from administrative rather than judicial proceedings are generally expected to provide less costly and more expeditious enforcement. They will also possibly be found more convenient from the perspective of offenders who accept the administrative determination of the contravention, a process that does not result in a criminal record. For precisely this reason, however, some observers question whether AMPs will serve as an effective deterrent.

Administrative penalty schemes will ordinarily involve a notification procedure setting out the details of the violation and the financial penalty determined to be applicable. British Columbia legislation provides an illustration:

> Subject to the regulations, if a director is satisfied on a balance or probabilities that a person has
> (a) contravened a prescribed provision of this Act or the regulations,
> (b) failed to comply with an order under this Act, or
> (c) failed to comply with a requirement of a permit or approval issued or given under this Act,
>
> the director may serve the person with a determination requiring the person to pay an administrative penalty in the amount specified in the determination.[52]

An administrative hearing on the appropriateness of the penalty, or possibly an administrative appeal or review of the entire offence and penalty proceeding, will generally be set out in legislation governing administrative penalty schemes of this type.[53]

---

51   See, for example, *CEPA, 1999,* above note 6, s. 310(1); *Wild Animal and Plant Protection and Regulation of International and Interprovincial Trade Act,* S.C. 1992, c. 52, s. 23; *Migratory Birds Convention Act, 1994,* S.C. 1994, c. 22, s. 19.
52   *Environmental Management Act,* above note 37, s. 115.
53   Environmental AMPs have been provided for in Alberta (*AEPEA,* above note 13, the *Public Lands Act,* the *Forests Act*), British Columbia (*Forest Practices Code,*

Alberta implemented an administrative penalty arrangement in the *AEPEA*, under which the director, if of the opinion that a contravention of designated sections of the Act or regulations has occurred, may impose a penalty as provided for by regulation.[54] Persons who elect to pay the administrative penalty in respect of a contravention are not subject to charges under the *AEPEA* in connection with the contravention. In case of non-payment, the province may recover the amount owing in an action in debt.[55]

With regard to the level of penalty to be assessed and the AMP scheme, the Alberta appeal board remarked:

> The Board believes the amount of the penalty must reflect the regulatory matrix and associated criteria. The Board believes that to achieve the goal of deterrence, the penalty must also be high enough so that those who violate the law without reasonable excuse will not be able to "write off" the penalty as an acceptable trade-off for the harm or potential harm done to Alberta's environment.[56]

Between April 2000 and March 2006, 138 AMPs were imposed under the *AEPEA*, resulting in total assessed penalties of $668,000. Individual penalties ranged from a low of $500 to a high of $29,500.

Ontario's venture into the realm of administrative penalties has been in operation since August 2007. The *Environmental Penalties Regulation*[57] designates "regulated persons" who may be subject to the new penalty regime in relation to certain specified contraventions. It establishes applicable procedures including notice of intention to issue a penalty and a request for review. In determining the amount of the environmental penalty to be assessed, a formula combining the "monetary benefit" received by the regulated person and a "gravity component" for the contravention is utilized. The monetary benefit is calculated in relation to avoided and delayed costs, while the gravity component is determined in accordance with a classification system intended to

---

Administrative Remedies Regulation, B.C. Reg 166/95), New Brunswick (*Clean Air Act, Administrative Penalties Regulation*), Nova Scotia, and Ontario (*EPA, OWRA, PA*). It is anticipated that AMPs, to be known as Environmental Penalties or EPs, will eventually be introduced in Ontario pursuant to the *Environmental Enforcement Statute Law Amendment Act*, S.O. 2005, c. 12. For discussion, see online: www.ene.gov.on.ca/envision/general/penalties/EPConsultationpaper. htm.

54   *Administrative Penalty Regulation*, Alta. Reg. 143/95.

55   *AEPEA*, above note 13, s. 223.

56   *Hayspur Aviation Ltd. v. Alberta (Department of Environmental Protection)*, [1997] A.E.A.B.D. No. 9.

57   *Environmental Penalties Regulation*, O. Reg. 222/07.

distinguish less serious, serious and very serious contraventions. In connection with a contravention of section 14 of the *Environmental Protection Act*, for example, a contravention is serious where it causes or may cause one or more of the following effects:

1. Localized injury or damage to any animal life.
2. Widespread or long-term interference with the normal conduct of business.
3. Widespread or long-term loss of enjoyment of the normal use of property.
4. Widespread damage to property, other than plant or animal life.
5. Damage to property, other than plant or animal life, such that the property cannot be restored, within a reasonable time, to the condition that existed immediately before the discharge occurred. [58]

On the other hand, a contravention of the same section is considered very serious where it causes or may cause the following:

1. Widespread injury or damage to plant or animal life.
2. Harm or material discomfort to any person.
3. An adverse effect on the health of any person.
4. The impairment of the safety of any person. [59]

Reductions to the basic administrative penalty are available in Ontario on the basis of such considerations as efforts to prevent or mitigate harm, or the existence of an environmental management system.

Although it had been assumed that AMPs would, apart from administrative reviews, operate more or less without legal challenge, questions have been raised about the availablity of a due diligence defence. [60] The controversy is in some respects a crossover from similar questions previously raised in other areas of the law. With regard to AMPs under the *Excise Tax Act*, the battle lines were sharply drawn by the unequivocal statement of Judge Bowman:

> That a person should be susceptible of being penalized administratively by a public servant without any possibility of exculpating himself by demonstating due diligence is not only extraordinary. It is abhorrent. It is not less abhorrent because it is mechanically and routinely imposed by anonymous revenue officials and therefore quali-

---

58   *Ibid.*, s. 10.
59   *Ibid.*
60   *MacMillan Bloedel Ltd. v. British Columbia* (1997), 23 C.E.L.R. (N.S.) 47 at 51 (B.C. Forest Appeals Commission).

fies for the essentially meaningless rubric "administrative" rather than "criminal." A punishment is a punishment. Neither its nature nor its effect is tempered by the use of palliative modifiers.[61]

Courts of appeal in at least two provinces have also indicated their understanding that a due diligence defence ought to be available in the context of administrative penalties.[62] They have done so, however, with specific reference to the gravity or severity of the consequence of an administrative finding. There is thus some continuing basis for uncertainty about due diligence defences, at least where the actual burden of the penalty might be perceived as modest.

The range of measures described in this chapter, from devices oriented towards information gathering through administrative orders to administrative penalty regimes, are intended to ensure, by and large in a "business as usual" context, an acceptable level of compliance. Nevertheless, as noted in the following chapter, environmental law includes offences that have increasingly been the subject of formal enforcement proceedings.

FURTHER READINGS

COMMISSION FOR ENVIRONMENTAL COOPERATION, *Special Report on Enforcement Activities* (June 2001)

CROWLEY, R. & F. THOMPSON, "Retroactive Liability, Superfund and the Regulation of Contaminated Sites in British Columbia" (1995) 29 U.B.C. L. Rev. 87

HUGHES, E.L., A.R. LUCAS, & W.A. TILLEMAN, eds., *Environmental Law and Policy*, 3d ed. (Toronto: Emond Montgomery, 2003) c. 10

---

61   *Pillar Oilfield Projects Ltd. v. R.*, [1993] 2 G.T.C 1005 at 1009 (T.C.C.). Now see *Canada (Attorney General) v. Consolidated Canadian Contractors Inc.* (1998), 231 N.R. 92 (F.C.A.).

62   *504174 N.B. Ltée (f.a.s. Choo Choo's) c. Nouveau-Brunswick (Ministre de la Sécurité Publique)* (2005), 279 N.B.R. (2d) 307 (C.A.); *Whistler Mountain Ski Corp. v. British Columbia (General Manager Liquor Control and Licensing Branch)*, [2002] B.C.J. No. 1604, 43 Admin. L.R. (3d) 294 (C.A.).

CHAPTER 8

OFFENCES, PROSECUTION, AND PENALTIES

A. AN INTRODUCTION TO ENVIRONMENTAL OFFENCES

Several of the more prominent environmental offences have already been mentioned, or their existence may readily be inferred from the preceding discussion of regulation and administrative supervision. The primary focus, not unexpectedly, relates to environmental damage: in general, prohibitions are established against certain forms of conduct that cause or threaten to cause damage to the environment. The *Environment Quality Act* of Quebec provides an example in declaring that

> [n]o one may emit, deposit, issue or discharge or allow the emission, deposit, issuance or discharge into the environment . . . of any contaminant the presence of which in the environment . . . is likely to affect the life, health, safety, welfare or comfort of human beings, or to cause damage to or otherwise impair the quality of the soil, vegetation, wildlife or property.[1]

The *Ontario Water Resources Act* makes it an offence to discharge or cause or permit the discharge of any kind of material in or into any waters where the discharge may impair water quality.[2]

---

1 R.S.Q. c. Q-2, s. 20.
2 *Ontario Water Resources Act*, R.S.O. 1990, c. O.40, s. 30(1) [*OWRA*].

> Every person that discharges or causes or permits the discharge of any material of any kind into or in any waters or on any shore or bank thereof or into or in any place that may impair the quality of the water or any waters is guilty of an offence.

Similarly, the federal *Fisheries Act* states that

> no person shall deposit or permit the deposit of a deleterious substance of any type in water frequented by fish or in any place under any conditions where the deleterious substance or any other deleterious substance that results from the deposit of the deleterious substance may enter any such water.[3]

As broadly formulated as such prohibitions appear to be, the existence of exemptions must be noted. The *Fisheries Act*, in fact, contains its own express limitation in that the legislation itself indicates that no one contravenes the prohibition just cited "by depositing or permitting the deposit in any water or place of waste or pollutant of a type, in a quantity and under conditions authorized by regulations applicable to that water or place."[4]

In addition to their anti-pollution provisions, environmental statutes ordinarily establish a series of further offences. Failure to comply with regulatory requirements is an offence, as is the failure to obtain required licences, permits, or approvals, or failure to comply with any terms and conditions set out in these instruments. Non-compliance with valid administrative orders may be addressed through prosecution, and environmental legislation also typically makes it an offence to interfere with or disregard the regulatory process by failing to supply required information, or by providing false or misleading information, or by obstructing enforcement officials or failing to assist them as required.[5] Other environmental reporting obligations that may become the subject of prosecutorial redress relate to the occurrence of spills.

Offences in the environmental context are generally described as *regulatory* or *public welfare offences.* They differ in principle from what are commonly referred to in Canada as "true crimes." The theoretical distinctions were summarized by Mr. Justice Cory in *R. v. Wholesale Travel Group Inc.*:

---

3   *Fisheries Act*, R.S.C. 1985, c. F-14, s. 36(3) [*FA*].
4   *Ibid.*, s. 36(4).
5   *Canadian Environmental Protection Act, 1999*, S.C. 1999, c. 33, ss. 272–73 [*CEPA, 1999*]; *FA*, above note 3, s. 63, as am. by S.C. 1991, c. 1, s. 18; *Migratory Birds Convention Act, 1994*, S.C. 1994, c.22, s. 13, as am. by S.C. 2005, c. 23, s. 9 [*MBCA*].

The objective of regulatory legislation is to protect the public or broad segments of the public . . . from the potentially adverse effects of otherwise lawful activity. Regulatory legislation involves a shift of emphasis from the protection of individual interests and the deterrence and punishment of acts involving moral fault to the protection of public and societal interests. While criminal offences are usually designed to condemn and punish past, inherently wrongful conduct, regulatory measures are generally directed to the prevention of future harm through the enforcement of minimum standards of conduct and care.[6]

Justice Cory then contrasted the nature of fault in the regulatory and criminal settings:

Since regulatory offences are directed primarily not to conduct itself but to the consequences of conduct, conviction of a regulatory offence may be thought to import a significantly lesser degree of culpability than conviction of a true crime. The concept of fault in regulatory offences is based upon a reasonable care standard and, as such, does not imply moral blameworthiness in the same manner as criminal fault. Conviction for breach of a regulatory offence suggests nothing more than that the defendant has failed to meet a prescribed standard of care.[7]

Regulatory offences themselves may be further subdivided into three classifications—*mens rea*, strict liability, and absolute liability—which have particular significance for prosecutions. Regulatory offences, including environmental offences, fall overwhelmingly within the strict liability category. Commission of such offences, as explained by Dickson J. in *R. v. Sault Ste Marie (City)*, will be established on a *prima facie* basis by the prosecution showing the doing of the prohibited act unaccompanied by evidence of the mental state of the accused. It is then "open to the accused to avoid liability by proving that he took all reasonable care. This involves consideration of what a reasonable man would have done in the circumstances." A second category of offences requires the prosecution to prove *mens rea*, "consisting of some positive state of mind such as intent, knowledge, or recklessness." This may be accomplished "either as an inference from the nature of the act committed, or by additional evidence." Absolute liability offences require proof

---

6   [1991] 3 S.C.R. 154 at 219 [*Wholesale*].
7   *Ibid.*

of the *actus reus*, but it is not then "open to the accused to exculpate himself by showing that he was free of fault."[8]

In the absence of an express statutory classification of the regulatory offence as one of strict or absolute liability or involving *mens rea*, analysis of legislative intent begins with the presumption of strict liability that—depending on other factors present—might be displaced in favour of either *mens rea* or absolute liability. To classify an offence as one involving *mens rea* requires language signalling the importance of the accused's state of mind as a factor to be established by the prosecution. Words such as *wilfully, knowingly,* or *with intent,* are comparatively clear in this regard. It is less certain that words such as *participate* satisfy the standard, although it has been determined that wilful blindness may be equated with the *mens rea* standard of knowingly. "Deliberately choosing not to know something when given reason to believe further inquiry is necessary can satisfy the mental element of the offence."[9]

On the other hand, distinguishing between strict and absolute liability offences presents the challenge of determining whether the legislative body responsible for the enactment "had made it clear that guilt would follow proof merely of the proscribed act."[10] The primary, but not exclusive, considerations relevant to this determination include the subject matter of the legislation, the overall regulatory pattern, the importance of the penalty provided, and the precision of the language employed.[11]

New complications and a reorientation of incentives have resulted from the *Charter of Rights and Freedoms.* Defence counsel traditionally argued that statutory provisions established strict liability rather than absolute liability offences. Due diligence defences rendered conviction less likely.[12] The strategic situation was somewhat altered by the *Charter:* "Counsel now perceive that any absolute liability offence accompanied by a possibility of imprisonment will contravene the *Charter* unless saved by section 1; therefore, they argue that provisions create absolute liability offences, in the hope that they will be struck down."[13]

---

8   R. v. *Sault Ste.-Marie (City),* [1978] 2 S.C.R. 1299 at 1325–26, 85 D.L.R. (3d) 161 [*Sault Ste.-Marie*]. The framework for the classification of offences is reiterated in *Levis (City) v. Tetreault,* [2006] S.C.J. No. 12.

9   R. v. *Jorgensen,* [1995] 4 S.C.R. 55 at 110, Sopinka J., with reference to s. 163(2)(a) of the *Criminal Code,* R.S.C. 1985, c. C-46 [*Code*].

10 *Sault Ste. Marie,* above note 8 at 1326.

11 J. Swaigen, *Regulatory Offences in Canada: Liability and Defences* (Toronto: Carswell, 1992) at 32.

12 For discussion of due diligence, see chapter 9.

13 Swaigen, above note 11 at 39.

Legislative revisions designed to ensure *Charter* conformity now make such opportunities less likely.[14]

B. INTERPRETING ENVIRONMENTAL OFFENCES IN THE COURTS

Notwithstanding the best efforts of those responsible for drafting legislation, disagreements will arise over the meaning and application of statutory provisions. Such disputes are most likely in the context of prosecutions where an accused business or individual faces potentially severe consequences upon conviction. In these circumstances, as can readily be illustrated with reference to offences mentioned in the previous section, judicial interpretation plays a significant role in elaborating the scope of liability.

The applicability of the strong general prohibition in section 20(3) of Quebec's *Environment Quality Act* was restricted on the basis of judicial analysis of its relationship to two other prohibitions, namely against discharging a contaminant prohibited by regulation and against discharging a contaminant in excess of the quantity authorized by regulation. In *Alex Couture Inc. v. Piette*, charges were brought under the general prohibition, section 20(3), against a company whose operations were subject to existing regulations. In the circumstances, the Quebec Court of Appeal concluded that the general anti-pollution clause had no application on the grounds that the government would hardly authorize and prohibit the same emission of a contaminant. Thus, the general prohibition against any discharge of a contaminant would not apply in the case of a contaminant whose discharge was governed by regulation.[15]

Prosecutions under section 36(3), the deleterious substance provision of the *Fisheries Act,* raise numerous issues. Of particular importance, it has been asked whether the nature of the substance or the condition of the water after the introduction of the substance is the focus of attention. When a trial court in British Columbia concluded that the Crown's obligation was to establish that the water had been rendered deleterious by the addition of some substance, in this case Bunker C oil, the issue of interpretation proceeded to the Court of Appeal.[16]

---

14   But see **Whistler Mountain Ski Corp. v. British Columbia (General Manager Liquor Control and Licensing Branch)**, [2002] B.C.J. No. 1604 (C.A.) for further discussion of the distinctions.

15   *Alex Couture Inc. v. Piette*, [1990] R.J.Q. 1262 at 1268 (C.A.).

16   *R. v. MacMillan Bloedel (Alberni) Limited* (1979), 47 C.C.C. (2d) 118.

Seaton J.A. decided that section 36(3) "prohibits the deposit of a deleterious substance, not the deposit of a substance that causes the water to become deleterious." As he explained: "once it is determined that Bunker C oil is a deleterious substance and that it has been deposited, the offence is complete without ascertaining whether the water itself was thereby rendered deleterious." Seaton J.A. was certain that Parliament could very well have expressed a prohibition against depositing a substance in water so as to render that water deleterious to fish, but that it had chosen a stricter prohibition.

The same provision was recently examined by the Ontario Court of Appeal in a high profile prosecution against a municipality. A unanimous panel determined that:

> The focus of s. 36(3) is on the substance being added to the water frequented by fish. It prohibits the deposit of a deleterious substance in such water. It does not prohibit the deposit of a substance that causes the receiving water to become deleterious. It is the substance that is added to water frequented by fish that is defined, not the water after the addition of the substance. A deleterious substance does not have to render the water into which it is introduced poisonous or harmful to fish; it need only be likely to render the water deleterious to fish. The *actus reus* is the deposit of a deleterious substance into water frequented by fish. There is no requirement in s. 36(3) . . . of proof that the receiving waters are deleterious to fish.[17]

A somewhat similar controversy regarding the scope of liability arose in connection with Ontario legislation prohibiting the discharge into water of any material that "may impair" the quality of the water. Toronto Hydro was charged when mineral oil contaminated with PCBs escaped from underground vaults housing transformers and entered the drainage and sewage system leading to Lake Ontario. The company argued that the small quantity involved would not have impaired water quality in Lake Ontario. The proposition that the quantity or concentration rather than the nature of the material is determinative of impairment was rejected. Corbett J. stated:

> the offence is constituted when the Crown proves that any material discharged . . . may impair the quality of the water course . . . The use of the words "may impair" shows the intention of the legislation is not to prohibit the results of certain acts but to prevent the discharge

---

17   R. v. *Kingston (City)*, 2004 CanLII 39042 at para. 65 (Ont. C.A.), leave to appeal to S.C.C. refused, [2004] S.C.C.A. No. 347.

of any material which, by its nature, may impair the quality of the water course.[18]

A different formulation of the test was subsequently articulated in connection with charges of discharging activated sludge, a substance that is not always associated with adverse impacts on water quality. In *R. v. Imperial Oil* it was stated that:

> the offence is made out where the Crown proves beyond any reasonable doubt that the discharge of the material may impair the quality of the water, based upon not only the nature of the material, but also the nature and circumstances of the discharge of that material, including its quantity and concentration, as well as the time frame over which the discharge took place.[19]

The Court of Appeal has recently endorsed the test as formulated in *Imperial Oil*, observing that:

> Inherently toxic substances will always fail that test, reflecting zero tolerance for discharging materials that, by their nature, may impair water quality. If the material in the discharge is not inherently toxic, then it will be necessary to consider the quantity and concentration of the discharge as well as the time frame over which the discharge took place.[20]

Another common source of interpretive uncertainty — the relationship between discharging, causing, and permitting — was addressed by the Supreme Court of Canada. As explained by Dickson J. in *R. v. Sault Ste-Marie*, the discharging aspect of the offence relates to direct acts of pollution, while the causing dimension is associated with activity by the defendant that it is capable of controlling and that results in pollution. Permitting involves a passive lack of interference by the defendant, that is, a failure to prevent an incident which it should have foreseen.[21]

Before returning to a more extended discussion of regulatory prosecutions, we will briefly explain the significance of the *Criminal Code* in environmental protection.

---

18 *R. v. Toronto Electric Commissioners* (1991), 6 C.E.L.R. (N.S.) 301 at 316 (Ont. Gen. Div.).

19 *R. v. Imperial Oil* (1995), 17 C.E.L.R. (N.S.) 12 at 18 (Ont. Prov. Div.).

20 *R. v. Inco Ltd.* (2001), 54 O.R.(3d) 495 at 513 (C.A.). The proceedings in Inco are ongoing. See *R. v. Inco Ltd.*, [2006] O.J. No. 1809 (S.C.J.).

21 *Sault Ste-Marie*, above note 8 at 184–85 (D.L.R.). For a recent discussion and application of the distinctions between deposit and permit, see www.petitcodiac. org/riverkeeper/Documents/Final_Decision(Gemtec).pdf.

C. THE *CRIMINAL CODE* AND THE ENVIRONMENT

The severity of potential sanctions available and the presumption of moral wrongdoing on the part of those convicted under criminal law makes criminalization attractive to those who regard environmental degradation as a serious affront to contemporary social values. However, Justice Cory acknowledged difficulties in the theoretical distinction between degrees of moral fault in criminal and regulatory offences: "For example, is the single mother who steals a loaf of bread to sustain her family more blameworthy than . . . the manufacturer who, as a result of negligence, sells dangerous products or pollutes the air and waters by its plant?"[22] As he further observed, the degree of moral blameworthiness attaching to certain types of conduct may change with changing social values.

The *Criminal Code* makes no express reference to environment. Nonetheless, certain existing provisions offer some scope to prosecute those responsible for environmentally harmful conduct, presuming that substantially similar charges have not been brought for alleged violations of the environmental regime itself.[23] For example, the *Code* indicates that everyone is criminally negligent who, in doing anything or in omitting to do anything that it is his or her duty to do, shows wanton or reckless disregard for the lives or safety of other persons.[24] The common nuisance provision makes it an offence to commit a common nuisance and thereby to endanger the lives, safety, or health of the public.[25] Other sections of the *Criminal Code* with environmental dimensions address mischief;[26] dangerous, offensive, volatile,[27] and explosive substances;[28] and certain offences against animals.[29]

Historically, some use was made of these provisions in relation to environmental damage, particularly in situations involving threats to public health. However, the *Criminal Code* provisions contain a number of

---

22   *Wholesale*, above note 6.

23   *R. v. Crowe* (1996), 20 C.E.L.R. (N.S.) 235 (Ont. Gen. Div.).

24   *Code*, above note 9, s. 219.

25   *Ibid.*, s. 180; *R. v. Goodyear Tire & Rubber Co. of Canada* (1996), 21 (C.E.L.R.) (N.S.) 176 (Ont. Prov. Div.).

26   *Code, ibid.*, s. 430.

27   *Ibid.*, s. 178.

28   *Ibid.*, ss. 79–82.

29   *Ibid.*, ss. 444–47. Despite repeated attempts to include new animal cruelty provisions, (most recently including Bill C-22: 3d Session, 37th Parliament,) no changes have been introduced.

important limitations that render them poorly suited and unreliable for use in the cause of environmental protection. A study for the Law Reform Commission of Canada (LRCC) found that some of the *Code*'s existing provisions were too vaguely worded to facilitate successful environmental prosecutions, while the focus of others on threats and injury to the lives and safety of persons, or on damage to property rather than on environmental interests *per se*, undermined their utility. Having concluded that "existing *Code* offences do not effectively encompass serious pollution, and could not be revised to do so in a manner which would highlight the importance of a safe environment; nor could they be revised without diffusing the present goals and purposes of those offences,"[30] the LRCC recommended a new and distinct category of offences against the environment. The scope of the proposed offence would extend to

(a) environmental pollution which
    (i) seriously and directly damages the quality of the environment, or
    (ii) seriously and directly endangers the quality of the environment;
(b) in either case listed in (a), unauthorized conduct, normally involving as a necessary condition a serious and dramatic breach of a federal or provincial statutory prohibition or standard;
(c) in either case listed in (a) conduct for which there is no overriding social utility which could result in otherwise seriously harmful or endangering pollution being minor in nature or even tolerable and justifiable;
(d) especially environmental pollution which thereby seriously harms or endangers human life or health;
(e) not only immediate and known harms and dangers to human life and health, but also those which are likely to result in the foreseeable future;
(f) only by express exception, that environmental pollution which deprives others of the use and enjoyment of one or more elements of the natural environment, causing very serious consequences although resulting in no serious harm or danger to human life or health; such instances would be in the nature of catastrophes, an example being the loss of livelihood of an entire community as a result of pollution.[31]

---

30 Law Reform Commission of Canada, *Crimes against the Environment* (Ottawa: LRCC, 1985).
31 *Ibid.* at 68. For a remarkable attempt to craft a comprehensive rule around "ecological sustainability" rather than pollution, see Bruce Pardy, "In Search of

The specific recommendations of the LRCC were not adopted, but the publication of the report coincided more or less with a serious strengthening of the enforcement capacity of many provincial environment ministries and with increasingly severe penalty regimes in a number of jurisdictions. In addition, section 274(1) of *CEPA, 1999* creates something in the nature of a crime against the environment provision triggered by violations of *CEPA, 1999* itself:

> Every person is guilty of an offence and liable on conviction on indictment to a fine or to imprisonment for a term of not more than five years, or to both, who, in committing an offence
> (a) intentionally or recklessly causes a disaster that results in a loss of the use of the environment, or
> (b) shows wanton or reckless disregard for the lives or safety of other persons and thereby causes a risk of death or harm to another person,

Subsection 274(2) specifically provides that sections 220 or 221 of the *Criminal Code* apply in the case of anyone contravening *CEPA, 1999* whose wanton or reckless disregard for the lives or safety of others in fact causes death or bodily harm.

D. ENFORCEMENT POLICY AND PROSECUTORIAL DISCRETION

As public concern mounted over the inadequacies of environmental protection, the question of appropriate strategies for ensuring that established environmental standards would be respected attracted increasing attention. As discussed in chapter 7, two general approaches — conciliatory and enforcement-based — were identified. The former generally consists of non-coercive measures and negotiations intended to encourage or promote environmental performance consistent with established environmental standards. Canada's approach has often been characterized as conciliatory in nature, or, in the words of one observer, as a "relatively closed, consensual and consultative approach with a small number of prosecutions."[32] An enforcement strategy, on

---

the Holy Grail of Environmental Law: A Rule to Solve the Problem" (2005) 1 Journal of Sustainable Development Law and Policy 29.

32   P.N. Nemetz, "Federal Environmental Regulation in Canada" (1986) 26 Natural Resources J. 551.

the other hand, relies more heavily on the use of prosecution and formal penalties or sanctions.[33]

There is an important ongoing debate about the effectiveness of the alternative strategies. A number of studies appear to confirm the utility of a sanctions-based approach to regulatory legislation.[34] However, there are indications that in certain circumstances significant reductions in the discharge of environmental contaminants may be brought about without resort to substantial sanctions or penalties.[35] Defenders of a conciliatory strategy also note its contribution to the dissemination of knowledge. There is an informal benefit, it is argued, from the work of inspectors who are sometimes in a position to facilitate the transfer of experience and learning between different companies which have encountered similar environmental compliance challenges.

Although each general strategy has advocates and detractors, the debate about their comparative merits is seriously complicated by the inevitable relationships between the two approaches. It has also been suggested that evaluation is problematic in that neither approach has been as actively or consistently applied as might be desirable. In relation to the linkage between the two approaches, advocates of a conciliatory process have often been willing to acknowledge that the existence of sanctions resulting from the possibility of prosecution provides some reinforcement for their efforts. On the other hand, it has been argued that effective enforcement action depends upon moral as well as legislative "legitimacy" and that this is likely to be absent where the institutions and processes of compliance are ignored. "What is sanctionable," in the opinion of Keith Hawkins, "is not rule-breaking as such, but rule-breaking which is deliberately or negligently done, or rule-breaking accompanied by unco-operativeness which amounts to a symbolic assault upon the enforcer's . . . authority and legitimacy."[36]

---

33   For a comprehensive discussion of differences between the two general approaches, see K. Hawkins, *Environment and Enforcement: Regulation and the Social Definition of Pollution* (Oxford: Clarendon Press, 1984); in the Canadian context see D. Chappell, *From Sawdust to Toxic Blobs: A Consideration of Sanctioning Strategies to Combat Pollution in Canada* (Ottawa: Supply & Services, 1989).

34   D. Saxe, "The Impact of Prosecution of Corporations and Their Officers and Directors upon Regulatory Compliance by Corporations" (1991) 1 J.Envtl. L. & Prac. 91; R. Brown & M. Rankin, "Persuasion, Penalties, and Prosecution: Administrative v. Criminal Sanctions" in M.L. Friedland, ed., *Securing Compliance: Seven Case Studies* (Toronto: University of Toronto Press, 1990) 325–53.

35   D.N. Dewees, "The Effect of Environmental Regulation: Mercury and Sulphur Dioxide" in Friedland, *ibid.*, 354–91.

36   Hawkins, above note 33 at xiv.

In relation to the issue of active implementation, a number of observers have argued that, although legislative and regulatory measures may be satisfactory in principle, enforcement efforts have been inconsistent and inadequate in practice. For example, studies and reports by the Canadian Environmental Advisory Council and by staff at the Law Reform Commission of Canada criticized Environment Canada during the 1980s for deficiencies in the enforcement of environmental legislation, or for what was described as an "implementation gap."[37] Various causes may be advanced to account for the "implementation gap" in environmental law, notably the fact that competition exists for the allocation of public prosecutorial resources. Justice officials carrying responsibility for the enforcement of a wide range of statutes applicable throughout the community must, in effect, allocate and ration personnel and available finances. In Saskatchewan, for example, before embarking upon a prosecution provincial justice decision makers systematically address the following questions:

i)   Is there a reasonable likelihood of conviction?
ii) Is it in the public interest to prosecute?

Consider the following in answering ii:

- The seriousness of the offence;
- Any mitigating or aggravating circumstances;
- The personal circumstances of the accused;
- The staleness of the alleged offence;
- The prosecution's effect on public order, morale, or public confidence in the administration of justice;
- The availability of alternatives to prosecution;
- The frequency of the offence in the community;
- The concern in the community over the offence;
- The likely sentence; and
- The attitudes and interests of the victim.[38]

An Alberta review panel on environmental law enforcement set out some of the considerations governing the operation of a sanctioning

---

37   L. Giroux, "A Statement by the Canadian Environmental Advisory Council on Enforcement Practices of Environment Canada" (June 1985); Law Reform Commission of Canada, *Pollution Control in Canada: The Regulatory Approach in the 1980s* (Study Paper) by K. Webb (Ottawa: The Commission, 1988).

38   Saskatchewan Department of Justice, "The Role of Public Prosecution in the Justice System," quoted in Michelle Bailey & Anthony Ikwueme, *Report on Saskatchewan Environmental Law Review* (Saskatoon, SK: Centre for Studies in Agriculture, Law and the Environment, 2001) at 28.

strategy. Prosecution, the panel explained, supplements the administrative process by signalling to polluters that prohibited conduct will not be tolerated. The imposition of a penalty deters not only the convicted accused but other potential offenders from future wrongdoing. The Alberta panel recommended that prosecution be used for clearly defined offences, with enforcement policy identifying certain crucial violations that constitute an automatic prosecutable offence:

> Since the current approach of Alberta Environment involving negotiation and abatement relies heavily on accurate monitoring and timely reporting, any breaches in this regard should be treated extremely seriously. Offences such as failure to report to authorities any uncontrolled releases, providing false information and failure to obtain a permit or license should also result in automatic prosecution.[39]

CEPA, 1999 came into effect during a period of intense interest in stricter enforcement, a situation that no doubt encouraged the federal minister to emphasize the severity of the sanctions to be embodied in the new legislation:

> Sanctions will include million-dollar-a-day fines. But more than fines are needed because they affect the balance sheet but not necessarily the polluters themselves. The new law will also place responsibility squarely where it belongs—on the shoulders of the chief executive officers and company presidents who commit violations or who permit them. They will be subject to jail sentences of one to five years. And the government intends to enforce the law with vigor.[40]

These widely quoted remarks contributed in an important way to the nature of the expectations attendant upon the introduction of *CEPA, 1999*. There was thus considerable interest when officials responsible for *CEPA, 1999*'s administration addressed the issues of enforcement and compliance in a policy statement:

> Compliance with the Act and its regulations is mandatory. Enforcement officials throughout Canada will apply the Act in a manner that is fair, predictable and consistent. They will use rules, sanctions and processes securely founded in law. Enforcement officials will ad-

---

39   Quoted in L.B. Huestis, "Enforcement of Environmental Law in Canada" in G. Thompson, M.L. McConnell, & L.B. Huestis, eds., *Environmental Law and Business in Canada* (Aurora, ON: Canada Law Book, 1993) 243 at 255. Now see "Enforcement Program for the Environmental Protection and Enhancement Act" (Alberta Environmental Protection, 2 September 1994).

40   Hon. Tom McMillan, Speech.

minister the Act with an emphasis on prevention of damage to the environment. Enforcement officials will examine every suspected violation of which they have knowledge, and will take action consistent with this Enforcement and Compliance Policy. Enforcement officials will encourage the reporting to them of suspected violations of the Act.[41]

These remain the guiding principles of compliance and enforcement in connection with the administration of *CEPA, 1999.*[42]

The specific measures envisaged to promote compliance include education and exchange of technical information, the elaboration of codes of practice and guidelines, inspections, oral and written warnings, increased monitoring, and the use of administrative orders, recalls, ticketing, and directions, as well as court-based proceedings, injunctions, civil claims for cost recovery, and prosecutorial action.

Environment Canada has reported annually on its enforcement efforts under *CEPA, 1999* using two broad categories and somewhat variable classification procedures. Enforcement *activities* include administrative verification, field, or site inspections and investigations. Enforcement *actions* include verbal and written warnings, directives, prosecutions, and some referrals to other agencies. By way of example, for the 1999–2000 reporting year, there were 327 administrative verifications and 129 inspections relating to the export and import of hazardous wastes. Nine investigations were also conducted. In the enforcement actions category, officials issued 4 verbal and 25 written warnings, referred 14 situations to others for follow-up and initiated 10 prosecutions.[43] For the 2002-2003 period, again with reference to enforcement initiatives relating to the export and import of hazardous wastes under *CEPA, 1999*, there were 866 inspections. Forty-one written warnings were issued. There were sixteen investigations, two prosecutions and one conviction.[44] The department has recently begun

---

41 Environment Canada, *Canadian Environmental Protection Act Enforcement and Compliance Policy* (Ottawa: Supply & Services, 1988) at 9. See also Environment Canada's directive on enforcement of DOE legislation, June 1995.

42 Environment Canada, *Compliance and Enforcement Policy for the Canadian Environmental Protection Act, 1999* (March 2001) at 5. See also *Compliance and Enforcement Policy for the Habitat Protection and Pollution Prevention Provisions of the Fisheries Act.*

43 For a complete record of annual enforcement activity, see Environment Canada, *CEPA Annual Report: April 1999 to March 2000* (2000) at 36.

44 Table 10, "Enforcement Activities Carried Out under *CEPA, 1999* during 2002–03" in Environment Canada, *CEPA Annual Report: April 2002 to March 2003*, online: www.ec.gc.ca/CEPARegistry/Archives/AR/ar02_03/enforce.cfm at 67.

to make significantly greater use of Environmental Protection Compliance Orders under section 235 to prevent or stop designated violations of *CEPA, 1999*.

In the provincial sphere, enforcement initiatives have also experienced ebb and flow. One major landmark in terms of environmental enforcement strategy was Ontario's decision in 1985 to reorganize its Ministry of the Environment by replacing a twelve-member special investigation unit with a new investigation and enforcement branch consisting of sixty-two staff. Shortly thereafter the ministry formulated an enforcement policy,[45] which resulted in a fourfold increase in the frequency of environmental prosecutions in the province.[46] A similar increase in investigative and prosecutorial activity occurred in British Columbia and Alberta.

Some observers of the enforcement record suggest that the greater frequency of prosecutions, combined with higher fines resulting from legislative amendments, had a discernible impact on corporate behaviour. In particular, more vigorous enforcement measures are thought to encourage more conscientious attention to the necessity for environmental compliance. Dianne Saxe surveyed senior corporate officials in major Canadian firms with respect to the impact that prosecution for environmental non-compliance might have on their decisions. She concluded that prosecution "has a strong, statistically significant impact upon the environmental behaviour of corporations, both in actual, past behaviour and in predictions of future behaviour." In terms of specific conduct, Saxe reported that corporations that had experienced prosecution had higher levels of environmentally related spending than firms that had not been prosecuted. She also found indications that corporate executives would be more likely to take action to have their companies avoid environmental offences if they could be prosecuted

---

45   D. Saxe, "Fines Go Up Dramatically in Environmental Cases" (1989) 3 C.E.L.R. (N.S.) 104 at 110.

46   From 1985 to 1991, the number of prosecutions initiated increased from 86 to 313 and convictions rose from 71 to 212. Ontario, Ministry of the Environment (Toronto: Ministry of the Environment, 1992). Prosecutorial activity was severely curtailed during a period of fiscal retrenchment following the provincial election of 1995. The recent creation of an environmental SWAT team may signal a renewal of the compliance and enforcement effort in Ontario. For a comparative assessment of provincial enforcement, see D.L. VanNijnatten, "The Bumpy Journey Ahead: Provincial Environmental Policies and National Environmental Standards" in D. VanNijnatten & R. Boardman, eds., *Canadian Environmental Policy: Context and Cases*, 2d ed. (Don Mills, ON: Oxford University Press, 2002) at 160–67.

personally for such offences.[47] More agnostic views are occasionally expressed, however:

> Most lawyers and judges do not pretend to be behavioural scientists
> and, for that reason, do not really know whether penalties gener-
> ate a higher standard of care among the general public. Parliament,
> however, is entitled to legislate on the basis that penalties have such
> an effect.[48]

E. INVESTIGATIONS

A search or investigation for the purpose of obtaining evidence relevant
to the prosecution of possible statutory violations differs in important
respects from routine administrative inspections, even if, as in some
jurisdictions, these activities may be conducted by the same officials.
The Supreme Court of Canada adopted the following distinction between searches and inspections in *Comité Paritaire de l'Industrie de la
Chemise v. Potash*:

> An inspection is characterized by a visit to determine whether there
> is compliance with a given statute. The basic intent is not to uncover
> a breach of the Act; the purpose is rather to protect the public. On the
> other hand, if the inspector enters the establishment because he has
> reasonable grounds to believe that there has been a breach of the Act,
> this is no longer an inspection but a search, as the intent is then es-
> sentially to see if those reasonable grounds are justified and to seize
> anything which may serve as proof of the offence.[49]

As one operational consequence of this distinction, officials involved in
investigations must pay particular attention to fact-finding techniques,
including the taking of witness statements and the identification and
safeguarding of evidence such as samples that could eventually be required in court.

Although courts have acknowledged the basic legitimacy of the inspection process where abatement officials gather information for ad-

---

47   Saxe, above note 34

48   *Canada (Attorney General) v. Consolidated Canadian Contractors Inc.* (1998), 231
     N.R. 92 at 107 (F.C.A.).

49   Translation from L. Angers, "La recherche d'une protection efficace contre les
     inspections abusives de l'état: la Charte québécoise, la Charte canadienne et
     le Bill of Rights américain" (1986) 27 C. de D. 723 at 727–28, quoted in *Comité
     Paritaire de l'Industrie de la Chemise v. Potash*, [1994] 2 S.C.R. 406 at 417.

ministrative compliance purposes, the potential use of information in prosecutions raises immediate concerns. In *Thomson Newspapers Ltd. v. Canada (Director of Investigation & Research)*, Justice La Forest referred to the suspicion and stigma attached to persons who are under investigation for a criminal offence when he asserted that "[f]or reasons that go to the very core of our legal tradition, it is generally accepted that the citizen has a very high expectation of privacy in respect of such investigations."[50] Certain *Charter* provisions are directly relevant to privacy interests in the course of investigative procedures. In particular, section 8 specifies that "everyone has the right to be secure against unreasonable search and seizure." This provision, according to the Supreme Court in *Canada (Director of Investigation & Research, Combines Investigation Branch) v. Southam Inc.*,[51] guarantees a reasonable expectation of privacy and makes warrantless searches presumptively unreasonable. A party seeking to justify a warrantless search faces the challenge of rebutting that presumption. Ordinarily, therefore, prior authorization obtained from an impartial arbitrator deciding on reasonable and probable grounds (established on the oath of the applicant) that an offence has taken place and that evidence can be found at the designated location will be necessary to establish the validity of the search or seizure.[52]

The interplay between the inspection/investigation distinction from *Comité Paritaire de l'Industrie de la Chemise* and the importance of protection against unreasonable investigative searches noted in *Thomson Newspapers* and *Hunter v. Southam* came to the fore in a prosecution against Inco for violations of the *Ontario Water Resources Act (OWRA)*.[53] After an officer of the Ministry of the Environment's Investigation and Enforcement Branch had been informed by abatement officials that a discharge had taken place from a mine waste treatment facility, the Investigation and Enforcement Branch (IEB) officer interviewed employees and requested documents relevant to the discharge. The company was subsequently charged.

It was the ministry's position that authority for the IEB officer's conduct was found in the warrantless inspection provisions of the OWRA section 15 which are reinforced by the possibility that charges of obstruction may be laid against those who fail to cooperate. In the Crown's submission, the statutory provisions involved no unreason-

---

50   [1990] 1 S.C.R. 425 at 507–8.

51   [1984] 2 S.C.R. 145.

52   *Ibid.* at 160–68.

53   *R. v. Inco Ltd.* (Ont. C.A.), above note 20, leave to appeal to S.C.C. refused, [2001] S.C.C.A. No. 436.

able incursion into the company's expectations of privacy as the information obtained corresponded to information to which the ministry was entitled within the general regulatory framework.

In the submission of Inco, on the other hand, the statutory provisions for inspections became inoperable at such point as the investigating officer had reasonable and probable grounds to lay charges. The Ontario Court of Appeal agreed that if reasonable and probable grounds existed before the interviews were conducted, the warrantless investigation was presumptively unreasonable as an interference with the company's expectation of privacy pursuant to *Hunter v. Southam.* In such circumstances, the investigating officer would be required to obtain a warrant to proceed.

The S.C.C. decision in *CanadianOxy Chemicals Limited* examined the scope of search warrants issued pursuant to section 487(1) of the *Criminal Code* in the context of strict liability or regulatory offences.[54] In particular, it was necessary to determine whether such warrants could authorize the collection of evidence relating to potential defences such as due diligence, or would they be confined to evidence related to the Crown's obligation to prove the offence. In *CanadianOxy*, following a reported discharge of chlorine into Burrard Inlet, a fisheries officer acting pursuant to a section 487(1) warrant had seized records relating to employee training, plant maintenance, and other matters that might permit a due diligence defence to be defeated by a demonstration of negligence.

Noting that the statutory phrase "evidence with respect to the commission of an offence" is a "broad statement," Major J. judged the ordinary meaning of the phrase to encompass "all materials which might shed light on the circumstances of an event which appears to constitute an offence." He further concluded that the gathering of evidence under warrant should not be restricted to the elements of the offence itself.

F. PRIVATE PROSECUTIONS AND OTHER CITIZEN INITIATIVES

Individuals and public interest groups who are dissatisfied with official efforts to ensure environmental compliance or to pursue violations have several enforcement options and environmental protection strategies.[55]

---

54 *CanadianOxy Chemicals Ltd. v. Canada (A.G.)* (1999), 29 C.E.L.R. (N.S.) 1.

55 J. Brunnée, "Individual and Group Enforcement of Environmental Law in Quebec" (1992) 41 U.N.B.L.J. 107; O.E. Delogu, "Citizen Suits to Protect the Environment: The U.S. Experience May Suggest a Canadian Model" (1992) 41 U.N.B.L.J.

Citizens may endeavour to compel public authorities to take enforcement action, or they may initiate private prosecutions. Individuals contemplating a private prosecution of an offence may be advised to complain formally and in writing to the appropriate enforcement agency in the hope that it may yet undertake the case. If this does not occur, the prosecution can be launched by laying an information concerning the alleged offence and preparing for trial.[56] Indeed, there have been some successful private prosecutions in the environmental context.[57] One important example is provided by the successful *Fisheries Act* prosecution of the City of Kingston which was initiated as a private prosecution.[58] And, if the entitlement of private prosecutors to share in the proceeds from fines becomes more commonly available, the incentive may encourage further use of this enforcement mechanism.[59] Such actions have served on occasion to draw attention to gaps in official enforcement action.[60]

Canadian commentators have generally expressed the view that private prosecutions are costly, difficult, and fraught with hazards; in the words of one observer, "[t]he weak-spirited need not even try."[61] In addition to the likelihood that the private prosecutor's investigative resources and access to legal services are limited, the attorney general retains authority under section 579(1) of the *Criminal Code* to stay proceedings at any time before judgment. In the absence of flagrant impropriety, the attorney general's decision to intervene and order a stay is unreviewable.[62] Elizabeth Swanson and Elaine Hughes also conclude that the courts have not proven effective as a means to compel government officials to undertake environmental enforcement actions. In support of their argument they cite *Canadians for the Abolition of the Seal*

124; R. Cotton & N. Johnson, "Avenues for Citizen Participation in the Environmental Arena: Some Thoughts on the Road Ahead" (1992) 41 U.N.B.L.J. 131.

56   L.F. Duncan, *Enforcing Environmental Law: A Guide to Private Prosecutions* (Edmonton: Environmental Law Centre, 1980).

57   *R. v. Sheridan* (1972), [1973] 2 O.R. 192 (Dist. Ct.).

58   *R. v. Kingston (City)*, above note 17. For the origins of the case, see *Fletcher v. Kingston (City)* (1998), 28 C.E.L.R. (N.S.) 229 (Ont. Prov. Div.).

59   *Penalties and Forfeitures Proceeds Regulations*, C.R.C., c. 827; *Environment Act*, S.Y. 1991, c. 5, , s. 19(2) [YEA]; *Environmental Rights Act*, R.S.N.W.T. 1988 (Supp.), c. 83, s. 5 [NWTERA].

60   S.A.G. Elgie, "Environmental Groups and the Courts: 1970–1992" in *Environmental Law and Business in Canada*, above note 39, 185 at 206–7.

61   R.W. Proctor, "Individual Enforcement of Canada's Environmental Protection Laws: The Weak-spirited Need Not Try" (1991) 14 Dal. L.J. 112 at 132.

62   *Kostuch v. Alberta (A.G.)* (1995), 174 A.R. 109 (C.A.), leave to appeal to S.C.C. refused, [1995] S.C.C.A. No. 512.

Hunt v. Canada (Minister of Fisheries & Environment),[63] an unsuccessful attempt to obtain an order of *mandamus* to require the federal minister of fisheries to enforce existing regulations as a means of minimizing cruelty in the hunt. Yet Swanson and Hughes acknowledge the value of judicial commentary in highlighting the controversy and the nature of public expectations.[64] The intense interest of concerned citizens in appropriate environmental enforcement activity in the face of limited public resources has underlined the need for governments to address regulatory negligence claims. Such actions might be brought by persons injured as a result of alleged deficiencies in enforcement practices.[65]

In addition to private prosecution, certain provisions in recent environmental legislation permit individuals to call for or initiate public investigation of alleged offences on the basis of documented applications to designated officials.[66] Thus, under *CEPA, 1999* any Canadian resident eighteen years of age or older who alleges an offence has been committed under the Act may apply to the minister to have the matter investigated.[67] Should the minister fail to investigate and report within a reasonable time or respond unreasonably to the investigation, the individual applicant is entitled to launch an environmental protection action under the Act.[68] Under the Ontario *Environmental Bill of Rights, 1993 (OEBR)*, any two residents of the province may apply for an investigation by the responsible minister of an alleged contravention of any Act, regulation, or instrument prescribed under the *OEBR*. Such applications are made in the first instance to the environmental commissioner, who forwards the request to the appropriate minister and thereafter monitors the response process.[69]

Between 1999 and 2005, roughly ninety applications or requests for investigations were received by the Environmental Commissioner of Ontario (ECO) and forwarded to the relevant ministry. One example will serve to indicate how such initiatives might proceed. In August 2002, the ECO forwarded to the Ministry of the Environment an ap-

---

63   (1980), [1981] 1 F.C. 733 (T.D.).

64   E.J. Swanson & E.L. Hughes, *The Price of Pollution: Environmental Litigation in Canada* (Edmonton: Environmental Law Centre, 1990) at 110–12.

65   M. Mittelstaedt, "Ontario Prepares Negligence Defence" *The [Toronto] Globe and Mail* (18 February 1997) A1; *Quebec (A.G.) v. Girard*, [2004] J.Q. no 13624 (C.A.).

66   *CEPA, 1999*, above note 5, s. 17.

67   *CEPA, 1999, ibid.* See also *NWTERA*, above note 59, s. 4; Alberta *Environmental Protection and Enhancement Act*, R.S.A. 2000, c. E-12, s. 186 [*AEPEA*]; *Environment Act*, S.N.S. 1994–95, c. 1, s. 115; *YEA*, above note 59, s. 14.

68   *CEPA, 1999, ibid.*, s. 22.

69   *Environmental Bill of Rights, 1993*, S.O. 1993, c. 28, Part V.

plication for investigation submitted by the Sierra Club. It was generally alleged that Ontario Power Generation's (OPG) five coal-fired plants were responsible for the deposition of mercury into bodies of water in Ontario. More specifically, the application alleged contravention of section 30(1) of the *OWRA* which prohibits the discharge into Ontario's waters of any material that "may impair" water quality.[70] The application also alleged that OPG contravenes section 36(3) of the federal *Fisheries Act*, which prohibits the deposit of a "deleterious" substance into Canadian waters frequented by fish.[71] MOE did not conduct an investigation under the *Fisheries Act* on the grounds that in Ontario "the investigation and enforcement of the *FA* is the responsibility of Environment Canada." The ministry carried out an investigation under the *OWRA* amounting to a paper review of the evidence. The ministry concluded that "there is not, at this time, a reasonable prospect of a successful prosecution of OPG or any of its officers or directors with respect to the mercury emissions from the coal-fired plants, nor would it now be in the public interest to commence such a prosecution under the *OWRA*."[72]

The *North American Agreement on Environmental Cooperation* (*NAAEC*) provides another mechanism to pursue grievances concerning environmental enforcement. Individuals and non-governmental organizations may make submissions to the secretariat of the Commission for Environmental Co-operation asserting that a "[p]arty [to the agreement] is failing to effectively enforce its environmental law." If the submissions satisfy criteria specified in *NAAEC*, the secretariat may request a response from the party named in the submission. Consideration of the response may lead to the preparation of a factual record for presentation to the council, the commission's governing body comprised of the environmental ministers of Canada, Mexico, and the United States, and on the basis of a two-thirds vote by council the factual record may be made publicly available.[73]

Certain interpretive issues arise in connection with the citizen submission process under the *NAAEC*. In particular, consideration must be given to the scope of "environmental law" within the context of the submission provision. Furthermore, there has been scope for dis-

---

70   *OWRA*, above note 2, s. 30(1).

71   Environmental Commissioner of Ontario, *Annual Report 2003–2004*, online: www.eco.on.ca/english/publicat/ar2003.pdf at 122.

72   *Ibid.* at 123.

73   *North American Agreement on Environmental Cooperation*, 12 and 14 September 1993, 32 I.L.M. 1480. For discussion of procedures applicable to citizen submissions, see online: www.cec.org/citizen.

agreement and uncertainty around what is meant by failure to enforce effectively. Chris Tollefson usefully describes what is and what is not contemplated by the arrangements:

> [T]he NAAEC does not require parties to protect the environment from harm. Parties are allowed to freely choose their own preferred level of environmetal protection. The NAAEC does, however, require that parties 'effectively enforce' environmental laws they enact, which are presumably designed to achieve their chosen level of environmental protection. In short, the citizen submission process is not about preventing environmental harm *per se*, but rather about holding governments responsible for enforcing environmental laws.[74]

Despite the obstacles and limitations of the citizen submission process, a number of Canadian applications have been successful in compelling the preparation of a factual record.[75]

G. PENALTIES, REMEDIAL ORDERS, AND SENTENCING PRINCIPLES

The sentencing of those convicted of environmental offences is generally intended to serve the same ends as penalties imposed on other wrongdoers. Punishment along with deterrence of further violations either by the convicted offender or by others are basic objectives, although considerable emphasis is placed on the goal of environmental protection in the public interest that underpins the overall regulatory regime.[76]

To promote compliance, a number of jurisdictions have revised their penalty provisions by increasing the severity of the potential consequences of ignoring environmental protection requirements. The level of fines authorized by statute was raised significantly in several jurisdic-

---

74 Chris Tollefson, "Stormy Weather: The Recent History of the Citizen Submission Process of the North American Agreement on Environmental Cooperation" in John Kirton & Virginia MacLaren, eds., *Linking Trade, Environment and Social Cohesion: NAFTA Experiences, Global Challenges* (Aldershot, UK: Ashgate, 2002) at 161.

75 For information on Canadian submissions resulting in factual records, see online: www.cec.org/citizen/status/index/cfm?varlan+english, accessible through www.cec.org/citizen, with particular reference to files on B.C. Hydro, B.C. Logging, B.C. Mining, Oldman River II, Ontario Logging, Ontario Logging II and Quebec Automobiles.

76 For discussion see Swanson & Hughes, above note 64 at 180–82.

tions during the 1980s. Individuals convicted under Manitoba's *Environment Act*, for example, are subject in the case of a first offence to a fine of not more than $50,000 or a term of imprisonment of up to six months, or to both. In the case of subsequent offences, the fine and potential prison term are increased to $100,000 and one year respectively. Corporate accused face a fine of up to $500,000 for a first offence and up to $1,000,000 for subsequent convictions.[77] In some jurisdictions, corporate offenders may also be subject to profit stripping.[78] As discussed more fully in the following chapter, increases in the personal exposure of corporate officers and directors to prosecution have appeared.[79]

Courts have considered and ordered prison sentences in a variety of circumstances involving environmental offences. These have included contempt as well as substantive offences under environmental legislation. In *R. v. Jetco Manufacturing Ltd.*,[80] a sentence of one year's imprisonment for contempt plus a further month up to a total of fifteen months for every day of delay in undertaking remedial work was ordered. The convictions of both the corporate defendant and the president were set aside on appeal on the grounds that it had not been satisfactorily established in evidence that the defendants had notice of the prohibition order, violation of which was the basis of the contempt.[81] In *R. v. B.E.S.T. Plating Shoppe Ltd.*,[82] Siapas, the president of B.E.S.T., was sentenced to a term of imprisonment not exceeding six months in an application for a contempt order arising from repeated violations of a prohibition order made pursuant to the former Ontario *Municipal Act* concerning discharges in contravention of Metropolitan Toronto's sewer-use bylaw. On *Charter* grounds, the contempt finding against the individual defendant was set aside on appeal.[83] Following a trial of the contempt charges, B.E.S.T.'s president was convicted and sentenced to six months' imprisonment.[84] In *R. v. Blackbird Holdings Ltd.*, a convicted director was jailed for violation of an environmental statute rather than

---

77   The *Environment Act*, C.C.S.M. c. E125, s.33. Substantially higher fines are now also anticipated in Ontario in connection with convictions under the OEPA, the OWRA, above note 2, and the *Pesticides Act*, R.S.O. 1990. c. P.11, as a result of the *Environmental Enforcement Statute Law Amendment Act*, S.O. 2005, c. 12.

78   AEPEA, above note 67, s. 216; *CEPA, 1999*, above note 5, s. 290; *MBCA*, above note 5, s. 13(5).

79   *Environmental Protection Act*, R.S.O. 1990, c. E.19, s. 194; *CEPA, 1999*, ibid., s. 280.1.

80   (1986), 1 C.E.L.R. (N.S.) 79 (Ont. H.C.J.).

81   *R. v. Jetco Manufacturing Ltd.* (1987), 57 O.R. (2d) 776 (C.A.).

82   (1986), 1 C.E.L.R. (N.S.) 85 (Ont. H.C.J.).

83   *R. v. B.E.S.T. Plating Shoppe Ltd.* (1987), 59 O.R. (2d) 145 (C.A.).

84   *Metropolitan Toronto (Municipality) v. Siapas* (1988), 3 C.E.L.R. (N.S.) 122 (Ont. H.C.J.).

on the basis of contempt.[85] Overall however, the use of imprisonment in Canadian environmental cases has been rare.[86]

In the context of public welfare offences such as environmental offences, consideration of imprisonment or significant financial penalties is closely associated with deterrence. The following discussion outlines the judicial basis of concern for this objective:

> In our complex interdependent modern society . . . regulatory statutes [such as ecological conservation statutes] are accepted as essential in the public interest. They ensure standards of conduct, performance and reliability by various economic groups and make life tolerable for all. To a very large extent the enforcement of such statutes is achieved by fines, imposed on offending corporations. . . Above all, the amount of the fine will be determined by the need to enforce regulatory standards by deterrence.
>
> With reference to these offences, deterrence is not to be taken only in its usual negative connotation of achieving compliance by threat of punishment. Recently [this court] . . . referred to deterrence in a more positive aspect:
>
>> But in a crime of this type the deterrent quality of the sentence must be given paramount consideration, and here I am using the term deterrent in its widest sense. A sentence by emphasizing community disapproval of an act, and branding it as reprehensible has a more educative effect, and thereby affects the attitude of the public. One then hopes that a person with an attitude thus conditioned to regard such conduct as reprehensible will not commit such an act.
>
> This aspect of deterrence is particularly applicable to public welfare offences where it is essential for the proper functioning of our society for citizens at large to expect that the basic rules are established and enforced to protect the physical, economic and social welfare of the public.[87]

The remedial powers of courts have been extended beyond fines and imprisonment to include authority to order restoration work, to

---

85 (1990), 6 C.E.L.R.(N.S.) 119 (Ont. Prov. Offences Ct.), var'd (1991), 6 C.E.L.R. (N.S.) 138 (Ont. Prov. Div), leave to appeal refused (1991), 6 C.E.L.R. (N.S.) 116 (Ont. C.A.).

86 *R. v. Varnicolor Chemical Ltd.* (1992), 9 C.E.L.R. (N.S.) 176, [1992] O.J. No. 1978 (Prov. Div.); *R. v. Demacedo*, [1992] B.C.J. No. 2254 (Prov. Ct.); *R. v. Fontaine*, [1992] B.C.J. No. 2640 (Prov. Ct.); *R. v Underwood*, (unreported, 29 March, 1996) (Alta. Q.B.).

87 *R. v. Cotton Felts Ltd.* (1982), 2 C.C.C. (3d) 287 (Ont. C.A.).

prevent or reduce the likelihood of recurrence of environmental harm, or to impose other potentially costly obligations in connection with a conviction.[88] In addition to any other punishment under *CEPA, 1999* the court—subject to the nature and circumstances of the offence—may make a variety of other enumerated orders:

(*a*) prohibiting the offender from doing any act or engaging in any activity that may result in the continuation or repetition of the offence;

(*b*) directing the offender to take any action that the court considers appropriate to remedy or avoid any harm to the environment that results or may result from the act or omission that constituted the offence;

(*c*) directing the offender to prepare and implement a pollution prevention plan or environmental emergency plan;

(*d*) directing the offender to carry out environmental effects monitoring in the manner established by the Minister or directing the offender to pay, in the manner prescribed by the court, an amount for the purposes of environmental effects monitoring;

(*e*) directing the offender to implement an environmental management system that meets a recognized Canadian or international standard;

(*f*) directing the offender to have an environmental audit conducted by a person of a class and at the times specified by the court and directing the offender to remedy any deficiencies revealed during the audit;

(*g*) directing the offender to publish, in the manner directed by the court, the facts relating to the conviction;

(*h*) directing the offender to notify, at the offender's own cost and in the manner directed by the court, any person aggrieved or affected by the offender's conduct of the facts relating to the conviction;

(*i*) directing the offender to post any bond or pay any amount of money into court that will ensure compliance with any order made under this section;

(*j*) directing the offender to submit to the Minister, on application by the Minister made within three years after the date of conviction, any information with respect to the offender's activities that the court considers appropriate and just in the circumstances;

---

88   For a well-documented review of environmental enforcement see Huestis, above note 39.

(k) directing the offender to compensate the Minister in whole or in part, for the cost of any remedial or preventative action taken by or caused to be taken on behalf of the Minister as a result of the act or omission that constituted the offence;

(l) directing the offender to perform community service, subject to any reasonable conditions that may be imposed in the order;

(m) directing that the amount of any fine or other monetary award be allocated, subject to the Criminal Code and any regulations that may be made under section 278, in accordance with any directions of the court that are made on the basis of the harm or risk of harm caused by the commission of the offence;

(n) directing the offender to pay, in the manner prescribed by the court, an amount for the purposes of conducting research into the ecological use and disposal of the substance in respect of which the offence was committed or research relating to the manner of carrying out environmental effects monitoring;

(o) directing the offender to pay, in the manner prescribed by the court, an amount to environmental, health or other groups to assist in their work in the community where the offence was committed;

(p) directing the offender to pay, in the manner prescribed by the court an amount to an educational institution for scholarships for students enrolled in environmental studies; and

(q) requiring the offender to comply with any other reasonable conditions that the court considers appropriate and just in the circumstances for securing the offender's good conduct and for preventing the offender from repeating the same offence or committing other offences.[89]

Some legislation, including the Manitoba statute whose penalty provisions were noted above, confers on judges a licence-revocation power that may be exercised "where in the opinion of the judge the individual [or corporation] is unwilling or unable to remedy the situation or condition giving rise to the offence."[90]

The task of determining the most appropriate sentencing option in the circumstances of a successful environmental prosecution rests with the court. The judiciary therefore constitute a vital element of the

---

89 *CEPA, 1999,* above note 5, s. 291; see also *Wild Animal and Plant Protection and Regulation of International and Interprovincial Trade Act,* S.C. 1992, c. 52, s. 22(6); *FA,* above note 3, s. 79.2.

90 Manitoba *Environment Act,* above note 77, s. 33.

compliance and enforcement structure, and so the principles applicable to their sentencing decisions are of considerable importance.

Principles on sentencing in environmental cases as articulated by Stewart J. in *R. v. United Keno Hill Mines Ltd.*[91] set out a framework for evaluating the available options. Relevant considerations include the nature of the environment affected by the offence; the degree of damage and the deliberateness of the offence, together with the accused's attitude and any indication of remorse; evidence of efforts made to comply; the nature and size of the corporation and any realization of profits from the offence; previous criminal record; and other evidence of the character of the convicted corporation or individual.

It is also possible for the legislature to address the matter of considerations relevant to sentencing, as was done in the case of pollution offences under the *Canada Shipping Act, 2001* which stipulates that a maximum fine of $1,000,000 may be ordered on conviction. The statute itself identifies factors to which the court may have regard in determining punishment:

(a) the harm or risk of harm caused by the offence;

(b) an estimate of the total costs of clean-up, of harm caused, and of the best available mitigation measures;

(c) the remedial action taken, or proposed to be taken, by the offender to mitigate the harm;

(d) whether the discharge or anticipated discharge was reported in accordance with the regulations . . .

(e) any economic benefits accruing to the offender that, but for the offence, the offender would not have received; and

(f) any evidence from which the court may reasonably conclude that the offender has a history of non-compliance with legislation designed to prevent or to minimize pollution.[92]

Notable even in the context of sentencing principles is the need to assess and balance direct environmental protection and restoration measures alongside more traditional punitive and deterrence considerations. Thus counsel, even at the time of argument on sentencing, must reflect carefully on the suitability of possible penalties to various underlying objectives of the environmental law regime, including prevention, restoration, and environmental protection.

---

91 (1980), 10 C.E.L.R. 43 (Y. Terr. Ct.).

92 *Canada Shipping Act, 2001*, S.C. 2001, c. 26, s. 191(4). See also *CEPA, 1999*, above note 5, s. 287. Whether the absence of explicit reference to general deterrence as an enumerated consideration will affect sentencing remains to be determined. See *R. v. B.W.P.*, 2006 SCC 27.

Creative sentencing decisions are beginning to emerge. When, during refuelling of the motor vessel "Lil Buddy LS 855," gasoline was discharged into the waters of British Columbia's Pitt River, contrary to oil pollution prevention regulations under the *Canada Shipping Act,* the court, upon conviction of the accused company, ordered a comparatively modest fine. In addition, however, the company was required to pay a further sum, ultimately to be made available to a community environmental organization to support its work on conservation and protection of fish and fish habitat.[93]

FURTHER READINGS

BERGER, S.D., The Prosecution and Defence of Environmental Offences (Toronto: Emond Montgomery, 1993)

CAMPBELL, G.S., "Fostering a compliance culture through creative sentencing for environmental offences" (2004) 9 Can. Crim. L. Rev. 1-33

COMMISSION FOR ENVIRONMENTAL COOPERATION, *Special Report on Enforcement Activities* (June 2001)

DUNCAN, L.F., *Enforcing Environmental Law: A Guide to Private Prosecutions* (Edmonton: Environmental Law Centre, 1990)

HALLEY, PAULE, *Le droit penal de l'environnement: l'interdiction de polluter* (Montreal: Yvon Blais, 2001)

LAW REFORM COMMISSION OF CANADA, *Sentencing in Environmental Cases* (Study Paper) by J. Swaigen & G. Bunt (Ottawa: the Commission, 1985)

SAXE, D., *Environmental Offences: Corporate Responsibility and Executive Liability* (Aurora, ON: Canada Law Book, 1990)

SWAIGEN, J., *Regulatory Offences in Canada: Liability & Defences* (Toronto: Carswell, 1992)

VALIANTE, M., "'Welcomed Participants' or 'Environmental Vigilantes'? The CEPA Environmental Protection Action and the Role of Citizen Suits" (2002) 25 Dal. L.J. 81

---

93   R. v. *Forrest Marine Ltd.* (29 April 2005) (B.C. Prov. Ct.).

WEBB, K., "Taking Matters into Their Own Hands: The Role of Citizens in Canadian Pollution Control Enforcement" (1991) 36 McGill L.J. 770

CORPORATE ENVIRONMENTAL OBLIGATIONS AND DIRECTORS' AND OFFICERS' LIABILITY

A. THE LIABILITY OF CORPORATIONS

Among the principal forms of business organizations—sole proprietorships, partnerships, and corporations—the last, corporations, has attracted particular attention from an environmental perspective. Despite many variations in corporate form, from small, not-for-profit entities to major multinational firms, in the environmental context corporations are regarded as serious sources of potential harm whose operations require careful supervision and control. Environmental risks inherent in the use of dangerous pollutants may be accentuated by competitive pressures on corporate profitability.

While the nature and magnitude of the risks create an obvious public interest in channelling corporate behaviour in ways that reduce the likelihood of environmental damage, the practical problems of influencing corporate behaviour through the legal regime must be faced. Those who rely on legal mechanisms, criminal sanctions in particular, have had to consider how a regime of prohibitions and penalties will affect corporate operations. In the context of corporate accused, some aspects of criminal law pose especially intriguing problems. The need, in relation to the prosecution of certain offences, to establish a guilty mind or some form of intent on the part of accused corporations is one obvious example.

Although it may be argued that corporate action ultimately depends on human agency, or that the corporation can never act alone, the tendency is to subordinate philosophical dilemmas in the context of holding corporations responsible for wrongdoing. One analysis sets out the normative and practical arguments. First, justice requires that everyone in breach of penal law be equally subject to prosecution. "It is hardly fair," the analysis continues, "that individuals committing rather petty crimes, almost always entailing only one or a few victims, are subject to prosecution and imprisonment while a corporation might cause harm on a far grander scale, yet escape punishment." Second, although individual actions within a corporate environment may not constitute a crime when considered separately, the cumulative impact can be criminal and blameworthy; to exempt the corporation from liability would be to permit such crime to go unchecked. Moreover, corporations, because of the collectivity of individuals involved, can and do behave as the persons that they, in strict point of law, are. Corporations are therefore susceptible to stigmatization (harm to status or reputation), and deterrence in the same way individuals are. Finally, access to resources, information, and expertise makes corporations better able to take measures to avoid the commission of criminal offences than individuals ordinarily are.[1]

Another approach to the conceptual challenges of holding corporations accountable for criminal offences attributed to them is to minimize the criminal dimensions of the situation. Such an approach is hinted at by Chief Justice Lamer, who expressed the opinion that "when the criminal law is applied to a corporation, it loses much of its 'criminal' nature and becomes, in essence, a 'vigorous' form of administrative law." Since the stigma attached to conviction is effectively reduced to a financial penalty, the corporation—which cannot be imprisoned—is in a completely different situation than is an individual.[2] As discussed below, recent changes to the *Criminal Code* in the aftermath of the Westray Mine disaster appear to have increased the direct exposure of corporations to criminal liability.

Corporate liability for environmental violations has rested on a variety of grounds. One means of linking the responsibility of the corporation directly with the conduct of individuals in its employ takes the form of vicarious liability. Such an approach appears in some regu-

---

1   M.A. Bowden & T. Quigley, "Pinstripes or Prison Stripes? The Liability of Corporations and Directors for Environmental Offences" (1995) 5 J. Envtl. L. & Prac. 209 at 222.

2   *R. v. Wholesale Travel Group Inc.*, [1991] 3 S.C.R. 154 at 182.

latory legislation, Alberta's *Environmental Protection and Enhancement Act*, for example, where it is provided that

> for the purposes of this Act, an act or thing done or omitted to be done by a director, officer, official, employee or agent of a corporation in the course of his employment or in the exercise of his powers or the performance of his duties shall be deemed also to be an act or thing done or omitted to be done by the corporation.[3]

Corporations may also be held liable directly if their actions are identified with the conduct of some individual, typically a senior official, who is seen for the purpose as being the "directing mind" of the corporation. Depending on the circumstances, there may be several directing minds, as the Supreme Court of Canada explained in *Canadian Dredge & Dock*,

> a corporation may . . . have more than one directing mind. This must be particularly so in a country such as Canada where corporate operations are frequently geographically widespread. The transportation companies, for example, must of necessity operate by the delegation and sub-delegation of authority from the corporate centre; by the division and subdivision of the corporate brain; and by decentralizing by delegation the guiding forces in the corporate undertaking.[4]

The inquiry required by this theoretical identification of the corporation with a directing mind was more fully explained by the S.C.C. in a subsequent decision:

> the focus of [the] inquiry must be whether the impugned individual has been delegated the "governing executive authority" of the company within the scope of his or her authority. I interpret this to mean that one must determine whether the discretion conferred on an employee amounts to an express or implied delegation of executive authority to design and supervise the implementation of corporate policy rather than simply to carry out such policy. In other words, the Courts must consider who has been left with the decision-making power in a relevant sphere of corporate activity.[5]

---

3   *Environmental Protection and Enhancement Act*, R.S.A. 2000, c. E-12, s. 239 [AE-PEA]. Clauses of this type address the attribution of conduct to the corporation, but are insufficient to attribute an employee's mental state to the corporation insofar as the mental element of an offence is concerned. See *R. v. Safety-Kleen Canada Inc.* (1997), 32 O.R. (3d) 493 (C.A.).

4   *R. v. Canadian Dredge & Dock Co.*, [1985] 1 S.C.R. 662 at 693.

5   *The Rhone v. The Peter B. Widener*, [1993] 1 S.C.R. 497 at 520–21.

For purposes of the *Criminal Code*, amendments were introduced following the Westray Mine experience where, in May 1992, twenty-six miners died in a coal mine explosion. A public inquiry found that management had either disregarded or even encouraged a number of hazardous or illegal practices which contributed to the explosion.[6] Legislative changes now set out principles for attributing criminal liability to "organizations" in relation to the conduct of individuals determined to be their "representative." As a result of the new provisions, corporations may now more readily face prosecution for both intentional offences and offences grounded on proof of negligence.[7]

Although a degree of uncertainty still surrounds the actual mechanisms of accountability for environmental offences, corporations are clearly expected to comply with the entire range of environmental requirements including anti-pollution provisions, licensing conditions, spills reporting, and cleanup obligations, the duty to implement administrative orders, and so on. They may accordingly face prescribed penalties.

B. DIRECTORS' AND OFFICERS' LIABILITY

Despite the imposition of liability on corporations, the practical impact remains uncertain, notably in relation to the potential of conviction to alter environmentally harmful behaviour. How, it is asked, can a monetary penalty—generally modest in relation to corporate assets, and possibly even paid for by consumers in the form of marginally higher prices—effectively promote environmental compliance? The assumption has been made that to ensure that corporations will devote adequate resources to compliance it is necessary to engage the attention of their most senior policy makers through personal liability. In the words of Chief Justice Stewart of the Yukon Territorial Court: "Fining corporations leaves the upper echelon policy makers relatively unscathed. Fining corporate policy makers reduces somewhat the impotency of levying fines against corporate assets." Personal liability, he argued, "is the most effective method of ensuring that persons with the power to shape corporate policy are deterred from either active or passive acquiescence in the development of corporate policies precipitating violations."[8]

---

6   Westray Mine Public Inquiry, *The Westray Story: A Predictable Path to Disaster, Report of the Westray Mine Public Inquiry* by Justice K. Peter Richard, Commissioner, online: www.gov.ns.ca/lwd/pubs/westray.

7   *Criminal Code*, R.S.C. 1985, c. C-46, ss. 22.1 & 22.2.

8   *R. v. United Keno Hill Mines Ltd.* (1980), 10 C.E.L.R. 43 at 52 and 55 (Y. Terr. Ct.).

In *R. v. Northwest Territories Power Corp.*, another northern judge insisted on the need to penalize individuals directly for corporate wrongdoing. Where it appeared that a regulated public corporation—having pleaded guilty to a violation of subsection 36(3) of the *Fisheries Act*—would simply recover the cost of a fine through its rate base, Justice Bourassa concluded that the defendant regarded the matter as "but an annoying, irritating obligation, rather than an important continuing responsibility."[9] To encourage a more responsible approach and to prevent future offences, Bourassa J. chose to involve directors in sentencing and concluded that he would require the directors and chief executive officer "to apologize to the public for the corporation's negligence."[10] In explaining the sentence, he formulated a rationale based on the fact that directors accept "the responsibility of overseeing and directing corporate management. They reflect the corporate character, and must be accountable for it."[11] The responsibilities of directors, he further observed, extend to "the policies, priorities and values inherent in the corporation's operations."[12] In making the link between individual conduct and corporate environmental performance, Bourassa J. stated:

> The public is never made aware of who these people are who, rhetorically speaking, love their children, go to church on Sunday and preside over the degradation of the public domain on Monday . . . . To impact upon the directors of a corporate defendant is likely . . . to prevent further offences, in that the directors will realize that they are and will be accountable for their acts (or omissions) on "Monday"—that they cannot shelter behind a corporate veil.[13]

Although Bourassa J.'s order for an apology was struck down on appeal,[14] the objective of promoting corporate compliance by means of imposing accountability on directors and other senior officers has gained acceptance.

Even in the absence of express statutory provision, corporate officials have long been liable to prosecution as parties to a corporate offence on the grounds that they aided or abetted the corporation in the commission of the wrongful act. But express liability provisions

---

9   *R. v. Northwest Territories Power Corp.* (1989), [1990] N.W.T.R. 115 at 119 (Terr. Ct.).

10   *Ibid.* at 123.

11   *Ibid.* at 122.

12   *Ibid.*

13   *Ibid.* at 122–23.

14   *R. v. Northwest Territories Power Corp.*, [1990] N.W.T.R. 125 (S.C.).

for directors and other corporate officials are now frequently found in environmental legislation. *CEPA, 1999*, for example, explicitly imposes personal liability on individuals, including officers and directors:

> Where a corporation commits an offence under this Act, any officer, director or agent of the corporation who directed, authorized, assented to, acquiesced in or participated in the commission of the offence is a party to and guilty of the offence, and is liable to the punishment provided for the offence, whether or not the corporation has been prosecuted and convicted.[15]

In addition to their customary responsibilities for corporate operations, officers and directors have also been more clearly singled out in provincial and territorial legislation for personal liability in relation to corporate environmental practices.[16] The liability of directors and officers under Quebec's *Environment Quality Act* (*EQA*) is associated with the use of an order, an authorization, advice, or encouragement that leads the corporation to commit an offence.[17]

A range of uncertainties relating to the necessary elements of offences formulated in this manner has somewhat limited the prosecutorial appeal of such provisions. In particular, the nature of conduct (passive or active) that would amount to assent or acquiescence has not been entirely clear.[18] Moreover, given the underlying assumption that directors' and officers' liability serves to improve corporate performance in the environmental field, prosecutors may be required to demonstrate actual influence and perhaps control of relevant aspects of corporate activity.

Partially as a consequence of the ambiguities, Ontario reformulated the environmental responsibility of directors and officers in 1986, imposing on them a "duty to take all reasonable care to prevent the corporation from causing or permitting . . . unlawful deposit, addition,

---

15   *Canadian Environmental Protection Act, 1999*, S.C. 1999, c. 33, s. 280 [*CEPA, 1999*]. Similar federal provisions are found in the *Transportation of Dangerous Goods Act, 1992*, S.C. 1992, c. 34, s. 39 [*TDGA*] and the *Fisheries Act*, R.S.C. 1985, c. F-14, s. 78.2, as am. by S.C. 1991, c. 1, s. 24.

16   *AEPEA*, above note 3, s. 218; *Environment Act*, C.C.S.M. c. E125, s. 35; *Environment Act*, S.N.S. 1994–95, c. 1, s. 164 [*NSEA*]; *Environmental Protection Act*, R.S.P.E.I. 1988, c. E-9, s. 32(3).

17   *Environment Quality Act*, R.S.Q. 1977, c. Q-2, s. 109.3.

18   For a discussion of the issues raised by s. 122 of *CEPA*. Now see *CEPA, 1999*, above note 15, s. 280.1, and similarly worded provisions, see D. Saxe, *Environmental Offences: Corporate Responsibility and Executive Liability* (Aurora, ON: Canada Law Book, 1990) at 131–36.

emission or discharge,"[19] and making failure to carry out that duty an offence. A roughly comparable duty is now found in section 280(2) of *CEPA, 1999*:

> Every director and officer of a corporation shall take all reasonable care to ensure that the corporation complies with
> (a) this Act and the regulations; and
> (b) orders and directions of, and prohibitions and requirements imposed by, the Minister and enforcement officers and review officers.

The intention of the Ontario initiative, according to one well-placed observer, was that the amendments would "serve a normative and educational function by bringing home to corporate officials their personal obligation to the public to govern the corporation in a manner that gives priority to the establishment and proper operation of pollution prevention systems."[20]

In the context of applying the new Ontario provision, an important procedural issue arose, one engaging underlying considerations associated with evidentiary responsibilities in the prosecution of regulatory offences, and directly affecting the utility and effectiveness of the provision. It was understood by some that the Crown would have the procedural burden of establishing not only that a corporation had engaged in a prohibited activity but also that the officer or director charged under section 194 had failed to take reasonable care in attempting to prevent the offence. On the other hand, it was argued that evidentiary responsibility regarding due diligence rested with the accused. In *R. v. Bata Industries Ltd.*,[21] the court concluded that, notwithstanding the statutory language, the failure to take all reasonable care was not an element of the *actus reus* that the prosecution must prove beyond a reasonable doubt. Rather, the defendants would continue to bear the burden of establishing due diligence on a balance of probabilities. This interpretation was subsequently rejected in another provincial court decision, *R. v. Commander Business Furniture Inc.*, where Hackett J. concluded that:

---

19   *Environment Enforcement Statute Law Amendment Act, 1986*, S.O. 1986, c. 68, s. 17.

20   J. Swaigen, "*Ontario's Environment Enforcement Statute Law Amendment Act, 1986*" (1987) 2 C.E.L.R. (N.S.) 14 at 19. For further discussion see J. Swaigen, *Regulatory Offences in Canada: Liability & Defences* (Toronto: Carswell, 1992) at 152–57.

21   (1992), 9 O.R. (3d) 329 (Prov. Ct.). Charges were laid under both the Ontario *Environmental Protection Act*, R.S.O. 1990, c. E.19 [*OEPA*] and the *OWRA*. Convictions were registered under the *OWRA*, while the *OEPA* charges were stayed.

the . . . wording . . . is such that the Crown must prove not only that the director is engaged in an activity that may result in the discharge of a contaminant, but it must also prove that he or she failed to take all reasonable care to prevent it. In my view, this goes beyond proof of an actus reus or a discharge which caused an adverse effect.

Hackett J. further explained his understanding of the content of the Crown's obligations as calling for actual evidence concerning the conduct or non-performance of the accused:

> To prove a failure to take all reasonable care, in my view, means that the Crown must prove an act or failure to act which amounts to negligent conduct or an objective intention beyond a reasonable doubt. The words . . . indicate to me that the legislature intended that the fault for this offence must be proved by the Crown rather than, as it is the case in most strict liability offences, disproved by the defence on a balance of probabilities.[22]

Further legislative amendment to the *OEPA* in 2005 more clearly asserts the conclusion reached in *Bata*. The amended section 194 (1) extends the range of environmental offences which "every director or officer or a corporation has a duty to take all reasonable care to prevent the corporation" from committing. Failure to carry out that duty is made an offence pursuant to section 194 (2), and the evidentiary burden relating to fulfilment of the duty is assigned to the accused as follows:

> If a director or officer of a corporation is charged with an offence under subsection (2) in connection with a specific contravention of the corporation, the director or officer has the onus, in the trial of the offence, of proving that he or she carried out the duty under subsection (1) in connection with that contravention.[23]

This provision has attracted considerable interest and attention on the part of corporate advisors seeking to ensure that appropriate means to demonstrate due diligence are in place, should an officer or director be called upon to establish the all reasonable care defence. Indeed, the early *Bata* proceedings were extremely successful from the perspective of "consciousness raising" for directors and officers. Publicity surrounding the Ministry of the Environment's decision to charge the chairman and chief executive officer of Bata, along with two other senior officials who were eventually convicted, contributed significantly to the level of

---

22   (1992), 9 C.E.L.R. (N.S.) 185 at 250–51 (Ont. Prov. Ct.).
23   *OEPA*, above note 21, s. 194 (2.1).

awareness of directors' and officers' responsibilities with respect to the environment.

Decisions to expand and make explicit the liability of directors and officers have been premised on some combination of perceived wrong-doing and the assumption that personal exposure to penalties would induce the individuals whose decisions govern corporate behaviour to address environmental considerations more forthrightly and system-atically.[24] Although the evidence is inconclusive, there is some support for the premise. For example, one survey found that "corporate execu-tives reported that attention to environmental matters at the highest levels of the firm, and corporate efforts to avoid pollution, would be greater if corporate executives faced the possibility of personal pros-ecution for pollution."[25] Another observer remarked anecdotally that, in the aftermath of written warnings to individual officers and dir-ectors of companies with three or more convictions under Metro To-ronto's sewage-control bylaws, at least eight of the nineteen companies involved initiated measures to prevent future contraventions.[26]

In *Bata* the trial judge had endeavoured to ensure that the personal liability of the officials convicted would not be diffused. He therefore issued an order prohibiting the corporation from indemnifying the in-dividual officers for the financial penalties imposed by the judgment. That order was subsequently determined by the Court of Appeal to have been improperly made against Bata in light of the purpose of the probation orders under the *Provincial Offences Act* and in light of de-tailed provisions governing indemnification set out in Ontario's *Busi-ness Corporations Act*.[27]

1) Strict Liability and Environmental Due Diligence

The defence of due diligence, which is available to an accused facing prosecution for a strict liability offence,[28] is often specifically incor-porated in environmental legislation. Whether expressed as "all due

---

24 For a review of the arguments, see Saxe, above note 18 at 31–45.

25 Saxe, *ibid.* at 53–54; see also D. Saxe, "The Impact of Prosecution of Corpora-tions and Their Officers and Directors upon Regulatory Compliance by Cor-porations" (1991) 1 J.Envtl. L. & Prac. 91.

26 H. Poch, *Corporate and Municipal Environmental Law* (Toronto: Carswell, 1989) at 60–62.

27 R.S.O. 1990, c. B.16, s. 136; *R. v. Bata Industries Ltd.* (1995), 25 O.R. (3d) 321 (C.A.) [*Bata*].

28 On the availability of a due diligence defence in the context of administrative penalties, see chapter 7.

diligence"[29] or as "all reasonable measures to comply"[30] or in the form of "a duty to take all reasonable care,"[31] the concept entails a demonstration that the accused's conduct prior to the offence satisfies the expected standard.

In the context of a prosecution, the due diligence standard has been subject to judicial consideration. It has been remarked, for example, that "[r]easonable care and due diligence do not mean superhuman efforts. They mean a high standard of awareness and decisive, prompt and continuing action."[32] What constitutes adequate due diligence for any particular defendant in the context of a given environmental offence will be a matter for determination by the court.

In the *Bata* decision, Ormston Prov. J. outlined certain general principles of a director's due diligence:

(a) Did the board of directors establish a pollution prevention "system" ... *i.e.*, was there supervision or inspection? Was there improvement in business methods? did he exhort those he controlled or influenced?

(b) Did each director ensure that the corporate officers have been instructed to set up a system sufficient within the terms and practices of its industry of ensuring compliance with environmental laws, to ensure that the officers report back periodically to the board on the operation of the system, and to ensure that the officers are instructed to report any substantial non-compliance to the board in a timely manner?

Directors, Ormston J. further observed,

(c) ... are responsible for reviewing the environmental compliance reports provided by the officers of the corporation, but are justified in placing *reasonable* reliance on reports provided to them by corporate officers, consultants, counsel or other informed parties.

(d) The directors should substantiate that the officers are promptly addressing environmental concerns brought to their attention by government agencies or other concerned parties including shareholders.

---

29 *CEPA, 1999* above note 15, s. 283, *Fisheries Act*, above note 15, s. 78.6.

30 *TDGA*, above 15, s. 40.

31 *OEPA*, above note 21, s. 194.

32 Fitzpatrick Prov. J. in *R. v. Courtaulds Fibres Canada* (1992), 9 C.E.L.R. (N.S.) 304 at 313 (Ont. Prov. Ct.).

(e) The directors should be aware of the standards of their industry, and other industries which deal with similar environmental pollutants or risks.

(f) The directors should immediately and personally react when they have noticed the system has failed.

Within this general profile and dependent upon the nature and structure of the corporate activity, one would hope to find remedial and contingency plans for spills, a system of ongoing environmental audit, training programs, sufficient authority to act and other indices of a pro-active environmental policy.[33]

In determining whether the due diligence standard has been met, the courts have identified a number of factors that must be weighed and balanced. These include: nature and gravity of the adverse effect; foreseeability of the effect, including abnormal sensitivities; alternative solutions available; legislative or regulatory compliance; industry standards; character of the neighbourhood; efforts (if any) made to address the problem; period of time over which such efforts were made, and promptness of response; matters beyond the control of the accused, including technological limitations; skill level expected of the accused; complexities involved; preventive systems; economic considerations; and actions of officials.

An active consulting industry has grown up to provide advice and due diligence "checklists" so that, in the event charges are laid for the violation of some relevant statute, the foundations of the defence will be available. Basic initiatives involve allocating environmental decision-making responsibilities, establishing regular reporting procedures, self-monitoring and internal reviews, staff training, and other more elaborate measures that may entail capital and ongoing operating expenditures. Since due diligence involves systematic efforts to detect possible environmental liabilities and to remedy them, the component activities have the potential to play a significant preventive role.

That general systems of due diligence may have been encouraged by recent jurisprudential pronouncements is welcome. But in a noteworthy decision, the British Columbia Court of Appeal made clear that while the structural framework of a system of due diligence may be a necessary component of a defence to strict liability offences, this will not always be sufficient. In R. v. Imperial Oil that court emphasized an important distinction between general systems of due diligence and

---

33 R. v. Bata Industries (1992), 7 C.E.L.R. (N.S.) 245 at paras. 134–35 (Ont. Prov. Div.).

due diligence in relation to the specific event giving rise to charges. While the defendant corporation, charged when plant effluent killed fish in Burrard Inlet, argued that it was entitled to rely on the advice of a chemical supplier that its product was not toxic to fish, and that its general program of identifying and remedying potential sources of environmental risk would shortly have addressed the situation, a majority of the court took a different view. The company had not specifically contemplated in a timely manner the implications of a release by means of its effluent discharge of what was in fact a toxic substance into neighbouring water.[34] Some further insight into what a corporation may be expected to contemplate for the purpose of safeguarding itself against the success of such charges is provided by the courts' observation in R. v. MacMillan Bloedel that the "foresight required will vary with the level of expertise generally acceptable in a given industry, and a link can be made to the factor of industry standards."[35]

The challenges of demonstrating due diligence will vary with particular circumstances—a fact which was highlighted in R. v. Petro Canada. Here, the company had been charged with causing a gasoline spill from an undetermined location in an extensive network of pipes. Given its inability to identify the specific source of the leak, and thus to point to directly-related due diligence measures, the company's due diligence defence emphasized the safety systems it had established to detect spills and leakage. The trial court rejected this attempt to show diligence on the grounds that the cause of the leak was not established. In setting this determination aside and ordering a retrial of the matter, the court of appeal indicated that it is unnecessary for a defendant to identify the exact source or cause of harm in order to invoke the defence. As Goudge, J.A. explained, however, there would be a clear advantage in being able to point more precisely to the source of harm:

> where the accused can do this, it may be able to narrow the range of preventative steps that it must show to establish that it took all reasonable care. However, where . . . the accused cannot prove the precise cause of the pipe failure that due diligence defence is not rendered unavailable as a result. That being said, it must be emphasized that to invoke the defence successfully in such circumstances, the accused must show that it took all reasonable care to avoid any foreseeable cause.[36]

---

34   R. v. Imperial Oil (2000), 36 C.E.L.R. (N.S.) 109 (B.C.C.A.).
35   (2002), 220 D.L.R. (4th) 173 (B.C.C.A.).
36   R. v. Petro-Canada (2003), 63 O.R. (3d) 219 at 224 (C.A.).

2) The Environmental Audit

An environmental audit process offers some measure of independent review, assessment or evaluation of performance in relation to expected and required standards. Although sometimes described as "self-inspection," the audit is most likely to be conducted by consultants or specialized professionals provided with authority to examine a company's operations, to make inquiries concerning practices and procedures, to compare these with corporate policy and existing regulatory requirements and to report their findings back to the senior administration. The audit serves increasingly as a vital element in systems of due diligence and in programs of prevention. That is, in the event of prosecution for a strict liability offence, the existence of an audit program may be of assistance in support of the reasonable care defence.[37] Audits and other forms of self-inspection also play a preventive role in that they allow conscientious management to identify sources of operational risk and to implement further measures to reduce the potential for environmental harm.

The precise nature of an adequate and effective environmental audit has not been standardized in Canada. However, one definition sets out the essential criteria and basic objectives this way:

> [E]nvironmental audit is a systematic, documented, objective evaluation of a facility's management, operations, and equipment that may have either a direct or indirect effect on the environment with a view to assessing (1) compliance with corporate policies, which should include meeting regulatory requirements; (2) risks of exposure to liability for environmental damage; and (3) opportunities for reducing, reusing or recycling wastes.[38]

In the context of *CEPA, 1999*'s enforcement and compliance policy, audits are described as

> [i]nternal evaluations by companies and government agencies to verify their compliance with legal requirements as well as their own internal policies and standards. They are conducted by companies, government agencies, and others on a voluntary basis, and are carried out by either outside consultants or employees of the company

---

37   See *Bata*, above note 27; *R. v. Rio Algom Ltd.* (1988), 66 O.R. (2d) 674 (C.A.); *R. v. J. Clark & Son Ltd.* (1979), 25 N.B.R. (2d) 488 (Prov. Ct.). See M.E. Deturbide, "Corporate Protector or Environmental Safeguard? The Emerging Role of the Environmental Audit" (1995) 5 J. Envtl. L. & Prac. 1 at 10, n. 30.

38   D.R. Cameron, *Environmental Concerns in Business Transactions: Avoiding the Risks* (Toronto: Butterworths, 1993) at 81.

or facility from outside the work unit being audited. Audits can identify compliance problems, weaknesses in management systems, or
areas of risk. The findings are documented in a written report.[39]

Audits may be initiated in a variety of circumstances and for a range
of purposes. Certain business transactions such as mergers, acquisi-
tions, and financings may trigger an audit requirement. Alternatively,
self-evaluation may be undertaken in the aftermath of new knowledge
concerning previously unanticipated sources of risk. Some operations
will conduct environmental audits on a more or less routine basis as a
matter of general due diligence, in connection with planning annual
programs of financial expenditure or risk-assessment and insurance
reporting.

The specific objectives selected will influence the scope of the audit
and the manner in which it is carried out. When employed as an ongoing management tool, for example, greater emphasis will be placed
on systems, processes, and practices in possible need of attention if
future environmental accidents and liability are to be avoided. On the
other hand, in the context of real estate transactions, preventive objectives may be much less significant; the parties may be primarily
concerned with legal compliance and indications of potentially costly
environmental liability existing at a specific time. Such knowledge may
allow the parties to a transaction to appreciate the risks involved more
fully and encourage them to structure their relationship or transaction-
al risks accordingly.

Although precise objectives dictate the manner in which self-evaluation processes are carried out, in general they will involve an intensive
site inspection including careful observation of facilities in operation,
a review of records and documentation, personnel interviews, and an
analysis and examination of adjacent properties. The findings at this
stage may suggest the need for follow-up work such as sampling and
testing to help in resolving uncertainties and in formulating appropriate recommendations for remedial action.

Those participating in the audit will have been selected on the
basis of the particular expertise each contributes to the investigation
and analysis. Other operational decisions in the conduct of an audit
or self-evaluation are often influenced by concern about the potential
for adverse consequences of the findings. Documented non-compliance
and identified deficiencies may expose the subject of the audit to legal
liability and negative publicity as well as to the expense of remedial

---

39   Environment Canada, *Canadian Environmental Protection Act Enforcement and
Compliance Policy* (Ottawa: March 2001) at 17 [*CEPA, 1999 Policy*].

measures. For these reasons the environmental-audit process is frequently treated as a confidential matter. Indeed, counsel have often recommended measures intended to secure a form of solicitor-client privilege for the audit report. It may be suggested, for example, that the audit team should report directly to counsel, that confidentiality agreements should be entered into with all consultants, and that copies should be marked "confidential" and access to them restricted.

Courts are diligent in scrutinizing claims of privilege, and it is not every report prepared for or under the direction of counsel that will satisfy the requirements of the privilege doctrine. In *R. v. McCarthy Tetrault*[40] certain documents seized by the Crown from counsel for a corporate accused pursuant to a search warrant were subject to a privilege claim. The documents had been prepared by counsel in the course of a meeting with the client in which discussion of a potential environmental prosecution took place. Although counsel insisted that the meeting was for the purpose of communicating confidential information and to prepare legal advice, notice circulated prior to the meeting had referred to it as an environmental audit. The Crown sought to characterize the meeting in this latter way to suggest that it occurred for internal corporate purposes rather than in relation to legal advice and was therefore not privileged. In assessing the competing characterizations, MacDonnell Prov. J. insisted that "[a] claim of privilege will not be established by merely asserting it." A sworn statement by the solicitor affirming his or her belief that a substantial and *bona fide* purpose of the communication was to obtain legal advice will generally be required. A solicitor who is aware of any other purpose for the communication which is subject to a claim of privilege is under a high duty to make disclosure so that the court can assess the claim fairly.[41]

As the origins of the *McCarthy* case indicated, enforcement officials may seek access to audit reports in connection with prosecutorial investigations.[42] Some reconciliation must therefore be established between the desire to promote self-assessments for their beneficial potential and the deterrent effect of using audits against those who voluntarily initiated them. As a matter of official practice, and more recently in legislation in some jurisdictions, attempts have been made to offer assurances against the abuse of audit reports in prosecution. These initiatives rec-

---

40   (1992), 9 C.E.L.R. (N.S.) 12 (Ont. Prov. Ct.).

41   *Ibid.* at 23.

42   Should questions arise concerning searches and seizure of law office records for which solicitor-client privilege is claimed, see *Lavallee, Rackel & Heintz v. Canada (A.G.)* (2002), 167 C.C.C. (3d) 1 (S.C.C.).

ognize the desirability of encouraging self-examination as a means of stimulating corrective action.[43]

CEPA, 1999 enforcement and compliance policy confirms that inspectors will not request environmental audit reports during routine inspections to verify compliance with the Act.[44] However, audit reports may be required in the course of investigations; if so, they may be obtained on the basis of a search warrant or without warrant in exigent circumstances "when the delay necessary to obtain a warrant would likely result in danger to the environment or human life, or the loss or destruction of evidence."[45]

Aspects of the matter are addressed by statute in Nova Scotia, where compliance with a negotiated agreement or with an administrative order will ensure that any person "who voluntarily provides the Department with detailed information obtained through an environmental audit or environmental-site assessment about non-compliance with the requirements of this Act by that person, shall not be prosecuted for the non-compliance."[46] There is no immunity, however, in cases where the department's knowledge of non-compliance was obtained independently prior to receiving information from the person.

Ontario, as a question of policy, provided protection from prosecution where a person responsible for a source of contamination disclosed an environmental evaluation voluntarily in connection with approval of an environmental plan to reduce pollution. To the extent they complied with such an approval, immunity from prosecution relating to matters dealt with in the approval was made available. Ontario, while it claimed access to environmental evaluations in the context of abatement inspections, enforcement investigations, and emergencies, indicated that such evaluations would not be used in prosecutions against the person for whom they were prepared if that individual or entity demonstrated good faith in taking environmentally responsible action to address deficiencies identified in the evaluation.[47]

43   *NSEA*, above note 16, s. 75.
44   *CEPA, 1999 Policy*, above note 39, at 17.
45   *Ibid.*
46   *NSEA*, above note 16, s. 70(1). Under the Nova Scotia legislation, environmental audit means "a process of independently obtaining and evaluating evidence about an environmental matter to determine the relationship between the environmental matter and the established standards and criteria," and environmental-site assessment means "the process by which an assessor seeks to determine whether a particular property is or may be subject to contamination."
47   Ontario, Ministry of the Environment, *Policy and Guideline on Access to Environmental Evaluations* (Toronto: Ministry of the Environment, July 1996) at 3–6.

Apart from judicial insistence on an audit or equivalent as a condition of avoiding conviction for strict liability offences, the environmental audit has not become a general legal requirement. Waste and packaging audits, however, may come to be seen as an exception.[48] In addition, other forms of disclosure, possibly involving information concerning environmental compliance and potential liabilities, among other performance measures, are increasingly common.

C. FINANCIAL-DISCLOSURE OBLIGATIONS, SHAREHOLDER ACCOUNTABILITY, AND SUSTAINABILITY REPORTING

The availability of information, expecially in combination with economic incentives, has considerable potential to influence behaviour. Not surprisingly, therefore, those anxious to enhance the foundations of environmental protection encourage corporate disclosure relating to environmental issues. In a summary that is perhaps equally applicable to the role of individual shareholders and ethical investment groups, one valuable commentary explains the importance of environmental information to financial institutions:

> Financial institutions must have timely and comprehensive information available to support efficient investment and lending decisions. Mandating disclosure of environmental liabilities and costs under securities laws and other company legislation can facilitate financiers' appraisal of the environmental behaviour of businesses. In theory, if accurate information is publicly available, market forces can respond by feeding environmental costs and performance into the cost and terms of finance.[49]

Financial reports prepared in accordance with generally accepted accounting principles will disclose certain environmental liabilities directly in financial statements where satisfactory estimates can be made, or in the form of accompanying notes where the nature of a potential liability is known but its magnitude or monetary significance remains too uncertain to quantify reliably. In this way the fact that assets have been devalued as a consequence of environmental contamination, that costs will be incurred to remediate property or to compensate injured

---

48   See *OEPA*, above note 21, ss. 176(4)(l) and 176(7)(p).
49   B.J. Richardson, "Financing Environmental Change: A New Role for Canadian Environmental Law" (2004) 49 McGill L.J. 145 at 195.

parties, or that pending litigation may affect operations and earnings, can be brought to the attention of investors. In addition, securities laws contribute to the dissemination of information about environmental matters affecting the financial position of businesses whose shares are offered to the public.

Securities legislation, supplemented by policy guidance, seeks to protect investors from unfair, improper, or fraudulent practices and to foster efficient capital markets supported by public confidence.[50] The connection between environmental law and securities regulation derives from the potential cost of corporate liability for environmental claims or cleanup and restoration obligations as well as the negative effects of adverse publicity associated with environmental damage. Thus, rules that require companies whose securities are offered to the public to disclose relevant information in a prospectus or other investor-oriented documentation and on a continuing basis during the course of operations are gradually being extended to include disclosure obligations concerning environmentally related liabilities.

In the United States, environmental disclosure obligations have been addressed directly during the past twenty-five years as the Securities and Exchange Commission responded to the requirements of the *National Environmental Protection Act*.[51] Companies registered under the securities regime have been required to disclose the material effects of compliance with federal, state, or local environmental protection measures on the capital expenditures, earnings, and competitive position of themselves and their subsidiaries.[52] Pending legal proceedings, including proceedings contemplated by government authorities, must be disclosed and described, again subject to the concept of materiality.[53] The SEC's requirement for management discussion and analysis encompasses certain anticipated environmental contingencies.[54] Other provisions impose liability for falsely presenting or failing to disclose material facts which cause damages to investors who relied upon the company's statements.[55]

Although not directly applicable in Canada (except as they apply to Canadian companies required to comply in the United States), de-

---

50 *Securities Act*, R.S.O. 1990, c. S.5, s. 1.1.
51 42 U.S.C. § 4321–370a (1988).
52 *Securities Exchange Commission Regulation S-K*, item 101.
53 *Ibid.*, item 103.
54 *Ibid.*, item 303.
55 Securities Exchange Commission Rule 10b–5.

velopments in U.S. securities law—with the *Sarbanes-Oxley Act*[56] serving as a striking example—are influential and have been considered relevant in the interpretation of securities legislation in Canada.[57] The significance of the U.S. experience for Canadian companies and investors makes it worthwhile to note the results of a recent attempt by the U.S. Government Accountability Office to assess the performance of the SEC in the environmental area:

> Little is known about the extent to which companies are disclosing environmental information in their filings with SEC. Determining what companies should be disclosing is extremely challenging without access to company records, considering the flexibility in the disclosure requirements. Despite strong methodological limitations, some studies provide tentative insights about the amount of environmental information companies are disclosing and the variation in disclosure among companies. However, the problem in evaluating the adequacy of disclosure is that one cannot determine whether a low level of disclosure means that a company does not have existing or potential environmental liabilities, has determined that such liabilities are not material, or is not adequately complying with disclosure requirements.
>
> The adequacy of SEC's efforts to monitor and enforce compliance with environmental disclosure requirements cannot be determined without better information on the extent of environmental disclosure.[58]

If these challenges continue to operate in the U.S., the situation in Canada is cloudier still.

In Canada, securities regulation has evolved as a provincial responsibility. Numerous recommendations and proposals to establish a national regulatory framework have foundered. However, initiatives such as national policy statements and a multijurisdictional disclosure system have been taken to reduce inconsistencies and to alleviate inconvenience. In addition, Ontario developments have been widely influential.

---

56   *Sarbanes-Oxley Act of 2002*, Pub. L. 107-204, 116 Stat. 745 (2002) [*Sarbanes-Oxley Act*].

57   *Pacific Coast Coin Exchange of Canada v. Ontario (Securities Commission)*, [1978] 2 S.C.R. 112.

58   U.S. Government Accountability Office, *Environmental Disclosure: SEC Should Explore Ways to Improve Tracking and Transparency of Information* (GAO-04-808, July 2004), online: www.gao.gov/cgi-bin/getrpt?GAO-04-808.

Initially through policy statements[59] accompanying legislation, and more recently through formally enforceable rules, regulatory bodies in all provinces have elaborated disclosure requirements. Disclosure principles concerning environmental liabilities flow from a basic obligation to provide full, true, and plain disclosure of matters that would reasonably be expected to affect the value of the issuer's securities. General obligations to disclose risk factors in a prospectus, while not specifically imposing environmental disclosure, strongly encourage due diligence investigations that may indicate the need to disclose and discuss environmental matters to potential investors. Complex legislation, diverse environmental circumstances, and real problems with quantification make it difficult to determine with precision whether there are matters requiring disclosure on the basis that some fact "significantly affects or would reasonably be expected to have a significant effect on the market price or value of the securities." To evaluate an environmental concern appropriately from the perspective of securities regulations not only "necessitates . . . an understanding of the laws that are in place but also requires an appreciation of the interplay between local sensitivity, local enforcement, the current state of the art of remediation, and the size and nature of the company."[60]

Companies recognized as reporting issuers of securities face continuous-disclosure obligations that require them to disclose on an ongoing basis, through press releases, all "material changes"; the latter have been defined as any "change in the business, operations or capital of the issuer that would reasonably be expected to have a significant effect on the market price or value of any of the securities." In 1993, the Ontario Securities Commission observed that an injunction application by environmental enforcement officials to restrain a securities issuer from pursuing a principal aspect of its operations on the basis of environmental non-compliance would appear *prima facie* to constitute a material change. Indeed, the commission added that

> given the current high public sensitivity to environmental issues, proceedings instituted . . . for non-compliance with environmental legislation [raise] something of a spectre and may be more likely to be a material change for an issuer than some other lawsuits, given

59 On the enforcement limitations of policy statements, see *Ainsley Financial Corp. v. Ontario (Securities Commission)* (1994), 21 O.R. (3d) 104 (C.A.).

60 S.H.T. Denstedt & S.R. Miller, "Due Diligence in Disclosing Environmental Information for Securities Transactions" (1995) 33 Alta. L. Rev. 231 at 250.

the impact it may have on the public image and consequently on the business affairs of the company.[61]

Ten years later, in a document addressing continuous disclosure obligations, the Canadian Securities Regulatory Authorities set out environmental disclosure requirements and explained their applicability to information forms and reports. A guidance statement provided in connection with what is referred to as Management's Discussion and Analysis Report offered the following advice to decision-maker's trying to determine whether an environmental matter relating to their company would be material and therefore subject to disclosure: "Would a reasonable investor's decision whether or not to buy, sell or hold securities in your company likely be influenced or changed if the information in question was omitted or misstated? If so, the information is likely material."[62]

Evolving Canadian securities law requirements for environmental disclosure, as introduced here, are supplemented by a further array of measures and initiatives that have enhanced the availability of corporate environmental information. In this regard, each of the following is of some interest: the influence of shareholder activism on corporate accountability and disclosure; voluntary corporate reporting associated with indicators of sustainability; the interest of financial institutions in environmental information; and, a potential acceleration in demands for specific environmental information linked to greenhouse gas emissions and climate change.

Legislation establishing the rights of shareholders in the context of corporate governance has established principles applicable to investors' participation in decision making, including opportunities to call for the circulation of proposed resolutions, the solicitation of proxies and so on. With regard to proxy circulation, an earlier version of the *CBCA* provided that

> a corporation is not required to comply with a shareholder's request if it clearly appears that the proposal is submitted by the shareholder primarily for the purpose of enforcing a personal claim or redressing a personal grievance against the corporation or its directors, officers

---

61   *Re Sheridan* (1993), 16 O.S.C. Bull. 6345 at 6349.

62   Canadian Securities Regulatory Authorities, National Instrument 51-102 *Continuous Disclosure Obligations* (NI-51-102) and Form 51-102F1, "Management's Discussion and Analysis" at 2. See also, Ontario Securities Commission, Staff Notice, 51-716, 29 February 2008, online: www.osc.gov.on.ca/Regulation/Rulemaking/Current/Part5/sn_20080229_51-716_enviro-rpt.pdf.

or security holders, or primarily for the purpose of promoting general economic, political, racial, religious, social or similar causes.[63]

Under this rule, several Canadian shareholder proposals associated with social or environmental causes were never circulated, and, accordingly, lost whatever opportunity advance circulation might have afforded to solicit additional support.[64]

New less restrictive legislation now appears to offer more potential for shareholder requests to receive the benefits of advance circulation in that the current rule states that a shareholder resolution need not be circulated when "it clearly appears that the proposal does not relate in a significant way to the business or affairs of the corporation."[65] Arguably, expanding requirements for environmental disclosure bring environmental considerations more closely within the well-recognized parameters of the business or affairs of the corporation.

In addition, on a voluntary basis, a number of firms have begun to produce environmental reports on their operations for the information of investors and the public generally. The environmental research and consulting group Stratos undertook a survey of "sustainability reporting" in Canada.[66] For the purposes of this survey, a "sustainability report" was defined

> to include reports that provide substantial information on a company's management and performance related to one or more aspects of sustainability beyond financial performance. This broad term encompasses environmental, social, community, corporate responsibility, and corporate social responsibility reports, along with annual reports that include five or more pages of environmental and /or social information, including performance data.

The Stratos survey documented substantial recent growth in the number of reporting companies, with significant sectoral variations. Financial institutions, utilities and companies in the resources sector were most common within the ranks of reporting businesses. Although much of the report is devoted to an assessment of the types of information provided (sustainabilility indicators) and to areas of potential improve-

---

63   *Canada Business Corporations Act*, S.C. 1974–75, c. 33, s. 131 (5)(b).

64   *Greenpeace Foundation of Canada v. Inco Ltd.*, [1984] O.J. No. 274 (H.C.J.); *Varity Corp. v. Jesuit Fathers of Upper Canada et al.* (1987), 59 O.R. (2d) 459 (H.C.J.), aff'd 60 O.R. (2d) 640 (C.A.).

65   *Canada Business Corporations Act*, R.S.C. 1985, c. C-44, s. 137(5)(b.1).

66   Stratos Inc., "Building Confidence: Corporate Sustainability Reporting in Canada" (November 2003), online: www.stratos-sts.com/publications/2003_Building_Confidence.pdf.

ment, a basic explanation was offered of the underlying business rationale for reporting. Three factors were of primary importance:

- Enhance corporate reputation by differentiating yourself from
  competitors and gaining a competitive advantage in capital, labour
  and customer markets;
- Improve internal operations through cost savings and more effective use of internal resources and building internal alignment and
  capacities of employees;
- Build stronger external relationships by publicly sharing information on your economic, environmental and social performance
  with key stakeholder groups.[67]

Sustainability reporting is a comparatively new undertaking, by no
means yet subject to the formal requirements associated with financial
reporting and securities regulation. Activity is nevertheless underway
to establish standards, identify best practices, and otherwise enhance
the comprehensiveness and reliability of information provided. The
Global Reporting Initiative (GRI), for example, is the outcome of collaboration between the United Nations Environment Program and the
Coalition for Environmentally Responsible Economies. The GRI has
formulated indicators and guidelines for sustainability reporting to address the following environmental dimensions of sustainability: materials use; energy use; water use; biodiversity; emissions, effluents and
waste; performance of suppliers; environmental impacts of products
and services; and compliance.[68]

Other factors are contributing to increasing interest in and requirements for corporate reporting on environmental performance. In particular, the emergence of markets for green house gas emissions brings
with it a need for transparent and verifiable reporting of a corporation's
assets and liabilities from an energy use and emissions perspective that
is likely to encourage further integration of financial and environmental disclosure.[69]

---

67   *Ibid.* at 6
68   Global Reporting Initiative, *Sustainability Reporting Guidelines* (2002), online:
     www.aeca.es/comisiones/rsc/documentos_fundamentales_rsc/gri/guidelines/
     gri_guidelines_2002.pdf .
69   For discussion of greenhouse gas trading and market instruments generally, see
     chapters 17 and 19.

FURTHER READINGS

ARCHIBALD, TODD, KENNETH E. JULL, & KENT W. ROACH, *Regulatory and Corporate Liability: From Due Diligence to Risk Management* (Aurora, ON: Canada Law Book, 2004–)

CAMERON, D.R., *Environmental Concerns in Business Transactions: Avoiding the Risks* (Toronto: Butterworths, 1993)

DETURBIDE, M.E., "Accessibility of Environmental Audit Reports: A New Business Privilege?" (1999) 8 J. Envtl. L. & Prac. 279

DONAHUE, M., "Proactive Environmental Management: More Than Staying Out of Jail" in D. Estrin, ed., *Business Guide to Environmental Law* (Toronto: Carswell, 1992) c. 4

GIROUX, ELIZABETH, "L'entreprise de l'audit environnemental: perspectives de developpement national et international dans les secteurs de l'environnement et du commerce" (1997) 38 C. de D. 71

MOFFET, J., "Ontario's Policy on Access to Environmental Evaluations: The Creation of an Audit Privilege" (1997) 7 J. Envtl. L. & Prac. 311

POCH, H., *Corporate and Municipal Environmental Law* (Toronto: Carswell, 1989)

SAXE, D., *Environmental Offences: Corporate Responsibility and Executive Liability* (Aurora, ON: Canada Law Book, 1990), cc. 5, 6, & 7

STRANZ, N.J., "Beyond *R. v. Sault Ste. Marie*: The Creation and Expansion of Strict Liability and the 'Due Diligence' Defence" (1992) 30 Alta. L. Rev. 1233

SWAIGEN, J., *Regulatory Offences in Canada: Liability & Defences* (Toronto: Carswell, 1992), cc. 5 & 6

ENVIRONMENTAL VALUATION AND COMPENSATION

A. THE NATURE OF ENVIRONMENTAL DAMAGE

Environmental damage and other losses suffered as a result of ongoing pollution, accidents or spills, general degradation, or the over-exploitation and mismanagement of resources may take many forms. Physical contamination of a short-or long-term nature is an obvious example, with or without destruction of plant and animal life, or biodiversity loss. In severe situations it is also possible to imagine that contamination will have permanently or irreversibly undermined the regenerative capacity or resilience of the affected ecosystem. Losses here may also entail the reduction or elimination of what we are coming to appreciate as ecological functions or services such as water supply, climate stabilization, nutrient cycling or pollination. Insofar as human populations are concerned, individuals may suffer adverse health effects, physical damage to property, or economic losses, singly or in combination. On occasion it is possible to speak of entire communities as the victims of environmental harm, arising, for example, from the contamination of food and water supplies. Financial compensation might then focus on payments to those—including the public—who have suffered losses or incurred expenses associated with remedying environmental damage or taking measures to prevent the spread of such damage.[1]

---

1   For discussion of restoration see the following chapter.

Many aspects of environmental damage as just discussed fall outside the scope of compensation as generally understood in the context of tort claims. For purposes of comparison it is worthwhile to review that approach prior to examining alternative approaches to environmental losses:

> Traditionally, the courts considered the only measure of compensation for damage to property to be the diminution in value caused by the tortfeasor's wrong, that is, the difference between the property value before and after the occurrence of damage. The cost of restoring or repairing the property, if considered at all, was simply regarded as a means of determining the diminution of value. However, in many cases, the distinction is irrelevant. Where the cost of restoration is equal to or less than the diminution of capital value, the repair is always recoverable, even if the plaintiff does not actually incur the cost. Moreover, where the repairs fail to restore the property to its original value, the plaintiff is entitled to the cost of repair and to an additional sum to compensate for the residual deficiency. However, where the cost of restoring the property is greater than the diminution of value the cases are divided as to which measure of damages should be applied. Most cases follow the traditional approach so that the plaintiff is only entitled to damages sufficient to compensate for a diminution of property value. However, damages will be measured according to the cost of repair if restoration alone will make good the plaintiff's loss . . . . The latter approach will only be adopted if the plaintiff actually intends to effect repairs and if the cost of such repairs is reasonable.[2]

As environmental losses are more fully appreciated in a context that encompasses recognition of such principles as polluter pay, intergenerational equity, and the values of biodiversity and ecological integrity, attention has shifted from individualized claims to a more broadly conceived framework for evaluating compensation. As seen in *British Columbia v. Canadian Forest Products Ltd.*[3] (discussed later in this chapter), the willingness of courts to explore new issues around the valuation of environmental losses introduces methodological and evidentiary challenges.

---

2   L.N. Klar *et al.*, *Remedies in Tort*, vol. 4, looseleaf (Toronto: Carswell, 1999–) at 27.

3   *British Columbia v. Canadian Forest Products Ltd.*, 2004 SCC 38 [*Canfor*].

B. EVALUATING ENVIRONMENTAL LOSSES

The issue of the value of environmental losses and of nature more generally has considerable significance for official attitudes towards resource development, sustainability, and the level of compensation. But it should be noted that "values toward nature have not been static in western society."[4] One stream of thinking promotes wise management of natural resources, recognizing both the limited extent of forests and waterways, for example, and their potential to contribute to economic development. Properly conserved and efficiently managed, natural resources represent an ongoing source of wealth for society. This attitude to the valuation of nature is essentially utilitarian: we value nature to the extent that we can use it for our purposes. "We" are human beings, and the purposes are very much our own.

Human purposes need not be confined exclusively to the consumption of resources for sale in the marketplace. As expressed by one commentator, important elements of human freedom may be associated with environmental quality: "Sustaining living standards is not the same thing as sustaining people's freedom to have — or safeguard — what they value and to which they have reason to attach importance. Our reason for valuing particular opportunities need not always lie in their contribution to our living standards."[5] Indeed, a good deal of thought has been devoted to the task of extending our understanding of the values and uses of the natural environment. Today, more decision makers will acknowledge recreational, scientific, aesthetic, and historical values in addition to other utilitarian measures of nature, even including the contribution of ecological services. There is less agreement, however, on the calculus to be applied if a dispute arises about preserving wilderness for public use and enjoyment or extracting its component parts. We have a fair idea of the market value of standing timber: some minor variation on "volume × unit price" will provide an approximation. It has proven much more difficult to place a value on pleasure and enjoyment, or the planetary advantages we are less able to take for granted now that they are being undermined.

---

4   R.B. Payne, "The Forest and the Trees: Non-Timber Values and Forest Management in Ontario" (Witness Statement Number 4, Filed on Behalf of Forests for Tomorrow); *Re Proposed Class Environmental Assessment by the Ministry of Natural Resources for Timber Management on Crown Lands in Ontario* (1990) 4 C.E.L.R. (N.S.) 50 (O.E.A.B.).

5   Amartya Sen, "Why We Should Preserve the Spotted Owl" 26:3 *London Review of Books* (5 February 2004).

How much is a wild river winding through an old-growth forest worth to lovers of the outdoors? Or, what is the value of a wetland region as habitat or for its role in filtering and restoring water? The formulae are of considerable interest, even if their practical utility is often unclear.[6] One might approach the challenge of valuing natural resources by posing the question as one of compensation for loss. That is, supposing that the environment suffered damage—or even destruction—as a consequence of some wrongful act, what amount of compensation should be paid by those responsible?

If everyone agrees that compensation should be based on the value or worth of the loss, there are great differences of opinion concerning the relevant factors. For some, the value of natural resources or the environment is equated with *utility* alone: we have lost value to the extent that we have lost use. Others are more willing to acknowledge additional bases of valuation associated with inherent or *intrinsic* qualities of nature or non-utilitarian considerations. Those who propose the inclusion of intrinsic values in the calculus might elaborate their position in several ways. Even if we do not use resources, we value them because of the option or potential for use that they represent. In addition, we value them on the basis of a desire to pass them on to future generations in the form of a bequest. Intrinsic valuation would also recognize the importance of the mere existence of environmental assets without regard to their actual use by present or future generations. Advocates of intrinsic value would defend their views with the further argument that in each case—option value, bequest value, and existence value—individuals would be willing to pay to protect environmental resources.

The analysis becomes even more complicated as the debate moves on from the kinds of values that might be recognized for purposes of compensation to the task of assigning numbers to those values. Methodology is a highly controversial matter. On the one hand are those who advocate a market-based approach to valuation. They suggest that compensation for loss or damage to a resource is simply the difference between its original market value and the commercial value or price after the damage has been done. The market-based approach is defended by its adherents with the claim that markets alone reflect real willingness to pay. In other words, only the actual behaviour of consumers establishes values. They might have some sympathy with the

---

6   For purposes of the following summary, I have relied heavily on an excellent condensation of some legal/economic literature prepared for the Ontario Law Reform Commission and published in Ontario Law Reform Commission, *Report on Damages for Environmental Harm* (Toronto: Queen's Printer, 1990).

use of surrogate markets to establish environmental values, but that is the extent of their flexibility. For example, the costs of travel and expenses associated with getting to wilderness might represent the value of the wilderness experience. However, even this methodology restricts the value of wilderness to the value of its use.

Critics, on the other hand, reject the market model, in part because it is just that, a model. Markets for most natural resources do not really exist, they say, and so even if you know what someone might pay for a quantity of lumber, the price is not indicative of the value of the forest. What gets left out includes the intrinsic value of the resource, its service as habitat, and values that attach to resources by virtue of public enjoyment of them. For people with this view, the challenge is to move from assertions about unpriced values to actual quantification. Various alternatives have been advanced.

One approximation of the value of a damaged natural resource centres on the cost of replacing it or of restoring it to its original condition.[7] Another suggested methodology known as the contingent-valuation approach involves the use of questionnaires and survey techniques in an attempt to determine the monetary value people would place on non-marketable items such as threatened species, free-running streams, and clear skies. Among the reservations expressed about an approach based on hypothetical transactions, serious controversy has arisen about whether sellers' hypothetical prices are more reliable measures than buyers' willingness to pay, for respondents differ in their valuations depending on whether they are gaining something or giving it up.

Yet alongside theoretical debates, practical attempts are underway to apply our current level of knowledge and understanding to environmental evaluation at regional and ecosystem levels.[8] A valuable example of this type of work is *Counting Canada's Natural Capital: Assessing the Real Value of Canada's Boreal Ecosystems*, a study intended by its authors "to begin to identify, inventory and measure the full economic value of the many ecological goods and services provided by Canada's boreal region."[9] The study, for which a distinctive accounting procedure was

---

7   For a class action claim by a group of cottage owners seeking the entitlement to be reimbursed for the cost of measures necessary to rehabilitate a lake injured by a fish-farming operation, see *Assoc. pour la protection du Lac Heney c. Gestion Serge Lafreniere inc.*, [2001] J.Q. no 1730 (S.C.).

8   Nancy Olewiler, *The Value of Natural Capital in Settled Areas of Canada* (Stonewall, MN: Ducks Unlimited Canada and Nature Conservancy Canada, 2004), online: www.ducks.ca/aboutduc/news/archives/pdf/ncapital.pdf.

9   Mark Anielski & Sara Wilson, *Counting Canada's Natural Capital: Assessing the Real Value of Canada's Boreal Ecosystems* (Ottawa: Canadian Boreal Initiative and

formulated, initially identified ecosystem services provided within the boreal region which covers just under sixty per cent of Canada's land mass. Those ecosystem functions or services include:

> atmospheric stabilization; climate stabilization; disturbance avoidance; water stabilization; water supply; erosion control and sediment retention; soil formation; nutrient cycling; waste treatment; pollination; biological control; habitat; raw materials; genetic resources; and recreational and cultural use.[10]

By way of results, the authors provided estimates of annual market values for natural capital extraction (timber, minerals, water) and non-market value estimates for the year 2002. The market value for natural capital extraction was adjusted to take account of environmental and social costs with the result that the *net* market value of natural capital extraction in the boreal region for the baseline year was $37.8 billion. For the same year, the total non-market value of boreal ecosystem services was estimated at $93.2 billion.[11] The principal components of the ecosystem services category with their estimated values were as follows:

- Flood control and water filtering by peatlands — $77 billion
- Pest control services by birds in the boreal forest — $5.4 billion
- Nature-related activities — $4.5 billion
- Flood control, water filtering and biodiversity value by non-peatland wetlands — $3.4 billion
- Net carbon sequestration by the boreal forests — $1.85 billion

In observing that non-market values of boreal ecosystem services amounted roughly to 2.5 times the net market value of natural capital extractions from the region, authors of *Counting Canada's Natural Capital* remark that the study "affirms the relative importance of ecosystem functions that have no markets in which their services are traded, and the potential cost of replacement if human-made infrastructure can replace their services."[12] Analyses such as this underline the significance of the judicial treatment of environmental losses when these matters reach court.

Pembina Institute, 2005), online: www.cpaws-sask.org/common/pdfs/Boreal_Wealth_Report_Nov_2005.pdf at 15. In light of limitations in publicly available data, the authors caution that their work is a first step towards an accounting of the ecological wealth of the boreal region.

10   *Ibid.* at 2.
11   *Ibid.* at 31.
12   *Ibid.* at 62.

C. VALUING ENVIRONMENTAL LOSSES IN COURT

In *British Columbia v. Canadian Forest Products Ltd. (Canfor)*,[13] the Supreme Court of Canada had an opportunity to consider several aspects of environmental valuation. While many matters remain unresolved, the court's discussion of the issues provides important guidance. To begin, an extended review and commentary on the use, existence and inherent values of ecosystems and natural resources was set out. This was accompanied by reference to measurement methodologies and U.S. cases where these have been adopted. Binnie J.'s majority opinion demonstrates acceptance of the conceptual framework for valuing environmental losses and also the judicial willingness to address the evidentiary and other implications when such cases come before the courts. The court's expectations were clearly stated, however: "A claim for environmental loss, as in the case of any loss, must be put forward based on a coherent theory of damages, a methodology suitable for their assessment, and supporting evidence."[14]

In *Canfor*, the Crown, in seeking damages for harm to public forest resources resulting from fire for which the defendant was largely responsible, failed to meet the applicable standard. Binnie J. stated:

> I do not . . . agree that the Crown can succeed in an unpleaded claim for "ecological" or "environmental" damage simply because the Crown on this issue occupies the moral high ground. The Court and the alleged wrongdoer are entitled to require the Crown to adduce a proper evidentiary basis. Such evidence would be subject to cross-examination. Citation of articles in scholarly journals . . . is no substitute for evidence.[15]

The type of evidence a court would expect to see was illustrated elsewhere in the judgement. It would relate, for example, to:

- The nature of the wildlife, plants and other organisms protected by the environmental resource in question, and in particular whether rare or commercially valuable species are put at risk by damage or destruction of the ecosystem.
- The uniqueness of the ecosystem from a biological perspective.

---

13   Above note 3.
14   *Ibid.* at para. 12.
15   *Ibid.* at para. 145.

- The environmental services provided by the resource, such as water quality and erosion control.
- The recreational opportunities afforded by the resource.
- The subjective or emotional attachment of the public to the damaged or destroyed area.[16]

Where an appropriate plaintiff is available to present relevant evidence for testing and scrutiny by the defendant, the court remains committed to fairness between the parties: "Quantification of the loss must be 'fair to both the plaintiff and the defendant . . . fairness is best achieved by avoiding both undercompensation and overcompensation'."[17] Some observers suggest that overcompensation for environmental losses is unlikely.[18]

Considerations somewhat related to environmental valuation may arise in injunction applications where the concept of irreparable harm must be addressed. Several British Columbia cases relating to old-growth forests and timber management provide some indication of judicial attitudes and approaches to the notion of irreparable harm. In *MacMillan Bloedel Ltd. v. Mullin*, an aboriginal community with undetermined land rights sought an injunction against forest operations.[19] Seaton J.A. stated in awarding the injunction that: "[i]f logging proceeds and it turns out that the Indians have a right to the area with the trees standing, it will no longer be possible to give them that right . . . . The courts will not be able to do justice in the circumstances."[20] As otherwise expressed, "[t]he forest that the Indians know and use will be permanently destroyed." In *Westar Timber Ltd. v. Gitskan Wet'suwet'en Tribal Council*, Esson J.A., in determining whether to grant an injunction against road construction designed to permit timber access, took into account the uniqueness of the area whose preservation was at stake.[21] On the other hand, in *Wiigyet v. Kispiox Forest District*, Thackrey J. indicated a concern for the impact on industry if an injunction were to be granted: "[t]he 'ripple down' effect of the consequences will be immeasurable. It is simply not possible to measure the damages of failed businesses, closed mills and people migrating from the area."[22]

---

16   *Ibid.* at para. 141.
17   *Ibid.* at para. 59.
18   For discussion of *Canfor's* implications for environmental valuation, see Martin Z.P. Olszynski, "The Assessment of Damages Following the Supreme Court's Decision in *Canfor*" (2005) 15 J. Envtl. L. & Prac. 257.
19   (1985), 61 B.C.L.R. 145 (C.A.).
20   *Ibid.* at 159.
21   (1989), 37 B.C.L.R. (2d) 352 (C.A.).
22   (1990), 51 B.C.L.R. (2d) 73 at 81 (S.C.).

And, having heard of the impact on the forest, he remarked: "[b]ut I cannot find that what is described makes the area in question any different than other pristine forest areas of British Columbia. It is sad that we cannot preserve every tract in a state that would be in total harmony with all calls of nature and of all claims of identifiable groups."[23]

Even where there are indications that matters of fundamental importance are at stake, as, for example, in the cause of action created under the Ontario *Environmental Bill of Rights, 1993* in the case of actual or imminent contravention of prescribed instruments causing or threatening "significant harm to a public resource of Ontario," it is specifically stated that "[n]o award of damages shall be made" even if the plaintiff is entitled to judgment.[24] Compensation, accordingly, has been more commonly associated with various forms of governmental losses and the damages or injuries of individuals.

D. STATUTORY APPROACHES TO COMPENSATION FOR ENVIRONMENTAL DAMAGE

Analysis of the difficulties associated with assessing damages and determining liability for compensating the victims of environmental injuries, notably those involving toxic and hazardous substances, has resulted in a variety of remedial proposals.[25] Although victim compensation has been referred to as "a grey area that has not been addressed in detail by legislation,"[26] innovative arrangements have been appearing.

Statutory compensation schemes are directed at a number of issues, including the scope and nature of compensable damages, the manner in which payments are to be distributed to eligible claimants, and possible limitations on the liability of those responsible for the environmental harm. There is a marked tendency to promote remedial action by facilitating the recovery of cleanup and prevention costs. The underlying assumption, especially evident in relation to spills legislation, is that quick responses can greatly lessen overall costs and losses in the

---

23 *Ibid.* at 80.
24 S.O. 1993, c. 28, ss. 84 and 93(2).
25 J.Z. Swaigen, *Compensation of Pollution Victims in Canada* (Study Prepared for the Economic Council of Canada) (Ottawa: Supply & Services, 1981).
26 G. Letourneau & B.A. Chomyn, "Contaminated Lands: A Canadian Perspective" (1991) 32 C. de D. 1073 at 1108.

area of environmental damage. British Columbia's *Environmental Management Act* section 47 provides an example:

(1) A person who is responsible for remediation of a contaminated site is absolutely, retroactively and jointly and separately liable to any person or government body for reasonably incurred costs of remediation of the contaminated site, whether incurred on or off the contaminated site.

. . .

(3) For the purpose of this section, "costs of remediation" means all costs of remediation and includes, without limitation,

(a) costs of preparing a site profile,

(b) costs of carrying out a site investigation and preparing a report . . . ,

(c) legal and consultant costs associated with seeking contributions from other responsible persons, and

(d) fees imposed by a director, a municipality, an approving officer or the commission under this Part.

(4) Liability under this Part applies

(a) even though the introduction of a substance into the environment is or was not prohibited by any legislation if the introduction contributed in whole or in part to the site becoming a contaminated site, and

(b) despite the terms of any cancelled, expired, abandoned or current permit or approval or waste management plan and its associated operational certificate that authorizes the discharge of waste into the environment.

(5) Subject to section 50 (3) [minor contributors], any person, including, but not limited to, a responsible person and a director, who incurs costs in carrying out remediation of a contaminated site may commence an action or a proceeding to recover the reasonably incurred costs of remediation from one or more responsible persons in accordance with the principles of liability set out in this Part.

. . .

(9) The court may determine in accordance with the regulations, unless otherwise determined or established under this Part, any of the following:

(a) whether a person is responsible for remediation of a contaminated site;

(b) whether the costs of remediation of a contaminated site have been reasonably incurred and the amount of the reasonably incurred costs of remediation;

(c) the apportionment of the reasonably incurred costs of remediation of a contaminated site among one or more responsible persons in accordance with the principles of liability set out in this Part;

(d) such other determinations as are necessary to a fair and just disposition of these matters.[27]

British Columbia courts have now begun to outline their approach to determining the scope of recoverable costs of remediation.[28]

The civil cause of action provided for in *CEPA, 1999* allows any person who has suffered loss or damage resulting from contravention of the Act or regulations to recover damages.[29] In addition to establishing a civil cause of action for damages *CEPA, 1999* authorizes court orders to be made at the time sentence is imposed to require the convicted offender to compensate an aggrieved person (on application) for loss or damage to property that resulted from commission of the offence.[30] Such orders, if not respected forthwith, may be made enforceable against the offender as a civil judgment by filing the order in the superior court of the province in which the conviction was obtained.[31] New to *CEPA, 1999* are Environmental Protection Alternative Measures (EPAMs). These are described as measures, other than judicial proceedings that are used to deal with a person who is alleged to have committed an offence under the Act. The outcome of the EPAM process, which has been likened to a criminal diversion program, will be embodied in an agreement. Satisfactory evidence of compliance with the agreement by the alleged offender will result in dismissal of the charge. From the perspective of the present discussion of compensation for environmental loss or damage, it should be noted that agreements reached through the EPAM process may contain terms similar to authorized terms for sentencing convicted offenders, including the taking of any action appropriate to remedy or avoid harm to the environment from the offence.[32]

Following a conviction under the *Transportation of Dangerous Goods Act, 1992,* the court is authorized to order monetary or other compensation "for any remedial action taken or damage suffered by another per-

---

27 *Environmental Management Act,* S.B.C. 2003, c. 53.

28 *Workshop Holdings Ltd. v. CAE Machinery,* 2006 BCSC 389; *Canadian National Railway v. A.B.C. Recycling,* 2006 BCCA 429.

29 *Canadian Environmental Protection Act, 1999,* S.C. 1999, c. 33, s. 40.

30 *Ibid.,* s. 292(1).

31 *Ibid.,* s. 292(2).

32 *Ibid.,* ss. 295–309.

son arising out of the commission of the offence."[33] In contrast to this broadly crafted eligibility provision, other statutory compensation opportunities are more closely circumscribed. Thus, only licensed commercial fishermen are eligible under the *Fisheries Act* to recover for "all loss of income" shown to have been incurred as a result of an unauthorized deposit of a deleterious substance.[34] Another special compensation regime operates for the benefit of farmers whose crops have been rendered unmarketable as a consequence of pesticide residues.[35]

The Maritime Pollution Claims Fund, established in 1973 under the *Canada Shipping Act* was subsequently replaced by the Ship-source Oil Pollution Fund (SOPF)[36] now authorized by the *Marine Liability Act*. Liability and compensation arrangements for oil pollution damage are integrated with the international framework on civil liability for oil pollution damage.[37] In the first instance, shipowners are liable for the cost of oil damage, clean-up and preventive measures caused by their ships.[38] Where damages cannot be recovered from shipowners or other relevant sources, compensation claims may be directed to the SOPF Fund.[39]

In the event of a nuclear incident at a Canadian nuclear facility (as defined in the *Nuclear Liability Act*, section 2), compensation for property damage and personal injury may be obtained through a nuclear power claims commission established under the federal *Nuclear Liability Act*.[40] Once created, such a commission would assume responsibility—subject to regulations—for determining eligibility for compensation. The establishment of a commission has the effect of staying all judicial proceedings relative to the particular incident in question. In *Energy Probe v. Canada (A.G.)*,[41] compensation provisions established under the *Nuclear Liability Act* were challenged on several grounds, including inconsistency with sections 7 and 15 of the *Can-*

---

33 S.C. 1992, c. 34, s. 34(1)(b).

34 *Fisheries Act*, R.S.C. 1985, c. F–14, s. 42(3).

35 *Pesticide Residue Compensation Act*, R.S.C. 1985, c. P-10.

36 For a discussion of the initial operation of the SOPF, see M.D.Faieta *et al.*, *Environmental Harm: Civil Actions and Compensation* (Toronto: Butterworths, 1996) at 396–403.

37 Protocol to Amend the International Convention on Civil Liability for Oil Pollution Damage, 27 November 1992, 1956 U.N.T.S. 255, as amended.

38 *Marine Liability Act*, S.C. 2001, c. 6, s. 51.

39 *Ibid.*, ss. 84 & 85.

40 R.S.C. 1985, c. N–28.

41 (1989), 68 O.R. (2d) 449 (C.A.), leave to appeal to S.C.C. refused (1989), 37 O.A.C. 160n (S.C.C.) [*Energy Probe*].

adian Charter of Rights and Freedoms.[42] As summarized by the Ontario Court of Appeal in preliminary proceedings, the applicants argued that the compensation ceiling actually promotes the use of nuclear energy:

> The thrust of the evidence is that the development of nuclear energy is encouraged by the Act, and may even be dependent upon the limitations of liability contained within it. Insurance or other forms of security against potential claims would be needed throughout the industry without the protection of the Act and this would add measurably to the costs of nuclear energy development, encouraging implementation of alternative energy sources. Thus a link is put between the Act and the creation and proliferation of nuclear reactors.[43]

The action was eventually dismissed.[44] However, failure to adjust the ceiling on liability upwards to take account of inflation and to keep pace with other jurisdictions has attracted renewed criticism of the framework.

Another specific compensation regime, in this case designed in the aftermath of regional environmental contamination, illustrates the precision with which compensation arrangements can be tailored. Following more than a decade and a half of intermittent and difficult negotiations involving the federal and provincial governments, the forest industry companies, and Indian communities, a settlement of claims regarding mercury pollution of the English and Wabigoon Rivers was reached in November 1985.[45] The settlement, whose implementation ultimately required legislative confirmation, provided for the creation of a special decision-making tribunal charged with the administration of applications for mercury-poisoning compensation by members of the Islington and Grassy Narrows Indian bands. The problematic issues of causation and entitlement to damages were resolved in the settlement by an agreement about the "known condition[s]" of mercury poisoning and by permitting the tribunal to determine eligibility on the basis of symptoms, signs, or conditions that were "reasonably consistent with mercury poisoning and capable of significantly impairing the quality

---

42 D. Poch, "The Nuclear Liability Act: Nuclear Power Versus Legal Rights" in *Report of the Canadian Bar Association Committee on Sustainable Development in Canada: Options for Law Reform* (Ottawa: Canadian Bar Association, 1990) 98.

43 *Energy Probe*, above note 41 at 452 (C.A.).

44 *Energy Probe v. Canada (A.G.)* (1994), 17 O.R. (3d) 717 (Gen. Div.). See also chapter 4.

45 *Energy Probe v. Canada (A.G.)*, ibid. The background is described in A.M. Shkilnyk, *A Poison Stronger than Love: The Destruction of an Ojibwa Community* (New Haven, CT: Yale University Press, 1985).

of life or limiting the activities of an applicant."[46] The settlement limited the financial obligations of the forest industry companies, placed the Ontario government in the position of underwriting costs exceeding the initial capacity of the fund to satisfy them, and eliminated any existing and future rights of action of the bands or their individual members "in respect of any claims and causes of action that are the subject of the settlement."

Compensation arrangements are frequently incorporated into the terms and conditions attached to land-use approvals where environmental losses may be anticipated or are expected to occur. Thus, landowners in the immediate vicinity of waste-disposal or management sites are often eligible for compensatory payments linked to market-value losses on their properties. Not all decision makers, however, have the authority to impose compensation funds in connection with approvals, and it has been held in an Ontario decision that "if the legislature intended that the Board should have the power to require compensation of those whose properties have or may lose value because of the operation of the site, it would have specifically so provided."[47]

Although they are therefore quite numerous,[48] statutory schemes for compensation for environmental damage have been criticized for their specificity and their tendency to force potential claimants to identify an appropriate pigeon-hole for their application.

D. LIABILITY AND COMPENSATION FOR SPILLS

Incidents involving adverse environmental consequences will occur despite reasonable efforts to avoid them. As one provincial public information guide paints the scene: "Equipment failure, accidents on highways, railways or waterways, human error, third party involvement—any number of factors may combine to create a spill incident."[49] Moreover, in the absence of prompt and appropriate responses, environmental damage may extend beyond the immediate location of the spill, increasing both the difficulty and cost of restoration. For a variety

---

46 *English and Wabigoon River Systems Mercury Contamination Settlement Agreement Act, 1986*, S.O. 1986, c. 23, s. 1, definition of "condition."

47 *Re Guelph (City)* (1995), 15 C.E.L.R. (N.S.) 241 at 245 (Ont. Div. Ct.).

48 See generally Faieta *et al.*, above note 36 at Part 4.

49 Environment Ontario, *Spills Response Program* (Toronto: Queen's Printer, 1988) at 4.

of substantive and procedural reasons, however, common law liability has provided an inadequate stimulus to immediate post-incident response.[50] Accordingly, several jurisdictions recognized the importance of remedial spills legislation.

Saskatchewan, in 1983, was first to implement legislation governing reporting and cleanup responsibilities for spills.[51] That province's former *Environmental Management and Protection Act* also authorized those who had suffered loss or damage from a pollutant discharge to take civil action against the owner or person having control of the pollutant, although recovery has, on occasion, proven to be problematic.[52] In November 1985 Ontario proclaimed its so-called "Spills Bill," which took the form of amendments to the province's *Environmental Protection Act* of 1978.[53] As explained by early commentators, the spills legislation "should superimpose liability over the common law, where intent, fault, reasonable use, escape, extent of damage, duty of care and foreseeability are not an issue. Rather, the ownership and control of the spilled pollutant is the primary question."[54]

To promote timely and effective measures in response to spills, the Ontario legislation proceeds on several fronts. Thus, a pollutant "spill" was broadly defined and the duties now arising in such an eventuality under the "Spills Bill" are such that "virtually any person could be affected by its provisions."[55] The legislation imposes a duty to give notice to the ministry and others of the circumstances of the spill and of remedial action taken or proposed. Where an "adverse effect" is associated with the spill, owners and persons having control of the pollutant prior to the spill have cleanup responsibilities requiring them to do "everything practicable to prevent, eliminate or ameliorate the adverse effects or to restore the natural environment."[56] But where appropriate actions are not forthcoming, the minister has extensive authority

---

50 J.W. Harbell, "Common Law Liability for Spills" in S.M. Makuch, ed., *The Spills Bill: Duties, Rights and Compensation* (Toronto: Butterworths, 1986) 1.

51 *Environmental Management and Protection Act*, S.S. 1983–84, c. E–10.2.

52 *Busse Farms Ltd. v. Federal Business Development Bank* (1998), 168 D.L.R. (4th) 27 (Sask. C.A.).

53 See now R.S.O. 1990, c. E.19 [*OPEA*]. Similar schemes are found in other jurisdictions. See *Waste Management Act*, R.S.B.C. 1996, c. 482, ss. 12 & 12.1 [*WMA*]; *Spills Reporting Regulation*, B.C. Reg. 263/90 and *Spill Cost Recovery Regulation*, B.C.Reg 250/98.

54 Harbell, above note 50 at 25.

55 D. Estrin, *Handle with Caution: Liability in the Production, Transportation and Disposal of Dangerous Substances* (Toronto: Carswell, 1986) at 5.

56 A claim under these provisions of the *OEPA* against a parent corporation which was not actually involved in activity on the site of its subsidiary at the time con-

to direct that suitable actions be taken by agents or employees of the ministry or by others.

In terms of compensation for losses associated with spills, the central provision of the Ontario legislation indicates that the Crown, in right of the province or of Canada, and any person are entitled to compensation for loss or damage incurred as a direct result of the spill and for all reasonable cost and expense incurred in carrying out preventive and remedial orders issued in connection with the spill.[57] Loss or damage for purposes of this section includes personal injury, loss of life, loss of use or enjoyment of property, and pecuniary loss, including loss of income.[58] As formulated, the legislation therefore addresses potential problems of standing and foreseeability for purposes of spills. Although strict liability applies to loss or damage from spills, the liability of owners and controllers of spilled pollutants is absolute in relation to the costs of cleanup.[59]

An organization known as the Ontario Environmental Compensation Corporation (ECC) was established in connection with the province's spills legislation.[60] Besides providing assistance to spills victims in the form of information and procedural advice, the ECC was authorized to make payments to eligible victims who were not otherwise able to secure compensation, generally in circumstances where the party responsible for the spill was insolvent. The scope of compensation claims did not include the victims of spills which may have taken place prior to the date on which the "Spills Bill" was proclaimed in force (29 November 1985).[61] Under the *Environmental Approvals Improvement Act*, Ontario took steps in 1997 to eliminate the ECC but not the remainder of the *OEPA*'s spills provisions.[62]

---

tamination occurred was rejected in *United Canada Malt Ltd. v. Outboard Marine Corp. of Canada* (2000), 48 O.R. (3d) 352.

57   *OEPA*, above note 53, s. 99(2).
58   *Ibid.*
59   See also *WMA*, above note 53, s. 10.
60   *OEPA*, above note 53, s. 111.
61   *McCann v. Environmental Compensation Corp.* (1990), 5 C.E.L.R. (N.S.) 247 (Ont. C.A.), leave to appeal to S.C.C. refused (1994), 15 C.E.L.R. (N.S.) 164.
62   S.O. 1997, c. 7, as amended by S.O. 2000, c. 26.

FURTHER READINGS

BOWMAN, M., "Biodiversity, Intrinsic Value, and the Definition of Environmental Harm" in Michael Bowman & Alan Boyle, eds., *Environmental Damages in International and Comparative Law: Problems of Definition and Valuation* (New York: Oxford University Press, 2002)

CROSS, F.B., "Natural Resource Damage Valuation" (1989) 42 Vand. L.R. 269

DAILY, G., *Nature's Services: Societal Dependence on Natural Ecosystems* (Washington DC: Island Press, 1997)

ELGIE, S., & A. LINTNER, "The Supreme Court's *Canfor* Decision: Losing the Battle but Winning the War for Environmental Damages" (2005) 38 U.B.C. L. Rev. 223

FAIETA, M.D., *et al.*, *Environmental Harm: Civil Actions and Compensation* (Toronto: Butterworths, 1996)

OLSZYNSKI, M., "The Assessment of Environmental Damages following the Supreme Court's Decision in *Canfor*" (2005) 15 J. Envtl. L. & Prac. 257

ONTARIO LAW REFORM COMMISSION, *Report on Damages for Environmental Harm* (Toronto: Queen's Printer, 1990)

SWAIGEN, J.Z., *Compensation of Pollution Victims in Canada* (Study prepared for the Economic Council of Canada) (Ottawa: Supply & Services Canada, 1981)

WORLD BANK, *How Much is an Ecosystem Worth: Assessing the Economic Value of Conservation* (Washington DC: World Bank, 2004)

WRUCK, J., "The Federal Environmental Damages Fund" (2004) 5 C.E.L.R. (3d) 120

CHAPTER 11

REMEDIATION AND RESTORATION OF CONTAMINATED LANDS

A. INTRODUCTION

Until recently Canadians devoted limited attention to the challenges of rehabilitating contaminated lands. The comparative familiarity of courts with financial mechanisms for compensating individual victims may have been one contributing factor. Moreover, the assumption was widespread that natural regenerative processes would operate satisfactorily or that the extent of degradation was still quite limited. In one case, for example, a provincial minister of the environment indicated that "[n]o inventory of existing or abandoned landfills has been conducted as the past history of industrialization in this province does not lead us to believe any significant quantities of toxic wastes have been deposited."[1] Persistent contamination is now recognized as a significantly more extensive and challenging problem than previously acknowledged. Canada now faces a costly remedial agenda.

In 1990, an inquiry conducted for the Law Reform Commission of Canada identified 8,784 waste disposal sites, many of which were considered to be sources of contamination. Only Quebec at that time had prepared a more comprehensive list in which the province identified some 11,000 properties known to be contaminated from waste or otherwise. A subsequent assessment undertaken on behalf of the

---

1   Quoted in P.N. Nemetz, "Federal Environmental Regulation in Canada" (1986) 26 Natural Resources J. 551 at 587.

National Round Table on Environment and Economy, resulted in an inventory of 30,000 locations under the general description of "brownfield sites," and originating in a variety of ways. In addition to known waste-disposal sites and scrapyards, hundreds of which may present continuing environmental and human-health risks, numerous other locations suffer toxic contamination. These include industrial sites associated with mining operations, with coal gasification plants, or metal and petroleum refineries. As well, there are old coking plants, chemical company facilities, electroplating establishments, and businesses whose operations once involved various forms of solvents, paints, and sealants or wood-preserving compounds.

The Sydney Tar Ponds in Nova Scotia, identified as problematic in 1982, represent one of the more intractable examples of widespread industrial contamination. The overall site contained 700,000 tonnes of toxic sludge accumulated over a century from the operations of a coking plant and steel mill. The condition of the site defied a series of federal-provincial cleanup efforts and continued to alarm nearby residents over health concerns.[2] Pursuant to a Memorandum of Agreement signed by the governments of Canada and Nova Scotia in May 2004, significant additional funding was committed and the province established a new organization, the Sydney Tar Ponds Agency (STPA), to implement a program of remediation. Some contaminants are to be removed for destruction elsewhere, while other materials will be treated on-site prior to the implementation of containment measures, restoration and landscaping. Detailed plans developed by the STPA have now been subject to joint environmental assessment review under federal and Nova Scotia legislation.[3]

Even rural lands, traditionally regarded as essentially pastoral and subsequently absorbed into suburban residential housing projects, have been found to contain toxic hazards. In some cases leaking underground fuel-storage tanks pose the risk, yet there have been examples of radioactive contamination in unexpected locations. The *Sevidal v. Chopra* and *Heighington* cases involved liability for radioactive contamination found in residential settings nearly half a century after wartime experimental use of agricultural property.[4]

Over and above historic sources of contamination, which are at least researchable and discoverable in principle, are spill and accident

---

2   For information from the Sydney Tar Ponds Agency on ongoing developments see online: www.TarPondsCleanup.ca.

3   Online: www.pwgsc.gc.ca/greening/text/rcjr-e.html.

4   *Sevidal v. Chopra* (1987), 64 O.R. (2d) 169 (H.C.J.); *Heighington v. Ontario* (1989), 69 O.R. (2d) 484 (C.A.).

sites. These are virtually impossible to locate reliably because of their largely random occurrence and the absence — until quite recently — of systematic reporting procedures and obligations.

There is a tendency to distinguish several dimensions of the cleanup task. Remediation is often understood to centre on the initial challenges of identifying and eliminating or neutralizing contaminants through a variety of mechanical, physical, chemical, and biological techniques.[5] A subsequent step, environmental restoration, may be described as "measures taken to return a site to previolation conditions"[6] or, somewhat more elaborately, as "*bringing a part of the natural environment from a state of decay, injury or loss back to its original self-sustaining condition, so that it will support all the forms of life which formerly inhabited it.*"[7] When used with reference to the spill of a contaminant under the OEPA, restoring the natural environment means to "restore all forms of life, physical conditions, the natural environment and things existing immediately before the spill of the pollutant that are affected or that may reasonably be expected to be affected by the pollutant."[8] However, statutory definitions combining remediation and restoration functions are not unknown.

Before discussing a number of issues associated with the legal framework for remediation, it is helpful to underline some of the distinctive challenges presented by contaminated lands. These have been usefully summarized by an experienced litigator in the field:

> Contamination is rarely static; its presence in the surface and subsurface of land, including groundwater, changes over time. Contamination does not respect property boundaries, so that site contamination can contribute toward liability for off-site migration, and a site contaminated by an off-site source may, after remediation, become recontaminated. Land exists in perpetuity; the use one party makes of it, its contamination today, and decisions respecting remediation, will affect future generations of owners, tenants and lenders. The regulatory environment dealing with contamination and people's perceptions of contamination can evolve, resulting in changes to the risk and liability occasioned by contamination over time, even without any change in the contamination itself. Remedial technologies can

---

5   Insight Educational Services, *Clean-up of Contaminated Sites: Regulations and State of the Art Technologies* (Mississauga: Insight Press, 1991).

6   W.A. Tilleman, ed., *The Dictionary of Environmental Law and Science* (Toronto: Emond Montgomery, 1994) at 244.

7   D. Saxe, "Reflections on Environmental Restoration" (1992) 2 J. Envtl. L. & Prac. 77 at 78 [emphasis in original].

8   *Environmental Protection Act*, R.S.O. 1990, c. E.19, s. 91(1) [*OEPA*].

develop and improve, but so can detection methods, finding contamination tomorrow where none was identified today. Finally there is a public interest in remediating contamination, and cases involving site contamination therefore necessarily affect the interests of persons who may not be parties to the lawsuit.[9]

One of the listed factors, the regulatory environment, has indeed been significantly transformed. We have recognized the extent of contamination across the country. We have formulated remedial programs, including programs influenced by a growing appreciation of the "polluter-pays" principle. And, as also noted among the factors listed above, we have increasingly recognized the interests of third parties.

In regard to broader interests, the National Round Table on Environment and Economy (NTREE) demonstrated important leadership in the course of its work on the redevelopment of brownfields. The initiative culminated in a call by the NRTEE for a national brownfields redevelopment strategy with an emphasis on sites where both clean-up costs and redevelopment potential are judged to be high. Typically, it is suggested, such properties will be found in urban centres and along transportation corridors where municipal services are already in place. The NRTEE anticipated that after clean-up, market values of such lands are likely to be slightly above or slightly below the combined cost of land plus clean-up.

In releasing its strategy, the NRTEE articulated the objective as being to provide all participants in brownfield redevelopment with a clear, fair and consistent public policy regime to bring greater certainty and efficiency to questions of liability and risk management and to promote a co-ordinated effort on liability and risk management among all levels of government. In connection with liability for contaminated lands in the context of brownfield redevelopment, a task force reported to the NRTEE with six recommendations:

2.1 Allow binding contractual allocation of liability.
2.2 Provide for termination of regulatory liability.
2.3 Provide for termination of civil liability after a limitation period.
2.4 Create an insurance fund [to deal with subsequent claims].
2.5 Apply site-specific assessment and approvals regimes.
2.6 Provide regulatory approvals for remediation.[10]

9   Katherine M. van Rensburg, "Deconstructing *Tridan*: A Litigator's Perspective" (2004) 15 J. Envtl. L. & Prac. 85 at 92.
10 NTREE, *Cleaning up the Past, Building the Future: A National Brownfield Redevelopment Strategy for Canada* (Ottawa: NRTEE, 2003) 25–30.

Not all of these proposals have been endorsed on a national basis, but coincident with debate encouraged by the NRTEE, several Canadian jurisdictions examined reforms to the legislative framework applicable to remediation and liability for contaminated lands. While the detailed arrangements operating in each province still often differ in important ways, they address a comparable range of questions: What process determines the designation of a site as contaminated? What instruments should be available to require or promote remediation of contaminated lands? What is the range of parties who may be considered responsible for the remediation effort or its costs; what principles ground their liability, and what is the extent of that liability? What standard of remediation is to be achieved; by whom should it be determined that the standard has been met? What form, if any, of official certification or approval of the remediation process or its results will be provided? In what circumstances, if any, might exposure to further liability be reopened following completion of the required remediation? What measures will be available to safeguard the interests of third parties in remediation initiatives? What exemptions may be applicable?

B. SITE REMEDIATION REQUIREMENTS

Requirements to remediate former industrial sites or to restore them after use to an environmentally acceptable standard will sometimes provide an illustration of the polluter-pays principle.[11] Such obligations may be imposed by general legislation, or they may appear as terms and conditions of operating approvals or administrative orders.[12] In some circumstances, remediation actions may be court ordered.[13] Moreover, in dealings with original owners, purchasers or leaseholders have become increasingly inclined to insist upon, or at least to bargain for, some level of cleanup, assurance about the condition of the property, or commitment to participate in remedial work that may be found necessary.[14] Owners, of course, are equally concerned that a property be returned to them in satisfactory condition after occupation by some other operation. Thus, private arrangements and obligations also figure in the delineation of cleanup requirements, both as to their existence

11   *Imperial Oil v. Quebec*, [2003] 2 S.C.R. 624.
12   See chapter 7.
13   *OEPA*, above note 8, s. 190(1); *Environmental Protection and Enhancement Act*, R.S.A. 2000, c. E-12, ss. 213(1) and 234(1) [*AEPEA*].
14   D.R. Cameron, *Environmental Concerns in Business Transactions: Avoiding the Risks* (Toronto: Butterworths, 1993) cc. 12 & 13.

and with respect to the standard of remediation that must be provided or financed. Before examining statutory schemes, aspects of possible private arrangements may be briefly noted.

In *Westfair v. Domo*, a gas bar operator, after occupying a leased site in Winnipeg for nearly twenty-five years, decommissioned the property and returned it to the landlord.[15] The remedial work cost about $400,000 and included excavation and removal of underground tanks and lines, the removal and treatment of contaminated soil, installation of a plastic liner or barrier, and backfill using clean material. Following this work, the property was considered to be in reasonable condition, generally in compliance with provincial guidelines and suitable for the site's highest and best use—commercial development. The property was not, however, in a condition equivalent to its original state at the time the leasing arrangement began. The landlord therefore sued to enforce a higher standard of remediation. Its claim, based on an implied contractual obligation for the lessee to return property in an uncontaminated condition, failed. Morse J. expressed the view that

> in the case of a commercial retail gasoline operation where a landlord must know of the likelihood of contamination of the soil arising merely from the day-to-day operation of the facility and where the landlord benefits financially from the sale of increased quantities of gasoline, a tenant, upon termination of the lease, should not, in the absence of a specific provision in the lease to the contrary, be required to restore the land to its original condition.[16]

Other courts have been more inclined to insist that leased property is to be returned in an uncontaminated condition on the basis of an implied term. In an Alberta decision, *Darmac Credit*, the view was expressed that

> in today's commercial world, unless a lease provides otherwise, it is implied within a lease that lands are to be returned uncontaminated. Contaminated lands are not saleable lands. Perhaps, when this particular lease was entered, environmental concerns were minimal, but they have become prominent in recent years. Although environment-

---

15   *Westfair Foods Ltd. v. Domo Gasoline Corp.*, [1999] M.J. No. 1 (Q.B.), aff'd (1999), 33 C.E.L.R. (N.S.) 93 (Man. C.A.).

16   In an Ontario case involving contamination of property by a significant leak from a neighbouring gas station, the court determined that the plaintiff was entitled to have its site restored to the "pristine" condition it had been in prior to the leak. See *Tridan Developments Ltd. v. Shell Canada Products* (2002), 57 O.R. (3d) 503 (C.A.), leave to appeal to S.C.C. refused, [2002] S.C.C.A. No. 98.

al damage was not directly addressed when this lease was entered, the tenants are responsible for any contamination they cause.[17]

Whatever their origin, cleanup obligations represent a cost of operations that might — in an earlier era — have been avoided altogether or at least deferred indefinitely. Indeed, Canada, like many other nations, contains sites that were contaminated by industrial by-products that are now difficult and costly to remove; a number of these sites have been abandoned. In numerous cases, persistent contamination is in fact the consequence of industrial operations that were carried out in compliance with previous permit standards. Accordingly, the situation has often presented governments seeking to promote the remediation of contaminated sites with a complex challenge from the perspective of allocating cleanup and restoration costs on a principled basis.

Where government agencies have incurred expenses in connection with environmental remediation or restoration measures, they are frequently authorized to recover the costs from persons responsible for the damage or from funds specifically created for the purpose. The *Arctic Waters Pollution Prevention Act*, for example, establishes the absolute liability of those engaged in resource exploration and development, shipping, or mainland or island-based undertakings in the Arctic and Arctic waters for costs and expenses incurred to repair or remedy any condition arising from unauthorized deposits of waste, or for the purpose of reducing or mitigating any damage to or destruction of life or property, so long as the expenditures "can be established to have been reasonably incurred in the circumstances."[18] Cleanup costs are also recoverable under the *Fisheries Act* and from the Maritime Pollution Claims Fund in connection with oil-spill damage.[19] Other remediation requirements have been imposed on a sectoral basis. Specific requirements apply, for example, to those whose activity involves the use of underground storage tanks, oil and gas wells, mineral properties, and forest resources.[20]

The widespread adoption of remediation requirements in recent legislation confirms the importance of the objective of environmental rehabilitation, and with experience a number of legal and operational

---

17 *Darmac Credit Corp. v. Great Western Containers Inc.* (1994), 163 A.R. 10 (Q.B.). For other decisions along similar lines, see *Progressive Enterprises Ltd. v. Cascade Lead Products Ltd.*, [1996] B.C.J. No. 2473 (S.C.) and *O'Connor v. Fleck* (2000), 35 C.E.L.R. (N.S.) 16 (B.C.S.C.).

18 *Arctic Waters Pollution Protection Act*, R.S.C. 1985, c. A-12, ss. 6–7.

19 *Fisheries Act*, R.S.C. 1985, c. F-14, s. 42.

20 See, for example, *Crown Forest Sustainability Act*, S.O. 1994, c. 25, ss. 55–64, and *Environmental Protection and Enhancement Act*, S.A. 1992, c. E-13.3, s. 220.

uncertainties are being addressed. Saskatchewan's original *Environmental Management and Protection Act*, dating from the early 1980s, offered limited guidance as to remediation of contaminated lands. However, the province's *Environmental Management and Protection Act, 2002* now explicitly provides for measures to deal with contaminated sites.[21] The process unfolds pursuant to designation of a contaminated site by the minister where he or she is of the opinion that a substance that is causing, may cause or has caused an adverse effect is present in the area. Designations are based upon any standards, guidelines or criteria adopted by the minister and may apply to adverse effects of discharges that occurred before or after the coming into force of the legislation in October 2002. The broad potential for designation is highlighted by its clear application even to activities that were, at the time of the discharge, giving rise to adverse effects, lawful or unregulated. In the words of section 11(8) of the Act, a contaminated site designation may be made notwithstanding that:

(b) the substance was discharged in accordance with this Act or any other Act, Act of the Parliament of Canada or regulations made pursuant to any of those Acts; or

(c) the discharge of the substance was not prohibited by this Act or any other Act, Act of the Parliament of Canada or regulations may pursuant to any of those Acts . . .

Public notice of the contaminated site designation, including a description of the site, will then be published in the *Gazette* while written notice must be given to parties specified in section 12 as follows:

(a) any person who, in the opinion of the minister, is a person responsible for the discharge that resulted in the contaminated site;

(b) any owner and occupier of land directly affected by the designation;

(c) the municipality in which the contaminated site is located . . .

In addition, written notice will also be provided to persons whose interests in land affected by the designation are on record under the land titles act or registry.

---

21   *Environmental Management and Protection Act, 2002*, S.S. 2002, c. E-10.21, s. 10 *et. seq.* For a detailed examination of remediation arrangements under the old and new *EMPAs* in Saskatchewan, see J. Kelly Brown, "Contaminated Site Liability in Saskatchewan: On the 'Right Track' to Remediation?" (2003) 12 J. Envtl. L. & Prac. 55.

Each "person directly responsible for a discharge" related to the designated contaminated site is then required to undertake a series of actions set out in detail according to section 14, together with the minister's authority to respond:

(2) (a) prepare a remedial action plan for the contaminated site; and
(b) if there are any other persons directly responsible for the discharge, enter into a written agreement with those other persons . . . that provides for:
(i)   the remedial action that must be taken; and
(ii) the apportionment of costs of taking that action.

(3) The person or persons directly responsible for a discharge shall submit the remedial action plan and any agreements for remedial action to the minister for approval.

(4) On receipt of a remedial action plan and an agreement . . . the minister may:
(a)   approve the remedial action plan and any agreement;
(b)   refuse to approve the remedial action plan and any agreement; or
(c)   direct that changes be made to the remedial action plan and any agreement.

(5) On approval by the minister . . . every person who submitted a remedial action plan and agreement . . . shall comply with the terms of the approved remedial action plan and any approved agreement.

Those who comply with the terms of an approved remedial action plan are immunized from further orders, known in the legislation as environmental protection orders (EPOs). Those failing to meet their obligations are subject to a broad range of administrative orders intended to bring about remediation of the contaminated site.

The general Ontario approach developed from a series of guidelines intended to elaborate on the Ministry of the Environment and Energy's use of its legislative authority in relation to remediation of contaminated lands. The Ontario guidelines described elements of three possible approaches for responding to contamination in the context of cleanup or redevelopment. The "background" approach has reference to naturally occurring, ambient, or background soil-quality criteria existing in the relevant area, while the "generic" approach associated specified land uses with soil and groundwater-quality criteria expected to safeguard against adverse environmental and human health effects. A third permitted approach was derived from site-specific risk assessment. New brownfields legislation has now provided a more detailed and comprehensive framework to address remediation and associated liability issues in the province.[22]

In addition to the new remediation requirements, in connection with a successful action under section 84 of the *OEBR* relating to significant harm to a public resource, the court has authority to order parties to the proceedings to negotiate a restoration plan. Such plans are expected to address, "to the extent that to do so is reasonable, practical and ecologically sound," such issues as

(a) the prevention, diminution or elimination of the harm;
(b) the restoration of all forms of life, physical conditions, the natural environment and other things associated with the public resource . . . ; and
(c) the restoration of all uses, including enjoyment, of the public resource.[23]

It is possible that *OEBR* restoration plans will also address harm to a public resource indirectly in that research on preventive technologies and community education or health programs might be incorporated.

In Alberta, specified lands, that is, lands identified by regulations and on or in respect of which an activity is carried out, are subject to the conservation and reclamation provisions of the *AEPEA* and must be restored to "an equivalent land capability." Operators on specified lands must conserve and reclaim such lands in accordance with any applicable approval, the terms and conditions of an environmental protection order dealing with conservation and reclamation, and official directions. An inspector, when satisfied that conservation and reclamation have been completed as required, may issue a reclamation certificate to the operator.[24]

In Nova Scotia, the minister, on the basis of departmental standards, criteria, or guidelines, may designate an area as a contaminated site, giving notice to "any person responsible for the contaminated site that the Minister considers appropriate." Persons responsible thereafter have the opportunity to prepare a remedial action plan for the minister's approval and to enter into a written agreement with the minister

---

22 Ontario, Ministry of the Environment, *Guideline for Use at Contaminated Sites in Ontario* (Toronto: Ministry of the Environment, 1996). Site-condition standards, similar to the current guidelines, are now prescribed by regulation pursuant to *An Act to Encourage the Revitalization of Contaminated Land (Brownfields Statute Law Amendment Act)*, R.S.O. 2001, c. 17. See O.Reg. 153/04.

23 *Environmental Bill of Rights, 1993*, S.O. 1993, c. 28, s. 95(2)

24 *AEPEA*, above note 13, Parts 5 & 6; *Conservation and Reclamation Regulation*, Alta. Reg. 242/99.

and other persons responsible for the remedial action to be taken and for the apportionment of costs. In the absence of agreement, the parties may utilize the legislation's provisions for alternative dispute resolution (ADR) although the minister retains authority to make an order resolving the matter where ADR is unsuccessful or "considered inappropriate" by the minister. Failure to fulfil a term of a remedial action-plan agreement is an offence.[25]

Where some form of certification or approval follows the completion of a remedial program, governments remain cautious about the implications of providing such documentation. British Columbia addressed this issue in connection with compliance certificates following satisfactory remediation of contaminated lands under the province's former *Waste Management Act* by providing that, other than in cases where bad faith can be established, "no action lies and no proceeding may be brought against the Crown, the minister or an employee of the ministry because of anything arising out of the issue of a certificate of compliance."[26]

C. LIABILITY ALLOCATION ISSUES

Among the most sensitive and controversial matters in the field of remediation is the issue of allocating cleanup costs among past and present property owners, business operators, financial participants, and other potential contributors to what will often be expensive undertakings.

To identify potential contributors requires important judgments about the principles to be applied to the allocation of cleanup costs. Are cleanup costs viewed as a matter of individual or social responsibility? Does it matter that waste discharges or the other practices that may have resulted in contamination were not unlawful, perhaps even permitted, at the time damages occurred? Is it significant that the community as well as individuals may have benefited from the environmentally harmful activity in the sense that an employment base was created, taxes paid, and so on? Where contributors have been identified—whatever the criteria—are there grounds for limiting the extent of that liability, or for apportioning it among a group of contributors?

---

25 *Environment Act*, S.N.S. 1994–95, c. 1, Part VIII. *Guideline for the Management of Contaminated Sites in Nova Scotia* (March 1996).

26 *Waste Management Act*, R.S.B.C. 1996, c. 482, ss. 26 & 27. Now see B.C.'s *Environmental Management Act*, S.B.C. 2003, c. 53, Part 4 and the *Contaminated Sites Regulation*.

These are the kinds of issues that have to be faced in designing liability regimes.[27] Saskatchewan's answers to some of these questions have been noted in the previous section.

Principles on contaminated sites liability formulated by CCME in 1993[28] were adopted by a number of administrative bodies[29] and variations can be found in some provincial legislation.[30]

A British Columbia legislative initiative on contaminated sites formalized principles of liability, including exemptions and cost-allocation mechanisms as well as possibilities for public consultation in a remediation program.[31] In the first instance, it defined current or former owners (including tenants) and operators. An "owner" means a person who is in possession of, has the right of control of, occupies, or controls the use of real property, including, without limitation, a person who has any estate, legal or equitable, in the real property. An "operator" is described as a person who is or was in control of or responsible for any operation located at a contaminated site.

Under specified conditions, secured creditors and other persons designated by regulations also face responsibility for remediation. Certain exemptions are then established, including exemptions for owners or operators who are able to establish that

(i) at the time the person became an owner or operator of the site,
   (a) the site was a contaminated site,
   (b) the person had no knowledge or reason to know or suspect that the site was a contaminated site, and
   (c) the person undertook all appropriate inquiries into the previous ownership and uses of the site and undertook other investigations, consistent with good commercial or customary practice at that time, in an effort to minimize potential liability,
(ii) if the person was an owner of the site, the person did not transfer any interest in the site without first disclosing any known contamination to the transferee, and

---

27 N. Vlavianos, "Creating Liability Regimes for the Clean-up of Environmental Damage: The Literature" (2000) 9 J. Envtl. L. & Prac. 145.

28 Canadian Council of Ministers of the Environment, *Recommended Principles* (May 1993). In 2003 the CCME reassessed the continuing applicability of the original principles. Now see *Recommended Principles on Contaminated Sites Liability, 2006*, online: www.ccme.ca/assets/pdf.csl_14_principles_e.pdf.

29 *Re 724597 Ontario Ltd.* (1994), 13 C.E.L.R. (N.S.) 257 (O.E.A.B.).

30 *AEPEA*, above note 13, s. 129(2).

31 B.C. *Environmental Management Act*, above note 26, Part 4.

(iii) the owner or operator did not, by any act or omission, cause or contribute to the contamination of the site.[32]

The B.C. Supreme Court had occasion to consider the scheme of the Act and particularly the scope of the definitions of owner and operator as these concepts relate to the concepts of control and responsibility in the case of *Beazer East Inc. v. British Columbia (Environmental Appeal Board)*.[33] The case centred on the potential liability of a parent corporation for contamination on the site of its subsidiary, though it is only necessary here to present Tysoe J.'s general remarks on the control and responsibility issues:

> In general terms, it is my view that the intention of the Legislature was to include persons who made decisions or had the authority to make decisions with respect to any operation on the site. These are the persons who are potentially culpable because they were the ones who made or could have made decisions in relation to operations on the site, which may have included operations that caused or contributed to the contamination. A person who makes the decisions with respect to an operation is "in control" of the operation and a person who has the authority to make the decisions with respect to an operation is "responsible" for the operation. In my opinion, a person who is responsible for an operation is one who is accountable for the operation but the accountability is not necessarily legally enforceable.
>
> I also believe in using the word "responsible," the Legislature intended to include persons who brought about an operation in the sense of causing the operation to be carried on or carried out. Such a person would be responsible for the operation because, but for the actions or decision of that person, the operation would not have been carried on or carried out.[34]

Manitoba legislation on contaminated sites approaches the question of allocating costs by providing, among other mechanisms, for "apportionment agreements." Those charged with deciding whether to approve such agreements are required to take all other relevant factors into account but must specifically "apply the principle that the primary responsibility for the remediation of a contaminated site lies with the

---

32   *Ibid.*, s. 46(d).

33   *Beazer East Inc. v. British Columbia (Environmental Appeal Board)* (2000), 36 C.E.L.R. (N.S.) 195 (B.C.S.C.).

34   *Ibid.* at 227. For discussion of the scope of remediation costs recoverable under the B.C. legislation, see *Canadian National Railway Co. v. A.B.C. Recycling*, [2005] B.C.J. No. 982 (S.C.).

person or persons who contaminated it and that they should bear the responsibility for the remediation in proportion to their contributions to the contamination."[35] Appeal mechanisms under the *Contaminated Sites Remediation Act* involve Manitoba's Clean Environment Commission (CEC) and the minister of the environment. Decisions of the CEC may, with leave, be appealed to the Manitoba Court of Appeal on questions of law or jurisdiction.

D. THE ENVIRONMENTAL LIABILITY OF LENDERS, RECEIVERS, AND TRUSTEES

The importance of environmental considerations for financial and real estate transactions has grown markedly since the 1980s, particularly as a consequence of statutory extensions of environmental liability to persons other than those who caused or were in some way directly responsible for environmental harm. In Ontario, for example, owners or former owners and a person who has or had the charge, management, or control of the source of a contaminant are liable to receive control orders or stop orders.[36] An order to take preventive measures may be issued to a person who owns or owned or who has or had management or control of an undertaking or property if the discharge of a contaminant from the property or undertaking will or is likely to result in an adverse effect and the required measures are necessary or desirable to prevent the discharge or lessen its adverse effects.[37]

Expansive approaches to such concepts as "person responsible," "owner," or "care, management, and control" had the potential to extend environmental liability to institutions and individuals whose original connection with contaminated properties was financial in nature rather than operational. Thus, lenders in general, mortgagees in particular, and others such as trustees and receivers acting on their behalf found their interests intertwined to a sometimes alarming degree with environmental legislation governing environmental protection and cleanup and restoration obligations on contaminated lands.

In *Re Canadian National Railway*, the Ontario Divisional Court considered a mortgagee's liability under an administrative order calling for study of contaminated industrial lands and an assessment of remedial

---

35   The *Contaminated Sites Remediation Act*, C.C.S.M. c. 205, Part 5 .

36   *OEPA*, above note 8, ss. 7 & 8. Comparable powers respecting waste removal are established under *OEPA*, s. 43.

37   *OEPA*, *ibid.*, s. 18.

alternatives.[38] Among the issues raised was the possibility that mort-gagees might exercise "control" so as to become "persons responsible" under the applicable legislation. In the circumstances of the case, and notwithstanding its knowledge of contamination amounting to breach of the covenant of good repair, the mortgagee who was not in posses-sion was not liable. The Ontario Divisional Court explained that the mortgagee might have exercised a power of re-entry and taken control of the property:

> Once in control of the property it could be a person responsible under the Act if, at that time, it was found that the plant was the source of contaminant . . . . The fact that the technical, legal ownership of the plant is in the mortgagee does not make it an owner within the defin-ition of a person responsible. To be an owner within the meaning of the Act, and subject to the serious responsibility imposed by it, there must be possession or dominion over the facility or property . . . . We do not believe it makes any difference whether a mortgagee . . . had knowledge of the contamination or not. If a mortgagee has taken no active steps with respect to gaining or obtaining control of the prop-erty, it is not responsible.[39]

The Divisional Court's decision, besides contributing to a fuller understanding of "care, management, and control" in Ontario legis-lation was also notable for the sensitivity of the surrounding policy implications. While some observers characterized the analysis as an obstacle to attempts by the Ministry of Environment to impose clean-up costs on private parties rather than the public at large, others wel-comed the result, arguing that "[i]t is too often assumed that current landowners should be made responsible for the condition of their land. However, where those conditions were created by others at a time when our current environmental sensitivity did not exist, is it unreasonable to suggest that society at large should pay for the cost of returning the environment to its natural state?"[40] But as *Re Canadian National Railway* was proceeding through the courts, the Ontario legislature ex-panded liability for cleanup costs to previous owners and other parties who may not themselves have caused pollution.[41]

---

38 *Canadian National Railway v. Ontario (Director appointed under the Environment-al Protection Act) (sub nom. Re Canadian National Railway)* (1991), 3 O.R. (3d) 609 (Div. Ct.), aff'd (1992), 7 O.R. (3d) 97 (C.A.).

39 *Ibid.* at 623–24 (Div. Ct.).

40 H. Dahme, "Northern Wood Preservers: A Case of Contaminated Land" (1991) 2:5 Env. L. Alert 1 at 2.

41 *OEPA*, above note 8, s. 7.

Concern about the developing pattern of liability prompted the Canadian Bankers Association to lament "that environmental protection law in Canada punishes the innocent as well as the guilty; that lenders and investors who are not polluters are being asked to pay the penalty for environmental damage caused by others." The association warned policy makers about the economic effects of environmental initiatives directed at "deep pockets" rather than actual polluters.[42] However, the policy issues were by no means one-sided. Aside from financing cleanup costs after damage has occurred, an important virtue of expanded liability lies in its potential to recruit financial institutions to the cause of systematic, preventive environmental monitoring. As one commentator concluded, "lenders must increasingly look to self-protection through careful investigation and the establishment and maintenance of on-going monitoring programs before a lending decision is made."[43]

When borrowers default, lenders may resort to receiverships to recover funds advanced, or bankruptcy proceedings may be initiated with the appointment of a trustee. In such circumstances of limited and uncertain financial resources, conflicts over environmental liabilities are particularly acute. In *Panamericana de Bienes y Servicios S.A. v. Northern Badger Oil & Gas Ltd.*, the Alberta Court of Appeal held that an order of the Alberta Energy Resources Conservation Board concerning well-abandonment procedures represented a general obligation for environmental work in the public interest, which the receiver/manager must pay out of the proceeds of disposition of a bankrupt company's assets prior to a distribution to secured creditors according to the scheme of the federal *Bankruptcy Act*.[44]

In the absence of statutory limitations on liability for costs of environmental cleanup and restoration, the possibility exists that receivers may face personal liability where such costs exceed the value of the assets under administration. To protect themselves from such risks, receivers and trustees, at the time of their appointment, have occasionally sought court assurances to limit the potential extent of environmental liabilities to the value of the debtor's assets, and to ensure that they will be paid for their services. Courts have shown some sympathy for these applications:

---

42   Canadian Bankers Association, *Sustainable Capital: The Effect of Environmental Liability in Canada on Borrowers, Lenders and Investors* (November 1991).

43   P. Lalonde, "Lenders and Their Agents Beware: The Northern Badger Case" (1991) 2:6 Env. L. Alert 1 at 3. For further consideration of the importance of financial arrangements in environmental protection, see chapter 17.

44   (1991), 81 D.L.R. (4th) 280 (Alta. C.A.).

The balancing of values in this case falls in favour of protecting the health and safety of society over the rights of creditors . . . but there is also a need in modern society for trustees to take on the duty of winding up insolvent estates. The evidence before me indicates that no trustee can be found who will take on the bankruptcy . . . without a guarantee that he or she will be entitled to trustee's fees to be deducted from the amount paid out under the Order, and will have no personal liability for the costs of cleanup of the contaminated site . . . . In keeping with the findings I have made . . . I direct that in the event there are insufficient funds to meet the requirements of the Order, the payment of funds pursuant to the Order must be subject to a reduction equal to the amount of the trustee's fees.[45]

Such willingness to accommodate the concerns of persons acting on behalf of creditors has certainly not been universal, and exemption from environmental liabilities has been denied where courts have felt this would amount to rewriting legislation.[46]

A series of amendments to section 14.06 of the federal *Bankruptcy Act* alleviated some of the uncertainties by providing that

Notwithstanding anything in any federal or provincial law, a trustee is not personally liable in that position for any environmental condition that arose or environmental damage that occurred,

(a) before the trustee's appointment; or

(b) after the trustee's appointment unless it is established that the condition arose or the damage occurred as a result of the trustee's gross negligence or wilful misconduct.[47]

Accompanying provisions address options available to trustees in the context of remedial orders.

In some circumstances, it has been possible for secured lenders, receivers, and others facing indirect environmental liabilities to consult with environmental officials in order to negotiate mutually satisfactory terms for the cleanup of contaminated sites. These arrangements may provide government representatives with assurances that basic environmental measures will actually be taken without public financing, while they offer lenders an acceptable measure of financial certainty in place of potentially unlimited obligations. Ontario officials formulated a *Global Agreement* concerning environmental investigations. The

45   *Re Lamford Forest Products Ltd.* (1991), 63 B.C.L.R. (2d) 388 at 396 (S.C.).

46   *Standard Trust Co. v. Lindsay Holdings Ltd.* (1994), 15 C.E.L.R. (N.S.) 165 (B.C.S.C.).

47   *An Act to Amend the Bankruptcy Act*, S.C. 1992, c. 27, S.C. 1997, c. 12.

arrangements made it possible for creditors, on a standard agreement basis, to undertake environmental evaluations and to address various health and safety issues to facilitate the resale of property without facing the risk that they would be deemed to have taken control in a manner that exposed them to statutory environmental liabilities.[48]

E. CONTAMINATED-SITES INVENTORY AND PUBLIC-REMEDIATION PROGRAMS

Practitioners have become more alert to potential environmental problems whether the indications are provided by historic use, topography, and the character of the neighbourhood or district, or based on specific information. Thus armed, legal advisers in real estate transactions may initiate on-site examinations or otherwise more actively pursue searches, investigations, and negotiations to protect their clients' interests in relation to environmental risk. Although neither the federal nor provincial governments have undertaken to produce a comprehensive contaminated-sites inventory, several public databases provide additional means of investigating environmental risks.

Despite the lack of a comprehensive inventory of contaminated lands in Canada, inquiries about the distribution of toxic substances and their use helped to identify extensive historic damage to the environment and refuted wishful thinking on the part of those who had assumed that nature would take care of the cleanup. Notwithstanding much effort to focus on preventive measures, the toxic legacy demands a costly and substantial response that is currently ongoing. That challenge, however, is a formidable one.

Following the announcement of federal funding in 1989, the CCME initiated a National Contaminated Sites Remediation Program (NCSRP). The jointly funded $250-million program was designed to pursue three objectives over a five-year period: to promote the remediation of contaminated lands on the basis of the polluter-pays principle; to encourage the development of innovative remediation technologies; and to fund the cleanup of abandoned or orphan sites that pose high

---

48   Significant elements of Ontario's *Brownfields Statute Law Amendment Act*, above note 22, Part II, ss. 89.9 and 89.12,, are directed to liability issues for those who undertake clean-up measures and others such as creditors, receivers, trustees, consultants, and municipalities who may become involved in contaminated sites.

risks.[49] The orphan category originally included about fifty of the estimated thousand contaminated sites that had been identified when the program was established. As of 1995 when the NCSRP was concluded, remediation was either completed or under way at forty-five of the orphan sites.[50] Although the NCSRP included some preliminary attempt to inventory and address contamination of federal government properties such as airports, government laboratories, ports and harbours, lighthouse stations and military facilities, the slow pace of progress in dealing with approximately 780 such contaminated sites has been the subject of repeated criticism.[51]

In the context of the IJC's concern for Great Lakes water quality, a restoration program was put in place in the form of so-called remedial action plans (RAPs) and forty-three areas of concern (AOCs), where a previous lack of action and the failure of preventive or cleanup initiatives had resulted in the persistence of toxic and other contaminants. As outlined in an annex to the 1987 *Great Lakes Water Quality Agreement* (GLWQA), the RAP process begins with the identification of impaired water uses and an analysis of the causes of that impairment. Remedial measures to restore impaired uses are then formulated and implemented with the involvement of all interested agencies and the local community. Systematic monitoring of progress identifies continuing problems and was intended to facilitate a transition towards ongoing ecosystem protection.

The IJC has a responsibility to review each RAP for compliance with the objectives of the *GLWQA* and to determine whether the remedial effort in place represents a systematic and comprehensive ecosystem approach. Despite persistent frustrations, the IJC judged the RAP program to be "one of the success stories" of the *GLWQA*.[52] The RAP process itself is considered to be a decentralized, "bottom-up" initiative whose operations should promote cooperation and coordination on the part of all levels of government and interested stakeholders. Nevertheless, the IJC has lamented the minor involvement of the two

---

49   G. Letourneau & B.A. Chomyn, "Contaminated Lands: A Canadian Perspective" (1991) 32 C. de D. 1073 at 1076.

50   Canadian Council of Ministers of the Environment, *National Contaminated Sites Remediation Program: Annual Report 1994–95* (Winnipeg: Canadian Council of Ministers of the Environment, 1995).

51   Office of the Auditor General of Canada, *2002 Report of the Commissioner of the Environment and Sustainable Development* (Ottawa: Office of the Auditor General, 2002) c. 2 "The Legacy of Federal Contaminated Sites."

52   International Joint Commission, *Seventh Biennial Report on Great Lakes Water Quality* (Ottawa: International Joint Commission, 1994) at 36.

federal governments in relation to many of the shared AOCs, in connecting channels between and below the Great Lakes: "The level of joint activity varies greatly and is generally too limited. The limited coordination and "cultural" differences in how RAPs are seen as part of governmental processes have led to considerable frustration for the individual jurisdictions and the public in these areas."[53]

On behalf of the IJC, the Great Lakes Water Quality Board undertook a review of government resources and changing program thrusts relating to operations under the *GLWQA* at the national and provincial/state levels.[54] Selected findings include:

- governments are making changes in what they do and how they deliver programs;
- a one-two-one relationship does not exist between resource expenditures and program delivery;
- a number of creative partnerships have been developed and are being developed that share responsibility for program delivery, create efficiencies, and build the institutional capacity to achieve ecosystem results;
- some agencies reported substantial reductions in resource expenditures for certain indicators;
- continued emphasis must be placed on evaluating program effectiveness based on measuring ecosystem results.

On the Canadian side, progress towards the elimination of Areas of Concern has fallen well short of expectations. In a twenty year period of operations, only two of the original Canadian Areas of Concern have been de-listed. Contaminated sediments and inadequate wastewater treatment facilities have yet to be effectively addressed. The 2001 *Canada–Ontario Agreement Respecting the Great Lakes Basin Ecosystem*, including provisions directed towards the remaining Areas of Concern in Canada is under renegotiation.[55]

---

53   *Ibid.* at 35.
54   Great Lakes Water Quality Board, International Joint Commission, *Review of Government Resources and Changing Program Thrusts as They Relate to Delivery of Programs under the Great Lakes Water Quality Agreement* (Detroit, MI: Great Lakes Water Quality Board, 1998).
55   Online: www.on.ec.gc.ca/coa/2001. See also Office of the Auditor General of Canada, *2008 March Status Report of the Commissioner of the Environment and Sustainable Development* (Ottawa: Minister of Public Works and Government Services, 2008) c. 7 "Areas of Concern in the Great Lakes Basin."

FURTHER READINGS

ABDEL-AZIZ, A., & N. CHALIFOUR, *The Canadian Brownfields Manual,* (Toronto: LexisNexis/Butterworths, 2004)

BERETI, RICHARD E., *British Columbia Environmental Management Legislation and Commentary* (Toronto: LexisNexis Canada, 2006–)

COBURN, F., & G. MANNING, *Toxic Real Estate Manual* (Toronto: Canada Law Book, 1999)

NRTEE, *Greening Canada's Brownfield Sites* (Ottawa: National Round Table on the Environment and the Economy, 1998)

SWAIGEN, J., *Toxic Time Bombs: The Regulation of Canada's Leaking Underground Storage Tanks* (Toronto: Emond Montgomery, 1995)

WINFIELD, M., & G. JENISH, *Troubled Waters? A Review of the Performance of the Governments of Canada and Ontario under the 1994 Canada–Ontario Agreement Respecting the Great Lakes Basin Ecosystem* (Toronto: Canadian Institute for Environmental Law and Policy, 1999)

CHAPTER 12

ENVIRONMENTAL ASSESSMENT

A. OVERVIEW OF ENVIRONMENTAL ASSESSMENT

Environmental assessment, in the opinion of the Supreme Court of Canada, has become "a planning tool that is now generally regarded as an integral component of sound decision-making."[1] It is important, again in the words of the court, because, "the growth of modern societies has shown the serious problems that can result from anarchic development and use of land, in particular those problems concerning public health and the environment."[2]

The basic idea is simple enough: certain proposed activities should be scrutinized in advance from the perspective of their possible environmental consequences. However, challenging operational questions may arise in the process of implementing this idea, and there has been considerable divergence of opinion about the legal status and weight to be given to assessment processes. At one extreme of the spectrum of opinion are those who think that assessment—not a bad idea in principle—is something that should be dispensed with in the interests of getting on with the real job of economic development. At the other end are those who view the satisfactory completion of a rigorous

---

1 *Friends of the Oldman River Society v. Canada (Minister of Transport)*, [1992] 1 S.C.R. 3 at 71 [*Oldman River*].
2 *R. v. Al Klippert Ltd.*, [1998] 1 S.C.R. 737 at para. 16.

and comprehensive environmental assessment as an essential precondition of proceeding with any proposal. Yet, even among those who accept the importance of environmental assessment, there are significant divergences of opinion concerning the scope and implications of such proceedings.

The components of a generic environmental assessment regime raise questions such as the following:

1. To what activities does the environmental assessment process apply? To large or small operations; public or private operations; projects only, or also plans, programs, and even policies that are less directly associated with immediate physical impacts?[3]
2. By whom should the assessment be carried out? By the initiator of the proposal, professional consultants or an independent body?[4]
3. What is the standard and scope of assessment, including the meaning of environment?[5] Does environment include social, cultural, and economic factors? Will the assessment deal only with "direct" and "significant" impact, or will "indirect" and "cumulative" impact also be addressed?[6]
4. Is environmental assessment primarily concerned with the technical dimensions of specific proposed activity, or should it extend to consideration of the very purpose and utility of the proposal, or to other means of accomplishing the same goals?
5. Will the assessment documents be subject to some further process of review and scrutiny? By departments of government; by the public; or through an administrative tribunal process? And are such reviews mandatory or discretionary?
6. What should a review body be authorized to decide or recommend?

---

3   Commissioner of the Environment and Sustainable Development, *2004 October Report* (Ottawa: Office of the Auditor General, 2004) c. 4.
4   Hugh Benevides, "Real Reform Deferred: Analysis of Recent Amendments to the *Canadian Environmental Assessment Act*" (2004) 13 J. Envtl. L. & Prac. 195.
5   Projects under assessment contribute, through CO_2 and other greenhouse gas emissions, to climate change at the global level with extraordinary environmental impacts outside the vicinity or locale of the the project itself, and well beyond the jurisdiction in which the proposed activity would be undertaken. How to incorporate these environmental impacts into the assessment process has been challenging and controversial. See, for example, Commissioner of the Environment and Sustainable Development, *2003 October Report* (Ottawa: Office of the Auditor General, 2003) c. 2 "Road Transportation and Urban Areas: Accountability for Reducing Greenhouse Gases."
6   C. Tollefson & K. Wipond, "Cumulative Environmental Impacts and Aboriginal Rights" (1998) 18 Environmental Impact Assessment Review 371.

7. What are the consequences of not completing, or not "passing," an environmental assessment? Can the proposed initiative be delayed or terminated?

8. Are follow-up measures available to ensure compliance with an assessment decision?

Following their introduction in the 1970s, the first generation of environmental assessment procedures was under almost continuous scrutiny by those who wished to strengthen the process and by those who believed that existing requirements or approaches were already too burdensome. Environmental groups actively promoted improvements through policy reform and used the courts to test environmental assessment standards.[7]

Costs and delays associated with compliance were frequently the subject of criticism from proponents. In fact, however, extended analyses of proposals by industry and other parties have been rare. One useful description of a private proponent's distinctive perspective on environmental assessment was formulated in a study of the Alberta-Pacific pulp mill application (Al-Pac):

> The proponent ... is ... the one party which has made a specific financial commitment to the project. It expects the project to be profitable, and the corporate proponent has a duty to its shareholders to make it so. It has therefore prepared financial projections, which will include a budget for the EIA review process, assumptions as to the date that it will be permitted to start work, and so on.[8]

Although approvals cannot be taken for granted, it is often assumed that a proponent has "a reasonable expectation for a process to be in place which it can predict with some degree of certainty."[9]

Some proponents have indeed experienced uncertainty in relation to such factors as "the time frame, the information requirements, the procedure for hearings, the outcome, and the policy that would be applied." The Al-Pac proponents faced most of these uncertainties and even the more fundamental "question of whether its project would be subject to hearings at all."[10] Over and above the actual requirements of environmental assessment if it is applicable, industry often raised

---

7   R.B. Gibson & B. Savan, *Environmental Assessment in Ontario* (Toronto: Canadian Environmental Law Research Foundation, 1986).

8   P. Edwards, *The Al-Pac Review Hearings: A Case Study* (Edmonton: Environmental Law Centre, 1990) at 126.

9   *Ibid.*

10   *Ibid.*

questions about inconsistencies and overlaps between Canadian jurisdictions, for, as discussed later in this chapter, the ambiguities of federalism have affected several major development proposals.

The concerns of industry and investors should be placed in context. Saskatchewan's Environmental Assessment Review Commission
(SEARC) re-examined the files on 636 proposals that had been considered by the Department of Environment and Public Safety during an
eleven-year period. A full environmental impact assessment (EIA) was
requested for 80 of these (13 percent), although only 35 EIAs were completed. Only one board of inquiry was established (Rafferty/Alameda)
and only two proposals were denied approval to proceed. SEARC concluded that "the existing EA process has not been a major roadblock
for those proposals it has affected."[11] Apart from occasional exceptions,
that evaluation is applicable across the country.

In terms of costs, some early estimates suggested that hearing costs
for projects considered under the federal environmental assessment and
review process ranged between 0.026 and 0.5 percent of total project
costs.[12] A subsequent survey carried out by the Economic Council of
Canada suggested that the average cost of environmental assessments
on major projects approximates 1 percent of the overall capital cost, with
major projects understood to be those involving more than $3 million.[13]

On the other hand, certain benefits have been claimed for environmental assessment. For example, it has been asserted that by providing timely opportunities for reflection and public input, environmental
assessments often serve to eliminate potential problems. Along with
the avoidance or reduction of environmental damage, benefits include
opportunities for public input into design and operational features, as
well as cost savings resulting from the downscaling or cancellation of
ill-conceived and unnecessary projects.[14] Negotiations over conditions
of approval have often been central elements of environmental assessment. In the sense that these produce consensus or agreement on the
means of resolving difficulties, they, too, have a positive impact.[15]

---

11   *Report of the Saskatchewan Environmental Review Commission: Environmental
     Challenges* (Regina: The Commission, 1991) at 83.
12   Gibson & Savan, above note 7 at 411.
13   G.E. Neufeld, *A Preliminary Survey of the Impact of Environmental Assessments on
     Competitiveness* (Ottawa: Economic Council of Canada, 1992). Roughly compar-
     able findings have been reported in other jurisdictions. See John Glasson, Riki
     Therivel, & Andrew Chadwick, *Introduction to Environmental Impact Assessment*,
     3d ed., (London: Routledge, 2005) at 233–35.
14   Gibson & Savan, above note 7 at 409.
15   M.I. Jeffery, "Accommodating Negotiations in EIA and Project Approval Processes"
     (1987) 4 E.P.L.J. 244; M.I. Jeffery, "Consideration and Analysis of Conditions of

B. THE *CANADIAN ENVIRONMENTAL ASSESSMENT ACT*

Procedures first adopted as Cabinet policy in 1973 and then reissued in 1984 as the *Environmental Assessment and Review Process Guidelines Order (EARPGO)* set out the original basis for federal environmental assessment.[16] Though treated by government officials as discretionary, the Federal Court of Canada eventually determined in litigation concerning Saskatchewan's Rafferty-Alameda dam proposals that the *EARPGO* was legally binding and that compliance with its procedures was required.[17] By this time, preliminary legislative efforts were well under way to provide formal statutory authority for the federal environmental assessment process and to address uncertainties that had arisen in connection with the *Environmental Assessment and Review Process (EARP)*. Enacted in 1992 and proclaimed in 1995 on the completion of supporting regulations, the *Canadian Environmental Assessment Act (CEAA)* reformulated the federal environmental assessment regime.[18]

By way of introduction, the scope of application of federal environmental assessments under *CEAA* proved to be remarkably problematic. Some insights may be gained from the Supreme Court of Canada's discussion of a similar issue in the context of the *Oldman River* decision under the *EARPGO*. After emphasizing the importance of first linking the exercise of legislative power in relation to the environment to the appropriate head of constitutional power, La Forest J. remarked that "the extent to which environmental concerns may be taken into account in the exercise of a power may vary from one power to another."[19] Accordingly, he observed that the exercise of Parliament's jurisdiction over fisheries, a resource, and over navigation, an activity, will each involve "a somewhat different environmental role."[20] He also offered a hypothetical example suggesting that, once the constitutional basis for federal action had been established, the scope of an associated environmental assessment might indeed be quite extensive:

Approval Likely to be Imposed by the Environmental Assessment Board in Granting Project Approval" (1988) 1 Can. J.Admin. L. & Prac. 21 ["Consideration"].

16   S.O.R./84-467.

17   *Canadian Wildlife Federation Inc. v. Canada (Minister of the Environment)*, [1989] 3 F.C. 309 (T.D.), aff'd (1989), 4 C.E.L.R. (N.S.) 1 (Fed. C.A.).

18   Controversies surrounding the transition between *EARPGO* and *CEAA* persisted for some time. See *Inter-Church Uranium Committee Educational Co-operative v. Canada (Atomic Energy Control Board)*, 2004 FCA 218.

19   *Oldman River*, above note 1 at 67.

20   *Ibid.*

[o]ne might postulate the location and construction of a new line which would require approval under the relevant provisions of the *Railway Act* .... That line may cut through ecologically sensitive habitats such as wetlands and forests. The possibility of derailment may pose a serious hazard to the health and safety of nearby communities if dangerous commodities are to be carried on the line. On the other hand, it may bring considerable economic benefit to those communities through job creation and the multiplier effect that it will have in the local economy. The regulatory authority might require that the line circumvent residential districts in the interests of noise abatement and safety. In my view, all of these considerations may validly be taken into account in arriving at a final decision on whether or not to grant the necessary approval. To suggest otherwise would lead to the most astonishing results, and it defies reason to assert that Parliament is constitutionally barred from weighing the broad environmental repercussions, including socio-economic concerns, when legislating with respect to decisions of this nature.[21]

Those who anticipated a less complex and controversial operation for the legislated federal environmental assessment regime have been disappointed.

As expressed in the preamble and a purposes clause, *CEAA* is intended both to ensure that the environmental effects of projects are carefully considered before the federal government takes action in connection with them and to promote sustainable development. In addition, the legislation seeks to ensure that projects within Canada or on federal lands do not cause significant adverse environmental effects on other jurisdictions and that opportunities are provided for public participation in the federal environmental assessment process. Environmental effects, the focus of the assessment exercise, are defined in respect of projects to which the Act applies as

(a) any change that the project may cause in the environment, including any effect of any such change on health and socio-economic conditions, on physical and cultural heritage, on the current use of lands and resources for traditional purposes by aboriginal persons, or on any structure, site or thing that is of historical, archeological, paleontological or architectural significance,

(b) and any change to the project that may be caused by the environment, whether any such change occurs within or outside Canada.

---

21   *Ibid.* at 66.

For *CEAA* to apply to a particular initiative, it must first be established that the initiative is a project within the terms of the legislation and not otherwise excluded. Projects, for the purposes of *CEAA*, are of two types—first, undertakings in relation to physical works, that is, "any proposed construction, operation, modification, decommissioning, abandonment or other undertaking in relation to that physical work," and, second, activities unrelated to a physical work if those activities are designated by regulation in what is known as the *Inclusion List*.[22] The *Inclusion List* identifies various physical activities associated with specified subject areas: national parks and protected areas; oil and gas projects; nuclear facilities; defence; transportation; waste management; fisheries;[23] wildlife; projects on aboriginal lands; the north, and forests. It is notable that initiatives of a policy or program nature do not fall within the *CEAA*'s conception of project, and assessment of their environmental impact would be conducted on a different basis.[24] These are generally known as strategic environmental assessments and have been described as "the systematic and comprehensive process of evaluating the environmental effects of a policy, plan or program and its alternatives."

The applicability of the *CEAA* regime further depends on the involvement of a federal authority in the exercise of one of a series of four statutorily defined powers, duties, or functions (commonly described as "triggers") in relation to the project. Ministers of the Crown, designated departments, and other statutory agencies, along with additional bodies prescribed by regulation, are federal authorities under *CEAA*.[25] If a federal authority proposes to exercise any of the following triggers in relation to the project, then a prior assessment may be required:

22 *Canadian Environmental Assessment Act*, S.C. 1992, c. 37, s. 2(1) [*CEAA*] and the *Inclusion List Regulations*, S.O.R./94-637, as amended by S.O.R./99-436, S.O.R./2000-309, S.O.R./2003-280, S.O.R./2003-349, S.O.R./2005-261, S.O.R./2005-314.

23 Arlene J. Kwasniak, "Slow on the Trigger: the Department of Fisheries and Oceans, the *Fisheries Act* and the *Canadian Environmental Assessment Act*" (2004) 27 Dal. L.J. 347.

24 Federal Environmental Assessment Review Office, *The Environmental Assessment Process for Policy and Program Proposals* (February 1993) and *Cabinet Directive on the Environmental Assessment of Policy, Plans and Program Proposals* (1999, amended 2004), online: www.ceaa.gc.ca/016/CEAA-StrategicFinal_e.pdf. See S. Hazell & H. Benevides, "Federal Strategic Environmental Assessment: A Legal Framework" (1997) 7 J. Envtl. L. & Prac. 349, and Commissioner of the Environment and Sustainable Development, *2004 October Report*, above note 3 at c. 4.

25 *Federal Authorities Regulations*, S.O.R./96-280, as amended by S.O.R./2000-44, and S.O.R./2001-44.

1. Is the federal authority the proponent of the project;
2. Does the federal authority plan to grant some form of financial assistance to the project;
3. Does the federal authority plan to dispose of an interest in federal lands to further the project; and
4. Does the project require the issuance of any permit, licence, or approval by either the federal authority or by Cabinet upon the recommendation of that federal authority, as specified in the regulation known as the *Law List*?[26]

Despite the fact that an undertaking constitutes a project within the meaning of *CEAA* and involves a triggering action by a federal authority, it might still be exempt from environmental assessment when carried out in response to certain emergencies or on the basis of an *Exclusion List*.[27] On the other hand, even where *CEAA* is not triggered by a federal authority, environmental assessment may be undertaken in relation to projects with an interprovincial or international impact or an impact on federal lands where the minister is of the opinion that significant adverse environmental effects may result.[28]

Where required, environmental assessment under *CEAA* will ordinarily begin with self-assessment by the responsible authority (RA), taking the form either of screening or a more extensive assessment for matters designated on a *Comprehensive Study List*.[29] The RA must ensure that the process is conducted as soon as practicable during the planning phase for the project and "before irrevocable decisions are made."[30] A public registry for each project, now encompassing paper and electronic materials[31] provides basic access to information. In the context of a screening, the lowest level of assessment, any further public consultation is entirely at the discretion of the federal authority.

Screening is overwhelmingly the dominant process of assessment: in the 2004–2005 federal fiscal year, over six thousand screenings

---

26 The *Law List Regulations*, S.O.R./94-636, as amended S.O.R./99-330; S.O.R./99-438; S.O.R./2000-308; S.O.R./2001-257; S.O.R./2003-281; S.O.R./2003-351; S.O.R./2005-261; S.O.R./2005-314. See *CEAA*, above note 22, s. 5(2).

27 *Exclusion List Regulations, 2007*, S.O.R./2007-108. See also *CEAA, ibid.*, s. 59(c.1).

28 *CEAA, ibid.*, ss. 46–48.

29 Projects subject to comprehensive study are designated by regulation: *Comprehensive Study List Regulations*, S.O.R./94-638, as amended.

30 *CEAA*, above note 22, s. 11.

31 *Ibid.*, s. 55. Recent statutory revision establishes the Canadian Environmental Assessment Registry.

were initiated in comparison with only eleven comprehensive assessments.[32]

Pursuant to section 16(1), screenings as well as comprehensive
studies involve consideration of the following factors, leading in each
case to the preparation of a report:

- environmental effects of the project, including cumulative effects
  likely to result from the combination of the project and other past or
  future projects and activities;
- significance of those effects;
- comments from the public;
- mitigation measures to address significant adverse environmental
  effects; and
- other relevant matters that the federal authority considers appropriate, including the need for the project and alternatives to the project.[33]

For those projects made subject to comprehensive assessment on the
assumption that their environmental effects will likely be significant,
section 16(2) requires that additional matters be addressed:

- purpose of the project;
- alternative means of carrying out the project and the environmental
  effects of those alternatives;
- follow-up program; and
- impact of the project on the capacity of renewable resources to meet
  present and future needs.[34]

The comprehensive-study process also differs from screening as a form
of initial assessment in that opportunities for public comment must be
made available and the results provided to the minister of the environment along with the report.[35]

The conclusion of the initial phase of assessment, whether by means
of screening or comprehensive study, establishes the basis for decision
making. In the case of screening, the RA faces three possible courses of
action. It may decide to proceed with a project whose adverse environmental effects, assuming the implementation of relevant mitigation
measures, are not likely to be significant. Where, despite mitigation,
significant and unjustified adverse environmental effects are likely, the

---

32 Online: www.tbs-sct.gc.ca/rma/dpr1/04-05/CEAA-ACEE/CEAA-ACEEd4502_e.
    asp#Anchor-Tabl-15556.
33 *CEAA*, above note 22, s. 16(1).
34 *Ibid.*, s. 16(2).
35 *Ibid.*, s. 22.

RA will not proceed. In cases of uncertainty, or where warranted on the basis of public concern, the RA will refer the project to the minister for further consideration by a review panel or through mediation.[36]

In the case of a comprehensive study concluding that significant adverse environmental effects are likely or uncertain, or where public concern warrants, the minister shall direct the project to a mediator or review panel for a further phase of environmental assessment.[37] Alternatively, the minister may determine either that the project (assuming the implementation of mitigation measures) is not likely to cause significant adverse environmental effects or that the project is likely to cause such effects that "cannot be justified in the circumstances."[38] In both of these latter instances the minister then refers the project back to the RA to proceed or not proceed.

The review panel and mediation provisions of *CEAA* offer additional mechanisms that, in controversial and uncertain cases, involve further scope for public participation.[39] Each of these additional phases of federal environmental assessment results in a report to the RA and to the minister, who is again responsible for making it available to the public.

In practice, the application of federal environmental assessment on a legislative basis under *CEAA* proved to be remarkably controversial. Particular concern arose about the scope, extent, or coverage of the environmental assessment process required by the Act. This concern had three aspects. Although they are closely interrelated, if not mutual substitutes, separate treatment will be offered here to clarify the statutory origins of each of the scoping issues.

1) The Scope of the Project

The first of the scoping issues relates to the project itself. Section 2 defines a project as being "in relation to a physical work, any proposed construction, operation, modification, decommissioning, abandonment or other undertaking in relation to that physical work," whereas section

---

36   *Ibid.*, s. 20(1).
37   *Ibid.*, s. 23(b). Canadian experience with mediation in the context of environmental assessment is extremely limited. For discussion see Tyson Dyck, "Standing on the Shoulders of Rio: Greening Mediations under the *Canadian Environmental Assessment Act*" (2004) 13 J. Envtl. L. & Prac. 335 at 342–44.
38   *CEAA, ibid.*, s. 23(a).
39   For discussion of the potential contribution but limited extent of public participation in *CEAA* panels, see Susan Rutherford & Karen Campbell, "Time Well Spent: A Survey of Public Participation in Federal Environmental Assessment Panels" (2004) 15 J. Envtl. L. & Prac. 71.

15(1) indicates that the responsible authority will determine the scope of the project in relation to which an environmental assessment is to be conducted. A liberal, generous determination of a project's scope will lead to a broader, more encompassing environmental assessment, whereas a narrower, more restricted approach to the scope of a project will confine the ambit of the associated environmental assessment. For example, a federal authority might be asked to approve bridge construction across a navigable waterway when a company engaged in forest operations wishes to establish a roadway between its cutting site and a mill. The project could be described as the construction of a bridge, or as the construction of a bridge in a roadway, or as the construction of a bridge in a roadway linking forest operations and milling facilities.

2) The Scope of the Environmental Assessment

The second scoping issue arises under section 15(3) and involves the scope of the environmental assessment:

> Where a project is in relation to a physical work, an environmental assessment shall be conducted in respect of every construction, operation, modification, decommissioning, abandonment or other undertaking in relation to that physical work that is proposed by the proponent or that is, in the opinion of the responsible authority . . . likely to be carried out in relation to that physical work.

Debate centred on whether (and the degree to which) this provision might require environmental assessment to extend outside the scope of the project. In other words, what activity or other undertakings are "in relation to" the physical work the proponent proposes or are, in the opinion of the responsible authority, likely to be carried out "in relation to" that physical work. To return to the previous example, and assuming the physical work constituting the scope of the project was construction of a bridge, could it now be argued that the roadway or the forest operations made possible by the roadway were undertakings "in relation to" the bridge?

3) The Scope of Factors to Be Considered in the Environmental Assessment

CEAA, having listed factors to be considered in either a screening or comprehensive study, provides further that the scope of the factors to be taken into consideration are to be determined by the responsible authority.

Divergent approaches to these three issues were apparent in trial court decisions before the Federal Court of Appeal judgment in a case known as *Sunpine*.[40] The facts in *Sunpine* correspond with the scenario presented above to illustrate points of uncertainty and debate associated with *CEAA* sections 15 and 16. When Sunpine Forest Products sought approval as required under section 5(1) of the *Navigable Waters Protection Act* to construct two bridges as part of a roadway connecting the company's timber harvesting operation to its mill, federal environmental assessment was triggered pursuant to *CEAA* section 5(1)(d). As responsible authority, the minister of fisheries and oceans scoped the project and prepared screening reports.

In scoping each bridge project, the responsible authority stated:

> The scope of the . . . Bridge Project includes: the construction and maintenance of a two-lane dual span bridge . . . including associated approaches and related works, storage areas or other undertakings directly associated with the construction of this bridge. The project involves preparation of the construction site . . . abutments and the bridge structure.[41]

Scoped in this way, the bridge projects did not encompass road work leading to the bridge or forest management operations made possible by their construction. Accordingly, the screening reports did not address the environmental implications of the roadway or the forest operations. Since the screening reports found that the bridge projects as scoped were "not likely to cause significant adverse environmental effects," the approvals were granted under the *Navigable Waters Protection Act*.

When the judicial review application reached the Federal Court of Appeal, that court confirmed the power of the responsible authority to exercise its discretion under section 15(1) in scoping the project subject to review. In the interpretation of section 15(3), the Federal Court of Appeal clarified the significance of the phrase "in relation to." Whereas the trial court had concluded that the road and possibly even the forest operations were undertakings in relation to bridge projects, the FCA firmly declared that section 15(3) was subordinate to the project scoping power in section 15(1). Accordingly, "the words in subsection 15(3) do not have the effect of rescoping a project to something wider than what was determined under section 15(1)."[42] As the FCA explained, the words "in relation to" do not encompass activity that has "any conceiv-

---

40   *Friends of the West Country Association v. Canada (Ministry of Fisheries and Oceans)* (1999), 31 C.E.L.R. (N.S.) 239 (F.C.A.).

41   *Ibid.* at para. 12.

42   *Ibid.* at para. 14.

able connection" to the project as scoped. In the opinion of the court, "the words refer to construction, operation, modification, decommissioning, abandonment or other undertakings that pertain to the life cycle of the physical work itself or that are subsidiary or ancillary to the physical work that is the focus of the project as scoped."[43]

The FCA also examined the question of whether the inclusion in section 16(1) of cumulative effects among the considerations to be addressed in an environmental assessment necessarily encompassed the effects of the road in combination with the bridges. The FCA emphasized that while section 16(1) is mandatory and that some consideration of each listed factor is therefore essential, discretion with regard to the scope of such consideration is clearly conferred on the responsible authority by section 16(3).[44]

4) *CEAA* Amendments

Pursuant to section 72 of the original enacting legislation, *CEAA* is subject to regular parliamentary review. The first review process was launched in 1999 on the basis of a Discussion Paper leading to more detailed studies on a series of issues targeted for closer consideration. Amendments to the legislation are now in effect.[45] The new provisions implemented numerous technical changes and adjustments to the underlying statute, beginning with additions to the purpose clause indicating the *CEAA* is intended to promote cooperation and coordinated action between the federal and provincial governments in the field of environmental assessment, and to enhance communication and cooperation between RAs and Aboriginal peoples. There were also changes to the description of federal authorities subject to *CEAA* requirements relating particularly to Crown corporations, port and harbour commissions and the Canadian International Development Agency. These organizations are now subject to distinctive environmental assessment procedures in light of the nature of their activities and financing.

Other significant amendments resulting from the legislative review included provisions for the coordination of federal environmental assessment where multiple federal authorities are involved. In addition new provisions clarify responsibility for mitigation measures where

---

43 *Ibid*, at para. 20.
44 For subsequent discussion by the F.C.A. of the scoping process and of the relationship between ss. 15 & 16, see *Prairie Acid Rain Coalition v. Canada (Minister of Fisheries and Oceans)*, 2006 FCA 31, and *Miningwatch Canada v. Canada (Minister of Fisheries and Oceans)*, 2007 FC 955.
45 S.C. 2003, c. 9.

these are called for, as well as the relationship between mitigation and follow-up programs with the latter now specifically associated with adaptive management. Funding to support public participation is now available not only in the case of panel reviews and mediation, but in connection with comprehensive studies and joint panel reviews.

C. PROVINCIAL ENVIRONMENTAL ASSESSMENT REGIMES

Provincial environmental assessment regimes have been established in all Canadian provinces (see table 12.1), although they differ, sometimes significantly, in detail.[46]

Table 12.1: Provincial Environmental Assessment Legislation

Alberta	*Environmental Protection and Enhancement Act*, R.S.A. 2000, c. E-12
	Activities Designation Regulation, Alta. Reg. 276/2003
British Columbia	*Environmental Assessment Act*, S.B.C. 2002, c. 43
	Environmental Assessment Reviewable Projects Regulation, B.C. Reg. 276/95, repealed by B.C. Reg. 290/2003
Manitoba	*The Environment Act*, C.C.S.M., c. E125
	Licensing Procedures Regulation, Man. Reg. 163/88
	Classes of Development Regulation, Man. Reg. 164/88
New Brunswick	*Clean Environment Act*, R.S.N.B. 1973, c. C-6
	Environmental Impact Assessment Regulation, N.B. Reg. 87/83
Newfoundland and Labrador	*Environmental Protection Act*, S.N.L. 2002, c. E-14.2
	Environmental Assessment Regulations, 2003, N.L.R. 54/03
Nova Scotia	*Environmental Act*, S.N.S. 1994–95, c. 1
	Environmental Assessment Regulations, N.S. Reg. 26/95
Ontario	*Environmental Assessment Act*, R.S.O. 1990, c. E-18
Prince Edward Island	*Environmental Protection Act*, R.S.P.E.I. 1988, c. E-9
Quebec	*Environment Quality Act*, R.S.Q. 1977, c. Q-2
	Regulation respecting environmental assessment and review, R.Q. c. Q-2, r.9
Saskatchewan	*The Environmental Assessment Act*, S.S. 1979–80, c. E-10.1

The application section of the Ontario *Environmental Assessment Act* states that the legislation applies to

---

46 For suggestions about reducing variations and inconsistencies, see the CCME Sub-Agreement on Environmental Assessment.

(a) enterprises or activities or proposals, plans or programs in re-
    spect of enterprises or activities by or on behalf of Her Majesty
    in right of Ontario or by a public body or public bodies or by a
    municipality or municipalities;

(b) major commerical or business enterprises or activities or propos-
    als, plans or programs in respect of major commercial or busi-
    ness enterprises or activities of a person or persons, other than a
    person referred to in clause (a), designated by the regulations.[47]

That is, in the absence of designation by regulation, private-sector initiatives in Ontario are not covered by provincial environmental assessment requirements. Most of the designations, until recently, involved
waste management, although as a consequence of deregulation energy
sector projects will now be subject to environmental assessment on the
basis of their environmental significance rather than their public or
private nature.[48]

Once the applicability of the Act to a given undertaking has been
confirmed, the Ontario requirements for environmental assessment are
comprehensive. According to the statute, an environmental assessment
ordinarily consists of the following:

(a) a description of the purpose of the undertaking;

(b) a description of and a statement of the rationale for,
    (i)   the undertaking,
    (ii) the alternative methods of carrying out the undertaking,
          and
    (iii) the alternatives to the undertaking;

(c) a description of,
    (i)   the environment that will be affected . . .
    (ii) the effects that will be caused . . .
    (iii) the actions necessary . . . to prevent, change, mitigate or
          remedy . . .

(d) an evaluation of the advantages and disadvantages to the en-
    vironment . . .[49]

Moreover, the province's Environmental Review Tribunal articulated
high standards for the process that must be followed by a proponent

---

47   *Environmental Assessment Act*, R.S.O. 1990, c. E.18, s. 3 [*OEAA*].
48   *Electricity Projects Regulation*, O. Reg. 116/01. *Waste Management Project*, O. Reg.
     101/07 and "Guide to Environmental Assessment Requirements for Waste Man-
     agement Projects" (15 March 2007) online: www.ene.gov.on.ca/en/publications/
     forms/6168e.pdf. Along with energy and waste management projects, the transit
     and transportation sector attracts reform attention.
49   *OEAA*, above note 47, s. 5(3).

in preparing an environmental assessment. The process should be systematic and replicable for, in the view of the tribunal, the Ontario Act calls for "a wide-ranging investigation that involves a reasonable and logical application of criteria, so that the final result is consistent with the steps taken along the way."[50] Subsequent amendments in Ontario, while preserving the existing description of the requirements for an environmental assessment, call for the proponent to submit terms of reference following consultations with interested persons and to obtain approval from the minister for those terms of reference. While this allows a proponent to seek approval for terms of reference tailored to a particular project, the generic elements identified in the statute remain presumptive requirements.[51] Provision was also made for time limits applicable to various stages in the environmental assessment process.[52]

Other provinces have more systematically provided for review of major resource and industrial projects and other private-sector initiatives, although the assessments required are not always as comprehensive as those provided for by Ontario. British Columbia's *Environmental Assessment Reviewable Projects Regulation*,[53] for example, specifically addressed a wide range of types of facilities and described the circumstances in which construction or modification projects would be considered reviewable. In particular, the regulation included reference to industrial projects in the organic and inorganic chemical industry; primary metals; non-metallic mineral product industries such as cement, glass, lime, and asbestos; forest products industries including pulp, paper, paperboard, de-inking, wood preservative, building-board manufacturers, and sawmills; pharmaceutical plants; fibre and textile facilities; tanneries; tire and tube plants; and lead-acid battery manufacturers. Additional types of activities that, depending on their size

---

50   *Re North Simcoe Waste Management Assn.* (1989), 5 C.E.L.R. (N.S.) 98 at 117 (O.M.B. & O.E.A.B.) [*North Simcoe*].

51   *Sutcliffe v. Ontario (Minister of the Environment)*, [2004] O.J. No. 3473 (C.A.). See M. Valiante, "Case Comment" (2003) 3 C.E.L.R. (3d) 219.

52   See M. Valiante, "Evaluating Ontario's Environmental Assessment Reforms" (1999) 8 J. Envtl. L. & Prac. 215, and Alan D. Levy, "A Review of Environmental Assessment in Ontario" (2002) 11 J. Envtl. L. & Prac. 173. Continuing refinements are underway, see "Codes of Practice for Ontario's Environmental Assessment Process: Preparing and Reviewing Environmental Assessments and Class Environmental Assessments" (Draft published for Comments, 17 April 2007).

53   B.C. Reg. 276/95, as amended. Now see *Environmental Assessment Act*, S.B.C. 2002, c. 43 [*BCEAA*] and *Reviewable Projects Regulation*, B.C. Reg. 14/2006. The *Environmental Management Act* also provides for ministerial designation of projects subject to environmental assessment, S.B.C. 2003, c. 53, s. 78.

and other characteristics, will be reviewable include mining projects, energy facilities, water-management and diversion projects, waste-disposal operations, food-processing and transportation projects, and tourism and recreational projects. In Alberta, environmental assessment is applicable to activities in the nature of "construction, operation or reclamation" if scheduled under the *Environmental Protection and Enhancement Act* or designated by regulation. For some initiatives environmental assessment is mandatory, but Alberta Environment's director may designate others on the basis of specified statutory criteria such as the location and size of the activity or the level of public concern.[54] The flexible and discretionary nature of requirements for environmental assessment has often become a subject of debate.[55]

The issues to be addressed in the provincial environmental assessment process itself will typically become the focus of discussion and negotiation between the proponent and the regulatory authority with overall supervisory responsibility. Legislative guidance on these matters again varies in detail. Alberta identified the following as issues for discussion in an environmental-impact assessment report (if required), whose final form is determined in terms of reference set by a provincially designated environment director:

(a) a description of the proposed activity and an analysis of the need for the activity;

(b) an analysis of the site selection procedure for the proposed activity, including a statement of the reasons why the proposed site was chosen and a consideration of alternative sites;

(c) an identification of existing baseline environmental conditions and areas of major concern that should be considered;

(d) a description of potential positive and negative environmental, social, economic, and cultural impacts of the proposed activity, including cumulative, regional, temporal, and spatial considerations;

(e) an analysis of the significance of the potential impacts identified under clause (d);

(f) the plans that have been or will be developed to mitigate the potential negative impacts identified under clause (d);

---

54   *Environmental Protection and Enhancement Act*, S.A. 1992, c. E-13.3, s. 42 [*AEPEA*]. Now see R.S.A. 2000, c. E-12.

55   N.J. Brennan, "Impediments to Environmental Quality and New Brunswick's *Clean Environment Act*: An Argument for a New Statute" (1996) 7 J. Envtl. L. & Prac. 93 at 103–7.

(g) an identification of issues related to human health that should be considered;

(h) a consideration of the alternatives to the proposed activity, including the alternative of not proceeding with the proposed activity;

(i) the plans that have been or will be developed to monitor environmental impacts that are predicted to occur and the plans that have been or will be developed to monitor proposed mitigation measures;

(j) the contingency plans that have been or will be developed in order to respond to unpredicted negative impacts;

(k) the plans that have been or will be developed for waste minimization and recycling;

(l) the manner in which the proponent intends to implement a program of public consultation in respect of the undertaking of the proposed activity and to present the results of that program;

(m) the plans that have been or will be developed to minimize the production or the release into the environment of substances that may have an adverse effect.[56]

The agencies with responsibility to conduct environmental assessments typically have authority in the context of their ultimate decision making to attach terms and conditions to approvals. They may, for example, impose certain safeguards on the manner in which projects are implemented, or they may require forms of compensation and assistance for the benefit of those whose interests will be adversely affected when developments proceed. Post-development monitoring and follow-up obligations are frequently considered to be vital elements in ensuring that environmental damages are controlled or that sustainability remains achievable.[57]

D. PUBLIC PARTICIPATION AND FUNDING

Whether or not public participation is formally required, some level of public involvement has ordinarily been encouraged in the interests of a better process. If nothing more, public involvement in the planning and assessment process can contribute to "minimization of confrontation and delays."[58] Potential contributions have also been recognized

---

56   *AEPEA*, above note 54, s. 49. See also *BCEAA*, above note 53.

57   See generally Jeffery, "Consideration," above note 15.

58   *North Simcoe*, above note 50 at 110.

in terms of legitimacy, accountability, and the importance of different perspectives, as well as, quite possibly, in terms of new information or more rigorous scrutiny of the proponent's case. In one decision concerning the lack of a formal requirement in the *EARPGO* to halt work on a project pending the completion of an environmental review, Madame Justice Reed of the Federal Court suggested that public scrutiny might serve an analogous end:

> it is the watchful eye of public opinion which is . . . to ensure that environmentally responsible decisions are taken . . . any obligation not to proceed while the project is under review also depends for "enforcement" on the pressure of public opinion and the adverse publicity which will attach to a contrary course of action.[59]

Statutory provision for some form of supplementary review and scrutiny of the assessment, including administrative proceedings and a hearings process, often permits public participation in decision making over and above opportunities for consultation that are ordinarily included in the initial preparation of the assessment document itself. Insofar as such hearings have generally been discretionary, however, several jurisdictions have experienced litigation directed at the status of these procedures. In particular, attempts have been made to require such procedures, rather than to leave decisions about their use to the discretion of officials.

Critics of the Nova Scotia Power Corporation's Point Aconi project were unsuccessful in their efforts to compel a public review of the proposal.[60] With reference to section 13 of the *EARPGO*, applicants asserted that the level and nature of public concern about the Point Aconi project was such that public review was desirable and that the minister of fisheries and oceans (representing the initiating department in the proceedings) had rejected panel review on the basis of irrelevant considerations. Efforts to compel reconsideration of the assessment process for road development to provide access to old-growth timber in Ontario's Temagami district or to "bump up" the assessment to a public-hearing process similarly failed,[61] as did claims for public participation require-

---

59   *Naskapi-Montagnais Innu Assn.* v. *Canada (Minister of National Defence)*, [1990] 3 F.C. 381 at 403–4 (T.D.).

60   *Cantwell* v. *Canada (Minister of the Environment)* (1991), 6 C.E.L.R. (N.S.) 16 (T.D.), aff'd (6 June 1991), (Fed. C.A.) [unreported].

61   *Temagami Wilderness Society* v. *Ontario (Minister of the Environment)*, [1989] O.J. Nos. 460 & 1522 (H.C.J.).

ments under Manitoba's *Environment Act*.[62] Despite insisting that basic environmental assessments must be undertaken where required, courts have demonstrated reluctance to scrutinize official judgments of those assessments with a high degree of intensity. In the words of Mr. Justice Strayer: "It is not the role of the Court . . . to become an academy of science to arbitrate conflicting scientific predictions, or to act as a kind of legislative upper chamber to weigh expressions of public concern and determine which ones should be respected."[63]

The contribution of public participation to the environmental assessment process depends not only on the nature of the decision to be made but on the actual involvement of the public and the quality of that involvement. The costs of effective participation are frequently substantial. This is particularly so in the context of resource-management hearings where decisions often depend heavily on complex evidence and expert witnesses. Litigation concerning the availability of financial support for public-interest intervenors in administrative proceedings[64] and related commentary[65] produced a number of *ad hoc* responses.

Ontario's *Intervenor Funding Project Act*[66] represented an attempt to deal more systematically with intervenor finances in relation to the proceedings of a small group of designated tribunals. The statute set out conditions and criteria for pre-hearing funding applications. Funding might be awarded in relation to issues that "affect a significant segment of the public" and "affect the public interest and not just private interests." In assessing eligibility for funding, panel members were directed to consider a series of criteria:

(a) the intervenor represents a clearly ascertainable interest that should be represented at the hearing;

(b) separate and adequate representation of the interest would assist the board and contribute substantially to the hearing;

(c) the intervenor does not have sufficient financial resources to enable it to adequately represent the interest;

(d) the intervenor has made reasonable efforts to raise funding from other sources;

---

62   *Swampy Cree Tribal Council v. Manitoba (Clean Environment Commission)* (1994), 94 Man. R. (2d) 188 (Q.B.).

63   *Vancouver Island Peace Society v. Canada*, [1992] 3 F.C. 42 at 51 (T.D.).

64   *Hamilton-Wentworth (Regional Municipality) v. Hamilton-Wentworth Save the Valley Committee Inc.* (1985), 51 O.R. (2d) 23 (Div. Ct.); *Reference Re Ontario Energy Board Act* (1985), 51 O.R. (2d) 333 (Div. Ct.).

65   R. Anand & I.G. Scott, "Financing Public Participation in Environmental Decision Making" (1982) 60 Can. Bar Rev. 81.

66   R.S.O. 1990, c. I.13.

(e) the intervenor has an established record of concern for and commitment to the interest;

(f) the intervenor has attempted to bring related interests of which it was aware into an umbrella group to represent the related interests at the hearing;

(g) the intervenor has a clear proposal for its use of any funds which might be awarded; and

(h) the intervenor has appropriate financial controls to ensure that the funds, if awarded, are spent for the purposes of the award.

However, the *Intervenor Funding Project Act* was dissolved in 1996. Costs awards, as distinct from advance funding for participants, are still available where applicable criteria are satisfied.[67]

E. INTERJURISDICTIONAL COORDINATION

Current environmental regimes evidence a greater willingness than their predecessors to acknowledge and take into account extrajurisdictional implications, including the international consequences of development. This latter characteristic may be evidence of efforts to fulfil Canadian obligations anticipated in connection with the 1991 international *Convention on Environmental Impact Assessment in a Transboundary Context (Espoo)*.

Some recent developments—notably, the incorporation of cumulative impact, and the environmental assessment of policy and sustainability—may represent new sources of uncertainty. However, the revised regimes may also provide mechanisms to promote convergence among neighbouring provinces.

Another possible source of convergence is federal-provincial agreements concerning the coordination of environmental assessments when both levels of government have responsibilities.[68] The CCME has been active in promoting discussion of interjurisdictional harmonization of environmental assessment. Several agreements have been reached embodying the principles of the 1998 Canada-wide Accord on En-

---

67 *OEAA*, above note 47, ss. 18–22. See also *CEEA*, above note 22, s. 58(1)(i); *Environment Act*, C.C.S.M. c. E125, s. 13.2.

68 *BCEAA*, above note 53, s. 86; Ontario, Bill 76, *An Act to Improve Environmental Protection, Increase Accountability and Enshrine Public Consultation in the Environmental Assessment Act*, 1st Sess., 36th Leg., 1996, cl. 3.1; *AEPEA*, above note 54, s. 55.

vironmental Harmonization and the sub-agreement on environmental assessment.[69]

Coordination efforts are also being taken in relation to situations involving native self-government. *CEAA*, for example, sets out a framework to deal with environmental assessment in the context of native lands, whether administered under the *Indian Act* or involving bodies established pursuant to land-claims agreements. As one illustration of the search for general consistency, environmental assessment regulations applicable to oil and gas exploration and exploitation under management by First Nations are currently being developed.

Innovative institutions with responsibility for environmental assessment have already emerged in the context of comprehensive aboriginal-claims agreements and other similar negotiations. In general, these are joint-management structures involving native and non-native participants in stages of decision making ranging from initial screening and recommendations through to final authority. Several of the recently created institutions are intended to operate in the northern territories. Of these, the arrangements provided in the *Inuvialuit Final Agreement* for an environmental impact screening committee and an environmental impact review board were not long in experiencing jurisdictional controversy vis-à-vis other approval bodies.[70]

In anticipation of further implementation of native self-government, several provinces have proposed or contemplated arrangements to coordinate decision making in relation to environmental assessment and planning.[71]

FURTHER READINGS

GREEN, ANDREW, "Discretion, Judicial Review and the Canadian Environmental Assessment Act" (2002) 27 Queen's L.J. 785

---

69 Beginning with environmental assessment agreements with several Western provinces in 1999 and 2000, agreements have been reached between the federal government and British Columbia, Alberta, Saskatchewan, Manitoba, Ontario, Quebec and Yukon.

70 M. Robinson & L. Binder, "The Inuvialuit Final Agreement and Resource-Use Conflicts: Co-Management in the Western Arctic and Final Decisions in Ottawa" in M. Passelac-Ross & J.O. Saunders, eds., *Growing Demands on a Shrinking Heritage: Managing Resource-Use Conflicts* (Calgary: Canadian Institute of Resources Law, 1992) 155.

71 See, for example, *BCEAA*, above note 53; *Crown Forest Sustainability Act, 1994*, S.O. 1994, c. 25.

HANEBURY, J., "Environmental Impact Assessment and the Constitution: The Never-Ending Story" (2000) 9 J. Envtl. L. & Prac. 169

HANNA, KEVIN S., ed., *Environmental Impact Assessment: Practice and Participation* (Don Mills, ON: Oxford University Press, 2005)

HAZELL, S., *Canada v. The Environment: Federal Environmental Assessment 1984–1998* (Toronto: Canadian Environmental Defence Fund, 1999)

HOBBY, B., D. RICARD, M. BOURRY, & J. DE PENCIER, *Canadian Environmental Assessment Act: An Annotated Guide* (Aurora, ON: Canada Law Book, 1997–)

KWASNIAK, A., "Slow on the Trigger: the Department of Fisheries and Oceans, the *Fisheries Act* and the *Canadian Environmental Assessment Act*" (2004) 27 Dalhousie L.J. 347

LEVY, ALAN D., "A Review of Environmental Assessment in Ontario" (2002) 11 J. Envtl. L. & Prac. 173

MEUNIER, P.B., & H.V. GAGNON, "Le Régime Québècois actuel d'évaluation environnementale et les réformes envisagées" (1996) 7 J. Envtl. L. & Prac. 43

NORTHEY, R., *The 1995 Annotated Canadian Environmental Assessment Act & EARP Guidelines Order* (Toronto: Carswell, 1994)

PHILLIPSON, M., & M.-A. BOWDEN, "Environmental Assessment and Agriculture: An Ounce of Prevention Is Worth a Pound of Manure" (1999) 62 Sask. L.R. 415

RENAUD, P., "The Environmental Assessment Process and Public Participation in Quebec: Concrete Elements for Sustainable Development" (1996) 27 R.G.D. 375

RUTHERFORD, SUSAN, & KAREN CAMPBELL, "Time Well Spent? A survey of public participation in federal environmental assessment panels" (2004) 15 J. Envtl. L. & Prac. 71

TOXIC SUBSTANCES

A. THE TOXICS CHALLENGE IN CANADA

The phrase *from sawdust to toxic blobs* has been used to describe a long-term transformation in the Canadian pollution-control agenda.[1] Public concern with a generalized and traditional understanding of pollution (visible emissions and discharges presumed to decompose without harm if released at "safe" levels) has given way to heightened anxiety over long-term threats to human and environmental health from certain types of contaminants. The concept of toxic substances offers the prospect of establishing some priorities for new regulatory and remedial efforts. Numerous American initiatives and references to "virtual elimination," to "zero discharge of toxic chemicals," and to the precautionary principle are increasingly part of these developments. For its part, Europe has proceeded further with the formulation of the an initiative known as REACH for Registration, Evaluation, and Authorization of Chemicals, a program that will increasingly influence chemicals management around the world.[2]

Designation of persistent toxics for special attention was an important step in the process of acknowledging that, if the environment

---

1   D. Chappell, *From Sawdust to Toxic Blobs: A Consideration of Sanctioning Strategies to Combat Pollution in Canada* (Ottawa: Supply & Services, 1989).

2   Marcos A Orellana, "Europe's REACH: A New Chapter in International Chemicals Law" (2006) 6 Sustainable Development Law and Policy 21.

is contaminated, so, in time, will be the species, including humans, who occupy the planet. But labelling the category of persistent toxics does not lessen the challenge of identifying the characteristics and ultimately determining the contents of that category. In general, concern with toxics focuses on substances that are highly resistant to natural processes of degradation even as they disperse through air, water, and soil. They bioaccumulate within food chains, but even in trace amounts they may be capable of bringing about biological changes.[3]

Toxic chemicals, although they are understood to pose significant risks to ecosystems and to human health, have often resisted precise definition and assessment. It has sometimes been difficult to determine exactly what human and environmental harm is caused by particular toxic substances. Substances differ in degree of toxicity and in terms of the nature of their impact, as well as in the timing in which those consequences appear. Moreover, toxicity varies in relation to concentration, length, and conditions of exposure; some segments of the population, children and the elderly, for example, may be more vulnerable than others. To complicate understanding still further, toxicity may be influenced by the presence of other substances in the environment, with such combinations and their synergistic consequences remaining largely unknown.

While toxic substances are numerous, historic limitations concerning data on their use, distribution, and effects on the environment and health have inhibited a comprehensive regulatory response. Yet, during the 1970s and 1980s, toxic contamination was recognized as a significantly more widespread and intractable problem than previously suspected or acknowledged.[4] Reference to a few much-discussed toxics serves as a reminder of recent developments and provides a partial setting for consideration of legal initiatives.

The displacement in 1988 of some 3,500 people as a consequence of PCB storage problems at Saint-Basile-le-Grand, Quebec, demonstrated the vulnerability of urban populations to toxic concentrations, just as the 1985 PCB spill on the Trans-Canada Highway near Kenora, Ontario, and revelations concerning the contamination of numerous Arc-

---

3   See Environment Canada, *The State of Canada's Environment* (Ottawa: Supply & Services, 1991) c. 21.

4   With advances in science and in measurement techniques, linkages between exposure and health impacts have often become more apparent. See Theresa McClenaghan *et al.*, "Environmental Standard Setting and Children's Health in Canada" (2003) 12 J. Envtl. L. & Prac 245; Devra Davis, *When Smoke Ran Like Water: Tales of Environmental Deception and the Battle Against Pollution* (New York: Basic Books, 2002).

tic sites and mammal populations demonstrated that remoteness was no guarantee of immunity. Although PCBs were already the subject of regulatory controls dating from the 1970s,[5] attention focused on PCBs again in the late 1980s amidst considerable controversy over storage, exports, appropriate disposal technology and costs, and the tainted fuel scam (in which gasoline was being laced with PCBs as a means of disposing of these wastes).[6]

Another symbolic episode in a decade of seemingly unexpected encounters with chemical hazards involved the mid-1980s "toxic blob" in the St. Clair River, a part of the Great Lakes system on the border with the United States. The origins of the "blob" were attributed at the time to the accidental spill of dry-cleaning fluid that combined on the river bottom with a number of more hazardous chemicals already present in sediment. Yet the precipitating incident was by no means an isolated occurrence; governmental research and journalistic investigation confirmed that, between 1972 and 1984, 275 toxic spills had taken place in the vicinity and that approximately half of these entered the river itself.[7]

Dioxins, the name referring to a family of chemical compounds including "the most toxic synthetic chemical ever tested in the laboratory," also secured a prominent place in the regulatory agenda of both the United States and Canada. Highly publicized incidents involving pulp mill effluents produced alarm and attracted federal and provincial reaction.[8] In *Gagnier* v. *Canadian Forest Products Ltd.*, a commercial crab fisherman sought damages from a pulp mill whose alleged discharge of dioxins and other toxic substances into B.C.'s Howe Sound resulted in closure of the crab harvest by government officials. The claim was dismissed without resolution of the scientific matters in conflict on the grounds that the plaintiff had, in any event, failed to establish damage.[9]

Our overall approach to the challenges presented by the proliferation of new potentially dangerous substances falls within the general framework of decision making for risk management. The complexities

---

5   J.F. Castrilli & C.C. Lax, "Environmental Regulation-Making in Canada: Towards a More Open Process" in J. Swaigen, ed., *Environmental Rights in Canada* (Toronto: Butterworths, 1981) at 349–59.

6   J. Ferguson, "Fuel Laced with Toxic Wastes Sold in Lucrative Scam" *The Globe and Mail* (8 May 1989) A1.

7   Chappell, above note 1 at 13.

8   K. Harrison & G. Hoberg, "Setting the Environmental Agenda in Canada and the United States: The Cases of Dioxin and Radon" (1991) 24 Can. J. Pol. Sci. 3.

9   (1990), 51 B.C.L.R. (2d) 218 (S.C.).

involved preclude any effective discussion here, but it may nonetheless be worthwhile to provide a condensed account of the evolving backdrop of contemporary risk management. William Leiss provides the following account:

> In Western industrial societies, with respect to the intrinsic difficulties of carrying out credible risk management decision making itself, all of the low-hanging fruit has been picked, so to speak: the easier victories have been won and the harder ones remain. These easier victories amounted to drawing firm conclusions from toxicology and epidemiology that unacceptable levels of risk exist, that exposures should be reduced, and that either governments or industry should pay the costs for risk reduction without further ado . . . . Now our risk management battles are almost entirely different, sometimes because the risk reduction gains are purchased at much higher prices, but even more importantly because the reasons for carrying on the battles themselves are so much murkier . . . .[10]

As Leiss explains, the significant advances in risk reduction achieved in the first half of the twentieth century were generally associated with quite distinct challenges in the fields of occupational health and safety, public health, and air pollution. This was attributable in part to the comparatively undeveloped state of such forms of risk-related inquiry as toxicology and epidemiology. Moreover, government acknowledgement of a degree of responsibility in relation to environmental risks came much later. Today, Leiss argues, "there is no significant risk factor in the lives of the population for which government cannot be expected to be called upon for a policy response." He describes the contemporary situation as follows:

> Now with far broader sets of responsibilities for risk management, with ever-increasing public expectations for risk control, and faced with the iron law of exponentially mounting costs for incremental risk reduction, in principle governments should look at risk factors synthetically, i.e., from the standpoint of comparative efficiencies in resource allocations for risk reduction opportunities . . . .
>
> With every advance our society makes in collective risk reduction, there are distinctive benefits to be reaped, both in terms of enhanced quality of life and longevity. But in most cases the marginal costs for risk reduction inexorably keep rising, so that with each passing day it becomes increasingly more important to allocate risk

---

10   William Leiss, *In the Chamber of Risks: Understanding Risk Controversies* (Montreal: McGill-Queen's Press, 2001) at 183–84

reduction resources wisely. This must mean, quite simply, that some public alarms would be addressed with dollars, while other concerns, however loudly expressed, would be answered only with explanations as to why the expenditures would not be made. Addressing this awkward state of affairs is such an enormous challenge for the government policy domain that it is perhaps unsurprising that no one wants to be first in line to do so. Sooner or later, however, it must and will be done.[11]

Chemicals introduced over the past decades constitute one broad category of risk to be managed within the broad framework sketched out above. In addition to the Canadian regulatory initiatives described below, a number of toxic substances have been subject to international controls such as the Stockholm Convention on persistent organic pollutants.

B. THE *CANADIAN ENVIRONMENTAL PROTECTION ACT, 1999 (CEPA, 1999)* AND TOXICS

An overview of the federal government's operations in relation to toxics concluded, early in 1982, that "no overall strategy or policy respecting toxic chemicals is in place to give guidance in priority setting and major resource allocation."[12] This report identified interdepartmental problems within the federal government and limitations in the availability of information from manufacturers and importers as among the challenges to be addressed. Although it regarded the federal government's involvement in the toxics field as essentially residual to the provincial role, a 1986 report also noted "a lack of coherence among programs and . . . a lack of overall priorities." Fifty-four acts administered by two dozen departments were found relevant to toxics in some way, but the *Environmental Contaminants Act,* perhaps the principal statute then involved, "has insufficient powers to deal with this area of increasing public concern."[13] Not long afterwards, the *Brundtland Report* noted toxics specifically as a subject to be addressed in terms

---

11   *Ibid.* at 183–87.
12   Environment Canada, *Toxic Chemical Related Activities within the Federal Government (FY 81/82): An Overview* by J.A.S. Walker & R.D. Hamilton (Ottawa: Supply & Services, 1982) at 19.
13   *Regulatory Programs: A Study Team Report to the Task Force on Program Review* (Ottawa: Supply & Services, 1986) at 211 [Neilson Task Force]. *Environmental Contaminants Act*, S.C. 1974–75, c. 72.

of "manufacture, marketing, use, transport, and disposal." The report added that the regulation "should normally be done at the national level, with local governments being empowered to exceed, but not to lower, national norms."[14] The challenges of coherence and priority-setting have persisted.

As enacted in 1988, the original *Canadian Environmental Protection Act, (CEPA)*, in addition to consolidating several existing federal environmental initiatives, was intended to address many of the limitations of the *ECA* in relation to toxic substances. Following a parliamentary review of *CEPA* by the House of Commons Standing Committee on Environment and Sustainable Development, legislation to amend *CEPA* was introduced in 1996 and finally implemented in 2000 as *CEPA, 1999*. The emphasis given to toxics in the legislation is evident in the preamble that includes several specific references to this issue and to the manner in which it is to be handled:

Whereas the Government of Canada is committed to implementing pollution prevention as a national goal and as the priority approach to environmental protection;

Whereas the Government of Canada acknowledges the need to virtually eliminate the most persistent and bioaccumulative toxic substances and the need to control and manage pollutants and wastes if their release into the environment cannot be prevented;

Whereas the Government of Canada is committed to implementing the precautionary principle that, where there are threats of serious or irreversible damage, lack of full scientific certainty shall not be used as a reason for postponing cost-effective measures to prevent environmental degradation;

Whereas the Government of Canada recognizes that the risk of toxic substances in the environment is a matter of national concern and that toxic substances, once introduced into the environment, cannot always be contained within geographic boundaries.

Building on the framework created by its predecessor, *CEPA, 1999* elaborated procedures for assessing the toxicity of designated substances and provided options for managing those substances ultimately determined to be toxic according to statutory criteria. Apart from substances understood to be "inherently toxic," a substance is toxic according to section 64 of *CEPA, 1999*

---

14   World Commission on Environment and Development, *Our Common Future* (Oxford: Oxford University Press, 1987) at 219–20.

if it is entering or may enter the environment in a quantity or concentration or under conditions that

(a) have or may have an immediate or long-term harmful effect on the environment or its biological diversity;

(b) constitute or may constitute a danger to the environment on which life depends; or

(c) constitute or may constitute a danger in Canada to human life or health.

For the purpose of assessing toxicity, several categories of substances have been established and various forms of evaluation have been provided. Approximately 23,000 existing substances, currently in use in Canada, were recorded on the Domestic Substances List.[15] Certain of these have already been designated as Priority Substances whose assessment must be completed within five years.[16] By September 2006, all substances on the Domestic Substances List were further classified to identify those requiring further screening or assessment as Priority Substances because of exposure, inherent toxicity, persistence, or bio-accumulation.[17]

Assessment procedures, following what is described as a risk-based approach, are conducted on the basis of information obtained from a range of sources[18] or may involve reference to decisions made by other jurisdictions.[19] It is intended that assessments of substances be conducted through the application of a weight of evidence approach and with reference to the precautionary principle as defined in *CEPA, 1999*.[20]

In section 77 the legislation contemplates several measures to be proposed by the responsible ministers following the assessments:

- no further action;

---

15   *Canadian Environmental Protection Act, 1999*, S.C. 1999, c. 33, s. 66 [*CEPA, 1999*]. Substances and activities new to Canada are subject to a distinctive set of procedures in ss. 80–89.

16   *Ibid.*, ss. 76(1) and 78.

17   *Ibid.*, ss. 73–74. Of the 23,000 existing substances reviewed, some 4,000 were determined to be in need of detailed scrutiny, with roughly 500 of these singled out for priority attention. For links to related documentation and details on the status of assessment processes, see online: www.chemicalsubstanceschimiques. gc.ca. A new Chemicals Management Plan was announced in December 2006. See also Commissioner of the Environment and Sustainable Development, *2008 March Status Report* (Ottawa: Office of the Auditor General, 2008) c. 1, Chemicals Management.

18   *CEPA, 1999, ibid.*, ss. 68, 70, & 71.

19   *Ibid.*, s. 75.

20   *Ibid.*, s. 76.1.

- add the substance to the Priority Substances List;
- add the substance to the Toxic Substances List;
- recommend virtual elimination in the case of persistent and bioaccumulative substances.[21]

In the case of substances determined to be toxic, their addition to the Toxic Substances List by order of the Governor in Council establishes the basis for a series of management alternatives. These include regulation, the implementation of pollution prevention planning, and the development of a program for virtual elimination.

On the recommendation of the ministers, listed toxic substances are subject to regulation by the Governor in Council respecting a wide range of issues:

(a) the quantity or concentration of the substance that may be released into the environment either alone or in combination with any other substance;

(b) the places or areas where the substance may be released;

(c) the commercial, manufacturing, or processing activity in the course of which the substance may be released;

(d) the manner in which and conditions under which the substance may be released into the environment;

(e) the quantity of the substance that may be manufactured, processed, used, offered for sale, or sold in Canada;

(f) the purposes for which the substance or a product containing it may be imported, manufactured, processed, used, offered for sale, or sold;

(g) the manner in which and conditions under which the substance or a product containing it may be imported, manufactured, processed, or used;

(h) the quantities or concentrations in which the substance may be used;

(i) the quantities or concentrations of the substance that may be imported;

(j) the countries from which or to which the substance may be imported or exported;

(k) the conditions under which, the manner in which, and the purposes for which the substance may be imported or exported;

(l) the total, partial or conditional prohibition of the manufacture, use, processing, sale, offering for sale, import or export of the substance or a product containing it;

---

21   *Persistence and Bioaccumulation Regulations*, S.O.R./2000-107.

(*m*) the total, partial, or conditional prohibition of the import or export of a product that is intended to contain the substance;

(*n*) the quantity or concentration of the substance that may be contained in any product manufactured, imported, exported, offered for sale, or sold in Canada;

(*o*) the manner in which, conditions under which, and the purposes for which the substance or a product containing the substance may be advertised or offered for sale;

(*p*) the manner in which and conditions under which the substance or a product containing it may be stored, displayed, handled, transported, or offered for transport;

(*q*) the packaging and labelling of the substance or a product containing it;

(*r*) the manner, conditions, places, and method of disposal of the substance or a product containing it, including standards for the construction, maintenance, and inspection of disposal sites;

(*s*) the submission to the Minister, on request or at any prescribed times, of information relating to the substance;

(*t*) the maintenance of books and records for the administration of any regulation made under this section;

(*u*) the conduct of sampling, analyses, tests, measurements or monitoring of the substance;

(*v*) the submission of samples of the substance to the Minister;

(*w*) the conditions, test procedures and laboratory practices to be followed for conducting sampling, analyses, tests, measurements, or monitoring of the substance;

(*x*) circumstances or conditions under which the Minister may . . . modify
  (i) any requirement for sampling, analyses, tests, measurements or monitoring, or
  (ii) the conditions, test procedures, and laboratory practices for conducting any required sampling, analyses, tests, measurements, or monitoring; and

(*y*) any other matter . . . necessary to carry out the purposes of this Part.[22]

For a selected list of existing regulations, see table 13.1.

Pollution prevention has been designated as a priority objective in the selection of options to manage risks associated with toxic sub-

---

22   *CEPA, 1999*, above note 15, s. 93(1).

stances.[23] To this end, *CEPA, 1999* authorizes the minister of the environment to call for the preparation and implementation of pollution prevention plans. Such a requirement may be applicable to single substances or groups of substances and may be directed to a person or to a class of persons by means of a notice under section 56. More particularly, notices under section 56 may specify:

(a) the substance or group of substances in relation to which the plan is to be prepared;

(b) the commercial, manufacturing, processing, or other activity in relation to which the plan is to be prepared;

(c) the factors to be considered in preparing the plan;

(d) the period within which the plan is to be prepared;

(e) the period within which the plan is to be implemented; and

(f) any administrative matter necessary.

Those required to draw up a pollution-prevention plan must provide written declarations confirming that such a plan has been prepared and that it has been implemented.[24] Plans should be available at the relevant location for examination by enforcement officials, but plans themselves will not ordinarily be submitted unless specifically required by the minister for the purpose of determining and assessing preventive or control actions in respect of a substance or group of substances.[25]

The management option applicable to substances that are persistent, bioaccumulative, and released to the environment primarily as a result of human activity is virtual elimination. In this context, virtual elimination means "the ultimate reduction of the quantity or concentration of the substance in the release below the level of quantification specified by the ministers" where the level of quantification (LoQ) for a substance is "the lowest concentration that can be accurately measured using sensitive but routine sampling and analytical methods."[26] With the LoQ established for a given substance, the ministers will prescribe the permissible quantity or concentration of the substance that may be released. Their decision in this respect may be based on "environment-

---

23   *Ibid.*, s. 90(1.1). In specified circumstances non-toxic substances affecting international air and water pollution may also be subject to pollution prevention initiatives.

24   *Ibid.*, s. 58.

25   *Ibid.*, ss. 59, 60(1), and 227(b). See also Environment Canada, *Guidelines for the Implementation of the Pollution Prevention Planning Provisions of Part 4 of the Canadian Environmental Protection Act, 1999 (CEPA, 1999)*, (February 2001).

26   *CEPA, 1999*, above note 15, s. 65.

al or health risks and any other relevant social, economic or technical matters."

As commentators have noted, the virtual elimination option does not, in fact, provide for elimination but only for controlled releases; and it does so, not with exclusive reference to environmental and health risks, but with respect to such risks set against or counterbalanced by social, economic, and technical matters.[27]

Table 13.1: Regulations for Toxic Substances (Selected)

Federal Regulations
Asbestos Mines and Mills Release Regulations, S.O.R./90-314
Chlor-Alkali Mercury Release Regulations, S.O.R./90-130
Chlorobiphenyls Regulations, S.O.R./91-152
Contaminated Fuel Regulations, S.O.R./91-486
Export and Import of Hazardous Wastes Regulations, S.O.R./2005-149
Gasoline Regulations, S.O.R./90-247
New Substance Notification Regulations (Chemicals and Polymers), S.O.R./2005-247
New Substance Notification Regulations (Organisms), S.O.R./2005-248
PCB Waste Export Regulations, S.O.R./97-109
Prohibition of Certain Toxic Substances Regulations, 2003, S.O.R./2003-99
Pulp and Paper Mill Defoamer and Wood Chip Regulations, S.O.R./96-313
Pulp and Paper Mill Effluent Chlorinated Dioxins and Furans Regulations, S.O.R./92-267
Prohibition of Certain Toxic Substances Regulation, 2005, S.O.R./2005-41

C. TRANSPORTATION OF DANGEROUS GOODS

The 1979 derailment of chlorine tank cars and the evacuation of some 200,000 Mississauga, Ontario residents revealed significant deficiencies in provisions governing the transportation of dangerous substances.[28] Existing legal controls were considered to be too particularized and sectoral either to provide an effective response capability or to reduce the likelihood of such occurrences in the first place.[29] The volume and

---

27   M. Valiante, "Legal Foundations of Canadian Environmental Policy: Underlining Our Values in a Shifting Landscape" in D.L. VanNijnatten & R. Boardman, eds., *Canadian Environmental Policy: Context and Cases*, 2d ed. (Don Mills, ON: Oxford University Press, 2002) at 15.

28   Report of the *Mississauga Railway Accident Inquiry* (Ottawa: Supply & Services, 1980).

29   M. Rankin, "Dangerous Moves: The Law Responds to the Transportation of Dangerous Goods" (1990) 24 U.B.C. L. Rev. 213.

diversity of hazardous substances being shipped throughout Canada clearly indicated the need for a more systematic and comprehensive framework for prevention and response.[30]

In order "to promote public safety in the transportation of dangerous goods," the federal government legislated in the immediate aftermath of the Mississauga disaster to establish such a framework, although the legislation anticipated provincial collaboration as well as detailed regulations.[31] Under the *Transportation of Dangerous Goods Act (TDGA)*, such goods included any product, substance, or organism contained either "by its nature" or by regulation in a scheduled classification list. Nine general classifications derived from the *International Convention for the Safety of Life at Sea* are used: explosives, compressed gases, flammable liquids, flammable solids, oxidizers and organic peroxides, poisonous and infectious substances, radioactives, corrosives, and a miscellaneous category including dangerous wastes and environmentally hazardous substances. Following revisions in 1992, the Act applied in relation to all matters within the legislative authority of Parliament, including dangerous goods outside Canada that are carried on a ship or aircraft registered in Canada.[32]

Statutory requirements include duties concerning registration and classification, labelling, packaging, and documentation as well as staff training. Section 5 of the *TDGA* specifically prohibits anyone from: handling, offering for transport, or importing "dangerous goods unless . . . the person complies with all applicable prescribed safety requirements; . . . [and] the goods are accompanied by all applicable prescribed documents."[33] Moreover, the means of containment and transport must

---

30   Estimates concerning the distribution of dangerous goods suggested that approximately 200 million tonnes of dangerous goods were transported in Canada in the 1990–91 year. Road, marine, rail, and air-transport modes accounted for 59 percent, 28 percent, 11 percent, and 2 percent respectively of the total volume; see *Transportation of Dangerous Goods Annual Report 1990–91*. More recently there has been an increase in the volume of intermodal consignments and in transborder shipping. Both developments have complicated regulation of dangerous goods movements.

31   *Transportation of Dangerous Goods Act*, R.S.C. 1985, c. T-19. By 1985, with the development of regulations completed, the new system was implemented (S.O.R./85-77, 1 July 1985).

32   *Transportation of Dangerous Goods Act*, 1992, S.C. 1992, c. 34, s. 3(1) [*TDGA*].

33   For examples of *TDGA* prosecutions, often combined with charges under *CEPA, 1999*, see *R. v. Snap-On Tools of Canada Ltd.* (2001), 44 C.E.L.R. (N.S.) 301, [2001] O.J. No. 5221 (Ct. J.); *R. v Alberta Public Works* (2001), 292 A.R. 157, 40 C.E.L.R. (N.S.) 99 (Prov. Ct.); *R. v. Leon-Ram Enterprises* (2001), 41 C.E.L.R. (N.S.) 179 (Sask. Prov. Ct.). See also *Canada (A.G.) v. Cariboo Pulp and Paper Co.*, [2007] B.C.J. No. 2418 (S.C.).

comply with all applicable prescribed safety standards and must display all applicable prescribed safety marks. "Handling" is also broadly defined to mean

> loading, unloading, packing, or unpacking dangerous goods in a means of containment for the purposes of, in the course of or following transportation and includes storing them in the course of transportation.

In anticipation that dangerous substances, despite precautions, might be released accidentally, the *TDGA* also imposes reporting requirements and an obligation to "take all reasonable emergency measures to reduce or eliminate any danger to public safety that results or may reasonably be expected to result from the release."[34] For the period 1995 to 1999, with roughly 25 million dangerous goods shipments estimated to have taken place in Canada each year, there were, on average, 395 reportable accidents involving the transportation of dangerous goods. Most of these accidents occurred in connection with road shipments. Possibly in response to security risks associated with dangerous goods, officials appear reluctant to offer estimates about the volume of shipments, but suggest that something in the vicinity of 500 accidents occur on an annual basis.

The *Transportation of Dangerous Goods Act, 1992* provides for controls on design and construction standards for containers and requires the preparation and prior approval by the minister of transport of emergency-response plans. The powers of inspectors, notably in relation to preventive orders, were increased. Arrangements have also been made for electronic computerized monitoring to allow firefighters and other front-line response-team members to identify the precise nature of goods in transit more promptly than has previously been possible.[35] The scope of penalties and remedial orders incorporates power to prohibit a convicted offender from engaging in activities regulated by the Act, and a duty to compensate those who undertook remedial work on the environment as a consequence of the offence. There are additional requirements to assist in repairing the environment and to conduct or to finance research to improve safety arrangements.[36]

The *TDGA* appears to have provided an effective framework for interjurisdictional cooperation in a field where coordination among

---

34   *TDGA*, above note 32, s. 18(2).

35   In November 1991, the CCME approved the implementation of a computerized monitoring system to track the movement of hazardous wastes in and out of the country.

36   *TDGA*, above note 32, s. 34.

jurisdictions and among agencies is a central element of an effective regulatory regime.[37] Consistent treatment of intraprovincial transportation is promoted through provisions to encourage negotiated agreements with the provinces concerning the implementation and administration of the Act.[38] The provinces acknowledged the virtues of consistency in relation to the transportation of dangerous goods and legislated accordingly in relation to their own constitutional responsibilities.[39]

TDGA regulations were produced in "clear language" for the first time in 2001.[40]

D. PCBs

Polychlorinated Biphenyls (PCBs) have been used for several decades in industrial and commercial applications. In electrical transformers, for example, their lubricating and insulating capability was particularly attractive. However, in the 1960s and 1970s, health concerns led to prohibitions and controls on their use and manufacture. Although such concerns later somewhat diminished, a complex regulatory regime addressing transportation, storage, and disposal issues remains in place.[41]

PCBs were banned in the United States in 1976 under the authority of section 6 of the *Toxic Substances Control Act*. In Canada, PCB production has been banned since 1980 and their continuing use has been restricted. Federal PCB storage controls were established on an interim basis under *CEPA* in the aftermath of the 1988 fire and evacuation at Saint-Basile-le-Grand, Quebec, and were subsequently implemented on a permanent basis.[42] The regulations establish storage requirements designed to prevent release of PCBs into the environment. Labelling and reporting duties, maintenance and inspection obligations, and emer-

---

37   Rankin, above note 29 at 198.
38   *TDGA*, above note 32, s. 4.
39   *CEPA, 1999*, above note 15, contains provisions for coordinating with the *TDGA*, *ibid.*, ss. 34(3) and 43.
40   S.O.R./2001-286.
41   In R. v. *Consolidated Maybrun Mines*, (sub nom. R. v. *Maybrun Mines Consolidated*) (1992), 9 C.E.L.R. (N.S.) 42 (Ont. Prov. Div.), Fraser Prov. J. found "no evidence presently available that would justify a finding that PCBs have an adverse effect on humans based on realistic exposure levels that could be obtained from environmental exposure."
42   *Storage of PCB Material Regulations*, S.O.R./92-507, amended by S.O.R./2000-102.

gency procedures are also addressed. Comparable and compatible requirements have been instituted at the provincial level.

Interprovincial PCB transportation within Canada is also governed by regulations, in this case pursuant to the *TDGA*. These call for equipment containing PCBs to be drained and sealed in suitable containers prior to shipment. Again, some provincial regimes are in place in connection with intraprovincial PCB transportation.[43]

The disposal of existing PCB stockpiles has remained extremely troublesome. PCBs have entered landfills, but the slow rate at which they break down has meant that destruction programs, primarily involving incineration, have been preferred. In Canada, disposal facilities were established at Swan Hills in Alberta, the first province to have eliminated its own stockpiled PCBs by means of a mandatory destruction program. To reduce risks associated with the transportation of PCBs, portable incineration units have been used elsewhere in the country. These facilities are costly and have not been available in sufficient numbers to address the overall problem. From 1988 to 1995 the federal government administered a PCB destruction program.[44] The apparent discharge of PCBs and other chemicals from the Montreal Technoparc, a household and industrial waste site, is now the subject of investigation under the auspices of the Commission for Environmental Cooperation.

PCBs have also been subject to the *Basel Convention on the Control of Transboundary Movements of Hazardous Wastes and Their Disposal*, whose effect was to encourage parties to the convention to dispose of their hazardous waste domestically, "as far as is compatible with environmentally sound and efficient management," thereby minimizing transboundary shipments. Canada and the United States addressed transboundary hazardous waste on a bilateral basis.[45]

The Canadian government introduced export-control regulations to eliminate the risk of Canadian PCB spillage in foreign countries.[46] An exception was permitted in order to facilitate the return to the United States of PCBs associated with American military installations. In 1995 an amendment to the *PCB Waste Export Regulations*[47] banned all PCB exports to the United States very shortly after that country had

---

43   *R. v. TNT Canada Inc.* (1986), 58 O.R. (2d) 410 (C.A.).
44   *Federal Mobile PCB Treatment and Destruction Regulations*, S.O.R./90-5, amended by S.O.R./93-231; S.O.R./2000-105.
45   (1986) 22 I.L.M. 1025.
46   *PCB Waste Export Regulations*, S.O.R./90-453.
47   *Ibid.*, as am. by *PCB Waste Export Interim Order*, P.C. 1995-2013, C. Gaz. 1995.I.4228.

relaxed its own import restrictions in the case of PCBs originating in Canada. The Canadian initiative was criticized as a measure to ensure PCB supplies for the Swan Hills facility and became the subject of a legal challenge on the part of many industrial operations that consider it invalid and unnecessarily costly.[48] As of February 1997, Canadian PCBs destined for destruction in the United States by incineration or other means were permitted under a detailed control regime requiring approvals, documentation, and insurance.[49]

In view of new federal authority relating to the export and import of hazardous waste and hazardous recyclable materials in sections 185 to 192 of *CEPA, 1999* consideration was redirected to regulatory revisions that would strengthen controls on imports of PCB wastes to Canada, harmonizing export and import requirements.

E. PESTICIDES

Although the Saint-Basile-le-Grand experience with PCBs and some other high-profile incidents might suggest that the primary focus of concern regarding toxics should be on accidental and comparatively isolated releases, other evidence points towards endemic practices creating systemic risks from toxics. Studies relating to pesticides demonstrate important concerns about the authorization and generalized application of chemical substances and continue to stimulate inquiry into the approvals process.[50]

As explained by Health Canada, the development and use of synthetic organic chemicals predates the Second World War and has subsequently grown steadily. Both insecticides and herbicides are extensively employed in a wide range of commercial as well as domestic applications. In addition to human exposure associated with direct contact, the general public is exposed to pesticides through residues on food and to a lesser extent in drinking water. The *Food and Drugs Act* provides mechanisms for constant monitoring of pesticide residues in foods, while the *Guidelines for Canadian Drinking Water* outline ac-

---

48 T. Weiler, "Application of the Federal Regulatory Policy to Regulatory Decision-Making: The Curious Case of the 1995 PCB Waste Export Interim Order" (1999) 8 J. Envtl. L. & Prac. 181.

49 *PCB Waste Export Regulations, 1996,* S.O.R./97-109, amended by S.O.R./2000-103.

50 G. Hoberg, "Risk, Science and Politics: Alachlor Regulation in Canada and the United States" (1990) 23 Can. J. Pol. Sci. 257; Pesticide Registration Review Team, *Final Report: Recommendations for a Revised Federal Management Regulatory System* (Ottawa: Supply & Services, 1990).

ceptable residue levels for pesticides that have entered the water system either directly through spills, off-target aerial spraying, run-off, or after filtering through the soil to groundwater.[51]

The Canadian regulatory regime combines a federal system of controls on the registration of chemical ingredients for use in pesticides with provincial regimes addressing licensing issues and the supervision of pesticide handling and application procedures. Municipal governments are increasingly involved in regulating the use of pesticides within their boundaries.[52]

1) The Federal Level

The federal *Pest Control Products Act*[53] established a registration requirement for any product, organism, or substance used to control, destroy, attract, or repel any pest. These so-called control products now also include control products derived from biotechnology. The pests targeted include any injurious, noxious, or troublesome animal, plant or other organism. The pesticide registration process, emphasizing health and risk assessments for control products, is carried out under the supervision of the Pest Management Regulatory Agency.[54]

Current federal legislation prohibits the sale, use or importation of any control product other than ones that have been registered, packaged, and labelled in the prescribed manner and that conform to prescribed standards, and requires that registered products be used in a manner consistent with the terms of registration. Additional offences relate to false, misleading, or deceptive advertising of control products or to manufacturing and distributing them contrary to regulations.[55] The previous Act, as described by Cullen J. of the Federal Court, was "clearly designed to protect the health of the general public from the impact of products that may be dangerous, and imposes significant control mechanisms before a product is permitted to be

---

51   Health Canada, *A Vital Link: Health and the Environment in Canada* (Ottawa: Supply & Services, 1992) at 54–58 [*A Vital Link*].

52   See for example City of Toronto, *Pesticides, Use of*, By-law No. 456-2003.

53   R.S.C. 1985, c. P-9

54   For a description of the assessment process under the previous regime, see the report of the House Standing Committee on Environment and Sustainable Development, *Pesticides: Making the Right Choice for the Protection of Health and the Environment* (2000), online: http://cmte.parl.gc.ca/cmte/CommitteePublication.aspx?COM=173&Lang=1&SourceId=36396 at c. 8. For information on the responsibilities and operations of PMRA, see online: www.hc-sc.gc.ca/pmra-arla/english/aboutpmra/about-e.html.

55   *Pest Control Products Act*, S.C. 2002, c. 28, s. 6 [*PCPA, 2002*].

registered."[56] The revised legislation now explicitly states in section 6(8) that "no person shall manufacture, possess, handle, store, transport, distribute, use or dispose of a pest control product in a way that endangers human health or safety or the environment."

Several hundred active chemical ingredients for pesticides have been registered in Canada, of which approximately 100 entered into regular use.[57] In the context of an application for registration, the applicant is required to furnish sufficient information to permit an assessment of the relevant control product and bears the burden of persuasion.[58] The decision to register is based ultimately upon a determination by the minister that the health and environmental risks and the value of the pest product are "acceptable." For purposes of that assessment, the legislation provides the following guidance:

> the health or environmental risks of a pest control product are acceptable if there is reasonable certainty that no harm to human health, future generations or the environment will result from exposure to or use of the product, taking into account its conditions or proposed conditions of registration.[59]

Considerable controversy has surrounded the manner in which determinations of acceptability are made, including the extent of public participation in the decision-making process.[60] Legal challenges under the previous legislation raised a number of issues which will be of contininuing relevance. In *Pulp, Paper & Woodworkers of Canada, Local 8 v. Canada (Minister of Agriculture)*, the registration of Busan 30WB, a chemical used to prevent discolouration from fungal growth in non-kiln-dried lumber, was challenged on several grounds in judicial review proceedings.[61] The Federal Court, Trial Division, held that the question of the sufficiency of the information provided in the application to enable the chemical to be properly evaluated was a condition precedent to the minister's discretion to register or not to register the control product. In the absence of sufficient information, the registration was therefore quashed. In another case, a claim for damages originating in the plaintiff's asser-

---

56   *Monsanto Canada Inc. v. Canada (Minister of Agriculture)* (1986), 1 F.T.R. 63 at 64 (T.D.).

57   *A Vital Link*, above at 51.

58   *PCPA*, 2002, above note 55, s. 7(6).

59   *Ibid.*, s. 2(2).

60   Commissioner of the Environment and Sustainable Development, *2003 October Report* (Ottawa: Office of the Auditor General, 2003) c. 1 "Managing the Safety and Accessibility of Pesticides."

61   (1991), [1992] 1 F.C. 372 (T.D.).

tion that she suffered from "delayed neurotoxicity" as a consequence of the negligent registration of a pesticide, the Federal Court of Appeal indicated that the decision to register a control product was a policy decision. In the absence of ministerial bad faith, that action could not succeed.[62]

In addition to amendments to the pest control products registration process, the new *PCPA* is also noteworthy for the introduction of post-registration controls, including requirements for the reporting of adverse effects and timely re-evaluations of older pesticides to ensure that new information is taken into account.[63]

2) The Provincial Level

At the provincial level, pesticide-management legislation has generally provided for a licensing and permit scheme governing the sale and use of pesticides in a range of applications including forest management operations, agricultural settings and commercial-extermination services.[64] Provincial pesticide regimes may include their own categorization of pesticide risks with corresponding requirements and conditions for the licensing, training and supervision of users in various settings, accompanied by enforcement provisions and penalties for non-compliance. Notwithstanding prior federal registration of the relevant control product, issues relating to pesticide risk and safety continue to arise in the specific context of licensing and on-site applications.

As approved by the British Columbia Court of Appeal,[65] the approach to toxicity and risk to be taken by the Environmental Appeal Board in considering licence applications for pesticide use under the province's former *Pesticide Control Act* merits repetition in light of recent criticisms of limitations in the federal regime. With regard to toxicity, the court supported the trial judge's observations to the effect that it was not a jurisdictional error to assume the general safety of a federally registered pesticide:

> Common sense dictates that the fact that a federally registered pesticide that has undergone extensive testing must have some probative

---

62   *Kuczerpa v. Canada* (1993), 14 C.R.R. (2d) 307 (Fed. C.A.).

63   The Chemicals Management Plan of December 2006 includes accelerated re-evaluation of older pesticides as one of its components, online: www.chemical substanceschimiques.gc.ca/plan/index_e.html.

64   *Environmental Protection and Enhancement Act*, R.S.A. 2000, c. E-12, Part 8; *Pesticides Act*, R.S.Q., c. P-9.3; *Pesticides Act*, R.S.O. 1990, c. P.11; *Pesticide Control Act*, R.S.P.E.I. 1988, c. P-4.

65   *Canadian Earthcare Society v. B.C. (Environmental Appeal Board)* (1988), 3 C.E.L.R. (N.S.) 55 (B.C.C.A.).

value. . . . It is important to bear in mind that the Board did not state that a federally registered pesticide could never cause an unreasonable adverse effect.

Indeed, the board showed a willingness to hear site-specific evidence on toxicity and evidence concerning the ability of the permit holder to apply the pesticide safely in conformity with the intent of the registration. With respect to the relevance of alternative approaches to pest control, the court also agreed with the trial judge's reasons:

> Should the Board find an adverse effect (i.e., some risk) it must weigh that adverse effect against the intended benefit. Only by making a comparison of risk and benefit can the Board determine if the anticipated risk is reasonable or unreasonable. Evidence of silvicultural practices will be relevant to measure the extent of the anticipated benefit. Evidence of alternative methods will also be relevant to the issue of reasonableness. If the same benefits could be achieved by an alternative risk-free method then surely the risk method would be considered unreasonable.

Failure to address site-specific and application-specific evidence relevant to the reasonableness or unreasonableness of an identifiable risk would be a reviewable error by the decision-maker.[66] In subsequent decisions, British Columbia's EAB demonstrated a greater willingness to impose additional controls over the conditions under which pesticides may be used and to explore alternatives to chemical pest control.[67]

The vital matters canvassed in these British Columbia decisions, may now be less relevant in that jurisdiction where the *Pesticide Control Act* has been replaced by the *Integrated Pest Management Act*.[68] The new legislation, in introducing "pesticide-free zones" and "no treatment zones," significantly reduces overall requirements for specific government approvals as a pre-condition of pesticide use in the province. One anticipated consequence of the new arrangements is a reduction in opportunities to ensure public accountability for the manner in which pesticides are used in British Columbia.[69]

---

66 *Weir v. British Columbia (Environmental Appeal Board)* (2003), 8 Admin. L.R. (4th) 71 (B.C.S.C.); *Eberhardt v. British Columbia (Ministry of Water, Land and Air Protection)* (2004), 5 C.E.L.R. (3d) 157 (B.C.E.A.B.).

67 See also *Re Proposed Class Environmental Assessment by the Ministry of Natural Resources for Timber Management on Crown Lands in Ontario* (1990), 4 C.E.L.R. (N.S.) 50 (O.E.A.B.).

68 S.B.C. 2003, c. 58.

69 West Coast Environmental Law, Bill 53, *The Integrated Pest Management Act* (Backgrounder) online: www.chemicalsubstanceschimiques.gc.ca/plan/index_e.html.

Provinces that recognize the continuing risks associated with the accumulation and storage of pesticides may initiate remedial programmes to reduce the danger of contamination. Alberta Environment, for example, through Operation Clean Farm, has worked in cooperation with non-governmental organizations over a three-year period to recover obsolete pesticides from the agricultural sector.[70] Other jurisdictions have set up depots to receive unused pesticides or containers from the agricultural setting, and several have introduced programs to reduce pesticide use in crop production.

3) The Municipal Level

For a variety of reasons, municipal initiatives to restrict and regulate the use of pesticides within municipal boundaries have proliferated.[71] The general legal foundation for these actions has been confirmed by the Supreme Court of Canada.

Having been licensed provincially, and using federally approved pesticides, a lawn care company challenged a municipal pesticide by-law enacted by the town of Hudson, Quebec. The company argued that such a bylaw was *ultra vires*, beyond the powers of the municipality, and that it was inconsistent with federal and provincial legislation. The S.C.C. upheld the bylaw as a valid exercise of the general power of the municipality to make bylaws "to secure peace, order, good government, health and general welfare in the territory of the municipality."[72] In upholding the validity of Hudson's pesticide regime, the S.C.C. noted that the bylaw regulated but did not prohibit pesticide use, that it was enacted for legitimate purposes, and that courts should exercise caution in holding that elected municipal bodies have exceeded their powers. In connection with the alleged inconsistency between the bylaw and the federal and provincial framework for pesticide management, Justice L'Heureux Dubé stated, "as a general principle, the mere existence of a provincial (or federal) legislation in a given field does not oust municipal prerogatives to regulate the subject matter." She concluded that there was no conflict sufficient to nullify the bylaw; indeed, Quebec's *Pesticide Act* was "meant to coexist with stricter municipal bylaws of the type at issue in this case."[73]

---

70   Alberta Environment, *Annual Report 2004–2005* (Edmonton: Alberta Environment, 2005) at 17.

71   J. Swaigen, "The *Hudson* Case: Municipal Powers to Regulate Pesticides Confirmed by Quebec Courts" (2000) 34 C.E.L.R. (N.S.) 162.

72   *114957 Canada Ltée (Spraytech, Société d'arrosage) v. Hudson (Town)*, 2001 SCC 40.

73   In the aftermath of the decision Quebec introduced a new *Pesticide Management Code* which is substantially more protective than its predecessor: *Pesticide Management Code*, R.Q. c. P-9.3, r. 0.01.

Municipalities have considered several alternative approaches to pesticide regulation. Some focus on the protection of populations considered to be facing the most severe risks, children in particular. Others emphasize the elimination of pesticide use by municipalities themselves. By way of example, the Regional Municipality of Halifax prohibits pesticide application on municipally owned property and within a specified distance of properties occupied by such institutions as schools and hospitals. Except in the case of "permitted pesticides" as designated by the Halifax Regional Council, and in cases where use has been specifically authorized in connection with a danger to human beings over an insect infestation, pesticide applications within the municipality were subject to a prohibition as of April 2003.[74]

Pursuant to By-Law No. 456-2003, the City of Toronto declared that "no person shall apply or cause or permit the application of pesticides within the boundaries of the City," although this restriction does not apply to pesticides used for disinfecting pools, purifying water, controlling termites or health hazards and certain other listed applications. Municipal authority to enact the bylaw in question was upheld pursuant to the power set out in s.130 of the Ontario *Municipal Act, 2001*:

> A municipality may regulate matters not specifically provided for by this Act or any other Act for purposes related to the health, safety and well-being of the inhabitants of the municipality.[75]

Muncipal pesticide regulation is now in place in over a hundred Canadian communities.

F. INFORMATION ON HAZARDOUS MATERIALS IN THE WORKPLACE AND WORKER HEALTH AND SAFETY LEGISLATION

The development and implementation of a nationwide system of information on hazardous materials in the workplace extended over the better part of the 1980s, largely as a consequence of the technical complexity involved and the constitutional division of relevant respon-

---

74   Regional Municipality of Halifax, By-Law P-800 Respecting the Regulation of Pesticides, Herbicides and Insecticides.

75   *Croplife Canada v. Toronto (City)* (2005), 75 O.R. (3d) 357 (C.A.), leave to appeal to S.C.C. refused, [2005] S.C.C.A. No. 329. Ontario's *Cosmetic Pesticides Ban Act*, S.O. 2008, c. 11 (awaiting proclamation), will further clarify municipal authority and the guidelines applicable to cosmetic pesticide use in the province.

sibilities. In 1982 a federal-provincial task force recommended that a combination of warning labels, data sheets on material safety, and worker-education programs would be required to address hazardous materials in the workplace comprehensively. Consultations involving governments together with representatives of labour and industry resulted in a more refined appreciation of the implementation issues at mid-decade. In 1988 the Workplace Hazardous Materials Information System (WHMIS) came into effect.

Through the combined operation of federal and provincial/territorial legislation, WHMIS establishes procedures regarding the disclosure of information concerning the nature and management of hazardous substances in the workplace. Described generally as "controlled products," the materials subject to the WHMIS arrangements are substances designated by regulation under the federal *Hazardous Products Act*[76] within the following categories: compressed gas, flammable and combustible material, corrosive material, and dangerous reactive material.[77] Other potentially harmful materials were expressly excluded from the WHMIS regime on the grounds that they were subject to existing legislation. Section 12 of the *HPA* excludes various materials governed by the *Explosives Act*, the *Food and Drugs Act*, the *Pest Control Products Act*, and the *Atomic Energy Control Act*, as well as hazardous waste and tobacco products.

Those who manufacture, process, package, or import or sell controlled products in the course of business (collectively known as suppliers) are required to provide material safety data sheets (MSDSs) and labels. This documentation will disclose prescribed information including the chemical identity and concentration of the controlled products present.[78] Other provisions are intended to respect the legitimate concerns of suppliers and employers regarding confidential business information. This reconciliation between workers' right to know about hazardous materials in the workplace and the confidentiality of certain business data is accomplished through exemption claims heard by the Hazardous Materials Information Review Commission.

Legislation governing workplace health and safety in various sectors and jurisdictions throughout Canada sets out further disclosure requirements and employee "right to know" provisions for the purpose

---

76   R.S.C. 1985, c. H-3.
77   *Ibid.*, s. 2 and Sch. II.
78   *Ibid.*, ss. 13 & 14; *Controlled Products Regulations*, S.O.R./88-66; *Ingredient Disclosure List*, S.O.R./88-64.

of making MSDS information available.[79] More recently, attention has focused on the status of products originally excluded from WHMIS, primarily because they were regulated elsewhere.

Worker health and safety legislation, supplemented by negotiated agreements, authorizes employees to refuse to work in dangerous conditions, including the presence of environmental hazards.[80] To promote compliance with regulations governing the workplace, legislation protecting employees from certain forms of reprisal has also been widely enacted. That is, employees who complain, report, or otherwise act in response to problems or hazardous situations in the workplace have some statutory means of redress against dismissal or other penalties that might ensue. In relation to environmental compliance, these "whistleblower" provisions not only offer workers job security if they seek to protect themselves from personal risk, but may also have the effect of encouraging those with detailed knowledge of environmental practices in the workplace to serve the public interest by promoting employer compliance through internal or external reporting.[81] Recent attempts to extend the level of whistleblower protection and to increase the likelihood that environmental harm will figure more prominently in decisions about the workplace include Ontario's *Environmental Bill of Rights, 1993*, and *CEPA, 1999*.[82]

FURTHER READINGS

BOYD, DAVID R., *Unnatural Law: Rethinking Canadian Environmental Law and Policy* (Vancouver: Univerity of British Columbia, 2003) c. 4.1

DOELLE, MEINHARD, *Canadian Environmental Protection Act and Commentary, 2008 Edition* (Markham, ON: LexisNexis Canada, 2008)

FISHER, ELIZABETH, "Risk and Environmental Law: A Beginner's Guide" in Benjamin Richardson & Stepan Wood, eds., *Environmental Law for Sustainability* (Portland, OR: Hart Publishing, 2006) c. 4

---

79   For example, in Ontario WHMIS is implemented via the regulation: *Workplace Hazardous Materials Information System (WHMIS)*, R.R.O. 1990, Reg. 860 promulgated under the *Occupational Health and Safety Act*, R.S.O. 1990, c. O.1.

80   See, for example, *Canada Labour Code*, R.S.C. 1985, c. L-2.

81   *Environmental Protection Act*, R.S.O. 1990, c. E.19, s. 174(2); *Kraan v. Custom Muffler Ltd.*, [1985] 2 O.L.R.B. Rep. October 1461.

82   S.O. 1993, c. 28; *CEPA, 1999*, above note 15, s. 16.

HEALTH CANADA, *A Vital Link: Health and the Environment in Canada* (Ottawa: Supply & Services, 1992)

LEISS, WILLIAM, "The CEPA Soap Opera" in William Leiss, *In the Chamber of Risks: Understanding Risk Controversies* (Montreal: McGill-Queen's University Press, 2001) c. 8

MCCLENAGHAN, THERESA, *et al.*, "Environmental Standard Setting and Children's Health in Canada: Injecting Precaution into Risk Assessment" (2003) 12 J. Envtl. L. & Prac. 245

NRTEE, *Managing Potentially Toxic Substances in Canada* (Ottawa: National Round Table on the Environment & the Economy, 2001)

Report of the House of Commons Standing Committee on Environment and Sustainable Development: It's About Our Health! Towards Pollution Prevention (Ottawa: Canada Communication Group, 1995)

ENDANGERED SPACES AND SPECIES

A. THE RATIONALE

Many features of environmental law safeguard human populations from the adverse effects and other impacts of environmental contamination and deterioration. Other initiatives, however, are specifically designed to protect the environment and its non-human inhabitants from seemingly inexorable human interventions, even where such interventions—a transportation corridor, or a drainage program, for example—might be perceived as "improvements." Along with pollution, developments of this kind impose severe costs on wildlife either by contamination, fragmentation of breeding territories, or destruction of certain types of vital habitat and migration routes. In addition, of course, humans themselves value and benefit from natural spaces for a range of economic, social, and spiritual reasons.

The *Canadian Wilderness Charter*, a document developed under the auspices of the World Wildlife Fund Canada and signed by more than half a million people, constitutes a powerful statement of the rationale for protecting wild and natural spaces. Humankind, the charter reminds us, is but one of millions of species sharing a planet whose future is severely threatened by our activities. Much of the Earth's former wilderness character is already lost, thereby endangering many species and ecosystems, but Canadians still have the opportunity to complete a network of protected areas representing the biological diversity of the country. For their inherent value, for their influence on national

identity, and in light of an intrinsic human need for spiritual rekind-
ling and artistic inspiration, Canada's remaining wild spaces should be
protected. Protected areas can serve a variety of purposes, including
preserving a genetic reservoir of wild plants and animals for future
use and appreciation; producing economic benefits from environmentally sensitive tourism; offering opportunities for research and environmental education; and maintaining options for traditional wilderness
use by aboriginal people.[1]

Very similar themes emerged from international discussions culminating in the *Convention on Biological Diversity* adopted at the United
Nations Conference on Environment and Development in Rio de Janeiro
in 1992. Since Canada was the first industrialized country to ratify the
CBD and since the Secretariat for the Convention is located in Montreal,
it may be worthwhile outlining current strategic goals under the *CBD* to
provide a point of reference for related Canadian initiatives.

In assessing progress and formulating a strategic plan with a target
for 2010, parties to the biodiversity convention identified seven focal
areas:

1) Reducing the rate of loss of the components of biodiversity, including:
   i)   biomes, habitats and ecosystems;
   ii) species and populations; and
   iii) genetic diversity;
2) Promoting sustainable use of biodiversity;
3) Addressing the major threats to biodiversity, including those
   arising from invasive alien species, climate change, pollution,
   and habitat change;
4) Maintaining ecosytem integrity, and the provision of goods and
   services provided by biodiversity in ecosystems, in support of
   human well-being;
5) Protecting traditional knowledge, innovations and practices;
6) Ensuring the fair and equitable sharing of benefits arising out of
   the use of genetic resources; and
7) Mobilizing financial and technical resources . . . for implementing
   the Convention and the Strategic Plan.[2]

---

1   M. Hummel, ed., *Endangered Spaces: The Future for Canada's Wilderness* (Toron-
    to: Key Porter, 1989) at 275.
2   Subsidiary Body on Scientific, Technical and Technological Advice, *Convention
    on Biological Diversity*, "Second Global Biodiversity Outlook: Draft Executive
    Summary" UNEP/CBD/SBSTTA/11/6 (5 October 2005) at para. 8.

Measures offering potential avenues of protection to spaces and species are found in many pieces of general legislation. The *Fisheries Act*, for example, prohibits the deposit of deleterious substances into water frequented by fish and the destruction of fish habitat, while environmental assessment procedures may be used to identify developmental threats to natural environments and non-human populations and to propose mitigative measures. As scientific and public understanding of the vulnerability of environmental systems to cumulative and wide-ranging impacts from human activity has increased, however, the search for more comprehensive responses has intensified. This chapter considers a number of other such broad approaches and legal mechanisms intended to safeguard spaces and species, ecosystems and biodiversity.[3]

B. PROTECTING ENDANGERED SPACES

Programs to safeguard a category known cumulatively as conservation lands include parks and wildlife-management areas or sanctuaries at the national, provincial, and territorial levels, as well as forest and ecological reserves, recreational land reserves, and a variety of special arrangements such as conservation easements and stewardship agreements to preserve private lands in their natural state. The total area protected in Canada according to the World Wildlife Fund's concluding report on the endangered spaces campaign (1989–2000) amounts to approximately 68 million hectares or 6.8 percent of the land base. The extent of protected areas as a percentage of each jurisdiction in Canada is as follows: Federal, 2.5 percent; Yukon, 10.38 percent; Northwest Territories/Nunavut, 5.2 percent; British Columbia, 11.4 percent; Alberta, 9.9 percent; Saskatchewan, 6.0 percent; Manitoba, 8.6 percent; Ontario, 8.7 percent; Quebec, 4.3 percent; New Brunswick, 3.2 percent; Nova Scotia, 8.3 percent; Prince Edward Island, 4.2 percent; Newfoundland, 4.3 percent.[4] An extensive and growing but still incomplete system of land-based and marine parks has been established under the authority of both federal and provincial legislation whose express purposes and

---

3   For commentary on the effectiveness of Canadian performance in relation to biodiversity protection, see *OECD Environmental Performance Reviews: Canada* (Paris: Organisation for Economic Co-operation and Development, 2004) c. 4; Stephen Bocking, *Biodiversity in Canada: Ecology, Ideas, and Action* (Peterborough: Broadview Press, 2000); David Boyd, *Unnatural Law: Rethinking Canadian Environmental Law and Policy* (Vancouver: UBC Press, 2003) c. 5.

4   *Endangered Spaces: The Wilderness Campaign that Changed the Canadian Landscape: 1989–2000* (Toronto: World Wildlife Fund, 2000) at 22.

administrative provisions appear to signal a significant long-term commitment to environmental protection.[5]

The National Parks of Canada are, by statute, "dedicated to the people of Canada for their benefit, education and enjoyment, subject to . . . [the *Canada National Parks Act*] and the regulations, and the National Parks shall be maintained and made use of so as to leave them unimpaired for the enjoyment of future generations."[6] Moreover, the *CNPA* reinforces a proposition that had previously served as departmental policy for years by establishing that "maintenance or restoration of ecological integrity, through the protection of natural resources and natural processes, shall be the first priority of the minister when considering all aspects of the management of parks."[7] The incorporation of the principle of "ecological integrity" into the federal legislative framework (as discussed below), raises issues around the standard to be met and its ultimate enforceability through the process of judicial review.

Echoing the federal initiative and previous recognition of ecological considerations by Quebec, Nova Scotia, Prince Edward Island, and Newfoundland and Labrador, Ontario has included within new legislation a statement to the effect that in planning and managing protected areas, "maintenance of ecological integrity shall be the first priority and restoration of ecological integrity shall be considered."[8] Nova Scotia's *Beaches Act* is another example of protected spaces legislation, devoted in this case to a particular type of environment: "The beaches of Nova Scotia are dedicated in perpetuity for the benefit, education and enjoyment of present and future generations of Nova Scotians." Among the Act's stated purposes are the protection of beaches and associated dune systems as significant and sensitive environmental and recreational resources; the regulation and enforcement of the full range of land-use activities on beaches, including aggregate removal, so as to leave them unimpaired for the benefit and enjoyment of future generations; and

---

5   Significant recent extensions of protected areas coverage were undertaken in connection with Ontario's Living Legacy program. A major expansion of national parks and wildlife areas throughout northern Canada was announced by the federal government in 2007. For comprehensive coverage of the latter developments, see online: www.newparksnorth.org.

6   *Canada National Parks Act*, S.C. 2000, c. 32, s. 4(1) [*CNPA*].

7   *Ibid.*, s. 8(2). As defined in the Act, ecological integrity with respect to a park means a condition that is determined to be characteristic of its natural region and likely to persist, including abiotic components and the composition and abundance of native species and biological communities, rates of change and supporting processes.

8   *Provincial Parks and Conservation Areas Act, 2006*, S.O. 2006, c. 12, s. 3.

control of recreational and other uses that may cause undesirable environmental effects.[9]

In practice, the interpretation of such provisions and their application has proven to be controversial. Across the country parks vary in terms of protection from potentially damaging activities and even in terms of the permanence and stability of their boundaries (see table 14.1). They remain subject to considerable developmental pressure from the resource, tourism, and transportation sectors, both within their boundaries and on the periphery.

Table 14.1: Selected Parks and Protected Areas Legislation

Alberta	*Provincial Parks Act*, R.S.A. 2000, c. P-35
British Columbia	*Park Act*, R.S.B.C., 1996, c. 344
Manitoba	*The Provincial Parks Act*, C.C.S.M. c. P20
New Brunswick	*Parks Act*, S.N.B. 1982, c. P-2.1
	National Parks Act, R.S.N.B. 1973, c. N-1
Newfoundland and Labrador	*Provincial Parks Act*, R.S.N. 1990, c. P-32
	Wilderness and Ecological Reserves Act, R.S.N.L. 1990, c. W-9
Nova Scotia	*Provincial Parks Act*, R.S.N.S. 1989, c. 367
	Wilderness Areas Protection Act, S.N.S. 1998, c. 27
Ontario	*Provincial Parks and Conservation Reserves Act, 2006*, S.O. 2006, c. 12[10]
Prince Edward Island	*Recreation Development Act*, R.S.P.E.I. 1988, c. R-8
Quebec	*Parks Act*, R.S.Q. c. P-9
Saskatchewan	*The Parks Act*, S.S. 1986, c. P-1.1
Federal	*Canada National Parks Act*, S.C. 2000, c. 32

In the context of a dispute over the expansion of skiing facilities in B.C.'s Cypress Provincial Park, opponents of the increased development sought a judicial declaration to the effect that the dominant purpose of the province's *Park Act* was the preservation and protection of the natural environment of parks.[11] Melnick J., while noting that the provision was not actually applicable to Cypress, analysed a key element of the legislation. Section 53 states that certain parks are "dedicated to

---

9   *Beaches Act*, R.S.N.S. 1989, c. 32. For a discussion of the history and operation of the Act, see *Mossman v. Nova Scotia (A.G.)* (1995), 140 N.S.R. (2d) 321 (S.C.).

10 The new legislation consolidates the statutory framework in Ontario for wilderness class parks, nature reserve class parks, cultural heritage class parks, natural environment class parks, waterway class parks, and recreational class parks.

11 *Friends of Cypress Provincial Park Society v. B.C. (Minister of Environment, Lands and Parks)* (2000), 33 C.E.L.R. (N.S.) 276 (B.C.S.C.).

the preservation of their natural environments for the inspiration, use, and enjoyment of the public." While acknowledging the importance of preserving the natural environment of those parks designated for such protection, Melnick J. noted a legislative intent to foster "recreational values" that were "not necessarily subsumed in the concept of nature conservancy." He concluded, accordingly, that the Act "provides a framework for the creation and preservation of parkland for a variety of purposes to serve a broad cross-section of the citizens of British Columbia whose interests are as diverse as its landscape."[12]

One prominent example of an attempt to reconcile the environmental protection dimensions of national parks with development was the subject of the Banff Bow Valley Study. Its report, *At the Crossroads*, formulated recommendations to address the study's principal finding that "[i]f current trends and pressures are allowed to continue, they will threaten the qualities that make Banff a national park" and the conclusion that "the ecological integrity of the Banff-Bow Valley cannot be sustained." The general thrust of the proposed actions responds to the injunction that "[a]d hoc decision making must give way to a more holistic approach, one that puts the Park ahead of human needs and desires." Although legal matters, including the application of federal parks legislation, international conventions and agreements, and an intricate web of local leasing arrangements, are all identified as sources of some support for the vision of the future as proposed by the task force, the overall need for accountable decision making, public participation, and effective use of scientific data remain as continuing challenges.[13] These were among the matters subsequently pursued on a more comprehensive basis by an expert panel appointed in 1998 to advise the minister of Canadian heritage.[14] Although this inquiry devoted particular attention to administrative and planning matters internal to Parks Canada, a number of principles advanced have wider significance. Of special interest in terms of broader legal implications is the suggestion

---

12   *Ibid.* at 291.

13   Banff-Bow Valley Task Force, *Banff-Bow Valley: At the Crossroads: Summary Report* (Ottawa: Supply & Services, 1996). The emergence of "Riverkeeper" organizations, including one dedicated to oversight of the Bow River valley, is one response to the need for a comprehensive approach to ecological protection, in such cases at the watershed level. For background on the riverkeeper movement, see John Cronin & Robert F. Kennedy Jr., *The Riverkeepers* (New York: Simon & Schuster Touchstone, 1999).

14   Panel on the Ecological Integrity of Canada's National Parks, *"Unimpaired for Future Generations?" Conserving Ecological Integrity within Canada's National Parks, Report of the Panel on the Ecological Integrity of Canada's National Parks* (Ottawa: Panel on the Ecological Integrity of Canada's National Parks, 2000).

that national parks must be more systematically viewed as elements of ecological networks rather than as "islands" in isolation from the surrounding landscape.

Judicial recognition of the status of environmental values in national-parks management is evident in numerous judgments, including a Federal Court of Appeal decision on the need for environmental assessment of the expansion of skiing facilities at Banff's Sunshine Village. The court's decision calling for an examination of the cumulative impact of ongoing development rather than an incremental assessment was forward-looking and appropriate.[15] Development proposals on or affecting parklands continue to generate litigation, often in relation to environmental assessment,[16] and now in relation to expectations surrounding the meaning of ecological integrity as a standard for parks management.

Parks Canada, in connection with its responsibility for 41 national parks, has undertaken significant steps to assess and to maintain or restore ecological integrity within the parks system. "State of the Park" reports will provide information over five-year cycles that will support the evaluation of management actions against benchmarks and objectives. On a system-wide basis Parks Canada anticipates that for all parks the necessary monitoring and reporting arrangements will be in place by 2009, that consistent and up-to-date management plans will be available by 2010 and that elements of ecological integrity will show improvement by 2014. An audit report carried out by the Commissioner of the Environment and Sustainable Development, while containing recommendations for improvements, appears generally favorable to the manner in which Parks Canada has begun to pursue ecological integrity on an administrative basis.[17]

---

15 *Sunshine Village Corp. v. Canada (Minister of Canadian Heritage)* (1996), 20 C.E.L.R. (N.S.) 171 (Fed. C.A.), leave to appeal to S.C.C. refused, [1996] S.C.C.A. No. 498 .

16 *Alberta Wilderness Association v. Canada (Minister of Fisheries and Oceans)* (1999), 29 C.E.L.R. (N.S.) 21 (F.C.A.); *Bowen v. Canada (A.G.)* (1997), 26 C.E.L.R. (N.S.) 11 (F.C.T.D.); *Bow Valley Naturalists Society v. Canada*, (1999), 32 C.E.L.R. (N.S.) 84 (F.C.T.D.); *Friends of Point Pleasant Park v. Canada (A.G.)* (2000), 36 C.E.L.R. (N.S.) 253 (F.C.T.D.); *Society of Friends of Strathcona Park v. B.C. (Minister of Environment, Lands and Parks)* (1999), 31 C.E.L.R. (N.S.) 274 (B.C.S.C.).

17 "Ecological Integrity in Canada's National Parks," in *Report of the Commissioner of the Environment and Sustainable Development, 2005* (Ottawa: Office of the Auditor General, 2005) c. 2 [*CESD Report 2005*]. For specific illustrations of the range of initiatives involved in Parks Canada's ecological integrity work,

In relation to the legal status of ecological integrity, however, doubts have been expressed on the basis of judicial review of a decision of the minister of Canadian heritage to approve winter road construction in Wood Buffalo National Park.[18] As noted above, ecological integrity is referred to as "the first priority" of the minister when considering parks management. The concept of ecological integrity itself is statutorily defined as "a condition that is determined to be characteristic of its natural region and likely to persist, including abiotic components and the composition and abundance of native species and biological communities, rates of change and supporting processes."[19] When a national environmental organization challenged the minister's approval of the winter road for failing to meet the statutory standard established by the definition and its designation as "the first priority," the trial court found no evidence that the concept of ecological integrity had even been addressed in the decision-making process. The trial judge further observed that ecological integrity was not, within subsection 8(2), the determinative factor and could be overridden "where impairment of such integrity can be minimized to a degree that the minister concludes is consistent with the maintenance of the Park for the enjoyment of future generations."[20] The Federal Court of Appeal, in upholding the lower court's dismissal of the judicial review application, roughly equated the ecological integrity standard with the screening test for federal environmental assessment. Accordingly, the FCA concluded that the minister's approval of the road was not "patently unreasonable" and therefore a legitimate exercise of the statutory authority under which it was made.[21]

Another doctrine, public trust, has also been invoked in litigation by those seeking to impose an obligation on governmental authorities to safeguard the environmental conditions and integrity of designated parklands. The argument, roughly stated, is that certain statutory provisions establish a trust in park areas for the benefit of the public

---

see Parks Canada, *Action on the Ground: Ecological Integrity in Canada's National Parks* (Ottawa: Parks Canada, 2005).

18 *Canadian Parks and Wilderness Society v. Canada (Minister of Canadian Heritage)* (2003), 1 C.E.L.R. (3d) 20 (F.C.A.).

19 CNPA, above note 6, s. 2 (1).

20 *Canadian Parks and Wilderness Society v. Canada (Minister of Canadian Heritage)* (2001), 212 F.T.R. 1 at paras 52–53 (T.D.).

21 For commentary and analysis of the decisions, see Shaun Fluker, "'Maintaining Ecological Integrity Is our First Priority' — Policy Rhetoric and Practical Reality in Canada's National Parks? A Case Comment on *Canadian Parks and Wilderness Society v. Canada (Minister of Canadian Heritage)*" (2003) 13 J. Envtl. L. & Prac. 131.

or some designated class of persons that the government as trustee is under a legally enforceable duty to uphold.

In *Green v. R.*, a researcher with the Canadian Environmental Law Association unsuccessfully attempted to persuade a court that the provincial government's conduct in relation to Sandbanks Provincial Park was in breach of such a trust.[22] In 1968, Ontario leased some of the sandbanks bordering Lake Ontario to a company that accordingly gained the right to excavate sand. The province subsequently established Sandbanks Provincial Park on adjacent land, thereby prompting Green to argue that by permitting excavation to continue on the leased property the province was in breach of certain trust obligations established by the then current *Provincial Parks Act*. Section 2 of that legislation stated that provincial parks are "dedicated to the people of the Province of Ontario . . . for their healthful enjoyment and education, and the provincial parks shall be maintained for the benefit of future generations in accordance with this Act and the regulations."[23]

Although Lerner J. resolved the conflict by ruling that Green lacked standing to proceed with the litigation, he addressed the argument that section 2 created a public trust imposing obligations on the provincial government. Lerner J. concluded that the elements of a trust were lacking in the circumstances of the case in that the existence of legislative authority to increase, decrease, or close the park meant that the subject matter of the alleged trust was uncertain; nor could the objects or beneficiaries of the trust be ascertained with sufficient certainty. In addition, Lerner J. found that the wide powers of discretion conferred upon the province to manage parks were inconsistent with the existence of a trust.

The failure of the public-trust argument in *Green* does not preclude its use in other settings where different legislative language has been employed. Indeed, the concept of the public trust was favourably remarked on in the context of a damage claim by municipal authorities against a builder whose operations negligently destroyed a number of mature maple trees within a city road allowance. Writing for a majority of the Ontario Court of Appeal, Lacourcière J. stated: "In our judgment, the municipality is, in a broad sense, a trustee of the environment for the benefit of the residents in the area of the road allowance and, indeed for the citizens of the community at large."[24] Public-trust claims

---

22 [1973] 2 O.R. 396 (H.C.J.) [*Green*].

23 *Provincial Parks Act*, R.S.O. 1990, c. P.34, s. 2.

24 *Scarborough (City) v. R.E.F. Homes Ltd.* (1979), 10 C.E.L.R. 41 at 41–42 (Ont. C.A.).

remain rare in Canada,[25] although they may ultimately be encouraged by an important decision on fiduciary relationships in which the Supreme Court of Canada rejected the assumption that the nature of fiduciary relationships is exhaustively established by the categories of agent, trustee, partner, director, and so on:

> It is the nature of the relationship, not the specific category of actor involved that gives rise to the fiduciary duty. The categories of fiduciary, like those of negligence, should not be considered closed.[26]

It would also appear that overall judicial attitudes towards the environment are more favourable than at the time of the *Green* case when Lerner J. dismissed the plaintiff's assessment of the importance of the sandbanks by remarking: "That 'the towering sand dunes . . . constitute . . . a unique ecological, geological and recreational resource . . .' is clearly a statement of opinion as much as a comment that a particular *objet d'art* is good or bad esthetically."[27]

Significantly, some legislation is now explicit in its reference to the existence of a public trust. Thus, the Yukon *Environmental Act* designates the government of the Yukon as "the trustee of the public trust," defined as "the collective interest of the people of the Yukon in the quality of the natural environment and the protection of the natural environment for the benefit of present and future generations." The statute formally requires the Yukon government to "conserve the natural environment in accordance with the public trust" subject to the Act and other scheduled enactments.[28] A comparable provision was introduced in the N.W.T. and has been referred to in judicial proceedings involving wildlife matters, essentially as an indication of the fundamental importance of the northern environment to the people resident there.[29]

---

25 A public trust argument was advanced in *Canadian Parks and Wilderness Society v. Wood Buffalo National Park* (1992), 55 F.T.R. 286 (T.D.), but was not addressed by the court when the parties settled the litigation.

26 *Guerin v. R.*, [1984] 2 S.C.R. 335 at 384.

27 *Green*, above note 22 at 401.

28 *Environment Act*, S.Y. 1991, c. 5, ss. 2 and 38. For discussion, see D.W.M. Waters, "The Role of the Trust in Environmental Protection Law" in D.W.M. Waters, ed., *Equity, Fiduciaries and Trusts* (Toronto: Carswell, 1993) 383. For discussion of the public trust concept in relation to the territorial legislation, see B. von Tigerstrom, "The Public Trust Doctrine in Canada" (1998) 7 J. Envtl. L. & Prac. 379. For discussion of public trust in relation to resources such as fisheries and forest lands, see Scott Kidd, "Keeping Public Resources in Public Hands: Advancing the Public Trust Doctrine in Canada" (2006) 16 J. Envtl. L. & Prac. 187.

29 *Environmental Rights Act*, R.S.N.W.T. 1988 (Supp.), c. 83. See *R v. Ram Head Outfitters Ltd.*, [1995] N.W.T.J. No. 29 (Terr. Ct.).

Several jurisdictions have used ecological reserves and other comparable designations to safeguard vulnerable sites from development. Typical reasons for such designations are set out in British Columbia's *Ecological Reserves Act*, which identified relevant criteria for selecting areas to be reserved:

(a) suitable for scientific research and educational purposes associated with studies in productivity and other aspects of the natural environment;

(b) that are representative examples of natural ecosystems within the Province;

(c) that serve as examples of ecosystems that have been modified by man and offer an opportunity to study the recovery of the natural ecosystem from modification;

(d) where rare or endangered native plants and animals in their natural habitat may be preserved; and

(e) that contain unique and rare examples of botanical, zoological or geological phenomena.[30]

The Act conferred upon the lieutenant governor in council the power to designate ecological reserves on Crown land and to cancel or amend such reserves once established. Reserves thus created are not subject to further disposition that might be granted under other provincial legislation such as the *Land Act*, the *Forest Act*, the *Mineral Act*, and the *Petroleum and Natural Gas Act*.[31]

Protection of endangered spaces extends beyond the terrestrial landscape to encompass marine areas and wetlands. The creation of marine parks and reserves is a comparatively recent initiative in Canada, and one that may be carried out under several pieces of legislation. The *Oceans Act* confers authority on the federal Minister of Fisheries and Oceans to lead the development of a system of marine protected areas.[32] These are intended to serve several purposes, including the protection of fisheries resources or habitat (including that for marine mammals); the protection of endangered or threatened marine species or habitat; the protection of unique habitats; the protection of marine areas of high biological diversity or productivity; and the protection of other marine resources. While there have been some delays in the

---

30 *Ecological Reserve Act*, R.S.B.C. 1996, c. 103, s. 2.

31 *Ibid.* See also *Ecological Reserves Act*, S.N.B. 1975, c. E-1.1; *Wilderness Areas, Ecological Reserves and Natural Areas Act*, R.S.A. 2000, c.W-9. The Alberta legislation has recently been extended to provide for "heritage rangeland" designations.

32 *Oceans Act*, S.C. 1996, c. 31. See also *Canada National Marine Conservation Areas Act*, S.C. 2002, c. 18 and the *Canada Wildlife Act*, R.S.C. 1985, c. W-9, s. 4.1.

designation of marine protected areas under the *Oceans Act*, and some uncertainty or lack of coordination between Fisheries and Oceans, Parks Canada and the Canadian Wildlife Service in relation to an over-all approach, a program to address such limitations was published in 2005.[33] Challenges remain to ensure the coordination and integration of federal and provincial measures.

In relation to wetlands, these have been profoundly affected by land use practices and policies affecting such matters as drainage, transportation and urban expansion. Twenty million hectares of Can-adian wetlands have been converted to agricultural use. Significant and widespread losses of habitat and ecological functions, notably relating to water quality, have thus already occurred. Some provinces, led by Al-berta, Manitoba, Nova Scotia, P.E.I., and New Brunswick, have begun to introduce various forms of wetland protection. For its part, the fed-eral government has formulated a policy on wetland conservation.[34] This document calls for cooperation with provinces and territories to pursue goals including the maintenance, enhancement and rehabilita-tion of wetland functions, and, in relation to federal responsibilities in particular, for no net loss of wetland functions on federal lands and for recognition of those functions in federal planning, management and decision making.

C. CONSERVATION MECHANISMS FOR PRIVATE LANDS

Measures to protect sensitive areas in private ownership from disrup-tion and development include conservation easements, related coven-ants, and other forms of stewardship either initiated by conscientious landholders or promoted more systematically by nature protection and conservation organizations.[35] Such mechanisms may be particularly

---

33   *CESD Report 2005*, above note 17, c. 1 at 15–20; *Canada's Federal Marine Pro-tected Areas Strategy* (June 2005), online: www.dfo-mpo.gc.ca/oceans-habitat/ oceans/mpa-zpm/fedmpa-zpmfed/pdf/mpa_e.pdf. For a detailed illustration of the planning process, see the Regulatory Impact Analysis Statement prepared in connection with proposed *Manicouagan Marine Protected Area Regulations* under the *Oceans Act*, in C. Gaz. 2006, Vol. 140, No. 39 (30 September 2006), online: http://gazetteducanada.gc.ca/partI/2006/20060930/html/regle3-e.html.

34   Environment Canada, *The Federal Policy on Wetland Conservation* (Ottawa: Min-ister of Supply and Services, 1991).

35   The Nature Conservancy of Canada is one important example. See online: www.natureconservancy.ca.

useful in relation to numerous small sites that fulfil vital ecological functions — wetlands, for example.

At common law, certain interests in land might be recognized through easements granted by the owner to an easement holder who would thereby gain a right to use the owner's land in some prescribed manner (a right of way, for example) or to prevent the owner from using the land for some specified purpose. These arrangements were known as positive and negative easements respectively. Covenants between the landowner and another contracting party or parties could also be used to create restrictions on the manner in which land could be used. In principle these mechanisms could be employed to safeguard environmental values, but limitations in transferability and enforceability severely undermined their utility for this purpose.

Statutory reforms in several jurisdictions[36] have alleviated many historic constraints on conservation easements. These often permit conservation easements to be granted to public bodies and to recognized non-governmental conservation organizations. The Ontario legislation now permits a landowner to "grant an easement to or enter into a covenant with a conservation body . . . for the conservation, maintenance, restoration, or enhancement of all or a portion of the land or the wildlife on the land; or . . . for access to the land for these purposes."[37] In addition, the easement or covenant is valid whether or not the conservation body or assignee owns appurtenant land or land capable of being accommodated or benefited by the easement or covenant and regardless of whether the easement or covenant is positive or negative in nature. The easement or covenant is enforceable against the owner of the land and, if registered, against any subsequent owner of the land.[38]

---

36 S. Lieberman, "New Game in Town: Conservation Easements and Estate Planning" (1995) 14 E. & T.J. 315. Note 23 lists B.C., Yukon, Manitoba, P.E.I., Sask., N.S., and Nfld., citing I. Attridge, "Canadian Land Trust and Conservation Easement Law: An Overview" in Land Trust Alliance, Land Trust Alliance National Rally '94 Workbook (Washington, DC: Land Trust Alliance, 1994). A.J. Kwasniak, Private Conservancy: The Path to Law Reform (Edmonton: Environmental Law Centre, 1994); W.J. Andrews & D. Loukidelis, Leaving a Living Legacy: Using Conservation Covenants in B.C. (Vancouver: West Coast Environmental Law Research Foundation, 1995); A. Silver, "Canadian Legislation for Conservation Covenants, Easements and Servitudes" (Ottawa: North American Wetlands Conservation Council, 1995); Land Title Act, R.S.B.C. 1996, c. 250; Environmental Protection and Enhancement Act, R.S.A. 2000, c. E-12, s. 22.

37 Conservation Land Act, R.S.O. 1990, c. 28, s. 3(2).

38 Ibid., s. 3(6).

Although legislation of this nature enables landowners to pursue statutorily approved conservation objectives with greater confidence that their intentions will not be thwarted by historic common law principles, these arrangements must nonetheless be implemented with care on an individual basis.[39] Their attractions to landowners have recently been summarized as follows:

- right to continued use of the land after the conservation objectives have been determined;
- significantly less disruption than total disposition of the property in that other elements of control are retained;
- flexibility and adaptability to particular individual circumstances relating to the land and to the interests of the owner; and
- a possible lowering of the tax burden.[40]

Other forms of private-stewardship agreements have been implemented through the efforts of conservation groups across Canada. Voluntary stewardship agreements, both oral and written, and varying in duration and permanence from short-term renewable to multi-year undertakings, have emerged from discussion between conservation interests and landowners. NGOs such as Wildlife Habitat Canada, Ducks Unlimited, and the Nature Conservancy of Canada have devoted extensive effort and resources to wetlands, sometimes leasing and sometimes aquiring property, and sometimes consulting on appropriate land-use practices. In Saskatchewan, the Prairie Pot-hole Project was designed to elicit the support of agricultural landholders for measures to safeguard waterfowl habitat. Other programs with provincial involvement include the Habitat Enhancement Land-Use Program (HELP) in Manitoba, the Co-operative Watershed Management Project in Prince Edward Island, and the Nature Heritage Stewardship Program in Ontario, where oral stewardship agreements predominated.[41]

An observer of many such initiatives has identified a series of considerations arising from the pilot projects now under way:

[A]re the handshake agreements used in Ontario strong enough to provide long-term protection? Are the leases used in the prairies

---

39   For a case study on the tools, (inlcuding conservation covenants) available to safeguard environmental values on private lands see Michelle Campbell, "Tools for the Protection of Ecologically Significant Private Lands in Ontario: A Case Study of Marcy's Woods" (2006) 17 J. Envtl. L. & Prac. 47.

40   Lieberman, above note 36 at 316.

41   Stewart Hilts, "Private Stewardship" in M. Hummel, above note 1 at 103–5.

going to become a long-term financial burden, and condition land-owners to expect payment for conservation of natural habitats?

. . . Is there an opportunity to bring an integrated conservation message to farmers; for example, pulling together the principles of soil and water conservation with natural-heritage values?[42]

D. THE PROTECTION OF ENDANGERED SPECIES

Plant and animal species have been and remain extremely vulnerable to the direct impact of human activities on their populations or habitat and to the indirect, cumulative and unintended consequences of human behaviour as well. In addition to such threats as hunting and capture whether for consumption, ornament, commerce or other purposes and to the demolition of habitat for agricultural use, urban expansion, or transportation, species have been adversely affected by pollution and the release of toxic substances. New threats whose ultimate impacts remain imperfectly understood include the introduction of invasive species, the release of genetically-modified competitors, and climate change. The loss of individual species furthers the loss of planetary biodiversity whose value has recently been articulated in the preamble to Ontario legislation:

> Biological diversity is among the great treasures of our planet. It has ecological, social, economic, cultural and intrinsic value. Biological diversity makes many essential contributions to human life, including foods, clothing and medicines, and is an important part of sustainable social and economic development.[43]

Many observers also find the destruction of other forms of life on the planet to be deeply disturbing from an ethical perspective. For this and other reasons legal measures have been introduced and proposed to safeguard endangered species and in some instances to endeavor to restore their numbers.

At the international level, the importance of species preservation has been a recurring focus of concern. Since 1975 the *Convention on International Trade in Endangered Species of Wild Flora and Fauna (CITES)* has been one of the more prominent international legal initiatives directly affecting the development of species protection measures

---

42   *Ibid.* at 105.
43   *Endangered Species Act, 2007*, S.O. 2007, c. 6.

within Canada and approximately 140 other parties to the convention.[44] With the support of national management and scientific authorities as well as an international secretariat, CITES protects wildlife by regulating international trade in designated species. Three categories of species are set out in the convention. First, subject to "exceptional circumstances" outside the commercial context, CITES prohibits trade in species that are threatened with extinction. Second, export permits are required for species that are not yet threatened but that might face pressures towards extinction in the absence of effective regulation. A third category comprises species identified by individual CITES members as protected under their own domestic regulatory regimes. Exports of such species from the listing state are subject to a system of export permits and to the presentation by importers of satisfactory documentation concerning origin.

Canada originally implemented CITES through the *Export and Import Permits Act*,[45] which established a permit program to control exports of listed goods and the *Game Export Act*.[46] The sentencing of a young man who entered a plea of guilty to a charge of attempting to export four falcon eggs in contravention of the legislation was the occasion for a moving analysis of the situation by Mr. Justice Bourassa of the Territorial Court of the Northwest Territories. Bourassa J. began by rejecting the view that this is an offence where there is no real victim and no real impact on the community. The victim, he argued, "is the community of Frobisher Bay, in fact, the community of the Northwest Territories, and indeed, the whole world." By contributing to a further decline of an endangered species of bird, the accused exacerbated a serious situation:

> Here in the Northwest Territories, wildlife is an essential feature of life, and not only that, it is a treasured resource to be conserved, husbanded, protected and fostered, so it can continue to provide sustenance for the body and for the spirit in future ages as it has in past ages. The placing of the gyrfalcon on the export permit control list is precisely for that purpose, to allow the community through its legislation to conserve and protect that species of wildlife. . . . If this type of conservation-oriented law, one of which is the *Export and Import Permits Act*, is to have any respect, then I think the Court's response to this particular offence must be more than a slap on the wrist. I

---

44   For a discussion of other international agreements dealing with species and habitat protection, see S. Lyster, *International Wildlife Law* (Cambridge: Grotius, 1985).

45   R.S.C. 1985, c. E-19.

46   R.S.C. 1985 c. G-1.

think such a response would be demoralizing and destructive for the rule of law, and especially the rule of law as it applies to conservation and wildlife management in the north.[47]

Subsequent legislation, the *Wild Animal and Plant Protection and Regulation of International and Interprovincial Trade Act*, replaced the previous game-export legislation.[48] The new legislation is again designed to conform to *CITES* while providing more effectively for federal-provincial cooperation to regulate interprovincial as well as international trade in designated plants and animals. Several key prohibitions have been formulated:

> 6. (1) No person shall import into Canada any animal or plant that was taken, or any animal or plant, or any part or derivative of an animal or plant, that was possessed, distributed or transported in contravention of any law of any foreign state.
>
> (2) Subject to the regulations, no person shall, except under and in accordance with a permit issued pursuant to subsection 10(1) import into Canada or export from Canada any animal or plant, or any part or derivative of an animal or plant.
>
> (3) Subject to the regulations, no person shall, except under and in accordance with a permit issued pursuant to subsection 10(1), transport from one province to another province any animal or plant, or any part or derivative of an animal or plant.

Moreover, the legislation requires importers, exporters, and transporters to maintain prescribed documentation and makes possession of illegally imported plants and animals an offence.

Regulations implementing *WAPPRITA* establish rules applicable to importation, exportation, and interprovincial transport while providing certain exemptions. In prosecutions to date it is not uncommon to combine charges under *WAPPRITA* with related charges under provincial or territorial wildlife legislation.

While restrictions on inter-jurisdictional trade offered one means of protection for species facing pressures associated with their commercial value and marketability, it has long been evident that more comprehensive measures were required to address a far broader range of threats to habitat, for example, and that the rationales for such measures might also be quite diverse. Thus, the World Conservation Strategy (1980) identified the "preservation of genetic diversity" as one of its

---

47   *Krey v. R.* (1982), 12 C.E.L.R. 108 (N.W.T. Terr. Ct.).

48   S.C. 1992, c. 52 [*WAPPRITA*]. *Wild Animal and Plant Trade Regulations* S.O.R./96-263.

principal objectives, while the World Commission on Environment and Development described protection of species and their ecosystems as "an indispensable prerequisite for sustainable development."[49] More recently, parties contracting to the *Convention on Biological Diversity* acknowledged "the intrinsic value of biological diversity and of the ecological, genetic, social, economic, scientific, educational, cultural, recreational, and aesthetic values of biological diversity and its components"[50] and agreed that, "as far as possible and as appropriate" each nation should "[d]evelop or maintain necessary legislation and/or other regulatory provisions for the protection of threatened species and populations."[51]

This prominent call for domestic measures did not inaugurate Canadian consideration of species protection legislation. Statutory and regulatory regimes for wildlife conservation are longstanding. However, international attention revitalized debate in Canada by underlining the significance of biodiversity, the importance of habitat protection, and the emergence of new risks.

Intergovernmental discussion of general wildlife matters takes place under the auspices of the Wildlife Ministers Council of Canada. Within this framework, agreement was reached in 1996 on a National Accord for the Protection of Species at Risk, a document in which the signatory jurisdictions undertook "to prevent species in Canada from becoming extinct as a consequence of human activity" as well as "to establish complementary legislation and programs that provide for effective protection."

Effective protection will ultimately be subject to assessment against the actual performance record of species protection measures that are put in place. On the nature of appropriate measures, however, there is some basic agreement. Legislation should provide a suitable mechanism for identifying and officially designating endangered species according to their degree of vulnerability. Direct harm to designated species should be prohibited and the habitat required for their survival should be protected, in each case with a suitable set of incentives, penalties and enforcement mechanisms. Procedures accompanied by adequate financial support should be in place to promote the recovery of endangered species in a timely manner.[52]

---

49   World Commission on Environment and Development, *Our Common Future* (Oxford: Oxford University Press, 1987) at 166.

50   *Convention on Biological Diversity*, 5 June 1992, 1760 U.N.T.S. 79, (1992) 31 I.L.M. 818, preamble.

51   *Ibid.*, art. 8(k).

52   David Boyd, *Unnatural Law: Rethinking Canadian Environmental Law and Policy* (Vancouver: UBC Press, 2003) at 190–92.

Several provinces enacted new legislation or amended existing arrangements subsequent to the intergovernmental accord. Manitoba's *Endangered Species Act* addresses some of the concerns typically raised in connection with such initiatives: What is the status of species protection in relation to other statutory provisions? Is habitat safeguarded in any way? The Manitoba legislation identified an important consideration in environmental law by indicating that the *MESA* provisions will apply in cases of conflict with other legislation, "unless the other Act expressly provides that the other Act prevails."[53] The Act also authorizes regulations relating to habitat[54] and prohibits the disturbance and destruction of the habitat of an endangered, a threatened, or an extirpated species that has been reintroduced.[55] On the other hand, developments may be exempted from the provision of the *Endangered Species* legislation where the minister is satisfied either that the protection and preservation of the species or habitat is assured, or that appropriate measures will be established to minimize the impact of the development on protected species and their habitats.

Another approach to the habitat issue appears in Nova Scotia legislation.[56] That province's *Endangered Species Act*, adopted in 1998, distinguishes between the dwelling places and the core habitat of an endangered or threatened species. In contrast with specific dwelling places such as a nest or den, core habitat for an endangered or threatened species encompasses areas that are essential for long-term survival and recovery. While interference, destruction, and disturbance of dwelling places is subject to a general prohibition, core habitat must first be designated by the minister before it will enjoy statutory protection. Core habitat will not be designated for a threatened or endangered species until a recovery plan has been prepared. Thus, while protection

---

53   *The Endangered Species Act*, S.M. 1989–90, c. 39, s. 2(2) [*MESA*]; *Endangered Species Act*, R.S.O. 1990, c. E.15, as amended by S.O. 1997, c. 41, s. 116; *Endangered Species Act*, S.N.B. 1996, c. E-9.101 [*NBESA*]; *Endangered Species Act*, S.N.S. 1998, c. 11 [*NSESA*]; *An Act Respecting Threatened or Vulnerable Species*, R.S.Q. c. E-12.01 [*Que. TVSA*]. In provinces lacking statutory protection for endangered species as such, analogous provisions may sometimes be found in wildlife legislation. See, for example, *Wildlife Act General Regulation*, B.C. Reg. 340/82. Other B.C. initiatives regarding endangered species are associated with the *Forest Management Code* or administered through the Conservation Data Centre at the Ministry of Sustainable Resource Management. *Saskatchewan Wildlife Act*, S.S. 1998, c. W-13.12, Part V.

54   *MESA, ibid.*, s. 9(1)(a).

55   *Ibid.*, s. 10(1).

56   *NSESA*, above note 53 .

may be extended to habitat, that process is subject to potentially significant delays.

On a national basis, significant shortfalls remain between the number of species understood on the basis of scientific assessment to be threatened or vulnerable to extinction and the number of species designated for protection under provincial endangered species or wildlife legislation.[57] The contribution of federal legislation to the overall framework for species protection in Canada is therefore of great importance.

E. FEDERAL SPECIES AT RISK LEGISLATION

Canada's first bird sanctuary was established at Last Mountain Lake in 1887. A noticeable decline in the population of migratory bird species then spurred federal legislative action nearly a century ago when Canada, in conjunction with the United States, enacted legislation in 1917 to implement a *Migratory Birds Convention* agreed upon the previous year. In 1994, the original statute was replaced by the *Migratory Birds Convention Act, 1994.* This statute provides for a licensing and permit scheme within the context of a general prohibition against possession of migratory birds or commercial transactions involving them.[58] Alongside severe fines for contravention, persons convicted under the *Migratory Birds Convention Act, 1994* are potentially subject to court orders requiring remedial action, community service, and other alternative forms of punishment.[59] In the case of certain offences prescribed by regulation, ticketing with a maximum fine of $1000 is established as

---

57   The shortfall in Ontario has been the subject of repeated comment. See Environmental Commissioner of Ontario, *Annual Report 2002–2003: Thinking beyond the Near and Now* (Toronto: Environmental Commissioner of Ontario, 2003) at 134–38; *Annual Report 2004–2005: Planning Our Landscape* (Toronto: Environmental Commissioner of Ontario, 2005) at 148–52; www.saveon-tariospecies.ca. The *Endangered Species Act, 2007*, above note 43, offers the possibility of substantially strengthening the provincial regime on the basis of scientific listing and automatic habitat protection. See also *Wildlife Act*, R.S.B.C. 1996, c. 488; *Forest Practices Code of British Columbia*, R.S.B.C. 1996, c. 159; *Forest and Range Practices Act*, S.B.C. 2002, c. 69; *Wildlife Act*, R.S.A. 2000, c. W-10; *Wildlife Act*, S.S. 1998, c.W-13.12; *Wildlife Habitat Protection Act*, S.S. 1983–84, c. W-13.2; *Que. TVSA*, above note 53; *NBESA*, above note 53.

58   *Migratory Birds Convention Act, 1994*, S.C. 1994, c. 22.

59   *Ibid.*, ss. 13 and 16. For discussion of the interaction of the *Migratory Birds Convention Act*, *ibid.*, provincial fish and game regulation and bylaws under the *Indian Act*, see *R. v. Blackbird* (2005), 74 O.R. (3d) 241 (C.A.).

an enforcement option.[60] Other federal legislation, the *Canada Wildlife Act*, provides for the designation of national wildlife areas and for other measures related to wildlife research, conservation, and interpretation.[61] The existing federal measures were widely judged to be inadequate in relation to the requirements for national legislation highlighted by the international *Convention on Biological Diversity*.[62]

In the aftermath of two unsuccessful attempts to enact legislation to fulfil public commitments in relation to endangered species, the federal government, following the November 2000 election, introduced Bill C-5 in February 2001. The resulting legislation, the *Species at Risk Act* (*SARA*) represents a federal initiative to complement provincial and territorial measures to promote the protection and recovery of endangered species.[63] Many of its provisions were also conceived to enhance other supportive partnerships with governments, aboriginal communities, conservation organizations, and individuals, or to promote voluntary activity relating to species protection.

The stated purposes of *SARA*, largely in force as of June 2003, are threefold. First, to prevent Canadian wildlife species from becoming extinct or extirpated; second, to provide for the recovery of species that are extirpated, endangered or threatened; and, finally, to provide for the management of species of special concern so as to prevent them from becoming endangered or threatened.[64] A narrower expression of the intent of the legislation as formulated by the Commissioner of Environment and Sustainable Development more accurately describes its essential scope of operation: "The purpose of the Act is to protect and recover species considered to be at risk that are found on federal lands or under federal jurisdiction and to protect their critical habitat."[65] The categories of risk—extinct, extirpated, endangered, and threatened—as well as the manner in which this status is determined and the responses then available are central elements of the federal act.

SARA formally constitutes the Committee on the Status of Endangered Wildlife in Canada, (COSEWIC), whose members bring scientific expertise from such fields as conservation biology or genetics, or

---

60 *Migratory Birds Convention Act, 1994, ibid.*, s. 19. In June 2008, federal *Migratory Bird Regulations* making it an offence to disturb or destroy the nest of a migratory bird without a permit were held to be constitutional in New Brunswick Provincial Court.

61 *Wildlife Act*, R.S.C. 1985, c. W-9.

62 *Convention on Biological Diversity*, above note 50.

63 *Species at Risk Act*, S.C. 2002, c. 29 [*SARA*].

64 *Ibid.*, s. 6.

65 *CESD Report 2005*, above note 17, cc. 8 and 12.

traditional aboriginal knowledge of wildlife conservation to the assessment of the status of wildlife species considered to be at risk.[66] This assessment involves classifying such species according to the categories noted above, or determining that insufficient information is available to make the determination, or that the species is not at risk. *SARA* explains the classifications as follows:

> A species is **extirpated** if it no longer exists in the wild in Canada, but exists elsewhere in the wild.
>
> A species is **endangered** if it is facing imminent extirpation or extinction.
>
> A species is **threatened** if it is likely to become an endangered species if nothing is done to reverse the factors leading to its extirpation or extinction.
>
> A species is of **special concern** if it may become a threatened or endangered species because of a combination of biological characteristics and identified threats.[67]

COSEWIC's status assessment reports, including the reasons for the assessment, are included on a public registry provided for under *SARA*.[68] A further designation beyond the expert assessment of COSEWIC is required, however, before a species will be included on the List of Wildlife Species at Risk. This crucial determination is made by the Governor in Council or cabinet with reference to recommendations from the federal Minister of the Environment.[69] Only species "listed" in this way are eligible for the protective measures available under *SARA*.

When the initial listing decisions under *SARA* were made in 2004, some species assessed as being at risk by COSEWIC were not recommended for listing by the minister, and some species recommended for listing by the minister were not listed by cabinet. Guidelines to suggest criteria for decision making with regard to listing have been under development, but early decisions indicated that socio-economic considerations which are not part of the COSEWIC status assessment influenced the outcome in several cases including a ministerial recommendation against listing Cultus Lake and Sakinaw Lake sockeye salmon.[70]

---

66   *SARA*, above note 63, ss. 14–16.
67   *Ibid.*, s. 2.
68   *Ibid.*, s. 120. See online: www.sararegistry.gc.ca.
69   *Ibid.*, s. 27.
70   *CESD Report 2005*, above note 17, cc. 8 and 14.

Table14.2:   Canadian Species at Risk, January 2007

Category	Birds	Mammals	Fish	Reptiles	Molluscs	Vascular Plants	Lichens and Mosses	Amphibians and Arthropods	Totals
Extinct	3	2	6	0	1	0	1	0	13
Extirpated	2	3	4	4	2	2	1	4	22
Endangered	26	20	32	9	15	81	9	20	212
Threatened	12	17	26	13	3	50	4	11	136
Special Concern	22	26	37	10	4	32	10	10	151
Total	65	68	105	36	25	165	25	45	534

Online: www.cosewic.gc.ca/eng/sct0/rpt/rpt_csar_e.pdf

By way of protective measures, section 32 prohibits killing, harming, harassing, capturing, or taking "an individual of a wildlife species that is listed as an extirpated species, an endangered species, or a threatened species." Section 33 would prohibit the destruction of the "residence" of species at risk.

These safeguards are subject to significant limitations, however. In particular, the protections apply in the first instance only to federal lands — national parks, military bases and Indian reserves, for example. That is, the general prohibitions against harming listed species and their residences do not apply to those species on provincial lands unless a further designation is made by the Governor in Council extending the prohibitions to provincial lands after it has been determined that provincial laws do not effectively protect the species or their residences.[71] Moreover, as observers have critically noted, the concept of "residence" is of limited scope. Residence for purposes of *SARA* means a specific dwelling place, such as a den, nest, or other similar area, place or structure, that is occupied or habitually occupied by one or more individuals during all or part of their life cycles.[72] The residence of a species is therefore far more restricted in scope than its habitat.

SARA calls for the preparation of recovery strategies for extirpated, endangered or threatened species, assuming that such a strategy would

71   *SARA*, above note 63, s. 34. The prohibitions do apply automatically in the case of migratory birds and aquatic species.
72   Provisions for the protection of "critical habitat" are included elsewhere in the legislation where such habitat is identified in a recovery plan or action strategy for a listed species. See *ibid.*, ss. 57–64.

be "technically and biologically feasible."[73] While the requirement for recovery strategies in the interests of listed species has been welcomed, particularly because these may extend protection to critical habitat, observers note that implementation of recovery strategies in the form of action plans calls for a substantial and ongoing financial commitment.[74]

FURTHER READINGS

BEAZLEY, K., & R. BOARDMAN, *Politics of the Wild: Canada and Endangered Species* (Toronto: Oxford University Press, 2001)

HUMMEL, M., ed., *Protecting Canada's Endangered Spaces: An Owner's Manual* (Toronto: Key Porter, 1995)

HUNT, C., "The Public Trust Doctrine in Canada" in J. Swaigen, ed., *Environmental Rights in Canada* (Toronto: Butterworths, 1981)

KILLAN, G.F., *Protected Spaces: A History of Ontario's Provincial Parks System* (Toronto: Dundurn Press, 1993)

LEIBERMAN, S., "New Game in Town: Conservation Easements and Estate Planning" (1995) 14 E. & T.J. 309

PASSELAC-ROSS, MONIQUE, *Overview of Provincial Wildlife Laws*, Wildlife Law Paper No. 3 (Calgary: Canadian Institute of Resources Law, 2006)

SWAIGEN, JOHN, "Parks Legislation in Canada: A Comparison of the New *Canada National Parks Act* and Ontario's Existing *Provincial Parks Act*" (2000) 10 J. Envtl. L. & Prac. 223

VANDERZWAAG, DAVID, & JEFFREY A. HUTCHINGS, "Canada's Marine Species at Risk: Science and Law at the Helm, but a Sea of Uncertainties" (2005) 36 Ocean Devel. & Int'l L. 219

WALTON, JANICE H., *Blake's Canadian Law of Endangered Species*, looseleaf (Toronto: Carswell, 2007–)

---

73   *SARA, ibid.*, ss. 37–40.
74   For a survey of reservations that have been expressed about the effectiveness of *SARA*, see David L. Vanderzwaag & Jeffrey A. Hutchings, "Canada's Marine Species at Risk: Science and Law at the Helm, But a Sea of Uncertainties" (2005) 36 Ocean Devel. & and Int'l L. 219 at 224–37.

WATERS, D.W.M., "The Role of the Trust in Environmental Protection Law" in D.W.M. Waters, ed., *Equity, Fiduciaries and Trusts* (Toronto: Carswell, 1993)

WORLD COMMISSION ON ENVIRONMENT AND DEVELOPMENT, *Our Common Future* (Oxford: Oxford University Press, 1987) c. 6

ENVIRONMENTAL LAW AND THE CITIZEN

The importance of individual commitment to environmental protection cannot by overemphasized. As Mr. Justice Gonthier of the Supreme Court of Canada remarked not long ago, "[e]veryone is aware that individually and collectively, we are responsible for preserving the natural environment,"[1] and legislation is replete with such observations as "all persons should be responsible for the consequences to the environment of their actions,"[2] or with references to "the shared responsibility of all . . . citizens for ensuring the protection, enhancement and wise use of the environment through individual actions."[3] It should be understood that the foundation for these responsibilities is more than exhortation. In the words of two experienced students of environmental law, responsibilities are conceptually integrated with environmental rights:

> Since the correlative of rights is responsibility, if we have these rights we also have the responsibility to respect those rights in others and must be prepared for constraints on our own conduct. So there is a notion of duty or responsibility, in addition to the notion of entitlement.[4]

---

1   *R. v. Canadian Pacific Ltd.*, [1995] 2 S.C.R. 1028 at 1075.
2   *Environment Act*, S.Y. 1991, c. 5, s. 5(2)(e).
3   *Environmental Protection and Enhancement Act*, S.A. 1992, c. E-13.3, s. 2(f) [*AEPEA*].
4   E.L. Hughes & D. Iyalomhe, "Substantive Environmental Rights in Canada" (1998–99) 30 Ottawa L. Rev. 240.

How, apart from liability under pollution laws and other general environmental legislation, law promotes and facilitates environmentally responsible individual action is considered in this chapter primarily with reference to the automobile, household waste and energy efficiency, and the Environmental Choice program for consumers.

A. THE AUTOMOBILE

In 1994 at least one member of almost two-thirds of Canadian households commuted to work; for nearly 80 percent of these households, the motor vehicle was the preferred mode of travel, and the overall situation was very much the same in 2006.[5] Many and varied environmental effects of the automobile demonstrate linkages between individual behaviour and environmental quality. The equally varied responses demonstrate the complexity and the persistence of the challenge of reducing the environmental impact of a way of life.

In terms of impact, now intimately associated with greenhouse gas emissions, automobile traffic makes continuing demands on land-use priorities, leading to the destruction of agricultural and other rural lands and in general undermining environmental amenities. The long-term transformation of Toronto's Don River, as described by the Royal Commission on the Future of the Toronto Waterfront, is a dramatic illustration:

> Much of what was once a lovely valley is now a transportation corridor and a repository for road salt, dirty snow, and illegally dumped garbage. The river's lower stretch is strait-jacketed in steel and concrete, while chain-link fences discourage strolls along its degraded banks. Long gone is its natural mouth, an expansive delta that once teemed with life.[6]

In responding to the environmental issues raised by automobile use, Canadian governments utilize an array of instruments and incentives. Attempts to address the problem of automobile traffic volume have included improved public-transit services, dedicated lanes to favour multipassenger vehicles, and, on occasion, tax measures designed

---

5   Statistics Canada, *Households and the Environment, 1994* (Ottawa: Statistics Canada, 1995) at 14–15 [*Households, 1994*]; Statistics Canada, *Households and the Environment, 2006* (Ottawa: Statistics Canada, 2007) at 26 [*Households, 2006*].

6   Royal Commission on the Future of the Toronto Waterfront, *Regeneration: Toronto's Waterfront and the Sustainable City: Final Report* (Toronto: Queen's Printer, 1991) at 227 [*Regeneration*].

to promote alternative forms of transport such as bicycles. However, in the early 1990s the only province to see an increase in public-transit use by commuters was British Columbia, where the light-rail transit system was expanded on the lower mainland.[7] Serious consideration is being given in some settings to toll charges on designated routes or surcharges for travel during rush hour. Although planning and urban-design principles are gradually being reassessed with a view to reducing actual needs for transport, courts still emphasize the conventional utility of highway corridors. Thus, in *St. Pierre v. Ontario (Minister of Transportation & Communications)*, when plaintiffs, rural landowners whose retirement residence was adversely affected by the construction of a highway nearby, brought a nuisance claim, McIntyre J. remarked:

> In the balancing process inherent in the law of nuisance, their utility [highways] for the public good far outweighs the disruption and injury which is visited upon some adjoining lands.[8]

The issue of automobile fuels, once predominantly associated with concern about energy shortages and pricing, is also the subject of renewed interest in relation to vehicle-emission standards, since these have been seriously implicated in the threat of global warming from greenhouse gases.

Like other provinces, British Columbia requires sellers and operators of designated types or classes of motor vehicle to have pollution-control devices installed according to regulatory specifications.[9] The province subsequently instituted annual inspection and certification of exhaust emissions as a precondition of the licence-renewal process for designated classes of motor vehicles in certain parts of the province.[10] In southern Ontario, roughly three million vehicles have been tested in a comparable program known as Drive Clean. Approximately 85 percent of those vehicles passed the initial emissions assessment.[11]

British Columbia has also been at the forefront of Canadian efforts to accelerate the introduction of cleaner-technology vehicles on provincial roads. In 1992, the *Motor Vehicle Emissions Reduction Regulation*[12] made low-emission exhaust standards formulated by California's Air

---

7   *Households, 1994,* above note 5 at 15.
8   *St. Pierre v. Ontario (Minister of Transportation & Communications),* [1987] 1 S.C.R. 906 at 916.
9   *Motor Vehicle Act,* R.S.B.C. 1996, c. 318, s. 47.
10 *Ibid.,* ss. 45.1–45.3; B.C. Reg. 321/9.
11 See online: www.driveclean.com.
12 B.C. Reg. 517/95. Now see *Exhaust Emission Standards Regulation,* B.C. Reg. 274/2000.

Resources Board applicable to all vehicles sold in British Columbia as of 2001. Manufacturers were previously requested to submit proposals for the model years 1997–2000, setting out measures to reduce net greenhouse gas emissions in British Columbia. The regulation also called for the creation of an advisory committee on cleaner technology to promote the use of hybrid electric vehicles and vehicles meeting California's low-emission standards.

The statutory foundations of fleet-wide emissions requirements are currently under review in the context of B.C. Bill 39-2008, the proposed *Greenhouse Gas Reduction (Vehicle Emission Standards) Act*. A further provincial initiative in B.C. set out to promote emissions reduction through an incentive program designed to reduce the number of vehicles pre-dating 1988, when catalytic converters were first used on a comprehensive basis. British Columbia's AirCare program, the first in the country, reports a 31 percent reduction in vehicle emissions for the period 1992–2006.[13]

Fuel-emission standards were strengthened significantly during the 1980s (lead was virtually eliminated[14]) although some anomalies remain. There has been less progress in relation to greenhouse gases originating in automobile use although attention is shifting towards this problem. Federal legislation also authorized the regulation of vehicle fuel-consumption standards, but until recently the power remained dormant.[15] Other measures have been instituted to promote oil recycling as a means of reducing the amount of used oil dumped in garages and yards across the country.[16]

Even after its useful life has come to an end, the conventional automobile presents environmental challenges and risks. The 1990 tire fire at Hagersville, Ontario, showed the hazardous implications of an accumulation of used tires that are ordinarily treated or classified as waste and brought within the overall regulatory framework for waste handling.[17]

---

13 Online: www.aircare.ca.

14 *Gasoline Regulations*, S.O.R./90-247. For further developments in relation to planned fuel-emission standards, see *Canada Gazette* (17 February 2001).

15 *Motor Vehicle Fuel Consumption Standards Act*, R.S.C. 1985, c. M-9, s. 3. The 2007 federal budget proposed a rebate to the purchasers of automobiles meeting a fuel-efficiency standard of 6.5 litres per 100 kilometres.

16 Hon. R. Grier, *Speaking Notes for Official Launch of Used Oil Depot Network* (21 September 1992).

17 Considerable litigation resulted from the Hagarsville incident: see *Ontario (A.G.) v. Tyre King Tyre Recycling Ltd.* (1992), 9 O.R. (3d) 318 (Gen. Div.); *Pilot Insurance Co. v. Tyre King Tyre Recycling Ltd.* (1992), 8 O.R. (3d) 236 (Gen. Div.); *Re Straza* (1992), 9 C.E.L.R. (N.S.) 314 (O.E.A.B.). See, generally, R.R.O. 1990,

Tire taxes have been introduced in several jurisdictions as a possible means of directing remedial resources at a specific problem.[18] Despite the attractiveness of the principle involved, the latter measures encountered considerable resistance at the administrative level, and only limited benefits appear to have been obtained.

In 1995 Manitoba designated motor vehicle tires under provisions of the *Waste Reduction and Prevention Act*[19] and provided for a Tire Stewardship Board with responsibility for establishing and administering a scrap tire waste-reduction and prevention program (WRAP).[20] Levies of $2.80 on each new tire are directed to a fund that will finance the scrap tire WRAP program and associated expenditures including research and education initiatives.[21] Ontario, with more than five million tires stockpiled and awaiting appropriate handling and disposal, also explored fees for tire stewardship and other initiatives.

Other automobile components such as air-conditioning units present a noteworthy post-consumer threat to the ozone layer as CFCs from cooling units leak out into the atmosphere. With respect to the challenge of CFCs and related chemicals, while the automobile represents only one element of the problem, significant efforts are under way to reduce or eliminate the use and release of these chemicals into the atmosphere. Steps taken in Ontario and British Columbia, among other provinces, to regulate automobile air-conditioning, servicing, and disposal practices, and eventually to eliminate designated chemicals from new vehicles, illustrate alternative means of achieving these objectives.[22] More generally, the automobile CFC process illustrates the way in which global concerns addressed internationally by means of

---

Reg. 347, s. 2(1)(9) and *Baldwin Rubber Recycler and Stephen Sager v. Ontario (Ministry of the Environment)*, [2001]O.E.R.T.D. No. 21.

18   *Retail Sales Tax Amendment Act, 1989 (No. 2)*, S.O. 1989, c. 38, s. 3; *Environment Tax Act*, S.P.E.I. 1991, c. 9; *Sustainable Environment Fund Act*, S.B.C. 1990, c. 27, s. 11. The Multi-Materials Stewardship Board of Newfoundland and Labrador embarked upon a scrap tire management program in 2001.

19   C.C.S.M. c. W40.

20   *Tire Stewardship Regulation*, Man. Reg. 33/95. See also *Scrap Tire Management Regulations*, R.R.S., c. E-10.2, Reg. 9 and *Tire Designation Regulation*, Alta. Reg. 95/2004 .

21   An earlier B.C. initiative along similar lines was successfully challenged on the grounds that it had been implemented on the basis of policy rather than by means of a regulation-making power that had been provided within the *Waste Management Act* for this purpose. *Valley Rubber Resources Inc. v. British Columbia (Minister of Environment, Lands and Parks)*, [2001] B.C.J. No. 629 (S.C.).

22   *Ozone Depleting Substances Regulation*, B.C. Reg. 53/93; *Ozone Depleting Substances and Other Halocarbons Regulation*, Man. Reg. 178/2005.

conventions and protocols have begun to have a direct impact on the operations of manufacturers, service personnel, and consumers.

B. THE HOME ENVIRONMENT

Initiatives directed at environmental problems emerging from residential settings often combine financial incentives with regulation and other inducements to lessen the cumulative environmental impact of contemporary lifestyles. While the most comprehensive reductions in residential environmental impacts will ultimately result from collective planning and land-use decisions to reduce urban sprawl and the associated burden of infrastructure requirements, and energy use, especially for transportation, the design of individual homes is also an important influence. Energy Solutions Alberta in association with Climate Change Central, a public-private partnership, offers information and advice to homeowners or prospective purchasers on a wide range of energy-saving and pollution-reducing innovations. These run from solar housing projects through transportation options to advice on detergents and Christmas lights.[23] Residential construction is itself a major contributor to the waste burden. Thus, some jurisdictions have taken steps to recover costs associated with the disposal of such materials as construction and demolition waste.[24]

Some measures to lessen residential environmental impacts are directed toward individual behaviour while others address the characteristics of household products and appliances at the point of manufacture and distribution. Waste reduction and energy-efficiency initiatives are often emphasized.

The importance of waste reduction for sustainable development is suggested by primary statistics. The residential, commercial, and non-hazardous industrial waste streams, which together constitute Canada's municipal garbage, amounted during the late 1980s to approximately 35 million metric tonnes each year.[25] As more graphically stated by *Regeneration: Toronto's Waterfront and the Sustainable City*, "every year, homes, institutions, industries and commercial establishments in the GTA [Greater Toronto Area] produce 4.5 million tonnes (5 million

---

23   Online: www.energysolutionsalberta.com; www.climatechangecentral.com.
24   See for example, Quebec's *Regulation respecting the charges payable for the disposal of residual materials*, R.Q. c. Q-2, r.18.1.3.
25   S. Shrybman, "Reducing Solid Waste" in *Report of the Canadian Bar Association Committee on Sustainable Development in Canada: Options for Law Reform* (Ottawa: Canadian Bar Association, 1990) at 113.

tons) of garbage—enough to fill six SkyDomes to the roof."[26] Another perspective highlighting the enormous environmental importance of certain forms of waste reduction is indicated by a commentary on the benefits of recycling aluminum soft drink cans:

> First, recycling these containers conserves very large amounts of energy and raw materials. Second, the extraction and processing of the raw materials needed to make new cans release large quantities of pollutants and greenhouse gases. In 2003, the World Watch Institute estimated that making 1 million tonnes of aluminum cans from virgin materials requires 4.95 million tonnes of bauxite ore and the energy equivalent of 35 million barrels of crude oil. Recycling the cans, in comparison, saves all of the bauxite and more than 75 per cent of the pollutants. Recycling just one aluminum can saves enough electricity to run a laptop computer for 4 hours. [27]

Various elements of the household component of the waste stream invite different treatment and responses. For example, significant efforts are now made to encourage the redirection of organic materials to composting either on a residential basis or at community composting facilities. Nearly 40 percent of British Columbia households composted in 1994, but this level of participation was almost double the national average of 22.7 percent. By 2006, the national average participation in composting had risen to 27 percent, a figure that encapsulates a wide range from 70 percent participation in Halifax down to below 10 percent in Quebec City.[28]

Perhaps the most visible symbol of environmental responsibility at the individual level are blue box recycling programs, implemented on an experimental basis in Kitchener, Ontario, in 1981 and subsequently introduced in other communities in various jurisdictions across Canada.[29] The original curbside recycling programs have become increasingly sophisticated. Once confined to private residences in urban settings, they have been introduced to multi-unit apartment complexes and in a growing number of rural communities. Once operated on the

---

26   *Regeneration*, above note 6 at 28.
27   Environmental Commissioner of Ontario, *Annual Report, 2003-2004: Choosing Our Legacy* (Toronto: Environmental Commissioner of Ontario, 2004) at 81.
28   *Households, 1994* above note 5 at 9 and *Households, 2006* above note 5 at 19–20.
29   For background information on the development and introduction of recycling programs and the optional design features available, see V.W. MacLaren, "Waste Management: Current Crisis and Future Challenge" in B. Mitchell, ed., *Resource Management and Development: Addressing Conflict and Uncertainty* (Toronto: Oxford University Press, 1991) 38.

assumption of voluntary participation, they are now occasionally implemented as mandatory programs. Once restricted to a limited range of recyclable materials including newsprint, glass, and tin cans, they have diversified to accept a wider range of recyclables. Once premised on the hope that markets for recycled material would emerge on the basis of reliable supply, the programs have subsequently attempted to address structural obstacles to the creation of markets. All these developments have taken place in the context of an ongoing debate about the relationship among reduction, reuse, and recycling as long-term strategies to deal with waste. In Alberta, a recycling fund was established to administer waste minimization and recycling programs and to encourage related educational and research activities.[30] To promote recycling, regulations made blue box management systems compulsory in designated Ontario municipalities. Additional measures to promote composting and the diversion of household and yard waste from landfill were implemented simultaneously.[31]

Despite high participation levels (especially in relation to paper recycling), blue box programs have encountered some criticism. The need for supplementary financial support for recycling where markets are not readily available or where prices remain below collection costs has presented challenges. Manitoba, under the Manitoba Product Stewardship Plan, arranged funding by means of a levy on newspapers and on beverage containers (other than dairy product containers and containers to which a deposit-refund scheme applies.)[32] In Ontario, where refillable bottles have been heavily displaced by cans and plastic containers, the industry contributed direct financial support to the Blue Box program. Pursuant to the *Waste Diversion Act*, companies responsible for paper and packaging in the consumer marketplace ("stewards") are expected to finance half the net cost of the municipal Blue Box waste diversion program.[33]

Another focus has been on an actual reduction in the level of curbside deposits. Thus, proposals to charge for waste collection have

---

30 *AEPEA*, above note 3, s. 164.

31 O. Reg. 101/94. See also *Waste Management Act*, R.S.B.C. 1996, c. 482, requiring municipal waste-management plans, including provisions for recycling.

32 *Waste Reduction and Prevention Act*, above note 19; *Multi-Material Stewardship (Interim Measures) Regulation*, Man. Reg. 39/95.

33 *Waste Diversion Act*, S.O. 2002, c. 6, s. 25(2); O. Reg. 273/02; online:www. bottlebill.org/legislation/canada/ontario.htm; www. stewardshipontario.ca. A comparable arrangement respecting the apportionment of recycling costs exists in Quebec where Eco Entreprises Quebec, on behalf of the container and packaging industries, contributes to municipal associations representing the municipal operators of curbside recycling programs.

emerged in some settings. These arrangements typically require the purchase of a tag or sticker which must be affixed to garbage bags set out for collection, or perhaps the use of specially marked bags. The arrangements may provide that all household waste be accompanied by confirmation of payment, or the system may permit a base level of one or more bags to be collected from each household before charges apply. In Peterborough, Ontario, a proposal for user fees was advanced in part to provide an incentive for the separation of recyclables, and in part to ensure more appropriate revenue contributions from users. Although this plan was defeated in a municipal referendum, amendments to the *Municipal Act* later confirmed the authority of municipalities to charge user fees in lieu of property rates for services.[34] User-pay approaches have been introduced in several other communities. The city of Edmonton introduced an elaborate curbside collection program as early as 1989 to provide for the pickup of about a dozen separate categories of household waste, and began to explore user-pay alternatives.[35]

Despite refinement and extension, the effectiveness as well as the cost of the blue box or curbside approach have been questioned, particularly in comparison with deposit/refund systems to promote reuse. The latter approach adds a direct economic incentive to reinforce the essentially voluntary underpinnings of curbside recycling. On the basis of effectiveness, that is, recovery rates, the western Canadian provinces resisted pressure from soft drink manufacturers to replace their established deposit/refund systems with curbside recycling. Instead, modifications to these systems were examined with a view to reducing the inequities and inconvenience associated with the chain of relationships among bottlers, distributors, retailers, and consumers.[36] In Nova Scotia, a deposit-refund scheme for beverage containers involving a series of payments linking distributors, retailers, and consumers was challenged on the grounds that it constituted an indirect tax that was outside the constitutional jurisdiction of the province. The Nova Scotia Court of Appeal concluded that the arrangement was within the

34   Now see *Municipal Act, 2001*, S.O. 2001, c. 25, Part XII "Fees and Charges."

35   MacLaren, above note 29 at 41. For further information on innovations in Edmonton, see City of Edmonton, Waste Management Centre, "The Edmonton Composting Facility", online: www.edmonton.ca/Environment/WasteManagement/CompostingWasteFacts.pdf.

36   For background discussion, see Recycling Council of British Columbia, *Reiterate: The Newsletter of the Recycling Council of British Columbia* (October 1992). Current arrangements are found in the *Beverage Container Stewardship Program Regulation*, B.C. Reg. 406/97. See also New Brunswick's *Beverage Containers Act*, S.N.B. 1991, c. B-2-2.

powers of the provincial legislature to enact as it was merely ancillary to a valid regulatory scheme.[37] Recycling as a strategy has also been questioned in relation to other materials, notably household hazardous wastes and packaging.

Several individual initiatives addressed the use and disposal of corrosive, toxic, flammable, and reactive consumer products that collectively constitute household hazardous waste (HHW). British Columbia's Waste Reduction Commission, for example, formulated a discussion paper on HHW strategy that reviewed both consumer-based and producer-based approaches to the problem. On the consumer side, the strategy identified several alternative approaches to collection and deposit arrangements, but it placed greater emphasis on the principle of product stewardship, which may be promoted through taxes, deposit/refund systems, or industry levies reinforced through regulation. Yet, in a conclusion similar to that reached in most other jurisdictions where the threats posed by HHW have been carefully examined, British Columbia's discussion paper argued that

> HHW is, first and foremost, a problem of *source reduction or product/ material substitution* . . . . The primary challenge is to increase source reduction and product/material substitution in order to reduce the amount of material entering the HHW stream.[38]

In British Columbia the brand-owners and sellers of consumer paint products (whether the coatings are latex, oil, or solvent-based) are responsible for ensuring that an approved post-consumer paint-stewardship program is in place.[39] Such stewardship programs provide for the collection, transportation, and final treatment of post-consumer paint and are expected to incorporate pollution-prevention principles by moving progressively from treatment or containment to recovery of energy, recycling, or reuse. Similar initiatives were subsequently introduced in relation to solvents, pesticides, gasoline, and pharmaceuticals in British Columbia.[40] Saskatchewan amended *The Environmental Man-*

---

37 *Cape Breton Beverages v. Nova Scotia (A.G.)* (1997), 24 C.E.L.R. (N.S.) 319 (N.S.C.A.).

38 British Columbia, Ministry of Environment, Lands and Parks, Toxic Reduction Branch, Environmental Protection Division, *Household Hazardous Waste Strategy* (Discussion Paper) (March 1993) at 6.

39 *Post-Consumer Paint Stewardship Program Regulation*, B.C. Reg. 200/94. For its part, the federal government has moved to reduce the initial presence of hazardous substances such as lead and mercury in products entering the home environment. See *Surface Coating Materials Regulation*, S.O.R./2005-109.

40 *Post Consumer Residual Stewardship Program*, B.C. Reg. 111/97.

agement and Protection Act to provide for comparable product-management programs.[41]

So called e-wastes associated with electronic devices pose distinctive and increasing challenges. To reduce the volume of these materials finding their way to landfills, the CCME has formulated Canada-Wide Principles for Electronics Stewardship and targeted responses have been contemplated. Alberta, for example, has introduced fees on computers and televisions sold in the province. These charges help to offset costs that must be borne somehow in relation to collecting, transporting and recycling the metal and chemical components of modern consumer technology.[42] While televisions and computers may be the most readily imagined examples of e-waste, the category extends to other audio-visual equipment, telecommunications devices, a range of products associated with sports and leisure pursuits, as well as numerous tools, navigational instruments and so on. An emerging focus of concern is the environmental impact of pharmaceuticals and a wide range of personal care products. These have been associated with abnormalities in aquatic species and initiatives have been introduced to reduce the volume of unused products entering the municipal waste stream en route to land fill or simply being flushed away in the course of household cleaning.[43]

Both the federal and provincial governments have enacted legislation to foster more efficient use of energy. At the national level, the *Energy Efficiency Act* provides for standard-setting, testing, research, and promotional initiatives to encourage the efficient use of energy and the use of alternative energy sources. Those involved in the manufacture, importation, sale, or leasing of energy-using products are required to ensure that such products comply with prescribed standards and labelling requirements.[44]

In parliamentary debate, the minister of energy, mines, and resources highlighted the advantages to be anticipated from the initiative:

---

41   *The Environmental Management and Protection Act, 2002*, S.S. 2002, c. E-10.21, ss. 38(1)(w.1)(iii)–(viii).

42   Alberta's environmental fees have been applicable to televisions and computers since 1 February 2005 under a program administered by the Alberta Recycling Management Authority. See online: www.albertarecycling.ca.

43   Environmental Commissioner of Ontario, *Annual Report 2004-2005: Planning Our Landscape* (Toronto: Environmental Commissioner of Ontario, 2005) at 179–85.

44   *Energy Efficiency Act*, S.C. 1992, c. 36 and *Energy Efficiency Regulations*, S.O.R./94-651. Amendments proposed in 2007 would facilitate the phasing out of most uses of incandescent lighting by 2012 and strengthen packaging requirements to enhance consumer understanding of included information.

By being energy efficient, Canadian consumers can reduce energy expenditures and businesses can become more competitive. Moreover, being energy efficient helps to improve air quality, to preserve water and land resources, and to reduce greenhouse gas emissions.[45]

While accepting these attractions and the desirability of federal legislation along the lines proposed, most participants in the parliamentary debates regarded the government's initiative as too limited a response to present circumstances. Speakers were particularly sceptical about the government's commitment in light of severe reductions in financing for energy conservation and renewable energy that had occurred during the preceding half-decade.[46]

Residential appliances and equipment have been an important focus of attention.[47] Ontario's *Energy Efficiency Act* specifically identified central air conditioners, clothes dryers, clothes washers, dishwashers, freezers, furnaces, heat pumps, ovens, ranges, refrigerators, room air conditioners, pool heaters, and water heaters as appliances to which provincial energy-efficiency standards will apply.[48] Quebec more generally defined "appliance" as "any new household, commercial, industrial or institutional electrical or hydrocarbon-fuelled appliance."[49] The House of Commons Standing Committee on Environment and Sustainable Development clearly envisaged an even broader effort, arguing that "energy efficiency should be more important in Canada than in other countries, and must be our first priority."[50]

C. GREEN MARKETING AND ENVIRONMENTAL CHOICE

Next we consider the position of the citizen as consumer, one illustration of the potential of pricing and markets to promote environmental

---

45 *House of Commons Debates* (20 February 1992) at 7421.

46 Between 1984 and 1990–91, federal spending on conservation and renewables dropped from $500 million to $30 million.

47 *Energy Efficiency Regulations*, S.O.R./94-651. See also Natural Resources Canada, *Report to Canada on the Administration and Enforcement of the Energy Efficiency Act 1994–95* (Ottawa: Supply & Services, 1995).

48 *Energy Efficiency Act*, R.S.O. 1990, c. E.17.

49 *An Act Respecting the Energy Efficiency of Electrical or Hydrocarbon-Fuelled Appliances*, R.S.Q. c.E-12, s. 1. Other provincial legislation includes the *Energy Efficiency Act*, R.S.B.C. 1996, c. 114; the *Energy-efficient Appliances Act*, S.N.S. 1991, c. 2, and the *Energy Efficiency Act*, S.N.B. 1992, c. E-9.11.

50 House of Commons, Standing Committee on Environment, *Out of Balance: The Risks of Irreversible Climate Change* (Ottawa: Queen's Printer, 1991) at 27.

benefits.[51] David Cohen, in examining arguments that are used to support the privatization of environmental protection through market-based incentives, identifies an underlying assumption that is directly relevant to the issue of green consumerism:

> Using markets to deliver environmental quality assumes that there is a substantial number of individuals who are demanding improvements in their local and global environments, and who will express that demand in their economic decisions. The vast untapped demand for environmental benefits can be harnessed to the dynamically efficient and creative engine of industry for the benefit of us all. Capital markets, industrial commodity, inventory and capital equipment markets, consumer markets and labour markets can all be exploited to deliver the environmental goods, it is said.[52]

Viewing the issue directly from the perspective of environmental quality, Cohen explains:

> The decision to privatize environmental regulation, thereby using the market to deliver environmental benefits, recognizes that through all of our personal, professional, and corporate decisions we are continuously creating and transforming the environment. The use of markets to deliver environmental benefits recognizes that consumers are environmental planners.[53]

There has been considerable debate about whether environmental considerations do, in fact, enter into the calculus of Canadian consumers of goods and services. It was suggested a decade ago, for example, that environmental considerations are relevant on a regular or continuous basis to only about 15 percent of Canadian food shoppers, leading one commentator to conclude:

> [W]hile on one hand the public expects businesses to improve their environmental performance, on the other hand, there has been no modification of consumption patterns to show support for this process. Consumers therefore fail to create demand for increasingly "greener" products and services. As a result, non-environmental consumer behaviour slackens the pace of environmental improvement.[54]

---

51   See chapter 17.
52   D.S. Cohen, "The Regulation of Green Advertising: The State, the Market and the Environmental Good" (1991) 25 U.B.C. L. Rev. at 228, n. 10.
53   *Ibid.* at 230.
54   Lila Barrera-Hernandez, "Consumer Behaviour and the Environment: An Environmental Law and Policy Approach" (1995) 5 J. Envtl. L. & Prac. 161 at 162.

More recent indications suggest that environmental consumerism is a more robust phenomenon. In the food sector, the demand for "organic" items has grown substantially. And, in relation to consumer electronic goods, by 2005, according to a Pollara survey, 88 percent of Canadians were prepared to pay more for such goods if they were more energy efficient, or generally less wastefully produced, or were produced using recycled materials.[55] Major retailers in other sectors have responded with initiatives intended to satisfy the expectations of more environmentally-conscious shoppers. In the service sector as well, programs are emerging to advise users of hotel or marina facilities, for example, that their environmental concerns are being addressed.[56] Apart from the theoretical base and these somewhat anecdotal illustrations, the policy-making challenge in employing market mechanisms to enhance environmental protection raises a number of issues around information, the reliability of that information, and mechanisms for communicating it to potential purchasers of goods and services. Consumers can be well meaning and wrong, just as one can be incapable of acting on a latent disposition to contribute to a better environment (even at some personal cost or sacrifice) because of unavailable or unreliable information. Regulated standards relating to disclosure or product-performance characteristics and approved-use and disposal practices were introduced to overcome some of these types of deficiencies.

The Environmental Choice[57] initiative was announced in 1988 and dubbed by one observer a variation on the "good housekeeping seals of approval."[58] Following identification of environmental considerations relevant to particular product categories and the formulation of performance guidelines, time-limited licences to use the "ecologo" were issued to applicants whose products complied with the established standards. The relevant criteria were not without controversy as commentators point variously to the importance of production considerations, characteristics associated with actual use, and concerns around

---

55   Sharp Canada, online: www.sharp.ca/pdf/release_Think_Green_mar3.pdf.

56   The Canadian hotel industry has developed a "Green Leaf" eco-rating program. Marina operators are involved in a comparable initiative. See online: www. marinasontario.com/clean_marine_marinas.asp.

57   For general information on the original framework of the Environmental Choice program, see Environment Canada, *Environmental Choice Program: Certification Overview* (Ottawa: Environment Canada, 2001).

58   M. Rankin, "Economic Incentives for Environmental Protection: Some Canadian Approaches" (1991) 1 J.Envtl. L. & Prac. 256. These programs are by no means confined to the Canadian market. See, for an international survey, the U.S. E.P.A. study *Environmental Labelling Issues, Policies and Practices Worldwide* (Washington, DC: Environmental Protection Agency, 1998).

ultimate disposal, noting that these are often difficult to determine, and perhaps even more difficult to compare. Even if relevant information on alternative products and alternative production processes has been developed, it is typically in the hands of private manufacturers who, for reasons of competitive advantage and on the basis of their research investment, will be reluctant to place it into general circulation.[59] Once certified or approved, licensees pay fees and submit to ongoing monitoring on the assumption that the logo will contribute to sales by attracting environmentally sensitive consumers. Purchasers presumably enjoy environmental satisfaction and are relieved of the otherwise burdensome tasks of searching for and assessing information.

The range of products and services certified under the Environmental Choice program was limited at the outset. Initial categories included re-refined motor oil; insulation made from recycled wood-based cellulose fibre; products made from recycled plastic; reduced-pollution water-based paints; fine paper made from recycled paper; newsprint made from recycled paper; reduced-pollution solvent-based paints; reusable cloth diapers; residential composters; ethanol-blended gasoline; reusable shopping bags; water conserving devices; and rechargeable batteries. The range of products has continued to expand, and alternative forms of certification emerged more recently when administration of the eco-labelling program was placed in the hands of an environmental marketing firm.[60]

One subject of particular significance in light of market growth is the use of the descriptor "organic." Controls on the use of the term were initially absent, allowing producers to self-declare. This era was followed by a more generalized set of characteristics developed by producer associations with a view to standardizing the concept to a greater degree. Most recently, the Canadian Food Inspection Agency has put forward a proposed regulatory framework to deal with continuing uncertainties through the creation of a "Canada organic" standard.[61] For

---

59   For a brief survey of issues associated with environmental standard-setting for labelling programs, see Kathryn Harrison, "Promoting Environmental Protection Through Eco-Labelling: An Evaluation of Canada's Environmental Choice Program" in Kernaghan Webb, ed., *Voluntary Codes: Private Governance, the Public Interest and Innovation* (Ottawa: Carleton University, 2004) 279–82.

60   TerraChoice Environmental Marketing.

61   CFIA, *Organic Products Regulation*, Canada Gazette Part I (2 September 2006). For additional information, see "Organic Production Systems—General Principles and Management Standards," online: www.tpsgc-pwgsc.gc.ca/cgsb/ on_the_net/organic/032_0310_2006-e.pdf.

its part, the government of British Columbia has established authority to control the manner and circumstances in which environmental
labels or certification may be used.[62]

The initiatives noted in this chapter are merely representative of
ways in which modifications in individual behaviour—induced through
informal mechanisms and education, or encouraged by changes in the
legal framework—have significant potential to lessen environmental
damage and reduce high levels of personal resource consumption.

FURTHER READINGS

BARTENSTEIN, K. & S. LAVALLÉE, "L'écolabel est-il un outil du protec-
tionnisme vert?" (2003) 44 C. de D. 361

COHEN, D., "Procedural Fairness and Incentive Programs: Reflections
on the Environmental Choice Program" (1993) 31 Alta. L. Rev.
544

DOELLE, M., "IT Waste Management in Canada: From Cost Recovery
to Resource Conservation?" (2006) 5 C.J.L.T. 59

HAGEN, PAUL E., "Product-based Environmental Regulations: Europe
Sets the Pace" (2006) 6 Sustainable Development Law and Policy
63

MACLAREN, V.W., "Individualized Waste Management: Integrated
Approaches" in Bruce Mitchell, ed., *Resource and Environmental
Management in Canada*, 3d ed. (Don Mills, ON: Oxford University
Press, 2004) 371

STATISTICS CANADA, *Households and the Environment 1994* (Ottawa:
Industry, Science & Technology, 1995)

URMETZER, P., *et al.*, Solutions to Environmental Problems: The Case
of Automobile Pollution" (1999) 25 Canadian Public Policy

WEBB, K., ed., *Voluntary Codes: Private Governance, the Public Interest
and Innovation* (Ottawa: Carleton Research Unit for Innovation,
Science and Environment Carleton University, 2004)

---

62   *Environmental Management Act*, S.B.C. 2003, c. 53, s. 118.

WINFIELD, M., *et al.*, *Looking Back and Looking Ahead: Municipal Solid Waste Management in Ontario from the 1983 Blue Print to 50 percent Diversion in 2000* (Toronto: Canadian Institute for Environmental Law and Policy, 1992)

CHAPTER 16

CONSULTATION, ALTERNATIVE DISPUTE RESOLUTION, AND VOLUNTARY MEASURES

Interest in innovative mechanisms for managing environmental conflicts has been stimulated by distinctive features of environmental decision making, notably those related to the element of uncertainty, and by the limitations of conventional forms of adjudication. Court-based proceedings, either civil or criminal, in which legal adversaries endeavour to persuade decision makers, who often lack environmental or scientific experience, that a particular standard of proof of controversial and uncertain scientific hypotheses has or has not been met, are both costly and slow. The scope for participation by interested parties who are not immediately affected by the matters in question is typically constrained by rules of standing, and the comparatively narrow range of remedial powers traditionally available to judicial decision makers has often frustrated the design of appropriate solutions. Administrative decision making by officials, boards, and tribunals is typically more flexible, but it often remains cumbersome and unsatisfying as well as being vulnerable to the complexities of judicial review. Further pressures for new approaches derive from financial constraints that severely restrict the ability of governments to pursue traditional enforcement strategies culminating in prosecution.

Several procedures associated with new forms of participation, or even "social learning" have been seen as increasingly attractive. Such approaches "emphasizing dialogue, mutual learning, and the continual evolution of ideas" are considered well-suited to "circumstances characterized by high uncertainty," for only arrangements of this type "enable individuals, organizations and communities to construct legitimate end points, identify appropriate technologies for reaching those end points, and navigate through the complexities of human-nature interactions."[1]

In the context of disputes, several mechanisms under the umbrella of alternative dispute resolution (ADR) have become quite common. Negotiation between or among interested parties, though certainly not a recent innovation, and mediation involving a disinterested third party are prominent examples. In addition, experiments with other mechanisms such as round tables, co-management councils, and commissions have been used to avoid conflicts or to minimize their scope and consequences.

A. CONSULTATIVE PROCEDURES AND THE ROUND TABLE MOVEMENT

As discussed elsewhere in this text, environmental assessment processes, environmental bills of rights, intervenor status, standing rules, and so on facilitate public participation especially in relation to specific projects or development initiatives.[2] But as Canada's National Task Force on Environment and Economy has emphasized, the participatory aspirations of constituencies such as business, labour, aboriginal peoples, and environmentalists extend beyond the project level to include an interest in the fundamental policy-making and planning processes that determine the framework for more concrete initiatives. The task force recommended that senior decision makers from these diverse groups be involved in a new process of consultations known as "round tables." It explained that

> [t]his process must involve individuals who exercise influence over policy and planning decisions and who can bring information and different views to the debate. The process should be designed to work towards consensus and to exert direct influence on policy and decision makers at the highest levels of government, industry, and non-government organizations.[3]

---

1   Alan Diduck, "Incorporating Participatory Approaches and Social Learning" in Bruce Mitchell, ed., *Resource and Environmental Management in Canada*, 3d ed. (Don Mills, ON: Oxford University Press, 2004) at 498.

2   For examples from the environmental assessment context, see Canadian Environmental Assessment Agency, "Reports from Consultation Activities" (Ottawa: CEAA, 2001), online: www.ceaa.gc.ca/index_e.htm.

3   Canadian Council of Resource and Environment Ministers, *Report of the National Task Force on Environment and Economy* (Downsview, ON: Canadian Council of Resource and Environment Ministers, 1987) at 10.

On the basis of deliberations concerning environment-economy issues, task force members concluded that round tables — each of which would include environment, resource, and economic development ministers — should make recommendations "directly to the First Ministers of their respective jurisdictions."[4]

Endorsement by a national task force whose membership included Cabinet ministers from seven jurisdictions contributed to the rapid adoption of the proposal. Round tables, however, were not implemented on a uniform basis across Canada, and some early observers doubted the ability of these new institutions as originally constituted to remedy the deficiencies that inspired their creation:

> [O]nly a few of the Round Tables are structured, composed, and mandated in such a way that they could reasonably be expected to legitimize the environmental policy process through enhanced representation and participation of non-corporate actors in the process of environmental policy formulation and implementation.[5]

Supporters emphasized the contribution of consensus-building and the benefits of the exchange of ideas, as well as the possibility of furthering mid-stream transformation of outlook without having to wait for intergenerational changes in leadership. Indeed, in announcing the membership of the National Round Table on the Environment and the Economy (NRTEE), Prime Minister Mulroney anticipated that "this new organization will help us all re-think how we make decisions, personally and within institutions, that affect our common environment."[6]

In 1993 legislative measures were taken to formalize the status of the National Round Table. As expressed in the statute, the Round Table's role is to be that of catalyst in identifying, explaining, and promoting the principles and practices of sustainable development through the following initiatives:

(a) undertaking research and gathering information and analyses on critical issues of sustainable development;

(b) advising governments on ways of integrating environmental and economic considerations into their decision-making processes and on global issues of sustainable development;

---

4   Ibid.

5   M. Howlett, "The Round Table Experience: Representation and Legitimacy in Canadian Environmental Policy-Making" (1990) 97 Queen's Quarterly 580 at 588.

6   Prime Minister's Office, Release, "Membership of National Round Table on Environment and Economy Announced" (28 March 1989).

(c) advising those sectors and regions on ways of incorporating principles and practices of sustainable development into their activities;

(d) promoting the understanding and increasing public awareness of the cultural, social, economic, and policy changes required to attain sustainable development; and

(e) facilitating and assisting cooperative efforts in Canada to overcome barriers to the attainment of sustainable development.[7]

The NRTEE has developed its mandate imaginatively and comprehensively over the years. Among projects of particular interest is a collaborative initiative with Statistics Canada on enviromental and sustainable development indicators. NRTEE anticipates that such indicators have the potential to assist environmental policy making in the same way that economic indicators contribute to economic and fiscal management.[8]

"Stakeholder" bodies similar to the NRTEE were established at the provincial level, though not always with the same durability, and the model has been adopted at the local level in several jurisdictions. The evolution of multi-stakeholder forums involves structural changes in participation. These bodies accommodate a greater range of interests and to some degree even suggest a transformation in philosophical attitudes towards a policy-making process in which the state no longer serves as the exclusive representative of environmental interests; instead, environmental groups and individuals would assume direct involvement.[9]

B. ALTERNATIVE DISPUTE RESOLUTION PROCEDURES

Processes of alternative dispute resolution, notably negotiation and mediation, are now regularly employed to assist in the resolution of environmental disputes. Possibilities for negotiation exist throughout the environmental regime, some more and some less attractive, depending

7   *National Round Table on the Environment and the Economy Act*, S.C. 1993, c. 31, s. 4.

8   NRTEE, *Environment and Sustainable Development Indicators for Canada* (Ottawa: NRTEE, 2003). Other areas in which the NRTEE has pursued collaborative and consultative initiatives include brownfields redevelopment, aboriginal interests in resource development, sustainable transportation, and regional environmental governance of the boreal forest.

9   G. Hoberg, "Governing the Environment: Comparing Canada and the United States" in K. Banting, G. Hoberg, & R. Simeon, eds., *Degrees of Freedom: Canada and the United States in a Changing World* (Montreal: McGill-Queen's University Press, 1997) at 341.

on the perspective of the observer. Negotiations are common in relation to the formulation and issuance of licences, approvals, or administrative orders.[10] This appears to some as a desirable means of providing for effective consultation and of ensuring flexibility and responsiveness in decisions that might otherwise be rigid and inappropriate. On the other hand, there are those who caution that bargaining between regulators and industry may constitute an abdication on the part of the former and an effort at manipulation on the part of the latter. In the context of non-compliance with the possibility of prosecution under contemplation, further negotiations are likely concerning remedial measures and the form of administrative orders.

Negotiations about environmental matters take place in settings other than licensing and prosecutorial confrontations. For example, a process approximating what is known in the U.S. context as negotiated rule-making was utilized in the original development of regulations under the *Canadian Environmental Assessment Act*. Representatives of several federal departments, provincial governments, and various industry associations, public-interest organizations, and aboriginal groups deliberated extensively in connection with the development of a set of regulations known as the Law List, the Inclusion List, the Exclusion List, and the Comprehensive Study List. In addition, negotiation has contributed to the resolution of controversies in relation to environmental assessment.[11] Thus, Ontario's EAB relied upon negotiations between the proponent and public-interest intervenors in the formulation of many of the terms and conditions that emerged from the province's Timber Management Class Environmental Assessment.[12]

The Sandspit Small Craft Harbour mediation exercise provides a further example of ADR procedures, in this case in the context of the federal Environmental Assessment and Review Process. The mediation was set up in 1992 to respond to concerns about the environmental impact of a proposed harbour for recreational boaters provided for under the Canada–British Columbia South Moresby Agreement. The matter was of interest to several federal departments, two B.C. ministries, and various parties on the Haida Gwaii/Queen Charlotte Islands. On the basis of initial terms of reference prepared by federal officials in consultation with a range of interested parties, the principal parties themselves subsequently formulated ground rules for the mediation.

---

10   For recent examples from B.C., see online: www.wcel.org/edrf, where operations of the Environmental Dispute Resolution Fund are discussed.

11   See chapter 12.

12   Ontario Environmental Assessment Board, Reasons for Decision, Class Environmental Assessment (EA–87–02) (20 April 1994).

As described in the ground rules, the objective of the mediation was to identify an acceptable way to provide Sandspit with small-craft harbour facilities pursuant to the South Moresby Agreement and to do so in a manner consistent with the principles of sustainable development and with the federal Environmental Assessment and Review Process. The potentially relevant options were broadly defined to encompass mitigation and/or compensation for fish and bird habitat, the possible relocation of the harbour to alternative sites, and alternative harbour designs. The parties agreed to operate on a consensus basis and to establish smaller working groups to address procedural and substantive issues as they arose.

Parties, at their own expense, were entitled to use appropriate experts. To preserve flexibility, and to encourage exploration of the options, the parties agreed "that any specific offers or statements made during the proceedings are not to be used by any other participant to attempt to bind any other party or person in any other forum including pending or future administrative procedures or litigation." The mediator, in addition to substantive contributions, was responsible for documenting discussions and for developing the text of any agreement as it was reached. From the fact that consensus was ultimately reached on an environmentally acceptable site and design for the harbour, observers have concluded that the process was successful.[13]

In some cases the use of alternative dispute resolution is based on general discretionary authority, but it is increasingly common to see formal statutory reference to ADR schemes.[14] One of the more elaborate provisions is found in the Nova Scotia legislation, which authorizes the minister of the environment to use conciliation, negotiation, mediation, or arbitration in the resolution of either procedural or substantive conflicts concerning disputes about various certificates and approvals under the statute, or concerning responsibility for rehabilitating a contaminated site.[15]

Given the wide range of settings in which ADR processes are now being employed—from the development of regulations to issues resolution in environmental assessment and the determination of terms

---

13   J. Mathers, *Sandspit Small Craft Harbour Mediation Process: A Review and Evaluation* (Ottawa: Supply & Services, 1995).

14   *Canadian Environmental Assessment Act*, S.C. 1992, c. 37, s. 30; *Environment Act*, C.C.S.M. c. E125, s. 3(3); *An Act to Amend the Environmental Protection Act*, R.S.N.W.T. 1988 (Supp.), c. 117, s. 4; *Environmental Assessment Act*, S.B.C. 2002, c. 43, s. 27(3)(f); *Environmental Assessment Act*, R.S.O. 1990, c. E.18, as amended by S.O. 1996, c. 27, s. 3.

15   *Environment Act*, S.N.S. 1994–95, c. 1, s. 14.

and conditions in the licensing context—several legal matters must be considered. What basis of authority exists for the use of ADR and what restrictions are inherent in that authority? It may be necessary to determine who, as a matter of law, is entitled to participate in ADR proceedings, especially when these are used to replace other mechanisms. In what respects can official decision makers commit themselves in advance to the substantive outcome of ADR without misusing their discretion through fettering or dictation? And to what degree or through what mechanisms can agreements be made enforceable on behalf of participants or by third parties whose interests may have been affected by the outcome?[16]

Although negotiated resolution of conflicts between aboriginal peoples and Canadian governments within the overall context of reconciling aboriginal rights and Crown sovereignty in Canada differs in important respects from other forms of dispute, it is instructive to recall judicial comment on consultation in relation to such situations, many of which do involve land use, resource and environmental issues. In *Delgamuukw*, the S.C.C. explained the duty of consultation as follows:

> The nature and scope of the duty of consultation vary with the circumstances. In occasional cases, when the breach is less serious or relatively minor, it will be no more than a duty to discuss important decisions that will be taken with respect to lands pursuant to Aboriginal title . . . (E)ven in these . . . cases . . . consultation must be in good faith, and with the intention of substantially addressing the concerns of the Aboriginal peoples . . . In most cases, it will be significantly deeper than mere consultation. Some cases may even require the full consent of an Aboriginal nation, particularly when provinces enact hunting and fishing regulations in relation to Aboriginal lands.[17]

Considerations of this nature have, in some circumstances, encouraged the introduction of joint management arrangements intended to provide on an ongoing basis for participation in operational decisions affecting environment and resources.

---

16   For an introduction to some of these questions, see Darshan Brach *et al.*, "Overcoming the Barriers to Environmental Dispute Resolution in Canada" (2002) 81 Can. Bar Rev. 396 at 410–14.

17   *Delgamuukw v. British Columbia*, [1997] 3 S.C.R. 1011 at para 168. See also *Mikisew Cree First Nation v. Canada (Minister of Canadian Heritage)*, [2005] 3 S.C.R. 388 at paras. 63–69.

C. CO-MANAGEMENT INSTITUTIONS

Co-management has been described as "power-sharing in the exercise of resource management between a government agency and a community or organization of stakeholders."[18] Co-management institutions, highly variable in their design, present opportunities for greater levels of direct citizen involvement in environmental decision making. Comprehensive co-management regimes may encompass a full range of resource-management functions including habitat protection, long-range planning, and even enforcement practices.

Although not restricted to situations involving native communities, co-management arrangements have been particularly attractive where aboriginal uses of fish and wildlife or other natural resources are involved.[19] The basis for evaluation of co-management in Canada remains fairly limited, but positive results have been anticipated on the basis of American experience: "The legal rights of tribes to protect habitat eventually led environmentalists and recreational fishermen to ally with them in the struggle to protect fish habitat, and a strong lobby which could no longer be identified on racial lines was created."[20] Yet, in Canada, co-management mechanisms involving aboriginal participation have been more readily implemented in areas far removed from centres of population. Arrangements concerning fish and wildlife management under the *Inuvialuit Final Agreement* and institutions to facilitate aboriginal participation in certain land-use decisions under the *James Bay and Northern Quebec Agreement* are prime examples.[21]

Revisions once proposed to the federal *Fisheries Act* contemplated fisheries-management agreements between the minister and "any organization that, in the opinion of the Minister, is representative of a

---

18   E.W. Pinkerton, "Overcoming Barriers to the Exercise of Co-management Rights" in M. Ross & J.O. Saunders, eds., *Growing Demands on a Shrinking Heritage: Managing Resource-Use Conflicts* (Calgary: Canadian Institute of Resources Law, 1992) 276 at 277. See also Diduck, above note 1 at 519–21.

19   *Wale v. British Columbia (A.G.)*, [1991] 1 S.C.R. 62.

20   E. Pinkerton, "Introduction: Attaining Better Fisheries Management through Co-Management—Prospects, Problems, and Propositions" in E. Pinkerton, ed., *Co-Operative Management of Local Fisheries* (Vancouver: University of British Columbia Press, 1989) at 12.

21   Indian Affairs and Northern Development Canada, *The Western Arctic Claim: The Inuvialuit Final Agreement* (Ottawa: Indian Affairs and Northern Development, 1984); *James Bay and Northern Quebec Native Claims Settlement Act*, S.C. 1976–77, c. 32; *An Act Approving the Agreement Concerning James Bay and Northern Québec*, S.Q. 1976, c. 46.

class of persons or holders."[22] The scope of the agreements as proposed would have included

- the harvest limits, and other conservation and management measures for a fishery;
- the number of licences that may be issued for the class of holders or persons;
- the fees payable to Her Majesty in right of Canada with respect to the issuance of the licences and the variation, recission, or addition to conditions of the licences;
- the obligations, responsibilities, and funding arrangements with respect to management of the fishery; and
- the conservation and management programs for the fishery.

In a somewhat similar manner, the *Oceans Act* calls for widespread collaboration in the development and implementation of a national strategy for the management of estuarine, coastal, and marine ecosystems.[23]

In 1992 British Columbia appointed a commissioner of resources and environment (CORE) with responsibility for advising Cabinet "in an independent manner on land use and related resource and environmental issues in British Columbia and on the need for legislation, policies and practices respecting these issues."[24] The mandate encompassed the development and monitoring of regional land-use planning, community-based participatory processes concerning land use, resources, and environmental management, and a related dispute-resolution system.[25]

In a public report entitled *Land Use Strategy for British Columbia*, the commissioner recommended shared decision making involving representatives of government and affected interests, while in a *Draft Land Use Charter* for the province he urged the use of processes to "promote decision-making through the building of consensus amongst diverse perspectives and stakeholders." Although influential in promoting many apparently promising initiatives, CORE was abolished in 1996.[26]

---

22 Bill C-115, *An Act Respecting Fisheries*, 1st Sess., 35th Parl., 1995, cl. 17(1). Bill C-115 died on the Order Paper as did a subsequent initiative along comparable lines, Bill C-62.

23 *Oceans Act*, S.C. 1996, c. 31, s. 29.

24 *Commissioner on Resources and Environment Act*, R.S.B.C. 1996, c. 59, s. 3(1).

25 *Ibid.*, s. 4(2).

26 For an assessment by a prominent participant in the CORE process, see S. Owen, "Land Use Planning in the Nineties: CORE Lessons" (1998) 25 Environments 14.

D. VOLUNTARY MEASURES

Environmental protection measures in Canada have historically relied on government intervention in the form of command and control regulation. However, the importance of supplementary and alternative approaches, particularly of a preventive nature, and implemented on a voluntary basis, is now widely—if not universally—accepted.

Voluntary environmental protection measures by industry may be implemented with or without government participation, assistance, and consent, and with or without the involvement of other interested parties. Thus, although the federal government established a National Office of Pollution Prevention in 1991 to promote voluntary efforts to reduce the use and emission of pollutants, programs can be initiated without the involvement of the office. They may be adopted at the level of individual companies with comparatively localized objectives, or they may be developed in relation to the needs and capacity of an entire industry or sector with much broader implications. Moreover, despite their voluntary nature originating in the consent of parties to them, voluntary measures can be designed to promote compliance through sanctions or financial and other penalties.[27]

Depending on the manner in which they are implemented, voluntary agreements may offer a range of potential attractions to participants. From the perspective of government, voluntary measures have the potential to enhance overall environmental performance with lower expenditures in financial and human resources terms. Insofar as government acknowledges the limitations and deficiencies of the command and control model, voluntary initiatives permit a more collaborative relationship with industry and may facilitate accelerated environmental improvement in comparison with more cumbersome and inflexible regulations. To the extent that voluntary measures are established for industry groups or industrial sectors, some of the burden of monitoring performance and encouraging backsliders may be assumed by industry associations rather than public officials.

For its part, industry may find voluntary measures attractive ways to forestall regulations that are often perceived as rigid and insufficiently tailored to the requirements and opportunities available to in-

---

27   See, for example, Canadian Council of Ministers of the Environment, National Task Force on Storage Tanks, *Environmental Code of Practice for Underground Storage Tank Systems Containing Petroleum Products and Allied Petroleum Products* (Ottawa: Canadian Council of Ministers of the Environment, National Task Force on Storage Tanks, 1993).

dividual businesses depending on their particular geographical and competitive setting. Opportunities to improve operational efficiency without lowering environmental performance are felt to be more readily available where industry has some scope to determine voluntarily the manner in which it will fulfil social, including environmental, obligations. In addition, public relations advantages may accrue to businesses and industries that can demonstrate a genuine commitment to the environment, particularly one that is independent of official coercion and perhaps produces beneficial results faster than or in excess of regulatory timetables.

Before proceeding to some illustrations of voluntary initiatives in Canada, it is important to note that the voluntary nature of participation in such arrangements does not mean they are without legal consequences or implications. The leading analysts of linkages between law and voluntary codes in Canada have provided an inventory of possible relationships, including the following observations:

- Voluntary standards can be referentially incorporated in law, with or without the approval of the initiators of the voluntary standard;
- Voluntary code initiatives may elaborate on and refine the generality of legislative requirements;
- Voluntary initiatives may be explicitly created pursuant to legislative instruments;
- Governments may support the development of voluntary initiatives that have extraterritorial application when it might be difficult to directly legislate these non-domestic operations;
- Non-compliance with voluntary standards can be a factor used by judges in determining liability, compliance with voluntary standards can aid firms in avoiding penal liability or reducing penalties, and the terms of voluntary programs can be judicially imposed on firms as part of sentencing;
- Consumers or affected members of a community may be able to use the commitments made in voluntary initiatives in legal actions to assist in establishing liability against individual firms and against those who develop voluntary standards;
- Disciplinary actions by code administrators against participating firms may be undertaken through contractual actions;
- The fairness of disciplinary actions taken by code administrators toward participating firms may be reviewed by the courts and, if found wanting, the actions can be overturned.[28]

---

28   Kernaghan Webb & Andrew Morrison, "The Law and Voluntary Codes" in K. Webb, ed., *Voluntary Codes: Private Governance, the Public Interest and Innova-*

The nature of several current possibilities is illustrated in the following examples.

1) Environmental Performance Agreements

Environment Canada's National Office of Pollution Prevention undertook to develop environmental performance agreements with individual companies, industrial sectors, other departments of the federal government and provincial and territorial agencies.[29] Such agreements have been described as "a complement, a precursor or an alternative to regulations." In developing guidelines for EPAs, Environment Canada identified four general principles: effectiveness, credibility, accountability, and efficiency. Design criteria were formulated in order to ensure overall compliance with those principles:

- clear objectives and measurable results;
- clearly defined roles and responsibilities;
- provision for consultation;
- public reporting;
- incentives and consequences;
- verification of results;
- a regulatory backstop;
- continuous improvement.

2) ARET

Beginning in the early 1990s, a program known as ARET (Accelerated Reduction/Elimination of Toxics) encouraged voluntary action on the part of industrial users of toxic substances in order to reduce or eliminate toxics. The ARET committee was constituted as a stakeholders' group including representatives from health and professional bodies and government along with eight industry associations. After screening some 2000 substances and grouping them on the basis of persistence, bioaccumulation, and toxicity criteria, the committee designated some for virtual elimination after a 90 percent reduction from 1993 levels by 2000. Others were targeted for a 50 percent reduction in emissions by the same year.

---

tion (Ottawa: Carleton Research Unit for Innovation, Science and Environment, Carleton University, 2004) 97 at 98–99.

29   Environment Canada, *Policy Framework for Environmental Performance Agreements* (Ottawa: Environment Canada, 2001).

Significant emission reductions were achieved by the participants who constitute approximately 70 percent of the members of ARET's sectoral stakeholder associations.[30] Despite the accomplishments attributable to the ARET initiative, overall assessments have been mixed.[31]

3) Responsible Care

Responsible Care, a set of initiatives of the Canadian Chemical Producers' Association, is intended to demonstrate at a sectoral level that the industry is capable on a voluntary basis of implementing effective measures for managing chemicals, chemical products, and processes. CCPA members have agreed to guiding principles that underlie the program and that require each to

- ensure that its operations do not present an unacceptable level of risk to employees, customers, the public, or the environment;
- provide relevant information on the hazards of chemicals to its customers, urging them to use and dispose of products in a safe manner, and make such information available to the public on request;
- make Responsible Care an early and integral part of the planning process leading to new products, processes, or plants;
- increase the emphasis on the understanding of existing products and their uses and ensure that a high level of understanding of new products and their potential hazards is achieved prior to and throughout commercial development;
- comply with all legal requirements that affect its operations and products;
- be responsive and sensitive to legitimate community concerns; and
- work actively with and assist governments and selected organizations to foster and encourage equitable and attainable standards.[32]

In addition, codes of practice have been formulated in relation to such issues as community awareness and emergency response; research

---

30   Environment Canada, Health Canada, & Industry Canada, *Environmental Leaders 1: Voluntary Commitments to Action on Toxics through ARET: Accelerated Reduction/Elimination of Toxics* (Hull: ARET Secretariat, 1995). For critical comment on the ARET initiative, see D.L. VanNijnattan, "The ARET Challenge" in R. Gibson, ed., *Voluntary Initiatives: The New Politics of Corporate Greening* (Peterborough, ON: Broadview Press, 1999) at 93–100.

31   D.L. VanNijnattan & Eric Darier, "Voluntary Instruments" in William Leiss, ed., *In the Chamber of Risks: Understanding Risk Controversies* (Montreal: McGill-Queen's University Press, 2001) at 221.

32   Canadian Chemical Producers' Association, *Responsible Care: A Total Commitment* (Ottawa: Canadian Chemical Producers' Association, 1992).

and development; manufacturing; transportation; distribution; and hazardous-waste management. Reported results suggest that substantial advances are being made. In particular, on the basis of aggregated member-company data, the CCPA reported a 50 percent reduction in chemical emissions between 1992 and 1996 and a decline in the frequency and severity of transportation incidents. The Responsible Care initiative is also associated with benefits to participating companies including anticipated insurance-premium reductions, a reduction in the potential for legal claims, lower workers' compensation costs, and reduced delays in permit-application proceedings.[33]

Responsible Care has been credited with certain direct accomplishments in the sense that the health and safety records of participating firms had improved while several categories of emissions to the environment were measurably decreased. In addition, the mere existence of the program is understood to have served indirectly to elevate the expected levels of performance of those seeking to demonstrate that they had exceeded the common law's negligence standard or that they had, in the context of a regulatory prosecution, demonstrated due diligence. The significance of this experience has raised interesting policy questions: "To what extent should resource strapped government enforcement officials use membership in Responsible Care as the basis for placing a CCPA company low on their list of inspection priorities? Is it valid to assume that a Responsible Care company will always comply with environmental regulations?"[34] As the authors of a comprehensive assessment of the program report in response to this inquiry:

> Even its strongest proponents do not argue that participation in Responsible Care is a guarantee of compliance. Instead, proponents argue, Responsible Care certification means that companies will more likely *want* to be in compliance. Thus, they say, a Responsible Care company will less likely be systematically non-compliant, and will more likely be willing to take remedial measures without a threat of prosecution if it inadvertently falls out of compliance. In short, it is argued, government enforcement officials should treat Responsible Care companies

33   Canadian Chemical Producers' Association, *Does Responsible Care Pay? A Primer on the Unexpected Benefits of the Initiative* (Ottawa: Canadian Chemical Producers' Association, 1996). For an overview of the evolution and effectiveness of the program, see J. Moffett & F. Bregha, "Responsible Care" in Gibson, ed., *Voluntary Initiatives*, above note 30, 69.

34   John Moffet, François Bregha, & Mary Jane Middelkoop, "Responsible Care: A Case Study of a Voluntary Environmental Initiative" in Webb, ed., *Voluntary Codes*, above note 28, 177 at 188.

differently from other companies by emphasizing a compliance-promotion approach versus a stricter enforcement approach.[35]

4) Environmental Management Systems, ISO 14000 and Certification

The International Standards Association (ISO), a Geneva-based federation of standards bodies, was recognized initially for its work in the formulation of technical product and design standards. The ISO subsequently ventured into the sphere of systems or quality management by means of the ISO 9000 series and has most recently begun to introduce environmental management standards, the ISO 14000 series.

The ISO 14000 series establishes environmental standards in two general categories, generally in the form of guidelines rather than as prescriptive specifications. In relation to management systems and organization evaluation, standards addressing environmental management systems, environmental auditing, environmental site assessments, and environmental performance evaluation have been formulated. In relation to product evaluation, the ISO 14000 series includes guidelines on environmental labelling and life-cycle product assessment, as well as a document dealing with terms and conditions relevant to self-declared environmental claims.

A general description of the nature of the ISO 14000 series may be helpful in understanding its scope and intent:

> The standards are "systems" standards, not legal standards and are intended to harmonize, not invent standards. They are designed to help organizations manage their environmental obligations such as compliance with legal requirements; the standards do not supplant nor do they add to existing legal requirements. They do not tell organizations how to run their businesses but rather define management processes to be followed to control the impact an organization will have on the environment. The organization identifies what environmental impacts are acceptable within the legal framework.

Nonetheless, it is of interest to note that Canadian courts, on sentencing a corporation convicted of an environmental violation, have occasionally ordered the company to obtain certification pursuant to ISO 14001, the Environmental Management Systems Specification.[36]

---

35   *Ibid.* at 189.
36   *R. v. Prospec Chemicals Ltd.* (1996), 19 C.E.L.R. (N.S.) 178 (Alta. Prov. Ct.); see also *R. v. Calgary* (2000), 35 C.E.L.R. (N.S.) 253 (Alta. Prov. Ct.).

The prevalence of environmental management system initiatives has already produced assessment and commentary designed to enhance their effectiveness. The CEC, for example, in a guidance document on improving environmental performance and compliance identified the following essential elements of an EMS:[37]

(a) The EMS should be based upon a documented and clearly communicated policy.

(b) The EMS should provide a means to identify, explain, and communicate all environmental requirements and voluntary undertakings to all employees, on-site service providers, and contractors, whose work could affect the organization's ability to meet those requirements and undertakings.

(c) The EMS should establish specific objectives and targets for:
   1) Achieving and maintaining compliance with environmental compliance.
   2) Environmental performance demonstrating continuous improvement in regulated and non-regulated areas.
   3) Pollution prevention that emphasizes source reduction.
   4) Sharing information with external stakeholders on environmental performance against all EMS objectives and targets.

(d) Sufficient personnel and resources should be provided to meet the objectives and targets of the EMS.

(e) The EMS should identify and provide for the planning and management of all the organization's operations and activities with a view to achieving the EMS objectives and targets.

(f) The organization should establish and maintain documented procedures for preventing, detecting, investigating, promptly initiating corrective action, and reporting (both internally and externally, in accordance with applicable laws) any occurrence that may affect the organization's ability to achieve the EMS objectives and targets.

(g) The EMS should establish procedures to ensure that all personnel whose job responsibilities affect the ability to achieve the EMS objectives and targets have been trained and are capable of carrying out their responsibilities.

(h) The EMS should describe how these elements will be integrated into the organization's overall decision making and planning.

---

37 Commission for Environmental Cooperation, *Improving Environmental Performance and Compliance: 10 Elements of Effective Environmental Management Systems* (Montreal: Commission for Environmental Cooperation, 2000).

(i) The EMS should establish procedures to ensure maintenance of appropriate documentation relating to its objectives and targets and should also ensure that those records will be adequate for subsequent evaluation and improvement of the operation of the EMS.

(j) The EMS should require periodic, documented, and objective auditing of the organization's performance in achieving the objectives and targets.

In certain sectors, with forestry a leading example, independent third party certification procedures to assess the sustainability of operations have achieved widespread acceptance.[38]

E. CONCLUSION

The proliferation of voluntary and alternative forms of decision making and performance setting may very well facilitate elaboration of the environmental management framework. Notwithstanding the enthusiasm with which these developments have been embraced in some quarters, certain criticisms and reservations have been voiced. These by and large concern the relationship between the new approaches and the prior regime to which they are described as alternatives. That prior regime, comprised of legislative, regulatory, and administrative rules and procedures, embodies or is subject to a number of fundamental public law values: opportunities for participation, the accountability of decision makers, review mechanisms of an administrative or judicial nature, formal monitoring and reporting procedures, and so on. The maintenance of these valued attributes is at some risk in the context of new forms of environmental governance and decision making unless steps are taken to ensure their continuation.[39] It is therefore unsurpris-

---

38 Gregory T. Rhone, David Clarke, & Kernaghan Webb, "Two Voluntary Approaches to Sustainable Forestry Practices" in Webb, ed., *Voluntary Codes*, above note 28. Benjamin Cashore, Graeme Auld, & Deanna Newsom, *Governing Through Markets: Forest Certification and the Emergence of Non-State Authority* (New Haven, CT: Yale University School of Forestry and Environmental Studies, 2003), online: www.yale.edu/forestcertification/pdfs/2003/03_modified_auld_newsom.pdf.

39 K. Beattie, "Fairness, Openness and Self-Regulation: An Examination of Administrative Law Values and the Use of Voluntary and Self-Regulatory Measures for Environmental Protection" (2001) 14 Can . J. Admin. L. & Prac. 1; A.R. Lucas, "Voluntary Initiatives for Greenhouse Gas Reduction: The Legal Implications" (2000) 10 J. Envtl. L. & Prac. 89. See also Commissioner of the Environment

ing that in its assessment of the federal government's initial approach to climate change, an approach heavily reliant upon voluntary action, the Commissioner of the Environment and Sustainable Development emphasized the fundamental importance of good management, notably the need for overall governance and accountability. The CESD emphasized, in particular, that those involved should clearly understand and agree to their roles and responsibilities. Results-based targets and time-tables will facilitate implementation and monitoring which in turn may identify necessary adjustments.[40]

FURTHER READINGS

BAETZ, M.C., & A.B. TANGUAY, "'Damned if You Do and Damned if You Don't': Government and the Conundrum of Consultation in the Environmental Sector" (1998) 41 Canadian Public Administration 395

BEATTIE, KAREN, "Fairness, Openness and Self-Regulation: An Examination of Administrative Law Values and the Use of Voluntary and Self-Regulatory Measures for Environmental Protection" (2001) 14 Can. J. Admin. L. & Prac. 1

DOELLE, M., "Regulating the Environment by Mediation and Contract Negotiation: A Case Study of the Dona Lake Agreement" (1992) 2 J. Envtl. L. & Prac. 189

GIBSON, R.B., ed., *Voluntary Initiatives: The New Politics of Corporate Greening* (Peterborough, ON: Broadview Press, 1999)

KRAHN, PETER K., "Enforcement versus Voluntary Compliance: An Examination of the Strategic Enforcement Initiatives Implemented by the Pacific and Yukon Regional Office of Environment Canada, 1983–1998" in *5th INECE Conference Proceedings*, vol. 1 (Washington, DC: INECE Secretariat, 1998) 25

LUCAS, A.R., "Voluntary Initiatives for Greenhouse Gas Reduction: The Legal Implications" (2000) 10 J. Envtl. L. & Prac. 89

---

and Sustainable Development, *2000 May Report* (Ottawa: Office of the Auditor General, 2000), online: www.oag-bvg.gc.ca/internet/English/aud_parl_cesd_200005_e_1137.html.

40   Commissioner of the Environment and Sustainable Development, *2006 September Report* (Ottawa: Office of the Auditor General, 2006) at 25, online: www.oag-bvg.gc.ca/internet/English/aud_parl_cesd_200609_e_936.html.

MOFFET, J., & F. BREGHA, "An Overview of Issues with Respect to Voluntary Environmental Agreements" (1998) 8 J. Envtl. L. & Prac. 63

PARDY, BRUCE, "Asking the Dog to Guard the Puppy Chow: Three Objections to Environmental Voluntarism" (2003) 12 J. Envtl. L. & Prac. 129

PINKERTON, E., ed., *Co-operative Management of Local Fisheries: New Directions for Improved Management and Community Development* (Vancouver: University of British Columbia Press, 1989)

ROUNTHWAITE, H. IAN, "Alternative Dispute Resolution in Environmental Law: Uses, Limitations and Potential" in E. Hughes, A.R. Lucas, and W.A. Tilleman, *Environmental Law and Policy*, 3d ed. (Toronto: Emond Montgomery, 2003) c. 14

SWANSON, E.J., "Alternative Dispute Resolution and Environmental Conflict: The Case for Law Reform" (1995) 34 Alta. L. Rev. 267

WEBB, K., ed., *Voluntary Codes: Private Governance, the Public Interest and Innovation* (Ottawa: Carleton Research Unit for Innovation, Science and Environment, Carleton University, 2004)

WINFIELD, M., "Alternative Service Delivery in the Natural Resources Sector: An Examination of Ontario's Forestry Compliance Self-Inspection System" (2005) 48 Canadian Public Administration 552

CHAPTER 17

ECONOMIC INSTRUMENTS

Economic instruments, another of the more recently prominent approaches to environmental protection, take a variety of forms. Not all of the economic incentives currently in place or under consideration are particularly innovative, even though efforts to appreciate the environmental implications of their operation have intensified in recent years. Nor is the focus entirely on initiatives that are explicitly directed at improving environmental conditions, for the environmentally-adverse impacts of other policy measures is of equal significance. A simple example is subsidies to the agriculture, energy, transportation and industrial sectors which have encouraged waste, pollution and excessive natural resource consumption.[1] Although this is an important matter, it will not receive much attention here.

After discussing the general attractions of economic instruments and market mechanisms from an environmental perspective, as well as noting some of the reservations that are expressed about them, this chapter describes non-tax instruments, tax incentives, and public funds dedicated to the environment. The chapter concludes with reference to insurance and financial institutions in light of their potential to use economic incentives in the interests of environmental protection.

---

1   OECD, *Improving the Environment through Reducing Subsidies* (Paris: OECD, 1998); OECD, *Environmentally Harmful Subsidies: Challenges for Reform* (Paris: OECD, 2005); OECD, *Subsidy Reform and Sustainable Development: Economic, Environmental and Social Aspects* (Paris: OECD, 2006).

A. SOME BASIC PROS AND CONS

Proponents of economic incentives anticipate that environmentally appropriate behaviour can be encouraged if the environmental costs of various activities are recognized, and then appropriately valued and allocated. Certain elements of the legal regime can already be seen as consistent with an economic approach to regulation. For example, statutory arrangements assigning financial liability for clean-up costs and other expenses to "persons responsible" for the damages express the general intention that the burden of compensation for environmental losses should be borne by those who stand to benefit from the activity that resulted in the damage. As the Supreme Court of Canada remarked in *Imperial Oil*, the polluter-pays principle "assigns polluters the responsibility for remedying contamination for which they are responsible and imposes on them the direct and immediate costs of pollution."[2] In this regard, profit-stripping provisions are expected to eliminate the financial attraction of disregarding environmental protection requirements. Legal implementation of the polluter-pays principle is also often assumed to create incentives for preventive measures and alternative approaches that serve to avoid environmental harm in the first place. Such an observation might be made in connection with the following provision from Newfoundland legislation:

> Where pollution occurs and the person or municipal authority that the minister considers responsible for the occurrence of the pollution fails to do the things that the minister considers are appropriate to prevent, control, eliminate or ameliorate the pollution, the minister may take appropriate action to prevent, control, eliminate or ameliorate the pollution and the costs incurred by the minister in taking that action are a debt due the Crown and are recoverable from the person or municipal authority that the minister considers responsible for the occurrence of the pollution.[3]

Although there are certain satisfactions in requiring those who pollute to assume the costs of the damage they have caused, prevention is more attractive. In general, advocates of economic instruments expect not only that harm to the environment will be less likely when those benefiting from the harmful activity must assume the costs, but that society's overall costs of achieving a given level of environmental protection will be lower because of a more efficient distribution among

---

2   *Imperial Oil v. Quebec*, [2003] 2 S.C.R. 624 at 642.
3   *Environment Act*, S.N. 1995, c. E-13.1, s. 21.

polluters of the costs of meeting that standard. It is also anticipated that appropriately designed economic incentives will promote the development of innovative means to safeguard and improve environmental quality on an ongoing basis.

A number of potential advantages have been claimed for economic instruments over traditional command and control regulation in achieving a given level of environmental protection.[4] First, insofar as they recognize and respond to the fact that pollution-abatement costs will vary among different sources of the same contaminant, economic instruments permit a specified level of environmental protection to be attained at lower cost than uniform emission standards applied under regulatory supervision. Secondly, economic instruments may provide greater ongoing incentives than regulation for polluters to design and implement more efficient processes and technology: if polluters are held responsible for cleaning up the environmental damage they cause, then being able to do so more cheaply saves them money. Finally, these instruments may accelerate progress towards environmental improvement, assuming either that more environmental protection may be realized for the same expenditure or, alternatively, that the operational flexibility they permit will allow for more stringent environmental targets in the first place. It is also claimed that economic instruments reduce the administrative burden and may more readily accommodate growth and the entry of new firms than the established regulatory approach.[5]

Other factors contributing to the attractiveness of economic instruments and incentives include greater appreciation of the competitive position of Canadian businesses in international markets, and a general concern to address the public debt and deficit situation through lowered public expenditures, including enforcement expenditures, and greater regulatory efficiency.

Notwithstanding the attractive features of economic incentives, there is strong resistance to their adoption, certainly as a complete re-

---

4   Environment Canada, *Economic Instruments for Environmental Protection* (Discussion paper) (Ottawa: Supply & Services, 1992); Stratos Inc., *Economic Instruments for Environmental Protection and Conservation: Lessons for Canada* (2003), online: www.stratos-sts.com/publications/Stratos_EIs_Smart_Reg_Ctee_Dec_2003_2.pdf; National Round Table on the Environment and the Economy, *Economic Instruments for Long-term Reductions in Energy-based Carbon Emissions* (2005), online: www.nrtee-trnee.ca/eng/publications/energy-based-carbon-emissions/index-energy-based-carbon-emissions-eng.htm; Marbek Resource Consultants, *Analysis of Economic Instruments for Water Conservation* (November 2005), online: http://ccme.ca/assets/pdf/ei_marbek_final_rpt_e.pdf.

5   Environment Canada, *Economic Intruments for Environmental Protection, ibid.* at 14–15.

placement for more traditional regulatory and enforcement practices. Some observers are reluctant to entrust government with responsibility for setting appropriate total emission and quality levels and for maintaining them through market-oriented mechanisms. Others claim that cost-benefit calculations associated with economic incentives could lead to the imposition of environmental burdens on minorities of some kind. Still more fundamental objections revolve around the assertion that no one should be able simply to buy the right to undertake activities that are inherently bad. And, from a practical perspective, critics charge that the tools of economic analysis currently available to us remain wholly inadequate to the task of assigning satisfactory values to the environment and its constituent elements. There are also critics who argue from the perspective of the rule of law that consistent application of legal standards is the desirable norm, both as a matter of fairness and in light of the need for governments as well as potential polluters to be held accountable for their actions.

B. CANADIAN EXPERIENCE WITH ECONOMIC INSTRUMENTS

The range of economic instruments is sometimes described as encompassing tax-based and non-tax-based mechanisms. Both are discussed in this section along with public funds dedicated to environmental programs.

1) Non-tax Instruments

On the non-tax side, economic instruments might include deposit and refund schemes such as those associated with consumer use of beverage containers, batteries, and so on.[6] User charges, that is, payments directly associated with the costs of resource use, waste management, or environmental damage arising from the discharge of pollution, have also been proposed.

New Brunswick's beverage container legislation is typical of deposit and refund regimes designed to encourage reuse of containers with resulting environmental savings from the perspective of reduced use of materials, reduced consumption of energy in container production, decreased demand on land fill facilities and so on. The legislation sets out requirements for distributors of beverages to establish arrangements

---

6   See, for example, *Beverage Containers Act*, S.N.B. 1991, c. B-2.2.

for receiving used containers, or redeeming them from consumers, and subsequently for refilling or recycling them. The deposit and refund level itself is provided for within the legislative framework. Thus, the deposit and refund level is prescribed by regulation, and consumers are statutorily required to pay this amount.[7]

National efforts to promote water conservation through pricing have been encouraged for twenty years in the aftermath of a valuable inquiry into water policy. *Currents of Change*, the report of the *Inquiry on Federal Water Policy*, made a major contribution simply by broadening awareness of the implications of pricing on the consumption of water, a highly valuable natural resource that is essential in domestic as well as industrial and institutional settings. The water inquiry identified several benefits anticipated from water pricing:

> It will create incentives to avoid waste and to use water efficiently, thus contributing to water conservation.
>
> By reducing the water needed and the waste disposal capacity, it will reduce infrastructure costs.
>
> The resulting lower demand will reduce environmental pressures on water resources.
>
> By demonstrating users' willingness to pay for water, prices help allocate supplies among uses and users so that the highest value is generated from limited resources.
>
> Pricing will generate revenue to cover the cost of water supply and waste disposal systems.
>
> Suitable pricing can ensure that the cost of water services is equitably borne by the beneficiaries according to the benefits they receive.[8]

In the aftermath of the report, more and more users who had become accustomed to receiving the benefits of water and related services at no charge or at nominal expense, are finding that their water usage is being measured through metering devices. On a national basis, between 1991 and 2001, the percentage of residential water consumers whose consumption is metered increased from 51.5 percent to 60.5 percent, although Quebec, British Columbia and Newfoundland continue to lag. The results strongly indicate that metering significantly lessens water consumption in comparison with use by customers who are on

---

7   *Ibid.*, ss. 4, 5, and 7(1).

8   P.H. Pearse *et. al.*, *Currents of Change: Final Report, Inquiry of Federal Water Policy* (Ottawa: Supply and Services Canada, 1985) at 98–99.

a flat rate and whose charges are not varied on the basis of volume consumed.[9] The next challenge, currently underway, is to refine the relationship between pricing clean water and the costs of supply. Further refinements in water pricing are thought to offer additional advantages, and in the aftermath of Walkerton it is widely assumed that the value of safe drinking water and the costs of securing it will soon be reflected in higher prices.[10] Under Ontario's new *Sustainable Water and Sewage Systems Act*, the full cost of providing water services is understood to include "the source protection costs, operating costs, financing costs, renewal and replacement costs and improvement costs associated with extracting, treating or distributing water to the public and such other costs as may be specified by regulation."[11]

Statutory authorization for economic instruments is apparent elsewhere. Thus, Manitoba's *Environment Act* anticipates the sale of emission rights for designated pollutants by authorizing the lieutenant governor in council to market units of allowable emission of specific pollutants, in accordance with the regulations. Such arrangements must be consistent with established environmental quality objectives. Resulting revenues may be held in trust by the provincial minister of finance as an environmental contingency fund, to be used at the request of the minister of the environment in cases of environmental emergency.[12] Alberta's *Environmental Protection and Enhancement Act* authorizes the use of economic and financial instruments and market-based approaches such as emission trading, incentives, subsidies, and emission, effluent- and waste-disposal fees as well as differential levies "for the purpose of protecting the environment, achieving environmental quality goals in a cost effective manner and providing methods of financing programs and other measures for environmental purposes."[13] Nova Scotia legislation contemplates research on and the eventual adoption of an even broader array of economic and market-based approaches including tradeable emission and effluent permits; offsetting environmental costs and benefits; user charges; resource pricing and physical-resource accounts; deposit-refund systems; emission, effluent- and waste-disposal

9   Environment Canada, Freshwater Website, online: www.ec.gc.ca/water/descrip/info/pubs/sss/e_chart2.htm.

10 M. Sproule-Jones, "User Fees" in A.M. Maslove, ed., *Taxes as Instruments of Public Policy* (Toronto: University of Toronto Press, 1994) at 19–23. For details on the Walkerton inquiry, see Dennis O'Connor (Commissioner), *Report of the Walkerton Inquiry* (Toronto: Ministry of the Attorney General, 2002).

11 *Sustainable Water and Sewage Systems Act*, S.O. 2002, c. 29, s. 3(7).

12 *The Environment Act*, C.C.S.M. c. E125, s. 45.

13 *Environmental Protection and Enhancement Act*, R.S.A. 2000, c. E-12, s. 13.

fees; product charges; charges on inputs or materials; tax incentives and tax differentiation; subsidies, loans, and grants.[14]

Tradeable emission permits that may be exchanged within a market of users (and sometimes even of non-users) are increasingly important examples of non-tax economic instruments. The particular attraction of tradeable permits (assuming an adequate number of participating purchasers) lies in their potential to control aggregate emissions of designated contaminants through the operation of market forces rather than the decisions of regulators.[15] Canada's use of such economic instruments remains limited when set against the use that has been made of similar mechanisms in other jurisdictions. But some sophisticated applications have been examined as part of an effort to provide environmentally beneficial economic incentives to industry and encouragement for individual Canadians to incorporate environmental considerations into the decisions they make as consumers. Significant studies have been carried out, including those for the CCME on emissions trading,[16] for the province of Alberta on air pollution,[17] and for the International Joint Commission on toxic substances in the Great Lakes.[18]

While discussions about the appropriate design and development of emissions trading regimes continue in the context of the Kyoto Protocol as a response to climate change from greenhouse gas emissions, a number of organizations have begun to acquire emission rights in private transactions that are being carried out in both the national and international contexts. This activity is providing experience that has been likened to the early development of negotiable instruments preceding legislation on bills of exchange. It is being carried out on the assumption that the public environmental goals of emission trading re-

---

14   *Environment Act*, S.N.S. 1994–95, c. 1, s. 15 [*NSEA*]; see also *Environment Act*, R.S.Y. 2002, c. 76, s. 57 [*YEA*]; *Canaadian Environmental Protection Act, 1999*, S.C. 1999, c. 33, ss. 322–27 [*CEPA*].

15   K. Hoey & A.J. Roman, "The Regulatory Framework" in G. Thompson, M.L. McConnell, & L.B. Huestis, eds., *Environmental Law and Business in Canada* (Aurora, ON: Canada Law Book, 1993) at 59–64.

16   Canadian Council of Ministers of the Environment, Emission Trading Working Group, *Emission Trading: A Discussion Paper* (Winnipeg: Emission Trading Working Group, 1992). Ontario adopted an emissions trading regulation for the energy sector in October 2001: O. Reg. 397/01.

17   For background, see National Economic Research Associates, *Market-based Approaches to Managing Air Emissions in Alberta* (Discussion paper) (Cambridge, MA: National Economic Research Associates, 1991). For implemenation, see *Emissions Trading Regulation*, Alta. Reg. 33/2006.

18   International Joint Commission, *Economic Instruments for the Virtual Elimination of Persistent Toxic Substances in the Great Lakes Basin* (Windsor: International Joint Commission, 1994).

gimes will eventually mesh with the private interests of rights holders, and that the vital issue of monitoring and verifying actual emissions will be satisfactorily addressed.[19]

2) Tax Incentives and Allowances

Taxes are popularly perceived as revenue-generating devices for governments; however, they can also serve to promote changes in behaviour, including behaviour intended to reduce environmental damage. Specific uses of taxation regimes to promote environmental quality are thus the subject of increased attention.[20]

Environmental taxes may be applied to industrial inputs, that is, on resources consumed during production, on pollution emissions discharged into the environment, or on waste. Taxes can also be applied at the point of consumption by individual purchasers. In each case, levels of taxation must be carefully monitored to reduce the risk of unwanted distortions and side effects. Such design features are crucial, and the need for fine-tuning and refinements appears to be ongoing.

One widely discussed possibility is the carbon tax, contemplated for its potential to lower the rate of production of carbon dioxide, a major greenhouse gas contributor to global warming. In principle such a tax could be applied to fossil-fuel energy inputs based on the proportion of carbon in their composition. Coal, a high carbon-content fuel, would be subject to a higher level of taxation per unit of energy potential than a comparatively low carbon-content fuel such as natural gas. Analysts see some potential for a carefully designed carbon tax to provide the economic incentive necessary to induce energy users to lower their use of fossil fuels or to reorient their consumption from high to low carbon-content fuel sources. Apart from the concerns of different aspects of the energy sector, most governments have also been preoccupied with the impact of carbon taxes on the competitive position of their domestic industries if other jurisdictions fail to implement similar measures.[21]

---

19 A.J. Black, "Emission Trading and the Negotiation of Pollution Credits" Energy Economist *Financial Times* (July 2000) at 14–18. At meetings in Montreal (2005) and Nairobi (2006), parties to the Kyoto Protocol have continued to discuss the operation and future administration of GHG emissions trading schemes. See chapter 19.

20 N. Olewiler, "The Case for Pollution Taxes" in G.B. Doern, ed., *Getting It Green: Case Studies in Canadian Environmental Regulation* (Toronto: C.D. Howe Institute, 1990) 188.

21 *Report of the Ontario Fair Tax Commission: Fair Taxation in a Changing World* (Toronto: University of Toronto Press, 1993) at 559–63.

At the time of writing, one operational initiative along these lines has been introduced by the province of Quebec.[22] Here it is proposed to charge the producers or importers of coal, gas and oil on the basis of their carbon dioxide emissions with the proceeds constituting an annual duty payable to a new provincial Green Fund intended to achieve compliance with Kyoto goals of GHG reductions. The provincial government has encouraged the producers and importers to absorb this additional charge, but the possibility that costs might be passed on to consumers is not foreclosed. Either way, GHG emitters would contribute financially to costs associated with efforts to address climate change either by reducing GHG emissions or through adaptation measures.

Tax-based instruments also include incentives in the form of eligibility for expense deductions or other inducements to stimulate particular forms of investment. One example of a tax-based incentive to investment is the availability under the federal *Income Tax Act* of accelerated depreciation write-offs for eligible pollution-control equipment. The legislation permits those who have incurred capital expenditures for the acquisition of pollution-control equipment to set off these costs against business income more rapidly than would otherwise be permissible.[23] At the provincial level, a sales-tax rebate on pollution-abatement equipment provided a comparable stimulus. In Ontario, tax measures on automobiles with high fuel consumption may promote greater awareness of the environmental consequences of vehicle choice.[24] The overall tax regime applicable to a particular business or undertaking may vary significantly as between one industry and another, depending upon location, the nature of assets utilized in production or operations—including land, equipment, technology, and so on—as well as the business structure involved. In the forest sector, for example, tax treatment of the resource itself, of machinery utilized in harvesting, transport and production, as well as expenditures on supporting infrastructure, and even research must all be considered.[25]

Apart from environmental tax measures as such, general provisions concerning allowable expense deductions affect the ultimate cost

---

22   *An Act Respecting the Implementation of the Quebec Energy Strategy*, S.Q. 2006, c. 46.

23   *Income Tax Regulations*, C.R.C., c. 945, Sch. II, Classes 24 and 27.

24   Ontario Tax for Fuel Conservation. *Retail Sales Tax Act*, R.S.O. 1990, c. R.31, s. 4, as am. by S.O. 1992, c. 13, s. 2, 1997, c. 19, s. 22.

25   For a valuable review of these and other relevant factors, see Nathalie Chalifour, "Encouraging the Transition to Sustainable Forestry in Canada with Ecological Fiscal Reform—Potential and Pitfalls" (2004) 14 J. Envtl. L. & Prac. 253 at 268–82.

of environmental compliance by business. That is, in the absence of explicit treatment of environmental costs, basic principles of business income taxation serve to determine the deductibility of environmental expenditures, including ordinary costs to avoid pollution, specific expenditures required to obtain and maintain necessary approvals, costs incurred through compliance with administrative orders, remedial work following the cessation of operations, or even penalty costs imposed for non-compliance.[26] Mining reclamation trusts and environmental trusts dedicated to waste disposal and other environmental restoration obligations have the effect of advancing the timing of the deduction of expenses in connection with reclamation work.

Economic incentives (or disincentives) are also highly relevant in the context of municipal property tax assessment. In a pair of Alberta property tax cases, the provincial assessment appeal board and the Edmonton Court of Revision reduced property taxes on contaminated lands to reflect lower market values. The two companies involved had been responsible themselves for the practices that resulted in pollution and, accordingly, lower land values. Although both companies were persuaded by public pressure to pay taxes at the original assessment level, commentators took the occasion to urge a more appropriate reconciliation of property taxes with the goals of environmental policy.[27]

3) Public Spending and Environmentally Dedicated Funds

The historic reluctance of Canadian governments to link specific revenue sources, taxes in particular, with expenditure programs is gradually being overcome to some degree in relation to environment and sustainability measures. The so-called tire tax levied in 1989 on new tire purchases in Ontario and dedicated to research issues and the disposal challenge was a small-scale example until its repeal in 1993.

---

26   R.J. MacKnight, "Taxation: Environmental Cost Write-Offs" in D. Estrin, ed., *Business Guide to Environmental Law* (Toronto: Carswell, 1992) c. 5. In response to public concern that fines, including environmental fines or penalties, might be eligible deductions from otherwise taxable business income as indicated by the Supreme Court of Canada in *65302 British Columbia Ltd. v. Canada*, [1999] 3 S.C.R. 804, the *Income Tax Act* was amended in the course of implementing the 23 March 2004 federal budget. See *A second Act to implement certain provisions of the budget tabled in Parliament on March 23, 2004*, S.C. 2005, c. 19, s. 16.

27   E.J. Sidnell, "Property Assessment of Contaminated Land in Alberta" (1993) 3 J. Envtl. L. & Prac. 231.

Alberta established a fund for environmental protection and enhancement that is also available for environmental emergencies.[28] As well, the province has a Recycling Fund, which in addition to any gifts or donations, is based on surcharges on designated material and may be used to support waste minimization and recycling programs along with research, education, and development activities in the same areas.[29] British Columbia operates a Waste Management Trust Fund to finance the clean up of waste-management facilities that were inadequately closed and for the long-term care of other such facilities.[30] The same province provided for a Sustainable Environment Fund in 1990.[31] Revenues for the fund are derived in part from fines and penalties under provincial environmental legislation and from approvals fees under the *Environmental Management Act* (previously the *Waste Management Act*.) British Columbia also established a Forest Renewal Fund in 1994, a resource-oriented initiative similar in some respects to Ontario's Forestry Futures Trust.[32] In Manitoba a dedicated fund exists to support environmental innovation[33] while in Nova Scotia an environmental trust administered by the provincial Round Table was established to support environmental research, management, and conservation.[34]

C. OTHER ECONOMIC INCENTIVES

1) Insurance

Insurance against environmental liabilities may be required as a matter of law either by statute[35] or pursuant to the terms of an environmental approval, or perhaps as a contractual precondition of borrowing funds. Where not required in any of these senses it may nonetheless be con-

---

28 *Environmental Protection and Enhancement Act*, R.S.A. 2000, c. E-12, s. 30, as am. by S.A. 2003, c. 2, s. 1(24) [*AEPEA*].

29 *AEPEA*, *ibid.*, s. 171; see also *YEA*, above note 14, s. 108.

30 *Environmental Management Act*, S.B.C. 2003, c. 53, s. 52.

31 *Sustainable Environment Fund Act*, R.S.B.C. 1996, c. 445.

32 *Crown Forest Sustainability Act, 1994*, S.O. 1994, c. 25.

33 *The Sustainable Development Act*, C.C.S.M. c. S270, s. 17.

34 *NSEA*, above note 14, s. 28. See also *Environmental Trust Fund Act*, S.N.B. 1990, c. E-93.

35 *AEPEA*, above note 28, s. 120(1); for Ontario statutes requiring insurance see D. Estrin & J. Swaigen, *Environment on Trial* (Toronto: Emond Montgomery, 1993) at 130; *Pesticides Act*, R.S.O. 1990, c. P.11. For discussion, see Benjamin J. Richardson, "Mandating Environmental Liability Insurance" (2002) 12 Duke Envtl. L. & Pol'y F. 293.

sidered prudent on the part of those undertaking activities that entail risk of environmental harm to safeguard themselves against certain forms of potential liabilities to the extent that appropriate insurance coverage is available. Insofar as insurance policies spread or reallocate risks and thus in some respects have the potential to alter incentives for preventive care or to facilitate or to impede certain forms of activity, they fall generally within the realm of economic instruments relevant to environmental protection.

Many design features of liability insurance can, in principle, be used to induce insured parties to take accident-avoidance measures, including measures to reduce the likelihood of environmental damages from industrial operations. Adjustments in the size of the insured's deductible, variations in premium levels and their specific relationship to risk, restrictions on repeat claimants, the elimination of coverage for certain activities or forms of damage, and duties to report or submit to inspections can all be used for this purpose. It is also possible to imagine insurers requiring, as a condition of insurability, that appropriate risk management systems be maintained.

Insurance coverage specifically designed for environmental risk and pollution is comparatively recent, although comprehensive general-liability policies (CGL) traditionally fulfilled this function. The costs and availability of environmental pollution-insurance coverage have been influenced by changes in general-liability coverage arrangements. In some respects, however, the general changes, such as higher deductibles, increased premiums, and a shift from "occurrence-based" claims towards "claims made" policies, were brought about by considerations that were most prevalent in the environmental context, notably the insurer's risk of pollution-damage claims arising years after comparatively modest premiums had been received.[36]

Particular difficulties have arisen in predicting the likelihood and severity of claims involving toxic substances. Scientific uncertainty, including uncertainty about the synergistic effect of chemicals that have been mixed together in waste deposits, is a significant factor here. Moreover, the pathways followed by hazardous contamination as it migrates from storage facilities into neighbouring properties and enters underground water supplies are difficult to anticipate. Disasters, sporadic in occurrence and by definition catastrophic in proportions, defy prediction. The extended latency period between exposure to a toxic

36   K.S. Abraham, *Distributing Risk: Insurance, Legal Theory, and Public Policy* (New Haven, CT: Yale University Press, 1986); *Final Report of the Ontario Task Force on Insurance* (Toronto: Ministry of Financial Institutions, 1986).

substance and manifestation of disease symptoms caused by exposure is a further complicating factor.[37]

The scope of protection available to insureds under comprehensive general-liability policies[38] experienced considerable redefinition and refinement as environmental claims proliferated during the 1960s and 1970s. Initially, claims for environmental liabilities were made under the general wording of comprehensive commercial-liability policies. Under one CGL policy in common use at the time environmental claims began to arise frequently, insurers undertook to "pay on behalf of the Insured all sums which the Insured shall become legally obligated to pay as damages because of property damage caused by accident."[39] Uncertainty with respect to the nature of "accident" led some insurers to replace this concept with the idea of "occurrence," defined as "an accident, including continuous or repeated exposure to conditions which results in bodily injury or property damage neither expected nor intended from the standpoint of the insured." Yet this language also failed to resolve the issue of whether certain forms of polluting activity were "occurrences" within the terms of the policy or were instead the consequence of the insured's normal operations. Other controversial questions arose in connection with the scope of damages, as policyholders sometimes sought to recover expenditures on preventive measures designed to contain pollutants or costs incurred on the basis of administrative orders requiring extensive cleanup programs.

In response to the size and frequency of claims made by policyholders whose interpretations of the contract were often sympathetically viewed by the courts, insurers sought to reduce their own financial risks by including some form of environmental or pollution-liability exclusion clause. Such clauses were intended to restrict coverage to pollution incidents that could be considered "sudden and accidental" rather than the result of general business operations. One such clause, dating from the mid-1970s, stated:

> It is agreed that this policy does not apply to bodily injury or property damage arising out of the discharge, dispersal, release, or escape of smoke, vapours, soot, fumes, acids, alkalis, toxic chemicals, liquids or gases, waste materials, or other irritants, contaminants, or pollutants into or upon land, the atmosphere or any water of any

37 *Ontario Task Force on Insurance, ibid.* at 45–49.

38 From about 1986, comprehensive general-liability policies have been known as Commercial General Liability.

39 M.D. Faieta, "Liability Insurance for Environmental Contamination in Ontario" (1991) 2 C.I.L.R. 125 at 129.

description no matter where located or how contained, or into any watercourse, drainage, or sewage system, but this exclusion does not apply if such discharge, dispersal, release, or escape is sudden and accidental.[40]

Other exclusion clauses were introduced, including clauses intended to address insurance industry concerns with judicial interpretation of "sudden and accidental." One such clause, known as an "absolute" pollution liability exclusion became the standard in both the United States and Canada by about 1986. When residents of an apartment complex claimed compensation for injury from exposure to carbon monoxide attributed to a faulty furnace, the insurer argued that an "absolute" pollution liability exclusion in the building owner's policy barred coverage for such damages. Following a review of the history of "absolute" pollution clauses and consideration of divergent lines of interpretation in U.S. and Canadian cases, Borins J.A. formulated his assessment in the context of insurance law generally and of pollution:

> When the full panoply of insurance contract construction tools is brought to bear on the pollution exclusion, defective maintenance of a furnace giving rise to carbon monoxide poisoning, like related business torts such as temporarily strong odours produced by floor resurfacing or painting, fail the common sense test for determining what is "pollution." These represent claims long covered by CGL insurance policies. To apply an exclusion intended to bar coverage for claims arising from environmental pollution to carbon monoxide poisoning from a faulty furnace, is to deny the history of the exclusion, the purpose of CGL insurance, and the reasonable expectations of policy-holders in acquiring the insurance . . . . Based on the coverage provided by a CGL policy, a reasonable policy-holder would expect that the policy insured the very risk that occurred in this case. A reasonable policy-holder would, therefore, have understood the clause to exclude coverage for damage caused by certain forms of industrial pollution, but not damages caused by the leakage of carbon monoxide from a faulty furnace. In my view, the policy provisions should be construed to give effect to the purpose for which the policy was acquired.[41]

---

40 Aspects of a clause along these lines were considered in *Ontario v. Kansa General Insurance Co.* (1994), 17 O.R. (3d) 38 (C.A.), leave to appeal to S.C.C. refused (1994), 19 O.R. (3d) xvi (note) (S.C.C.).

41 *Zurich Insurance Company v. 686234 Ontario Limited* (2002), 62 O.R.(3d) 447 at 462–63 (C.A.). See also *Boliden Ltd. v. Liberty Mutual Insurance Co.*, [2008] O.J.

Apart from distinctive situations along the lines apparent in this case, the effect of the "absolute" pollution liability exclusion clauses, sharply increased premiums, and higher deductibles, was that by the early 1980s environmental pollution coverage had more or less disappeared or was not considered to be affordable.[42]

A limited pollution-liability policy (LPL) may now be obtained as a special endorsement to the CGL policy. The LPL coverage was introduced in 1985 with the support of an association of insurers and reinsurers known as the Pollution Liability Association, which offers reinsurance for certain pollution incidents, frequently those associated with manufacturing, farming, and dry-cleaning operations. Where the risks appear especially hazardous, measures may be taken to have the insured respond to the concerns, or the association may introduce a policy surcharge.[43]

The LPL contains several provisions that illustrate the relationship between compliance with environmental regulations and the availability of protection for the insured. In addition to the fact that coverage is not provided in connection with waste-management operations, transportation services, nuclear facilities, "war, invasion, act of foreign enemy, hostilities . . . or any other act of deliberate destruction or property, or terrorism," there are several notable general exclusions. Thus, the insurance does not apply to claims arising out of a pollution incident that "results from or is attributable to a failure to comply with any applicable statute, regulation, ordinance, directive, or order relating to the protection of the environment and promulgated by any governmental body, provided that failure to comply is a wilful or deliberate act or omission of any insured." Nor does coverage extend to

> "cleanup costs" caused by a "pollution incident" if any insured is convicted of an offence under any applicable statute or regulation, relating to the protection of the environment and promulgated by any governmental body, as a result of any insured's failure to comply with a legal duty to report the "pollution incident" to a governmental body or to take remedial steps after the "pollution incident."

Other general exclusions address pollution incidents determined to be "expected or intended from the standpoint of any insured."

No. 1438 (C.A.) and *Dave's K.& K. Sandblasting (1998) Ltd. v. Aviva Insurance Co. of Canada* (2007), 30 C.E.L.R. (3d) 74 (B.C.S.C.).

42 *Ontario Task Force on Insurance*, above note 36.

43 Faieta, above note 39. For judicial consideration of an LPL policy, see *Harvey Oil Ltd. v. Lombard General Insurance*, [2003] N.J. No. 273 (S.C), aff'd [2004] N.J. No. 47 (C.A.).

In *Pilot Insurance Co.* v. *Tyre King Tyre Recycling Ltd.*,[44] several aspects of the PLA policy were judicially considered in the aftermath of the Hagersville tire fire of February 1990. Tyre King managed a storage compound containing approximately fourteen million used tires in three piles surrounded by exterior walls of interwoven tires. When a group of teenagers set fire to tires in the compound, nearly all of the tires were consumed over a two-week period and some 60,000 litres of oil and other contaminants entered the environment. When compensation claims arose, the insurer advanced several arguments in an attempt to avoid responsibility under the PLA policy for defending the action or for indemnifying Tyre King in the event that damages were awarded. In response to the insurer's assertion that the fire was not "unexpected or unintentional," Jarvis J. indicated that the intent of third parties such as the vandals had no bearing on the provision in the insurance contract. Nor could possibly negligent conduct on Tyre King's part support an allegation that the company intended the conflagration and its consequences. The court also dismissed Pilot's argument that no pollution incident was involved because pollutants were not discharged from a structure or container by determining that the interwoven tire wall itself constituted a structure in that it was a thing "which is constructed." In addition, Jarvis J. rejected the suggestion that the teenagers' conduct constituted an "act of 'deliberate destruction of property'" within the meaning of the contract. The judge indicated that the conduct excluded must be similar in kind to other elements listed in the war-risk exclusion. Finally, when the insurer claimed an exclusion on the ground that the damage was "expected or intended from the standpoint of the insured," Jarvis commented as follows:

> It is notorious that some handlers of pollutants do so in a careless manner, without regard for the safety of others. A court might well find that such actions were so careless that the resulting injury or property damage was "expected or intended" and that coverage would therefore not be available to indemnify such an insured. I think it likely that such conduct was intended to be caught by this exclusion. However, the exclusion clearly does not apply to intentional acts of third parties. The acts of vandals are not covered.[45]

Although also subject to significant exclusions, and available only on a claims-made basis, another type of policy known as environmental impairment insurance may offer appropriate coverage in some circum-

---

44 (1992), 8 O.R. (3d) 236 (Gen. Div.).
45 *Ibid.* at 241.

stances. Environmental impairment rather than accidents or pollution incidents is the subject of protection, with environmental impairment defined as bodily injury; property damage; interference with or diminution of any environmental right or amenity protected by law; liability to clean up outside the premises of the insured arising out of any and all emissions, discharges, dispersals, disposal, seepages, releases, or escapes of any liquids, solids, gaseous, or thermal irritants into or upon land, the atmosphere, or any watercourse or body of water; or generations of smells, noises, vibrations, light, electricity, radiations, changes in temperature, or any other sensory phenomenon but not fire or explosion.

The ongoing challenges of designing appropriate environmental insurance and making it available at affordable rates have raised questions about the continuation of policies in this field and about the economic implications of their possible disappearance. Some attention has therefore shifted to alternative means of administering whatever environmental liability policies remain, and there is speculation to the effect that insurers themselves will become surrogate regulators, actively involved in monitoring the performance of their insureds for the purpose of more precisely controlling the extent to which they, as insurers, are exposed to the risk of claims.

Three important advantages have been identified in a greater level of insurance industry involvement in this unofficial regulatory role. First, loss prevention would replace reactive management as the primary basis for decision making. Second, insurers would not only consider the nature and potential scope of physical risks inherent in whatever particular activity is under consideration, but they might also be expected to investigate the track records and past performance of their prospective insureds. Finally, to the extent that environmental decision making by government bodies has embodied political considerations, the influence of these factors would likely be lessened.[46]

2) Financial Institutions and Environmental Monitoring

As previously discussed, there are circumstances in which those other than the actual operators of polluting businesses have been held legally responsible for cleaning up contaminated lands or for other costs associated with environmental protection (see chapters 7, 11). Lenders and those acting on their behalf such as trustees and receivers have experi-

---

46 L.A. Reynolds, "New Directions for Environmental Impairment Liability Insurance in Canada" (1996) 6 J. Envtl. L. & Prac. 89.

enced losses that have encouraged some critics of the lender-liability provisions to label such statutes as "deep-pocket" statutes in contrast to more widely accepted polluter-pays legislation. Even where those advancing funds do not face direct environmental costs, they are increasingly aware that the value of their security may be undermined if environmental charges and liabilities threaten a borrower's solvency.

The Canadian Bankers Association, among others, predicted the implications for financing:

> [e]nvironmentally risky borrowers will find it difficult, or perhaps impossible, to make credit arrangements, whether from a bank or any other lender. Since additional investigations will be required to alleviate lenders' environmental concerns and an increased risk premium will be built into the cost of borrowing to cover possible loan losses arising from environmental liability, all borrowers will pay increased costs to obtain funds.[47]

Although unable to quantify the impact on Canadian financial markets, the CBA reported "an increasing number of instances" where member banks refused to advance certain forms of credit on the basis of the risk of environmental liability. As regular participants or "repeat players" in business development, major lending institutions have moved quickly along the learning curve to introduce environmentally specific loan documentation and to require environmental audits.[48]

Some lament the loss of specific economic activity in those cases where lenders, having investigated the nature of the environmental risk and the applicant's capacity to manage it, decline to advance funds. On the other hand, systematic pre-screening stimulated by a broader assessment of risk and financial viability strikes many as highly desirable in the general interest of environmental protection and accident avoidance. It is a mechanism, in other words, integrating environmental considerations directly into economic decision making. As such, the systemic concern of financial institutions with environmental liability in commercial and real estate transactions significantly increases the

---

47 Canadian Bankers Association, *Sustainable Capital: The Effect of Environmental Liability in Canada on Borrowers, Lenders, and Investors* (Toronto, Canadian Bankers Association, 1991) at 3–4.

48 For a general guide to environmental concerns from a banker's perspective, see Canadian Bankers' Association, *Your Business, Your Bank and the Environment: An Overview of How Banks Address Environmental Risk in the Credit Review Process* (Toronto: Canadian Bankers' Association, 2000). For further discussion, see online: www.cba.ca/en/viewPub.asp?fl=304&docid=34&pg=1.

likelihood that environmental factors will be integrated to some degree into business planning on a comprehensive basis.

D. CONCLUSION

The introduction of a variety of economic instruments for environmental protection raises questions about the relationship between such initiatives and more traditional forms of regulation. Economic instruments remain anathema to some, while certain advocates enthusiastically appear to anticipate the dismantling of governmental controls in the environmental field. It is more likely that economic and regulatory approaches will coexist indefinitely. Bruce Doern has described one perspective on the challenge of identifying the appropriate interrelationship:

> It calls for a more sensible pairing of functions for those aspects of environmental policy that only the state can do well—setting standards in a democratic way and ensuring overall compliance—with those that only markets can do well—doing it at least cost, through the use of competitive technologies and price signals, by choices made at the firm or micro-organizational level.[49]

An Ontario study on taxation has gone somewhat further in an attempt to spell out, though still at a general level, the advantages of regulation and taxation as instruments of environmental protection:

> Regulation tends to be most appropriate . . . where the number of individual activities giving rise to the environmental problem is relatively limited. . . . Regulation, because it establishes the basis for direct control over the amount of environmental damage caused by the product or process, is also better suited to situations where there is a desire either to eliminate an environmentally damaging product or process altogether, or to limit its impact in a predetermined fashion.
>
> In contrast, taxation is most appropriate where there are large numbers of individual sources of pollution and where the objective is to reduce, rather than eliminate, activities that cause environmental damage. . . . Similarly, it may be impractical to eliminate an activity entirely, or even to reduce it substantially in the short term, but it may still be appropriate to impose a tax to compensate society for

---

49 G.B. Doern, "Regulations and Market Approaches: The Essential Environmental Partnership" in G.B. Doern, ed., *Getting It Green: Case Studies in Canadian Environmental Regulation* (Toronto: C.D. Howe Institute, 1990) 1 at 2.

environmental damage caused by the activity and to provide an incentive for change in the longer term.[50]

Canada was the subject of a general assessment of national environmental performance conducted by the OECD in which it was argued that increased use of economic instruments should be treated as a "matter of urgency." The study identified a series of contraints which, in the authors' view, had impeded more general adoption of such tools:

> Industry is concerned about day-to-day competitive pressures, especially in relation to cost competitiveness with the U.S. It has difficulty understanding how to implement new instruments such as trading. Within governments, economic agencies have supported economic instruments in principle, but resisted specific proposals for targeted incentives on allocative efficiency grounds. The public is wary of new fees and charges, and of the allocation of "rights to pollute." There is a general resistance to external pressure to change consumption patterns. Small but influential groups have blocked some proposals.[51]

FURTHER READINGS

CHALIFOUR, NATHALIE, "Encouraging the Transition to Sustainable Forestry in Canada with Ecological Fiscal Reform" (2004) 14 J. Envtl. L. & Prac. 253

DOERN, G.B., "Regulations and Market Approaches: The Essential Environmental Partnership" in G.B. Doern, ed., *Getting It Green: Case Studies in Canadian Environmental Regulation* (Toronto: C.D. Howe Institute, 1990)

DOLDEN, E.A., "The Comprehensive General Liability Policy: Responding to Modern Business Risks" (1991) 2 C.I.L.R. 11

DUFF, D.G., "Tax Policy and Global Warming" (2003) 51 Can. Tax J. 2063

FAIETA, M.D., "Liability Insurance for Environmental Contamination in Ontario" (1991) 2 C.I.L.R. 125–70

GRANDBOIS, M., "Entre la déréglementation et la surréglementation : le droit québécois de l'environnement" (1999) 78 Can. Bar. Rev. 111

---

50   *Report of the Ontario Fair Tax Commission*, above note 21 at 554.
51   *OECD Environmental Performance Reviews: Canada* (OECD, Paris, 2004) at 124–25.

JUTLAH, R.S., "Economic Instruments and Environmental Policy in Canada" (1999) 8 J. Envtl. L. & Prac. 323

Report of the Ontario Fair Tax Commission: Fair Taxation in a Changing World (Toronto: University of Toronto Press, 1993)

REYNOLDS, L.A., "New Directions for Environmental Impairment Liability Insurance in Canada" (1996) 6 J. Envtl. L. & Prac. 89

RICHARDSON, BENJAMIN J., "Financing Environmental Change: A New Role for Canadian Environmental Law" (2004) 49 McGill L.J. 145

SARGENT, JOHN H., "The Economics of Energy and the Environment: The Potential Role of Market-based Instruments" (2002) 28 Can.-U.S.L.J. 499

SWAIGEN, J.Z., *Compensation of Pollution Victims in Canada* (Study prepared for the Economic Council of Canada) (Ottawa: Supply & Services, 1981)

TEITELBAUM, M.S., & L.J. BRABANDER, "Environmental Insurance Coverage Issues: Will U.S. Developments Filter into the Canadian Courts?" (2003) 21 Can J. Ins. L. 57

WEERSINK, A.J., *et al.*, "Economic Instruments and Environmental Policy in Agriculture" (1998) 24 Can. Pub. Pol'y 309

ENVIRONMENTAL REPORTING AND INFORMATION SOURCES

A. INTRODUCTION

Under the auspices of the Economic Commission for Europe an agreement was reached at Aarhus, Denmark, in 1998 concerning access to information, public participation in decision making and access to justice in environmental matters. In this context, the Aarhus Convention formally defined "environmental information" as any information, in whatever form, relating to:

(a) The state of elements of the environment, such as air and atmosphere, water, soil, landscape, and natural sites, biological diversity and its components, including genetically modified organisms, and the interaction among these elements;

(b) Factors such as substances, energy, noise, and radiation, and activities or measures, including administrative measures, environmental agreements, policies, legislation, plans, and programmes, affecting or likely to affect the elements of the environment within the scope of subparagraph (a) above, and cost-benefit and other economic analyses and assumptions used in environmental decision-making;

(c) The state of human health and safety, conditions of human life, cultural sites and built structures, inasmuch as they are or may be affected by the state of the elements of the environment or,

> through these elements, by the factors, activities, or measures referred to in subparagraph (b) above.[1]

Although Canadian environmental law has not yet provided an all-encompassing approach to information nor formally recognised the significance of its availability along the lines set out in the Aarhus Convention, there are indications that the rationales for making information more widely available are equally applicable to environmental information. Freedom of information legislation has been introduced across the country and aspects of its contribution to democracy have been recognized by the Supreme Court of Canada:

> Access to information legislation . . . helps to ensure first, that citizens have the information required to participate meaningfully in the democratic process, and secondly, that politicians and bureaucrats remain accountable to the citizenry.[2]

In addition to arguments oriented around democracy, that is, to claims around informed public decision making, the availability of environmental information facilitates individualized decision making, as citizens may, to a greater or lesser extent depending on the circumstances, make choices about the environmental risks to which they or their families should be exposed. An initiative of the National Round Table on the Environment and the Economy (NRTEE) and the minister of finance to promote a new set of environmental and sustainable development indicators (ESDI) was specifically intended to advance understanding of the overall progress of Canadian society in ways that are largely overlooked by current measures such as gross domestic product:

> The Minister of Finance instigated the ESDI Initiative because of widespread agreement . . . that the national-level, macroeconomic indicators currently in use to judge a society's success provide only part of the information needed: they exclude many of the factors on which we depend for continued development as a society, particularly the services provided by a clean environment and by our education system. Moreover, macroeconomic indicators emphasize current income rather than wealth, but it is the latter that is the basis for generating income in the future. By neglecting the needs of future

---

1   *Convention on Access to Information, Public Participation in Decision-Making and Access to Justice in Environmental Matters*, adopted at Aarhus, Denmark, 25 June 1998, art. 2.

2   *Dagg v. Canada (Minister of Finance)*, [1997] 2 S.C.R. 403 at para. 61.

generations, macroeconomic indicators ignore the main concern of sustainable development.[3]

B. STATE OF THE ENVIRONMENT REPORTS

Attempts to meet the challenge of describing the state of the environment at the global and national levels have become more common since the publication in 1987 of the WCED report, *Our Common Future.*[4] A prototype report on Canada's state of the environment was published in 1986, using fifteen terrestrial ecozones and four aquatic ecosystems for organizational purposes. This approach, it was explained,

> allows characteristics of the environment to be compared within ecosystems over time and between one ecozone and another at any one time. It also makes possible, for the first time, an examination of an ecosystem based not on a general description and subjective interpretation, but on quantitative data of physical, biological, and dynamic response characteristics. Thus the extent and seriousness of potential or actual environmental change, or the amount and condition of a specific natural resource and its relation to other resources, may be identified in a way not previously possible.[5]

In subsequent editions, those responsible for preparing the report refined the presentation of data, and facilitated access to the document by publishing it as a CD-ROM and on the Internet.[6] As of 2004, the challenge set out by the NRTEE in its environment and sustainable development initiative has been at least partially met on the basis of a new data series, Canadian Environmental Sustainability Indicators, a collaborative project involving Environment Canada, Health Canada and Statistics Canada.[7]

The concept of state of the environment reporting arranged along jurisdictional lines has been adopted in legislation in several provinces

---

3   NRTEE, *Environment and Sustainable Development Indicators for Canada* (Ottawa: NRTEE, 2003) at 9.

4   From a global perspective, see the *Millennium Ecosystem Assessment* (2005).

5   Environment Canada, *State of the Environment Report for Canada* by P.B. Bird & D.J. Rapport (Ottawa: Supply & Services, 1986) at viii.

6   Online: www.ec.gc.ca/soer-ree/English/SOER/1996report/Doc/1-1.cfm.

7   Statistics Canada, *Canadian Environmental Sustainability Indicators, 2005* (Ottawa: Statistics Canada, 2005), online: www.statcan.ca/english/freepub/16-251-XIE/16-251-XIE2005000.htm.

and territories.[8] Government reporting obligations differ somewhat in terms of the frequency of report-publication and in terms of the required scope or coverage of the reports. Yukon legislation is most explicit in relation to the purposes of state of the environment reporting and with regard to content requirements. In the words of the statute, the Yukon State of the Environment report is intended to "provide early warning and analysis of potential problems for the environment; . . . to allow the public to monitor progress toward the achievement of the objectives of this Act; and . . . to provide baseline information for environmental planning, assessment and regulation."[9] In addition to baseline information on the environment, the Yukon report is required to establish indicators of impairment or improvement and to analyse changes in the indicators as these emerge over time. The report is further expected to identify emerging environmental problems, particularly any that involve long-term and cumulative effects.[10]

Other forms of environmental reporting requirements have frequently been established for individual departments or in connection with specific pieces of legislation. The federal minister of the environment, for example, must report annually on the administration and enforcement of *CEPA, 1999*[11] while Natural Resources Canada is under a statutory duty to report annually on the state of Canada's forests. Canada's *Fisheries Act* provides for the creation of additional data sources. Specifically, the responsible minister is required to report annually "on the administration and enforcement of the provisions . . . relating to fish habitat protection and pollution prevention."[12]

Certain designated federal departments have prepared sustainable-development strategies for presentation to the House of Commons. These were originally due by 15 December 1997 and are to be updated at least every three years. To monitor and report on departmental progress towards sustainable development, the office of the federal commissioner of the environment and sustainable development (CESD) was established to work with the auditor general of Canada, whose responsibil-

---

8   *The Environment Act*, S.M. 1987–88, c. 26, s. 4; *Environment Act*, S.N.S. 1994–95, c. 1, s. 16 [*NSEA*]; *Environmental Protection and Enhancement Act*, S.A. 1992, c. E–13.3, s. 15 [*AEPEA*].

9   *Environment Act*, S.Y. 1991, c. 5, s. 47.

10   *Ibid.*

11   *Canadian Environmental Protection Act, 1999*, S.C. 1999, c. 33, s. 342 [*CEPA, 1999*].

12   *Fisheries Act*, R.S.C. 1985, c. F-14, s. 42.1(1) [*FA*]. See also *Wild Animal and Plant Protection and Regulation of International and Interprovincial Trade Act*, S.C. 1992, c. 52, s. 28.

ities were extended to include bringing to the attention of the House of Commons any cases where "money has been expended without due regard to the environmental effects of those expenditures in the context of sustainable development."[13] The CESD has recently completed a review and assessment of departmental progress towards meeting commitments set out in earlier sustainable development strategies.[14]

Statistics Canada's survey of consumer behaviour in relation to the environment, *Households and their Environment*, last produced in 1994, has recently been updated. With reference to the 2006 year, information is now available concerning consumption and conservation of water, energy use and home heating, gasoline powered equipment use, pesticide and fertilizer use, recycling, composting and waste disposal practices, air and water quality, and transportation decisions.

C. CORPORATE INFORMATION

As noted in the previous discussions of environmental regulation (chapter 6) and corporate environmental obligations (chapter 9), businesses will frequently be required by legislation, governance principles, or under the terms and conditions of operating permits and licences to file information and reports on the environmental dimensions of their operations. Separate reporting obligations apply in the case of spills. Other specialized pieces of legislation also impose reporting and disclosure obligations.

Included in this inventory of new or refined sources of information are disclosure requirements relating to the workplace or the transportation of dangerous goods, and notice provisions applicable to other regulatory initiatives. In some jurisdictions, vendors of real estate may be required to file information concerning the condition of their property. In addition, those convicted of offences under the *Fisheries Act* may, for a three-year period following conviction, be ordered to report on their activities.[15]

The increasingly widespread practice of undertaking an environmental audit or self-evaluation (see chapter 9) has resulted in a further source of information on business operations and environmental compliance. The existence of such detailed information raises questions

---

13 *Auditor General Act*, R.S.C. 1985, c. A–17, s. 7(1)(f).

14 Commissioner of the Environment and Sustainable Development, *2006 September Report* (Ottawa: Office of the Auditor General, 2006) c. 4.

15 *FA*, above note 12.

about access and about the uses to which such information may be put.

Some environmental legislation addresses the release on request of environmental information in the possession of government. Information to be disclosed may include documentation received from licence or permit applicants, emission-monitoring results, and reports provided by those operating under approvals or orders. Although the disclosure provisions generally provide for confidentiality in certain specified circumstances, the presumption of public access to requested environmental information seems firmly established.[16] Under *CEPA, 1999*, for example, apart from certain specific exceptions, the minister may disclose information where:

(a) the disclosure is in the interest of public health, public safety, or the protection of the environment; and

(b) the public interest in the disclosure clearly outweighs in importance

(i) any material financial loss or prejudice to the competitive position of the person who provided the information or on whose behalf it was provided, and

(ii) any damage to the privacy, reputation or human dignity of any individual that may result from the disclosure.[17]

Notwithstanding a widely acknowledged presumption in favour of disclosure of information held in public hands, data and documentary materials are not always forthcoming and their release may be contested.[18]

A further challenge to the issue of disclosure of information is the complexity of identifying relevant environmental information, assuming its availability. One partial response is the creation of an environmental registry, or a central listing of decisions and instruments concerning environmental operations in a given jurisdiction. Modern technology greatly facilitates access to such databases. Nova Scotia

---

16   *AEPEA*, above note 8, s. 33; *Environmental Rights Act*, R.S.N.W.T. 1988 (Supp.), c. 83, s. 3; *Freedom of Information and Protection of Privacy Act*, R.S.O. 1990, c. F.31, s. 18; *Municipal Freedom of Information and Protection of Privacy Act*, R.S.O. 1990, c. M.56. See also Bill 48, *An Act to Provide a Charter of Environmental Rights and Responsibilities*, 2d Sess., 22d Leg., Saskatchewan, 1992, cl. 9.

17   *CEPA, 1999*, above note 11, s. 315(1). See generally ss. 313–21.

18   Lynda M. Collins, Jerry V. De Marco, & Alan D. Levy, "Accessing Environmental Information in Ontario: A Legislative Comment on Ontario's *Freedom of Information and Protection of Privacy Act*" (2004) 13 J. Envtl. L. & Prac. 267.

legislation now provides for a registry along these lines, as do the *OEBR* and *CEPA, 1999*.[19]

In some jurisdictions, the long-standing difficulty of lack of public information concerning the compliance status of industry has been at least partially addressed. In 1990, for example, the British Columbia government began systematic reporting of non-compliance in relation to waste-management permits and more general "pollution concerns." Environmental charges laid by provincial officials were also included.

D. THE NATIONAL POLLUTANTS RELEASE INVENTORY

A national inventory of releases of pollutants (NPRI) established under the legislative authority of *CEPA, 1999* provides published information on releases to the environment of a wide range of substances.[20] In 1993, its first year of operation, the NPRI collected data on 178 substances that were released to air, land, or water or that were transferred off-site in the form of waste. The selection was initially based on a review of the United States Toxic Release Inventory and the Canadian Chemical Producers' Association National Emissions Reduction Masterplan.

The most recent NPRI for 2005 presents information relating to approximately 300 substances released at 8000 reporting facilities in Canada. The information base is expected to assist in further environmental protection by identifying priorities, permitting progress to be monitored, stimulating voluntary efforts to reduce releases, and generally supporting regulatory programs.[21] The Canadian Institute for Environmental Law and Policy, the Canadian Environmental Law Association, and the Canadian Environmental Defence Fund provide location-specific information on pollutant releases in cooperation with a U.S. organization, Environmental Defense.[22]

---

19   NSEA, above note 8, s. 10; *Environmental Bill of Rights, 1993*, S.O. 1993, c. 28; *CEPA, 1999*, above note 11, s. 12.

20   *CEPA, 1999*, *ibid.*, ss. 46–50. These provisions shore up the statutory basis for information requests from industry in comparison with the *CEPA* era. See *IPSCO v. Canada (Minister of Environment)* (2000), 33 C.E.L.R. (N.S.) 223 (Sask. Q.B.).

21   Online: www.ec.gc.ca/pdb/npri. At the time of writing preliminary data for 2006 were available but not yet analyzed.

22   Online: www.pollutionwatch.org.

FURTHER READINGS

Canadian Environmental Directory 1996/97, 6th ed. (Toronto: Canadian Almanac & Directory Publishing Co., 1996)

COMMISSION FOR ENVIRONMENTAL COOPERATION, *Public Access to Government-held Information* (Montreal: Commission for Environmental Cooperation, 2003)

COMMISSION FOR ENVIRONMENTAL COOPERATION, *Taking Stock: 2004 North American Pollutant Releases and Transfers* (Montreal: Commission for Environmental Cooperation, 2007)

ESTRIN, D., & J. SWAIGEN, eds., *Environment on Trial*, 3d ed. (Toronto: Emond Montgomery, 1993) appendix

OECD, *Environmental Performance Reviews: Canada* (Paris: OECD, 2004)

CHAPTER 19

CLIMATE CHANGE: CANADIAN LEGAL AND POLICY RESPONSES

The causes and consequences of climate change, as discussed in connection with the international legal context for Canadian environmental law, now command attention at all levels of government and throughout society for the range and complexity of challenges they present. Even as it has become increasingly urgent to endeavour to mitigate the factors and processes that contribute to ongoing climate change, simultaneous efforts are essential to facilitate adaptation to the impact and effects of climate change that are already underway. Following a brief review of climate change information, notably the work of the Intergovernmental Panel on Climate Change (IPCC), this chapter surveys recent Canadian responses at the federal level, in intergovernmental settings, in a number of provinces and within the municipal context.

A. CAUSES AND CONSEQUENCES

For the benefit of policy-makers, experts from the physical sciences associated with the IPCC summarized their current understanding of the contribution of human activity to changing atmospheric conditions:

> Global atmospheric concentrations of carbon dioxide, methane and nitrous oxide have increased markedly as a result of human activities since 1750 and now far exceed pre-industrial values . . . . The global increases in carbon dioxide concentration are due primarily to fossil

fuel use and land-use change, while those of methane and nitrous oxide are primarily due to agriculture.[1]

In the view of the same IPCC assessors, "warming of the climate system is unequivocal, as is now evident from observations or increases in global average air and ocean temperatures, widespread melting of snow and ice, and rising global average sea level."[2]

Long-term changes in climate have been observed at the continental and regional bases and on the ocean basin level as well. These observations include significant increases in Arctic temperatures and changes in ice conditions, pronounced alteration in precipitation levels, shifting wind patterns as well as weather extremes such as droughts, heavy precipitation, heat waves and more intense tropical cyclones. IPCC scientists have concluded that "most of the observed increase in globally averaged temperatures since the mid-20th century is *very likely* due to the observed increase in anthropogenic greenhouse gas concentrations."[3] Projections based on modelling support the expectation that

> [c]ontinued greenhouse gas emissions at or above current rates would cause further warming and induce many changes in the global climate system during the 21st century that would very likely be larger than those observed during the 20th century.[4]

Examinations of climate change and its anticipated sectoral impacts on agriculture, forestry, and fisheries, for example, have also been conducted from the Canadian perspective.[5] On a broad scale, ecosystems and habitat are transformed by climate change with disruptive implications for biodiversity and dependent human populations. Regionally-focused studies, including studies of the Canadian Arctic, the Prairies and the Great Lakes have pursued the inquiry in more detail.[6] The lat-

---

1   Intergovernmental Panel on Climate Change, *Climate Change 2007: The Physical Science Basis — Summary for Policymakers* (Cambridge: Cambridge University Press, 2007) at 2, online: http://ipcc-wg1.ucar.edu/wg1/docs/WG1AR4_SPM_PlenaryApproved.pdf.

2   *Ibid.* at 4.

3   *Ibid.* at 8 [emphasis in original].

4   *Ibid.* at 10.

5   Canada, Climate Change Impacts and Adaptation Program, *Climate Change Impacts and Adaptation: A Canadian Perspective* (Ottawa: Climate Change Impacts and Adaptation Program, 2004).

6   George W. Kling *et al.*, *Confronting Climate Change in the Great Lakes Region: Impacts on Our Communities and Ecosystems* (Cambridge, MA: Union of Concerned Scientists, 2003); S. Nickels *et al.*, *Unikkaaqatigiit — Putting the Human Face on Climate Change: Perspectives from Inuit in Canada* (Ottawa: Inuit Tapiriit Kanata-

ter have often identified potential social, economic and health consequences of continuing climate change. Health-related implications of
climate change—both direct and indirect—have been explained along
the following lines:

> A growing body of research shows climate change can affect health
> through different pathways that vary in their directness, temporal
> scale and complexity. Climate change can affect health *directly* as a
> result of exposure to climatic extremes (e.g. high temperatures caus-
> ing dehydration and heat stroke) or sudden, intense changes in the
> environment (e.g. tornadoes causing injury). While direct pathways
> such as these often result in immediate health impacts, in some cases
> the impacts are not apparent until years of prolonged environmental
> exposure (e.g. ultraviolet (UV) radiation and skin cancer).
>
> Health can also be affected *indirectly* as a result of climate-in-
> duced changes in biological and geochemical systems, for instance
> by creating conditions favourable for disease (e.g. warmer, wetter
> weather favours the life cycle of mosquitoes, influencing the spread
> of the West Nile virus). Climate change can also indirectly have an
> impact through economic and social systems, for example through
> loss of employment or property after a natural disaster resulting in
> stress and other illnesses. These indirect pathways generally result in
> longer-term health impacts.
>
> Virtually all aspects of life, from food production and water man-
> agement, and energy production and consumption, to storm sewer,
> drainage and sanitation systems, and housing and health infrastruc-
> tures, including disease surveillance and control, are designed for a
> specific climate. Health risks arise when any one of these systems fails
> or becomes compromised—as they may in a changing climate.[7]

Increasingly severe threats posed by the continuing process of climate change have encouraged many jurisdictions to take steps intended to reduce the emission of greenhouse gases,[8] while economic studies

---

mi, 2006). For additional information on a regional basis, including teaching
materials, see online: http://adaptation.nrcan.gc.ca/posters/curriculum/index_e.
php.

7   Kaila-Lea Clarke, "Health in a Changing Climate" Health Policy Research Bulletin, Issue 11 (2005), online: www.hc-sc.gc.ca/sr-sr/pubs/hpr-rpms/bull/2005-
climat/2005-climat-5-eng.php.

8   For valuable and influential overviews of climate change and policy options, see
Tim Flannery, *The Weather Makers: How We Are Changing the Climate and What
It Means for Life on Earth* (Toronto: HarperTrophyCanada, 2007) and George
Monbiot, *Heat: How to Stop the Planet from Burning* (Scarborough, ON: Double-
day, 2006). Important legislative developments in other jurisdictions include

have indicated the virtue of prompt action rather than delay. One of the most prominent of these, known as the Stern Review, after the author of the report, Sir Nicholas Stern of the United Kingdom, utilized a number of techniques to analyse the economic costs of climate change.[9]

Evidence accumulated by the Stern Review supports, in the view of its author, "a simple conclusion," namely that "the benefits of strong and early action far outweigh the economic costs of not acting."[10] The report estimates that the long-term costs and risks of inaction in relation to climate change "will be equivalent to losing at least 5 percent of global GDP each year, now and forever,"[11] whereas the costs of acting now to reduce greenhouse gas emissions in order to avoid the worst climate change impacts "can be limited to around 1 percent of global GDP each year."[12] It is unnecessary and inappropriate, the study insists, to imagine conflict between economic development and measures to avert climate change:

> The world does not need to choose between averting climate change and promoting growth and development. Changes in energy technologies and in the structure of economies have created opportunities to decouple growth from greenhouse gas emissions. Indeed, ignoring climate change will eventually damage economic growth.[13]

As the Stern Review provides strong recent impetus to the current round of policy development and action, highlights from its findings are a valuable backdrop to consideration of Canadian climate change efforts:

> If no action is taken to reduce emissions, the concentration of greenhouse gases in the atmosphere could reach double its pre-industrial level as early as 2035, virtually committing us to a global average temperature rise of over 2°C. In the longer term, there would be more than a 50% chance that the temperature rise would exceed 5°C. This rise would be very dangerous indeed; it is equivalent to the change in average temperatures from the last ice age to today. Such a radical change in the physical geography of the world must lead to major

---

the Australian *Energy Efficiency Opportunities Act* (2006) and California's *Global Warming Solutions Act* (2006).

9   Nicholas Stern, *The Economics of Climate Change: The Stern Review* (Cambridge: Cambridge University Press, 2007).

10   *Ibid.* at vi.

11   *Ibid.*

12   *Ibid.*

13   *Ibid.* at viii.

changes in the human geography—where people live and how they live their lives . . . .

The risks of the worst impacts of climate change can be substantially reduced if greenhouse gas levels in the atmosphere can be stabilised between 450 and 550 ppm CO_2 equivalent (CO_2e). The current level is 430 ppm CO_2e today, and it is rising at more than 2 ppm each year. Stabilization in this range would require emissions to be at least 25% below current levels by 2050, and perhaps much more . . . .

The power sector around the world would need to be at least 60% decarbonised by 2050 for atmospheric concentrations to stabilise at or below 550 ppm CO_2e, and deep emissions cuts will also be required in the transport sector.[14]

By way of policy prescription, Stern highlights the importance of increased energy efficiency, changes in demand, and the adoption of clean power, heat and transport technologies. The Stern Review characterizes climate change as the greatest market failure in history and identifies three core ingredients of an effective global response:

The first is the pricing of carbon, implemented through tax, trading or regulation. The second is policy to support innovation and the deployment of low-carbon technologies. And the third is action to remove barriers to energy efficiency, and to inform, educate and persuade individuals about what they can do to respond to climate change.[15]

These objectives provide a valuable framework within which to outline steps that have been taken to address climate change within the Canadian context. It might also be added that implementation of effective climate change policy within each jurisdiction should be carried out in a manner that is consistent with principles of good governance and the rule of law.

Canada's lamentable national failure to respond effectively to emission reduction commitments assumed under the Kyoto Protocol 1997 has significantly increased the challenge of adjustment that lies ahead. As an Annex I Party to the UN *Framework Convention on Climate Change*,

---

14   *Ibid.* at vi–viii.
15   *Ibid.* at viii. In an interim report released in June 2007, the National Round Table on Environment and the Economy reviewed alternative Canadian response scenarios, arguing that an immediate and aggressive response is more likely to be effective in avoiding environmental damage, and might ultimately be less disruptive to the economy overall. See NRTEE, *Interim Report to the Minister of the Environment* (June 2007), online: www.nrtee-trnee.ca/eng/publications/ecc-interim-report/index-ecc-interim-report-eng.htm.

Canada is required to submit a national inventory of anthropogenic sources and sinks of greenhouse gases. The *National Inventory Report 1990–2005: Information on Greenhouse Gas Sources and Sinks in Canada* was updated for 2005.[16] In 2005, Canadian emissions were 25.3 percent above 1990 levels and thus at a level 32.7 percent above the Kyoto target. However, data for 2003–2005 indicate that there was a flattening of the emissions growth curve due primarily to a significant reduction in emissions from electricity production, a reduced demand for heating fuels due to warmer winters, and a reduction in the increase in fossil fuel production.[17] Yet Canadian GHG emissions are still increasing on a long-term basis. This is attributable, to a significant degree, to oil and gas production, much of which is ultimately exported to the United States. On a geographic basis, the province of Alberta produced the largest amount of greenhouse gas emissions in 2005, and also has had the largest increase since 1990. On a sectoral basis, changes in total emissions in megatons for the period 1990 to 2006 are as follows:

Table 19.1: Changes in Greenhouse Gas Emissions 1990–2006

Sector	Change
Energy Industries	Increase 113.4 Mt (+24.2 percent)
Transportation	Increase 46.7 Mt (+32.1 percent)
Industrial Processes	Decrease 0.3 Mt (-0.7 percent)
Agriculture	Increase 12.3 Mt (+25 percent)
Waste	Increase 2.7 Mt (+15.2 percent)

Source: Environment Canada, "Canada's Greenhouse Gas Inventory: A Summary of Trends," online: www.ec.gc.ca/pdb/ghg/inventory_report/2006/tab_eng.cfm.

B. FEDERAL CLIMATE CHANGE INITIATIVES

Since 1997, the date of the Kyoto negotiations setting out emissions reductions targets to be achieved during the 2008-2012 period by industrialized nations subject to the terms agreed, several climate change plans have been produced at the federal level. The *Government of Canada Action Plan 2000 on Climate Change*[18] was followed in 2002 by the

---

16   Environment Canada, *National Inventory Report 1990–2005: Information on Greenhouse Gas Sources and Sinks in Canada* (Ottawa: Environment Canada, Greenhouse Gas Division, 2007).

17   *Ibid.*

18   Online: http://env.chass.utoronto.ca/env200y/ESSAY2001/gofcdaplan_eng2.pdf.

Climate Change Plan for Canada[19] which in its turn gave way to *Project Green—Moving Forward on Climate Change: A Plan for Honouring Our Kyoto Commitment*[20] in 2005, the year in which the underlying international agreement came into legal force. In general terms, this sequence of proposals, accompanied by public funding announcements, relied heavily upon voluntary emission reduction measures. These were to be adopted on a sectoral basis, and by individual Canadians. The utility and appropriateness of economic incentives to promote behavioural transformation eventually received some acknowledgement: *Project Green* emphasized the role of large final emitters (LFEs) in the mining, oil and gas, manufacturing and thermal electricity sectors, and anticipated a combination of regulations and tradable emissions credits and other incentive programs to encourage compliance.[21]

These initiatives overall were evaluated by the House of Commons Standing Committee on Environment and Sustainable Development as *ad hoc* in nature, lacking strategic coherence, and generally devoid of an accountability framework. As assessed by the Commissioner of the Environment and Sustainable Development, progress has been sporadic. No effective governance structure has been established for the management of climate change activity at the federal level, and in the case of the most prominent voluntary agreement—an arrangement with the automotive industry—no provision was made to verify the model, data, or results to be employed in measuring progress.[22]

On the legislative front, a government proposal known as *Canada's Clean Air Act* was introduced in the House of Commons in October 2006. This measure, Bill C-30, *An Act to amend the Canadian Environmental Protection Act, 1999, the Energy Efficiency Act and the Motor Vehicle Fuel Consumption Standards Act* was severely criticized and extensively amended in the course of the parliamentary process before it was finally abandoned. In contrast, a private member's bill, Bill C-288, *An Act to*

19 Online: http://dsp-psd.pwgsc.gc.ca/Collection/En56-183-2002E.pdf.

20 Environment Canada, *Project Green—Moving Forward on Climate Change: A Plan for Honouring Our Kyoto Commitment* (Ottawa: Environment Canada, 2005).

21 To facilitate regulation of greenhouse gas emissions, carbon dioxide, methane, nitrous oxide, hydrofluorocarbons, perfluorocarbons, and sulfur hexafluoride were listed, upon assessment, as toxic substances under section 64 of the *Canadian Environmental Protection Act, 1999*, S.C. 1999, c. 33 [*CEPA, 1999*] . See C. Gaz. 2005.II.2568.

22 Commissioner of the Environment and Sustainable Development, *2006 September Report* (Ottawa: Office of the Auditor General, 2006) c. 1 "Managing the Federal Approach to Climate Change," online: www.oag-bvg.gc.ca/internet/English/aud_ch_cesd_200609_1_e_14983.html.

ensure Canada meets its global climate change obligations under the Kyoto Protocol was enacted at the close of the parliamentary session in June 2007.[23] This legislation is intended by its proponents to encourage Canadian compliance with commitments under the Kyoto Protocol. It calls upon the federal Minister of the Environment to establish an annual Climate Change Plan, and to make regulations consistent with Canada's emissions reduction targets under Kyoto. The statute calls upon the National Round Table on the Environment and the Economy to advise the minister on the effectiveness of the plans and would require the Commissioner of the Environment and Sustainable Development to report to the Speaker of the House of Commons concerning progress in the implementation of the national climate change plan.

The Conservative government's current plan to regulate GHGs, together with other air pollutants, is embodied in *Turning the Corner: An Action Plan to Reduce Greenhouse Gases and Air Pollution*.[24] *Turning the Corner* confirmed energy efficiency measures related to fuel consumption standards for vehicles to apply effective the 2011 model year, and calls for the elimination of most incandescent lighting by 2012. *Turning the Corner* was not intended to address Canada's Kyoto commitment of a 6 percent GHG reduction from 1990 levels by 2012. Instead, a new *Regulatory Framework for Air Emissions* was proposed with the intention of reducing GHG emissions 20 percent from 2006 by 2020.[25] It is anticipated that these reductions will be realized on the basis of regulations applicable to large final emitters (LFEs): fossil-fuel electricity generation, oil and gas, forest products, smelting and refining, iron and steel, iron-ore pelletizing, potash, lime, and chemical production, and cement. The proposal calls for emission intensity targets rather than absolute reductions and will apply on a differential basis to existing and new facilities. The operational implications of this approach are explained by Environment Canada as follows:

> The April 2007 framework set an initial required reduction of 18% percent from 2006 emission-intensity levels in 2010 for existing facilities. Every year thereafter, a 2% continuous improvement in emission intensity would be required. By 2015, therefore, an emission-intensity reduction of 26% from 2006 levels would be required, with a further reduction to 33% by 2020. The emission-intensity approach ties the

---

23 *Kyoto Protocol Implementation Act*, S.C. 2007, c. 30.
24 Introduced 26 April 2007, online: www.ecoaction.gc.ca/turning-virage/index-eng.cfm.
25 Environment Canada, *Regulatory Framework for Air Emissions*, introduced 26 April 2008, online: www.ec.gc.ca/doc/media/m_124/toc_eng.htm.

emission reduction targets to production. This allows emission reductions to be achieved while accommodating economic growth.

New facilities, which are those whose first year of operation is 2004 or later, would be granted a three-year commissioning period before they would face an emission-intensity reduction target. After the third year, new facilities would be required to improve their emission intensity each year by 2%. A cleaner fuel standard would be applied, thereby setting the target as if they were using the designated fuel. A flexible approach would be taken in special cases where the equipment or technology used in a new plant facilitates carbon capture and storage or otherwise offers a significant and imminent potential for emission reductions.

The purpose of this policy is to provide an incentive for new facilities to choose cleaner fuels or to invest in the technology needed for carbon capture and storage or in other less emission-intensive technologies.

For both existing and new facilities, fixed process emissions, which are emissions tied to production and for which there is no alternative reduction technology, would receive a 0% target in the regulations. In other words, for these types of emissions, there is no way, with current technology, for them to be reduced except by shutting down production.[26]

Regulated sectors have three options available to achieve their target objectives: actual reductions in emissions intensity; financial contributions to a technology fund payable at an initial rate of $15 per tonne on excess emissions of CO_2; or the purchase of emission credits generated for exchange within Canada, or derived from domestic "offsets," or associated with international mechanisms established under the Kyoto Protocol.[27]

Additional measures to promote carbon capture and storage at oil sands facilities and to eliminate coal-fired energy production were announced in March 2008 as refinements to the *Regulatory Framework*. Draft regulations are expected to be released for comment in the second half of 2008 in anticipation of the coming into force of final Canadian GHG regulations in 2010.

---

26 *Ibid.* at para. 2.1, online: www.ec.gc.ca/doc/virage-corner/2008-03/541_eng.htm#targets.

27 See Meinhard Doelle, "Global Carbon Trading and Climate Change Mitigation in Canada: Options for the Use of the Kyoto Mechanisms" in Steven Bernstein *et al.*, eds., *A Globally Integrated Climate Policy for Canada* (Toronto: University of Toronto Press, 2008) 189.

On a longer horizon, the *Regulatory Framework* called for further emission reductions to be achieved by mid-century. In response to a formal request for guidance in achieving longer-term GHG emission reductions, ultimately in the order of a 45 percent to 60 percent reduction from 2003 levels by 2050, the NRTEE set out the following recommendations:

> Implement a strong, clear, consistent and certain GHG emission price signal across the entire Canadian economy as soon as possible in order to successfully shift Canada to a lower GHG emissions pathway, achieve the targeted reductions for 2020 and 2050, avoid higher emission prices that a delay would entail, and reduce cumulative emissions released to the atmosphere.
>
> Institute a market-based policy that takes the form of an emission tax or a cap-and-trade system or a combination of the two.
>
> Develop complementary regulatory policies, in conjunction with the emission price signal, to address sectors of the Canadian economy that do not respond effectively to such a price signal or where market failures exist. Complementary policies should also provide support for research, development and demonstration of technologies, as well as strategic investments in infrastructure.
>
> Establish a Canada-wide plan, in the earliest possible time frame, that leads to better coordination or complementary federal, provincial and territorial GHG emission reduction policies aimed at common or shared targets, time frames and actions.
>
> Apply GHG emission reduction policies that incorporate adaptive management practices and have built-in monitoring and assessment mechanisms to allow for regular reviews to ensure efficiency and effectiveness. This approach will ensure that progress is monitored, compliance issues are addressed, and policies are adjusted to match the required level of abatement effort, and will minimize and mitigate unanticipated adverse outcomes.[28]

At the political level, the Liberal Party of Canada now advocates a program encompassing many features of the NRTEE recommendations. The proposal, centred on a carbon tax and the anticipated behavioural effects of economic incentives is explained in this form:

> Currently, there are very few costs to Canadian polluters for the greenhouse gases they dump into our atmosphere, even though we all pay a price for the impact of those emissions . . . . As long as it is

---

28 National Round Table on the Environment and the Economy, *Getting to 2050: Canada's Transition to a Low-emission Future* (Ottawa: NRTEE, 2007) at 49.

free to pollute, it is easy to forget about the impact of that pollution on others . . . . It should no longer be free to dump greenhouse gases into our atmosphere. The true cost of that pollution must be built into the decision-making process of every polluter . . . . by putting in place a comprehensive price on carbon alongside effective regulations, we can let the market determine the most cost-effective means of reducing greenhouse gas emissions. Putting a price on carbon will spur our industry to pollute less, either by using cleaner energy or innovating to become more energy efficient. This will create new demand in Canada for green products and technologies . . . .[29]

As Canadian climate change law and policy continues to evolve, litigation is already underway to accelerate decision making or to promote compliance. In the spring of 2007, the environmental NGO Friends of the Earth commenced litigation in order to compel the federal Minister of the Environment to take action in response to national greenhouse gas emissions. This application for judicial review asserts that the minister has failed to comply with section 166 of *CEPA, 1999*, a provision that addresses international air pollution.[30] Resort to the courts in Canada for judicial enforcement of climate change response roughly parallels litigation in other jurisdictions including Australia and the United States where recent judgments have confirmed and reinforced the existence of administrative authority to take action to assess and control greenhouse gas emissions.[31] Thus, a federal permit associated with an oil sands development in Alberta was determined to be invalid because the environmental assessment report on which it was based failed to address greenhouse gas emissions in an adequate manner.[32] In

---

29 Liberal Party of Canada, *The Green Shift: Building a Canadian Economy for the 21st Century* (2008) at 21–23, online: http://thegreenshift.ca/pdfs/green_shift_book_en.pdf.

30 For information on the judicial application by Friends of the Earth see online: www.foecanada.org/index.php?option=content&task=view&id=318&Itemid=135. *CEPA, 1999*, above note 21.

31 In *Massachusetts v. EPA* (2 April 2007) case no. 05-1120 (U.S. Supreme Court), the Court required the agency to include CO_2 emissions in its regulatory work (online: www.supremecourtus.gov/opinions/06pdf/05-1120.pdf). The Land and Environment Court of New South Wales, Australia decided on 29 November 2006 that an environmental assessment prepared by the Centennial Coal company did not adequately account for greenhouse gas emissions that would result from coal produced by the proposed Anvil Hill mine if approved. See *Gray v. The Minister of Planning and Ors*, [2006] NSWLEC 720.

32 *Pembina Institute for Appropriate Development v. Canada (A.G.)*, [2008] F.C.J. No. 324 (Fed. Ct.) and *Imperial Oil Resources Ventures v. Canada (Minister of Fisheries and Oceans)*, 2008 FC 598.

addition, a petition has been addressed to the Inter-American Commission on Human Rights from representatives of the Inuit Circumpolar Conference who are seeking relief from the United States for the adverse consequences of climate change on their health and livelihoods.[33]

C. PROVINCIAL RESPONSES TO CLIMATE CHANGE

In Alberta, initiatives associated with greenhouse gas emissions and climate change have been underway in the aftermath of a 2002 report, *Albertans and Climate Change: Taking Action*[34] which encouraged progress towards mandatory reporting by large industrial emitters in the province. Subsequently, legislation in the form of the *Climate Change and Emissions Management Act*[35] provides for a provincial emission target aimed at a reduction of specified gas emissions relative to GDP to 50 percent of 1990 levels or less. The legislation also allows sectoral arrangements to facilitate achievement of that target, among other technical matters.[36]

It is notable that the approach taken by Alberta addresses *emission intensity* relative to the overall level of economic activity in the province. This focus on emission intensity may reduce the rate of growth in greenhouse gas emissions, but is not directed at the more fundamental question of reducing the total level of such emissions. Accordingly, Alberta's intensity-based approach has been criticized for failing to rigorously address the urgent need for lower overall emissions.

Like Alberta, Nova Scotia enacted legislation, the *Environmental Goals and Sustainable Prosperity Act*, to establish a provincial framework on climate change.[37] This statutory landmark establishes a wide range of environmental and economic goals. Those provisions most directly linked to climate change and greenhouse gas emissions include the adoption of emission standards for greenhouse gases and pollutants from new vehicles by 2010 and targets for emissions of nitrogen oxides and greenhouse gases

---

33   Sheila Watt-Cloutier, *Petition to the Inter American Commission on Human Rights Seeking Relief from Violations Resulting from Global Warming Caused by Acts and Omissions of the United States* (7 December 2005).

34   Online: http://environment.gov.ab.ca/info/library/6123.pdf.

35   *Climate Change and Emissions Management Act*, S.A. 2003, c. C-16.7. Now see *Climate Change and Emissions Management Amendment Act*, S.A. 2007, c. 4, online: www.assembly.ab.ca/bills/2007/pdf/bill-003.pdf.

36   *Climate Change and Emissions Management Act*, ibid., ss. 3 & 4.

37   *Environmental Goals and Sustainable Prosperity Act*, S.N.S. 2007, c. 7.

are proposed. The legislation also states that 18.5 percent of the province's electricity needs will be met from renewable sources by 2013.[38]

Quebec's initial response to climate change dating from 1995 took the form of an essentially voluntary action plan to encourage the stabilization of greenhouse gas emissions in keeping with the general goals of the *Framework Convention on Climate Change*.[39] Following Kyoto, a somewhat more ambitious action plan was introduced in 2000 and recently replaced by a third formulation, *Quebec and Climate Change: A Challenge for the Future, 2006–2012*.[40] This latest program is comprised of some two dozen sectorally-oriented actions. It is anticipated that these will allow the province to reduce emissions of greenhouse gases by 10 megatons of CO_2 or equivalent gases. In conjunction with existing measures, the six year program is expected to reduce emissions by 2012 to approximately 1.5 percent below 1990 levels. Four guiding principles underpin the design of the current Quebec plan:

1. Assuming our responsibilities in our fields of jurisdiction
2. Economic efficiency to preserve the competitiveness of Quebec's companies
3. Complementarity of interventions in such manner as to maximize the positive impacts
4. The participation of all members of Quebec society: citizens, companies, municipalities and public institutions.[41]

Ontario made a number of announcements with the intention of formally presenting a more coherent program in 2007. Early policy initiatives included proposals to replace coal-fired electricity generation with cleaner sources of power and renewable supplies, as well as demand reduction measures. Other steps involve the introduction of ethanol to gasoline,[42] and more recently, financial encouragement to the automobile sector to pursue significantly increased fuel efficiency. Statutory proposals advanced by legislators to strengthen the formal framework for advancing emissions reductions in the province have not yet been successful.[43] In 2008, Ontario and Quebec agreed to more

---

38 *Ibid.*, s. 4.
39 Online: www.mddep.gouv.qc.ca/changements/agir_ensemble/action2.htm# demarche.
40 Online: www.mddep.gouv.qc.ca/changements/plan_action/2006-2012_en.pdf.
41 *Ibid.* at 17.
42 Ontario, Ministry of the Environment, News Release, "Ontario Makes Progress on Climate Change" (16 February 2005).
43 Bill 179, *Ontario Climate Change Act, 2006*; Bill 200, *Ontario Climate Change Act, 2007*.

vigorous joint action and have begun to explore participation in the Western Climate Initiative, discussed below in connection with British Columbia's climate change policy.

In the Speech from the Throne, 13 February 2007, British Columbia outlined three key initiatives on climate change. The provincial government expressed its intention to set a target to reduce greenhouse gas emissions by 33 percent below current levels by 2020, to set new tailpipe emissions standards for all new vehicles sold in B.C., and to identify practical options for making the Government of B.C. carbon neutral by 2010.[44] Subsequently, British Columbia announced its participation in the Climate Registry, a greenhouse gas database and reporting system operating in jurisdictions whose cumulative population exceeds 200 million. The registry will allow members to track progress in emissions reduction. In collaboration with California, the province has also undertaken to cap greenhouse gas emissions, such that, by 2020, levels would be reduced to at least 1990 levels. The two Pacific coast jurisdictions will also work together to reduce greenhouse gases from the transportation sector by adopting a low carbon fuel standard and greenhouse gas tailpipe emissions. Additional elements of the 31 May Memorandum of Understanding involve aggressive clean and renewable energy policies, and a "Hydrogen Highway" linking B.C. and California.[45]

British Columbia's February 2008 budget announced the proposed introduction of a carbon tax to take effect in July 2008. The tax, initially set at $10 per tonne of CO_2, is scheduled to increase annually in increments of $5 until it reaches $30 in July 2012. Upon introduction, it will apply to gasoline, diesel fuel, natural gas, home-heating fuel, propane, and coal. The measure is intended to be "revenue neutral," in that income tax reductions corresponding to the value of the new tax will be made. The province has now also introduced draft legislation, including the *Greenhouse Gas Reduction (Cap and Trade) Act*, which will permit trading under a hard cap within the framework of the Western Climate Initiative.[46]

---

44   British Columbia, Speech from the Throne (13 February 2007).

45   Online: www2.news.gov.bc.ca/news_releases_2005-2009/2007OTP0075-000704-Attachment1.pdf.

46   British Columbia, Bill 18, *Greenhouse Gas Reduction (Cap and Trade) Act, 2008*. See also British Columbia, Bill 31, *Greenhouse Gas Reduction (Emissions Standards) Statute Amendment Act, 2008*; British Columbia, Bill 16, *Greenhouse Gas Reduction (Renewable and Low Carbon Fuel Requirements) Act, 2008*; British Columbia, Bill 39, *Greenhouse Gas Reduction (Vehicle Emissions Standards) Act, 2008*.

British Columbia was the first Canadian province to join the Western Climate Initiative (WCI), a multi-jurisdictional consortium launched by the U.S. states of California, Washington, New Mexico, Oregon, and Arizona in February 2007. One central objective of the WCI is the creation of a versatile regional carbon-trading mechanism to encourage an efficient and effective market-based approach to greenhouse gas emissions reduction.

In July 2008, the WCI announced a recommended design for a cap-and-trade emissions reduction program intended to operate initially from 2012 through to 2020.[47] In contrast with regulatory measures oriented around emissions intensity standards, the WCI trading program is grounded upon an aggregate regional cap, representing a level of total regional emissions which will progressively decline over the course of successive three-year compliance periods.[48] The methodology for apportioning allowances amongst participating jurisdictions within the capped aggregate regional emissions level is currently under development.[49] Participating governments will then arrange for the distribution of allowances within their own jurisdictions, having regard to such considerations as consumer impacts, worker and industrial transition requirements, adaptation to climate change impacts, recognition of early reduction efforts, and so on.[50] The WCI cap-and-trade program applies initially (2012) to facilities or entities in electricity generation, industry, and commerce with an emission threshold of 25,000 metric tons of CO_2. Coverage will be extended in the second compliance period (2015) to smaller facilities and transportation.[51]

The proposed WCI cap-and-trade framework anticipates the use of offsets whereby regulated facilities that do not meet their reduction targets directly from internal operations may purchase substitute credits from other eligible activities, including use of the Kyoto Protocol's Clean Development Mechanism and Joint Implementation arrangements.[52] As explained by the WCI, offsets are emission reduction projects undertaken to address emissions not included in a cap-and-trade program. An offset mechanism enables covered entities to offset their own emissions by purchasing emission reduction credits generated through pro-

---

47   Western Climate Initiative, "Draft Design of the Regional Cap-and-Trade Program" (23 July 2008), online: www.westernclimateinitiative.org/ewebeditpro/items/O104F18808.PDF.

48   *Ibid.* at para. 6.1.

49   *Ibid.* at para. 7.

50   *Ibid.* at para. 8.

51   *Ibid.* at para. 1.

52   *Ibid.* at para. 9.

jects that address emissions not covered by the cap. Participants in the WCI cap-and-trade mechanism have also recognized the significance of other policies in meeting greenhouse gas-reduction targets and are exploring ways to integrate such other policies, including B.C.'s carbon tax, with the cap-and-trade system.[53]

Saskatchewan's Energy and Climate Change Plan was underpinned by a frank acknowledgement of the impacts of climate change on provincial forests, on the prairie landscape and on the availability of fresh water within the jurisdiction. The program highlighted five elements known as "emissions reductions wedges:"

- Conservation and efficiency measures by industry, business and homeowners;
- Carbon dioxide capture and storage measures in Saskatchewan's oil and gas industry and in the province's electricity sector;
- Increased use of renewable energy, including wind, solar power and hydrogen, and further development of Saskatchewan's ethanol and biodiesel resources;
- Reduction of methane and other emissions in the oil and gas industry, and methane and nitrous oxide emissions in the agriculture industry; and
- Creation of more natural carbon sinks in Saskatchewan's forests and soils.
- These measures are intended to advance the province through a series of targets, beginning with a stabilization of greenhouse gas emissions by 2010, a 32 per cent reduction from 2004 levels by 2020 and an 80 per cent reduction from 2004 levels by 2050.[54]

The direction of future initiatives following recent provincial elections is unclear.

D. MUNICIPAL ACTION

For their part, Canadian municipalities have also moved to address the climate change concerns of their constituents. They have acted, often in advance of provincial or federal guidance, in areas of responsibility available to them. In relation to transportation, for example, specific legal measures have included the creation of dedicated multi-passenger

---

53 *Ibid.* at para. 5.
54 Saskatchewan, News Release, "New Plan Attacks Climate Change in Saskatchewan" (14 June 2007).

lanes. In the construction field, we have seen stricter regulation of building in flood plains or other vulnerable areas. Some communities have begun to deal either through guidelines or bylaws with idling vehicles. Other municipal programs seek to encourage residential, commercial and industrial renovation to enhance heating and cooling efficiency. Some Canadian municipalities have also demonstrated initiative in relation to the energy use and emissions of their own fleets of vehicles, and in relation to emergency preparedness. These efforts are now widespread and can merely be illustrated here.

In 2003, Vancouver's city council sought expert guidance on the challenges of climate change at the municipal level. Recommendations from the Cool Vancouver Taskforce culminated in two sets of climate change goals. The first set of objectives targeted municipal operations with a *Corporate Climate Change Action Plan*. The second set of goals, embodied in a *Community Climate Change Action Plan*, was oriented towards citizens and residents.

Approved by Council on March 15, 2005, the fundamental goal of the *Corporate Climate Change Action Plan*[55] is for Vancouver to reduce GHG emissions from its own facilities and operations by 20 percent of 1990 levels by 2010. The corporate plan rests on eight fundamental priorities:

1. Energy efficient retro-fits for facilities
2. Green design for new and replacement civic buildings
3. Green energy and sustainable dense development
4. Active and public transportation
5. Fuel-efficient fleets and fleet management
6. Energy efficient street/park lighting and traffic control signals
7. Corporate waste reduction and landfill gas utilization
8. Educating people to curb energy demands

Approved at the same time as the corporate plan, the *Community Climate Change Action Plan*[56] sought to engage residents in efforts to reduce their own GHG emissions 6 percent from 1990 levels by 2012 on the basis of six priority initiatives:

1. Home renovations for energy efficiency
2. Energy efficient retro-fits for institutional facilities
3. Energy efficient retro-fits for large commercial buildings
4. Bio-diesel fuel blends
5. Efficient driver training and anti-idling
6. Transportation alternatives

---

55 Online: http://vancouver.ca/sustainability/climate_protection.htm.
56 *Ibid.*

In Halifax, the SMART Community Action Guide to Climate Change and Emergency Preparedness dates from September 2006.[57] The guide combines encouragement to reduce GHG emissions with discussion of adaptation to the effects of climate change. Thus, it highlights recent weather disruptions, such as ice storms, torrential rains and flooding, and advises residents on how to adapt and protect themselves from such occurrences. It then encourages behaviour that reduces GHG emissions by drawing the connection between adverse weather phenomena and GHG emissions.

Quebec City provides an additional example, indeed one predating the Vancouver and Halifax initiatives. In 2004, Quebec adopted a *Plan de réduction des émissions de gaz à effet de serre.*[58] The initiative aimed to reduce municipal GHG emissions by 60,000 tonnes by 2010. By 2005, just one year after the adoption of the policy, the city had reached 75 percent of its objective, in that 46,000 tonnes of GHG emissions had already been eliminated by measures directed at four key sectors:

1. waste and recycling,
2. motorized equipment and transportation,
3. municipal installations, and
4. other sectors of intervention.

The City of Quebec's plan emphasizes that substantial savings can be expected from reducing GHG emissions. Specifically, the plan estimates that by 2010 if reductions remain on track, approximately $15,527,000 could be saved annually and reinvested back into the local economy.

E. CLIMATE CHANGE ADAPTATION

Alongside initiatives intended to reduce GHG emissions and thereby lessen the impact of human behaviour on the atmosphere, it is now necessary to take steps to adapt a wide range of operations and infrastructure to the effects of climate change. Adaptation challenges will vary with regional circumstances. Thus, the impact of heat in large urban centres such as Toronto may pose particular risks from the perspective of public health. In northern Canada, melting permafrost threatens to destabilize transportation and other infrastructure. In British

---

57　*Community Action Plan for Climate Change*, available on the Halifax Regional Municipality Website, online: www.halifax.ca/climate/index.html.
58　*Plan d'action* (2005), online: www.ville.quebec.qc.ca/fr/ma_ville/environnement/air/implication_ville.shtml.

Columbia milder temperatures have already undermined the effect of cold weather to control populations of mountain pine beetles, while the Prairies may now be exposed to more prolonged periods of devastating drought. Financial arrangements such as disaster relief, crop insurance or income stabilization funds constitute elements of an adaptation program, as do initiatives such as the National Disaster Mitigation Strategy formulated under the leadership of Public Safety and Emergency Preparedness Canada.[59]

Once again, the Stern Review provides useful general guidance about the range of measures likely to be highly relevant in adapting to the local and regional effects of climate change.

> Adaptation to climate change—that is, taking steps to build resilience and minimize costs—is essential. It is no longer possible to prevent the climate change that will take place over the next two to three decades, but it is still possible to protect our societies and economies from its impacts to some extent—for example, by providing better information, improved planning and more climate-resilient crops and infrastructure.[60]

Governments at all levels will be called upon to support adaptation measures, ranging from the possibility of strengthened water-rationing programs in the municipal context, through provincial land-use controls intended to reduce the vulnerability of buildings and their inhabitants to natural disasters. At the federal level, climate modelling and research are expected to receive increased attention. Natural Resources Canada is currently overseeing two programs along these lines, the *Climate Impacts and Adaptation Program*, and a second initiative on *Reducing Canada's Vulnerability to Climate Change*.

FURTHER READINGS

BERNSTEIN, STEVEN, *et al.*, eds., *A Globally Integrated Climate Policy for Canada* (Toronto: University of Toronto Press, 2008)

BOTHE, MICHAEL, & ECKARD REHBINDER, *Climate Change Policy* (Utrecht: Eleven International, 2005)

---

59   Commissioner of the Environment and Sustainable Development, *2006 September Report*, above note 22, c. 2 at 4–5.

60   *The Stern Review*, above note 9 at vii.

BURTON, IAN, *et al.*, *Adaptation Policy Framework for Climate Change: Developing Policies, Strategies, Measures* (Cambridge: Cambridge University Press, 2005)

DOELLE, MEINHARD, *From Hot Air to Action?: Climate Change, Compliance and the Future of International Environmental Law* (Toronto: Thomson/Carswell, 2005)

INTERGOVERNMENTAL PANEL ON CLIMATE CHANGE, *Climate Change 2007: the Physical Science Basis, Summary for Policy Makers* (Cambridge: Cambridge University Press, 2007), online: http://ipcc-wg1.ucar.edu/wg1/docs/WG1AR4_SPM_PlenaryApproved.pdf

LANTZ, VAN, & JOE RUGGERI, eds., *The Kyoto Protocol and Environmental Policy in Atlantic Canada* (Fredericton, NB: Policy Studies Centre, University of New Brunswick, 2003)

OECD, *Harmonisation between National and International Tradeable Permit Schemes* (Paris: OECD, 2003), online: www.oecd.org/dataoecd/11/63/2957623.pdf

PAEHLKE, ROBERT C., *Some Like It Cold: The Politics of Climate Change in Canada* (Toronto: Between the Lines, 2008)

PEW CENTER ON GLOBAL CLIMATE CHANGE, *The Agenda for Climate Action* (Arlington, VA: Pew Center on Global Climate Change, 2006)

SIMPSON, JEFFREY, MARK JACCARD, & NIC RIVERS, *Hot Air: Meeting Canada's Climate Change Challenge* (Toronto: McClelland & Stewart, 2007)

STERN, NICHOLAS, *The Economics of Climate Change: The Stern Review* (Cambridge: Cambridge University Press, 2007)

TRUDEAU, HÉLÈNE, & SUZANNE LALONDE, "La mise en oeuvre du Protocole de Kyoto au Canada: concertation ou coercitation?" (2004) 34 R.G.D. 141

CONCLUSION

Not long ago, the agility of pre-robotic, pre-mutant and pre-digital cartoon characters such as rabbits and roadrunners was constantly being tested at the brink of disaster, notably in proximity to terrifying cliffs. As they approached the edge of a daunting precipice, some of these colourful creatures would attempt — with mixed and limited success — to screech to a halt; others seemed capable of launching themselves into the air and then, with an incredible reversal of spinning feet, defying gravity to return to the safety of the ledge. An assessment of the adequacy and prospects for the contemporary environmental protection regime is likely to be influenced by metaphor: do we still have a little traction to work with on the ledge, or have we already gone over the brink? Those readers whose imaginations require the stimulus of further drama and suspense, may factor in the destabilizing effects of climate change: anyone hoping to screech to a halt or return to the safety of the ledge after overshooting the mark must now remember that the ledge itself is crumbling.

In these circumstances, to contemplate a future for environmental law — even in general terms — is something of a cause for celebration. It is also to acknowledge defeat. This paradox derives from sharply divergent perceptions of the efficacy of law as a response to environmental problems. For those who anticipated ecological apocalypse, mere survival must constitute something of a success, while from the perspective of those who have championed one legal innovation after another as *the* magic answer, the continuation of struggle against environmental degradation will be something of a setback. But so it will be, a future much like the past in which a wide range of instruments will be employed against an equally wide range of multifaceted problems in a complicated and dynamic context.

The first of the contextual elements is the continuation of environmental crises and resource depletion. Arctic ice cover is retreating rapidly; the collapse of fish stocks on a global basis is predicted; increasing average temperatures around the world threaten irreversible and accelerating transformation of planetary climate control systems. Despite significant advances in Canada, including some progress in terms of the rehabilitation of particular sites and ecosystems, there can be no illusion about general success in bringing severe threats of continuing environmental risk under control. Old bad habits die hard, and it is only realistic to anticipate new indications of significant environmental deterioration, further toxic and industrial accidents, and ongoing resource depletion.

The economic context will also continue to affect environmental regimes. One effect of the combined impact of habitual deficits and accumulated debt, trade liberalization, and international competition has been longstanding pressure to relieve "regulatory burdens." To some degree this has been attempted through the downloading of environmental responsibilities to local governments. Several jurisdictions have also witnessed severe reductions in public expenditures for environmental research, monitoring, and enforcement, although the pattern may now be reversing.

There has also been evidence of a tendency to consider harmonization measures in order to mitigate the potential—if poorly documented—impact of so-called "pollution havens" on domestic investment and employment. International legal developments relating to the environment are another continuing influence, an increasing one, perhaps, as compliance and enforcement mechanisms become a focus of attention.

Federalism and *Charter* considerations also remain highly relevant in litigation and to the design and effectiveness of the overall Canadian environmental regime. The *Charter's* influence on the environmental regime to date has been indirect. By formalizing the procedural protections applicable in the context of investigation and prosecutions, the *Charter* may have increased the cost and complexity of the enforcement process. On the other hand, this situation has probably helped to redirect attention to other and perhaps more efficient means of promoting compliance and environmental protection.

Lawyers can no longer remain as professionally isolated from scientific and ecological considerations as they have often been in the past, for resource use and management decisions require continuing reassessment from the perspective of health and environmental consequences. Cooperative problem-solving and alternative dispute-resolution approaches in the environmental context present additional opportunities and challenges for the corporate bar, government lawyers, and public-interest counsel alike. New institutions need to be designed and managed, while those participating in business and environmental policy-making will require the assistance of counsel with strategic planning skills. These requirements for a more informed scientific understanding and for more sophisticated approaches to dispute resolution are examples of ways in which members of the legal profession are being asked to grapple with the implications of sustainability as an emerging environmental norm and a contending economic paradigm.

An extended commentary on the status of sustainability cannot be attempted here, but it can at least be noted that statutory affirmations have proliferated. Corporate and institutional endorsements—though sometimes cautious and qualified—have been commonplace. Moreover, numerous sustainable-development research centres have been established. However, while the conceptual foundations are gradually being laid, the utility of sustainability as an enforceable legal standard remains to be determined. And, regrettably, the notion of sustainability seems as yet poorly connected to the challenge of global population growth.

The precautionary approach also offers great promise. As an antidote to an unfortunate pattern of underestimating the severity of environmental risks and overestimating our capacity to respond, it is long overdue. But, again, an uphill battle is in store for its advocates. And, in some of its most recent Canadian statutory formulation as "erring on the side of caution," the justiciability of this principle appears challenging indeed.

If the developments described in this volume in relation to toxics, environmental assessment, economic incentives, and the extension of responsibility have anything in common, it is perhaps to be found in the potential now in place for systematic preventive action rather than the more *ad hoc* remedial impact of earlier initiatives. By moving towards the consideration of policy, planning, and cumulative impact, environmental assessment procedures should become better able to identify the underlying causes of environmental damage. By identifying specific toxics for rigorous controls—or in some cases "virtual elimination"—government can more effectively direct administrative resources towards preventing harm. And by extending liability to financial institutions that facilitate economic activity, government and the courts will sensitize these institutions to the campaign for environmental quality. Measures taken to highlight the personal responsibility of directors and officers, to expand opportunities for public participation in environmental decision making, and to mitigate the adverse consequences of consumer behaviour are further important dimensions of the Canadian environmental law regime on whose success the well-being of future generations depends. For some time we have been doing better, but we are not yet doing well enough.

APPENDIX

WEBSITES

Arctic Council: www.arctic-council.org
Alberta Department of Environment: www.environment.alberta.ca

British Columbia Ministry of Environment: www.gov.bc.ca/env

Canadian Council of Ministers of the Environment: www.ccme.ca
Canadian Environmental Assessment Agency: www.ceaa.gc.ca
Canadian Chemical Producers' Association: www.ccpa.ca
Canadian Environmental Law Association: www.cela.ca
Canadian Parks and Wilderness Society: www.cpaws.org
Canadian Water and Wastewater Association: www.cwwa.ca
Canadian Wildlife Service: www.cws-sfc.ec.gc.ca
Commission for Environmental Cooperation: www.cec.org
Committee on the Status of Endangered Wildlife in Canada: www.
   cosewic.gc.ca
Commission on Sustainable Development: www.un.org/esa/sustdev/
   csd
Commissioner of the Environment and Sustainable Development:
   www.oag-bvg.gc.ca
Convention on Biological Diversity: www.cbd.int
Convention on International Trade in Endangered Species: www.cites.
   org

Environment Canada: www.ec.gc.ca
Environmental Commissioner of Ontario: www.eco.on.ca

Environmental Law Centre (Alberta): www.elc.ab.ca

Federation of Canadian Municipalities: www.fcm.ca

Intergovernmental Panel on Climate Change: www.ipcc.ch
International Joint Commission: www.ijc.org

Manitoba Department of Conservation: www.gov.mb.ca/conservation

National Pollutants Release Inventory: www.ec.gc.ca/pdb/npri
Nature Conservancy of Canada: www.natureconservancy.ca
New Brunswick Department of Environment: www.gnb.ca/environ-
    ment
Newfoundland and Labrador Department of Environment: www.gov.
    nf.ca/env
Nova Scotia Department of Environment: www.gov.ns.ca/nse
Nunavut Department of Environment: www.gov.nu.ca/env

Ontario Ministry of the Environment: www.ene.gov.on.ca

Prince Edward Island Department of Environment, Energy and For-
    estry : www.gov.pe.ca/enveng

Quebec Department of Environment: www.menv.gouv.qc.ca

Saskatchewan Department of Environment and Resource Management:
    www.environment.gov.sk.ca

United Nations Environment Program: www.unep.org

West Coast Environmental Law Association: www.wcel.org
World Conservation Union: www.iucn.org
World Wildlife Fund Canada: www.wwf.ca

Yukon Department of Environment: www.environmentyukon.gov.
    yk.ca

TABLE OF CASES

INDEX

ABOUT THE AUTHOR

Jamie Benidickson, Faculty of Law, University of Ottawa, teaches Environmental Law, Administrative Law, Water Law, and Legal History. He is the author of *The Culture of Flushing: A Social and Legal History of Sewage* (UBC Press, 2007). His previous publications include *The Temagami Experience: Recreation, Resources and Aboriginal Rights in the Northern Ontario Wilderness* (University of Toronto Press, 1989), *Getting the Green Light: Environmental Regulation and Investment in Canada* (C.D. Howe Institute, 1994), and *Idleness, Water, and A Canoe: Reflections on Paddling for Pleasure* (University of Toronto Press, 1997). In 2004 he was appointed Director of the IUCN Academy of Environmental Law.